T0328544

THOMAS JEFFERSON:
DIPLOMATIC CORRESPONDENCE

THOMAS JEFFERSON:
DIPLOMATIC CORRESPONDENCE
PARIS, 1784–1789

BRETT F. WOODS

Algora Publishing
New York

Library of Congress Cataloging-in-Publication Data —

Names: Jefferson, Thomas, 1743-1826, author. | Woods, Brett F., editor.
Title: Thomas Jefferson: diplomatic correspondence, Paris, 1784-1789 /
    [edited by] Brett F. Woods.
Description: New York: Algora Publishing, [2016] | Includes bibliographical
    references and index.
Identifiers: LCCN 2016031124 (print) | LCCN 2016032018 (ebook) | ISBN
    9781628942224 (soft cover: alkaline paper) | ISBN 9781628942231 (hard
    cover: alkaline paper) | ISBN 9781628942248 (pdf)
Subjects: LCSH: Jefferson, Thomas, 1743-1826—Correspondence. | Jefferson,
    Thomas, 1743-1826—Political and social views. | Statesmen—United
    States—Correspondence. | Diplomats—United States—Correspondence. |
    United States—Foreign relations—France—Sources. | France—Foreign
    relations—United States—Sources. | United States—Foreign
    relations—1783-1815—Sources.
Classification: LCC E332.86 2016 (print) | LCC E332.86 (ebook) | DDC
    973.4/6092—dc23
LC record available at https://lccn.loc.gov/2016031124

Printed in the United States

Table of Contents

Editor's Note

> "So ask the travelled inhabitant of any nation, In what country on earth would you rather live? Certainly in my own, where are all my friends, my relations, and the earliest & sweetest affections and recollections of my life. Which would be your second choice? France."
>
> — Thomas Jefferson

Thomas Jefferson did not follow a straight Cartesian road from Virginia to Paris. But the collaboration of the French army in the American Revolution had helped pave the way and build a bridge of understanding between New World and Old. When Filippo Mazzei, Jefferson's Albemarle neighbor, reported from Paris in 1780 that the French were afraid the Americans might settle for a separate peace with Britain, Jefferson, then governor of Virginia, was shocked. "Believe me no opinion can have less foundation," he replied immediately. "The disinterested exertions of France for us have not only made real impression on the leaders of the people, but are deeply felt by the people themselves....Whenever the French and American troops have acted together the harmony has been real, and not given out merely to influence the opinion of the world."[1]

Thomas Jefferson was born in 1743 in Albemarle County, Virginia, inheriting from his father, a planter and surveyor, some 5,000 acres of land, and from his mother, a Randolph, high social standing. He studied at the College of William and Mary and then read law. In 1772, he married Martha Wayles Skelton, a widow, and took her to live in his partly constructed mountaintop home, Monticello. Freckled and sandy haired, he was rather tall and awkward. And while eloquent as a correspondent, he was certainly no public speaker and in the Virginia House of Burgesses and the

---

[1] Adams, 1997, 25.

Continental Congress, he contributed his pen rather than his voice to the patriot cause. Still, as the "silent member" of the Congress, at 33 Jefferson drafted the *Declaration of Independence*. Then, in following years, he worked to make its words a reality in Virginia, most notably crafting a bill establishing religious freedom that was enacted in 1786.[1]

After Jefferson left Congress in 1776, he returned to Virginia and served in the legislature. Elected governor from 1779 to 1781, he suffered an inquiry into his conduct during his last year in office that, although finally fully repudiated, left him with a life-long prickliness in the face of criticism. Still, he remained prolific. During the brief private interval in his life following his governorship, Jefferson wrote *Notes on the State of Virginia*. Then, in 1784, he entered public service again, in France, first as trade commissioner and then as Benjamin Franklin's successor as minister.[2]

Before he departed for Paris, Jefferson was interviewed by a visiting Dutch nobleman, who asked his opinion of the current American government. Comparing the Confederation Congress to those heady days of 1775–76 in the Continental Congress, Jefferson saw a precipitous decline. "The members of Congress are no longer, generally speaking, men of worth or distinction," he lamented. "For Congress is not, as formally, held in respect; there is indeed dread of its power, though it has none." Benjamin Harrison, the governor of Virginia, concurred, observing that the very survival of the Congress "seems to be problematical." Like Jefferson, Harrison looked back to better days, "when the eyes of the world were upon us, and we were the wonder and envy of all," whereas now "we are sinking faster in esteem than we rose," and European nations were waiting "like buzzards to feast on the spoils of our demise." "Let the Blame fall where it ought," wrote one delegate to Washington, "on those whose attachment to State Views, State Interests, & State prejudices is so great as to render them eternally opposed to every Measure that can be devised for the public good."[3]

But, as Jefferson cast an eye toward Europe, America, he believed, could be the bearer of a new diplomacy, founded on the confidence of a free and virtuous people that would secure its ends based on the natural and universal rights of man: innate means that escaped war and its multiple corruptions. This new diplomacy broke radically, Jefferson thought, from the practices and principles of the old European tradition of reason of state, with its settled belief in the primacy of foreign over domestic policy. That the security and even aggrandizement of the state ought to have priority over domestic welfare, and that the actions of the state ought to be judged according to a different moral calculus than the conduct of individuals, were ideas that Jefferson found utterly antithetical to human progress and enlightenment.[4]

---

[1] Freidel and Sidey 2006.
[2] U.S. Department of State 2016.
[3] Ellis 2015, 1422-1431 Kindle
[4] Tucker 1992, iix-ix.

To be sure, he emerged as an excellent ambassador, for he possessed the same capacity to combine symbolic and practical representation that made Franklin's stay in France such an important episode in Franco-American relations; but, too, in a court almost paralyzed by ceremony and bored with excesses in dress and ornamentation, Jefferson's republican asceticism, his directness and apparent candor, lent him a distinction and significance which no amount of modishness could have gained for him. But the work he did was more important. He had begun his ambassadorial labors even before he left America, making a detailed survey of the needs of northern commerce as he traveled to Boston for embarkation, following up this personal investigation with a questionnaire "concerning government, labor, commerce etc." Once in France he began an endless series of negotiations in behalf of American commerce which he pursued tirelessly through the last twists of intrigue. His indefatigable but unsuccessful efforts to break the general monopolistic control of French imports of American tobacco led him into the intricacies of French cabinet politics and the secret recesses of commercial privilege. His more successful campaign to reopen the markets for American whale oil forced him into a sharp encounter with a ruthless, apolitical clan of Nantucket whalers who, in defense of the special advantages they enjoyed at Dunkirk, in all probability had conspired with French officials to impose the anti-American restrictions. He did not triumph in all such situations — in some, no one could have succeeded — but his successes were notable, and throughout he was shrewd and aggressive.[1]

But, perhaps because he was recognized in Europe as the author of the *Declaration of Independence*, Jefferson quickly became a lightning rod for revolutionaries in Europe and the Americas. And, as the United States minister to France when revolutionary fervor was rising toward the storming of the Bastille in 1789, he soon became an ardent supporter of the revolution, even allowing his residence to be used as a meeting place for revolutionaries, led by Lafayette. This relationship is straightforwardly illustrated by Lafayette's 1789 draft of the *Rights of Man* that contained Jefferson's annotations. Following this model, Lafayette drew up a French *Declaration of the Rights of Man* — and the new National Assembly began writing a Constitution embracing it. Among other principles, it held that "men are born and remain free and equal in rights," which are natural and inalienable, namely "liberty, property, security, and resistance to oppression." King Louis XVI, influenced by conservative ministers and his equally conservative queen, Marie Antoinette, confronted the people with troops instead of reforms, and Jefferson witnessed the first popular uprisings in Paris, which led to the storming of the Bastille, the fortress-prison in Paris where political prisoners were kept, and a symbol of the government's power. He wrote of the attack on the Bastille led by his friend, Monsieur de Corny, and also of the surrender of the prison: "July 19; carried the Governor and Lieutenant Governor to the Place de Grève (the place of public execution), cut off their heads, and sent them through the city, in triumph, to the Palais royal." The king went to bed, Jefferson remarked, "fearfully impressed" and "had he been left to himself,

---

[1] Bailyn 2011, 778-790 Kindle

he would have willingly acquiesced" in whatever the people decided was best for France.[1]

To be sure, Jefferson's preoccupation with France went far beyond revolutionary fervor, pursuing with equal attention, the development of a Franco-American commercial axis. While this focus could be seen as a simple, natural result of the position he now occupied, Minister Plenipotentiary to France, in fact the concern stemmed from the conviction, firmly implanted in Jefferson's mind, that France held the key to America's commercial problem. The existing British monopoly could be overthrown, the main avenues of American trade shifted to France and her colonies, if Versailles would abolish antiquated regulations, open the ports to American productions, and pay for them in manufactures, oils, wines, tropical produce, and other articles. France had everything to gain. Her hopes of permanently displacing Britain in the American market as a result of the war had been cruelly disappointed; but the commercial war was still on, in Jefferson's opinion, and France might yet succeed. The Vergennes ministry hated Britain, a hatred that played into Jefferson's hand, and he did not have to look far in the French capital — to Americanists like Lafayette, to physiocrats like Dupont, to *philosophes* like Condorcet, even to Vergennes himself — for men of influence who sympathized with the commercial goals of the American Revolution.[2]

Indeed, the task was not without some measure of difficulty. From the French ministry's perspective, the Americans seemed irrevocably attached to English merchandise and English commercial practices. Jefferson combatted these ideas, saying "that were national Prejudice alone listened to, our Trade would quit England and come to France." The difficulty, he insisted, was the inability of the Americans to trade directly and make exchanges in the French market. The remedy was no less obvious: the eradication of monopoly and restriction in France. Of course, this was not the whole of the problem. As a Virginian, himself deeply in debt to British merchants, Jefferson knew all too well that the chains of bondage were the invisible chains of credit. The French merchants, not as adventuresome as their British counterparts, unaccustomed to advancing credit and trading on consignment, lacking established connections in American ports, were necessarily at a disadvantage. Diplomacy alone would not slay the hydra of British credit, nor could Jefferson change the conservative habits of French merchants, though he tried. Commercial restrictions were more readily assailed, and, as reflected in his correspondence, Jefferson centered his efforts on opening the French market to direct trade in American productions.[3]

A word regarding methodology. While there are any number of texts that, to greater or lesser degrees, touch on various interludes in Jefferson life, I have elected to approach his time in France from more of a documentary perspective, an interesting journey, to say the least. For whether he is writing to peers such as James Madison, Patrick Henry, and George Washington; to French associates such as the Marquis de Lafayette and Hector St. John de Crevecoeur; or even

---

[1]   Moscow 2015, 1045-1057 Kindle.
[2]   Peterson 1965, 595.
[3]   Ibid, 596.

to his more social acquaintances such as Maria Cosway and Abigail Adams, Jefferson writes with, at time, surprising candor. And whether the subject might be an impassioned argument against Federalism, addressing the detail of international trade agreements, or even commenting on botany and agricultural issues, his words reflect remarkable clarity, insight, and eloquence.

I have long believed that the most comprehensive portrait of the founding fathers can be seen in their personal letters and journal entries. Jefferson is no exception, and those he wrote during his time as Minister to France — through many of the more critical episodes in both American and French history — are of singular importance. This is particularly true when one reviews them in their entirety, as opposed to selected excerpts that, if indeed they have been reprinted at all, have been available only in part, reduced to excerpts, citations, or references which, in many instances, have been repeatedly cited as the foundation for a particular interpretation of events, or conclusion of fact. Accordingly, in this selection of a comparatively few letters from the voluminous body of Jefferson correspondence that has been preserved, my intention is twofold: first, to add to the body of literature exploring early American consular history; and secondly, and perhaps more importantly, to provide an additional glimpse into the character and thought processes of Jefferson the diplomat.

The source material for this compilation is primarily *The Works of Thomas Jefferson, vol. 5 (Correspondence 1786–1789)* edited by Paul Leicester Ford which was published in 1905 by G.P. Putnam and sons. The format of the letters, as Jefferson wrote them, has been preserved whenever possible, while my efforts have been directed to refining the presentation, addressing formatting and spelling issues, correcting formatting, identifying the addressees, many of whom have been lost to history, and, where indicated, providing explanatory notes so as to assist the reader in placing the correspondence in its particular historical, political, or conceptual context. This methodology, I believe, serves to make the material more palatable to a general readership, as well as to students of military, diplomatic, or political history. Additionally, it will also permit — or, at a minimum, encourage — readers to arrive at their own conclusions as to the intention of a particular piece of correspondence.

Any errors in selection, fact, transcription, and interpretation remain, of course, my responsibility.

Brett F. Woods, Ph.D.

Chronology[1]

1784

May 7, 1784. Congress appoints Jefferson minister plenipotentiary to join John Adams and Benjamin Franklin in negotiating treaties of amity and commerce with European nations. Jefferson eventually replaces Benjamin Franklin as minister to France.

July 5. Jefferson sails for Europe from Boston, accompanied by his twelve-year-old daughter Martha (Patsy) and William Short as personal secretary. James Hemings, his nineteen-year-old slave, follows soon after. William Short (1759-1849) is a young relative and protégé, who trained as a lawyer with George Wythe and served on the Executive Council of Virginia. James Hemings is the son of Betty Hemings and brother of Sally. Jefferson intends that he learn the art of French cooking in Paris.

August 3. Jefferson and his party arrive in Le Havre and travel on to Paris. Jefferson takes up residence first at the Hôtel de Landron and then at the Hôtel de Langeac on the Champs-Elysées. David Humphreys, secretary to commissioners Jefferson, Franklin, and Adams, joins Jefferson's household. Jefferson hires a Frenchman, Adrien Petit, to manage the household. At about the same time, Abigail Adams and her children John Quincy and Abigail arrive in Paris to join John Adams, who will be appointed the first ambassador to the Court of St. James's in London.

1785

April–May. John Adams and Jefferson successfully negotiate a loan from Dutch bankers to consolidate U.S. debts, pay long overdue salaries to French officer veterans of the American Revolution, and ransom American captives held by Algerian

---

[1] U.S. Department of State 2016.

and Moroccan rulers who exact tribute from commercial shipping in the Mediterranean and hold hostage seamen of those countries unable or unwilling to pay.

Fall. Jefferson begins work with the Abbé Morellet on a French translation of his *Notes on the State of Virginia.* Having heard that a bad French translation is already in the works, Jefferson hopes to preempt it with his own. However, he is dissatisfied with Morellet's translation, published in 1787 as *Observations sur la Virginie.*

1786

January 7. Jefferson writes to New Hampshire governor John Sullivan, giving him directions on how to find and convey to Paris the skeleton and hide of a moose. Jefferson aims to refute the argument of famed French naturalist Georges de Buffon that nature, animals, and by implication humans in the New World are less developed and smaller in stature than those on the European continent.

January–March. Jefferson drafts a proposal to form a concert of powers led by the United States to oppose the North African regimes, known as the "Barbary Pirates," who levy tribute on American and European commercial ships. Friends present his proposal in Congress, but it is rejected because of its expense, as John Adams had predicted to Jefferson.

March–April. Jefferson visits the Adamses in London. John Adams and Jefferson take a tour of the English countryside. During his visit to London, Jefferson is presented at court and snubbed by King George III.

Late Summer. Jefferson is introduced to Maria Cosway by the American artist John Trumbull at the Halle aux Bleds, the French grain market in Paris. Cosway is a talented English artist, raised in Italy, and married to the miniaturist Richard Cosway. She and Jefferson develop a close personal relationship.

October 12. After recovering from a broken wrist, Jefferson writes Maria Cosway a carefully crafted letter in which his "Head" debates with his "Heart" contesting the merits of love and pleasure, on the one hand, and intellect and rationality, on the other. Jefferson's letterpress copy survives.

October–November. Jefferson learns of "Shay's Rebellion" in western Massachusetts, first from John Adams in a November 30 letter, and later from John Jay in an October 27 letter (that was delayed in delivery). The rebellion, led by Daniel Shays, is directed by Western debtor farmers against Eastern creditors and the courts. Abigail Adams, who corresponds regularly with Jefferson, also writes him about the insurgency, and Jefferson, who is not as alarmed as the Adamses, replies in a February 22, 1787, letter that "I like a little rebellion now and then. It is like a storm in the atmosphere."

1787

March–June. Jefferson travels through the south of France and in northern Italy.

May–September. The Constitutional Convention meets in Philadelphia, presided over by George Washington. Madison has been keeping Jefferson informed of the developments leading up to it, and Jefferson generally supports the effort. Under the Articles of Confederation, the government has the power to negotiate treaties but cannot regulate trade, and this has hampered Jefferson's efforts to negotiate commercial treaties with France. In November, Jefferson receives a copy of a draft of the Constitution and generally approves it, but urges Madison and others to add a bill of rights and to limit the number of terms that a president can serve.

July. Jefferson's other daughter, nine-year-old Mary (Polly), arrives in Paris with the fourteen-year-old slave, Sally Hemings. They first go to London, where they stay for a short while with John and Abigail Adams before proceeding to Paris.

1788

March–April. Jefferson travels through Holland and central Europe. June 19, he writes his "Hints to Americans Travelling in Europe" for Thomas Lee Shippen and John Rutledge Jr.

1789

May 5. Jefferson attends the opening of the French Estates-General and its debates at Versailles. The Estates-General have been called in the wake of the crown's increasing fiscal difficulties. Jefferson drafts a charter of rights with Lafayette in June. It serves as the basis for the French Declaration of Rights that Lafayette presents to the National Assembly in July.

July. Riots and mob actions, including the storming of the Bastille on July 14, occur in the streets of Paris. August, Lafayette and other French liberals meet secretly at Jefferson's home, the Hôtel de Langeac, just outside the city, to discuss a new French constitution.

September 26. The United States Senate confirms Jefferson's appointment as secretary of state in the administration of George Washington, first president of the United States.

September 28. Jefferson departs for home from the French port of Le Havre on board the *Clermont*. He does not learn of his appointment as secretary of state until he arrives in Norfolk, Virginia, on November 23. On February 14, 1790 he accepts it reluctantly, because he had hoped to devote his time to Monticello and his private affairs.

SELECTED CORRESPONDENCE

1784

To the Governor of Virginia (Benjamin Harrison)
Paris, Aug. 20, 1784.
Sir,

A few days after my arrival here Colo. Le Maire, writer of the enclosed letter called & asked me to forward it to you with such explanations as I could give.[1] As to his commission, having lost the original as he therein mentions, he asks an authenticated copy of it, which he thinks will enforce some application he is making to this government. As to lands, I remember the gift of 2000 acres, & think the entry of it will be found in the minutes of the council sometime in the summer or autumn of 1779. A letter was written to Colo. Shelby or to Majr Martin, (the Cherokee agent) to locate the warrant on the best lands possible; and I believe it was meant that every expense should be borne by the state so that Le Maire should receive an actual grant clear of all charges & trouble. But of these things the minutes & letters of the Executive will give more certain information; or if these should have been lost, Mr. Blair will probable recollect the circumstances.

---

[1] The son of a prominent French family, Jacques Le Maire had come to Virginia with the permission of the French court in 1777 in search of a political future in America. Virginia Governor Patrick Henry quickly accepted his offer of assistance, provided him with a list of needed materials for the state, and commissioned him with the rank of captain. Le Maire returned to Paris where he met with Virginia's commercial agent, Arthur Lee, who directed him to Strasbourg where, for 40,000 *livres*, he purchased 1,200 complete swords at the at the Klingenthal factory. Jefferson's acknowledgement of this service is reflected in both this letter, as well as his 11 November 1785 correspondence with James Madison. (Hartzler 2015, 89)

To James Madison[1]
Paris, November 11, 1784

I am obliged to you for your information as to the prospects of the present year in our farms. It is a great satisfaction to know it & yet it is a circumstance which few correspondents think worthy of mention. I am also much indebted for your very full observations on the navigation of the Mississippi. I had thought on the subject, & sketched the anatomy of a memorial on it, which will be much aided by your communications.

You mention that my name is used by some speculators in western land jobbing, as if they were acting for me as well as for themselves. About the year 1776 or 1777 I consented to join Mr. Harvey and some others in an application for lands there; which scheme, however, I believe he dropped on the threshold, for I never after heard one syllable on the subject. In 1782 I joined some gentlemen in a project to obtain some lands in the western part of North Carolina. But in the winter of 1782 and 1783, while I was in expectation of going to Europe, and that the title to western lands might possibly come under the discussion of the ministers, I withdrew myself from this company. I am further assured that the members never prosecuted their views. These were the only occasions in which I ever took a single step for the acquisition of western lands, & in these I retracted at the threshold. I can with truth therefore declare to you, & wish you to repeat it on every proper occasion, that no person on earth is authorized to place my name in any adventure for lands on the western waters, that I am not engaged in any but the two before mentioned. I am one of eight children to whom my father left his share in the loyal company, whose interests, however, I never espoused, and they have long since received their quietus. Excepting these, I never was nor am I now interested in one foot of land on earth off the waters of James River.[2]

---

[1] The 50-year friendship between James Madison and Thomas Jefferson illustrates the development of an adult friendship. That friendship is also evocative of some of the leadership qualities the two men brought to the founding era. Madison and Jefferson became friends because each needed an intellectual compatriot in the political arena to replace a lost relationship. However, their initial relationship was more a mentor-student relationship rather than an egalitarian partnership. As illustrated through their letters, the friendship itself grew and deepened until Madison and Jefferson had their first and only serious intellectual break over the inclusion of a bill of rights in the proposed constitution. The friendship that emerged after this break was one of equality. (Wilkins 1991, 593)

[2] As soon as Jefferson arrived in Paris, sparkling exchanges began to flow with his best friend on his impressions and discoveries of the "transatlantic world." Jefferson thus made it possible for Madison to share his experience of France. Madison, on the other hand, made it easy for Jefferson to know the true complexion of political developments in America. Madison at once took up his role of safeguarding the interests of his vulnerable, absent friend. The first letter that Madison sent to Jefferson in Paris informed him that a rumor was circulating to the effect that Jefferson was an active party to some land speculation in Kentucky. Grateful for Madison's protective intervention, in this letter Jefferson replied conscientiously that he had on two earlier occasions joined with others to obtain Western lands, but that upon taking up a European posting when "the

I shall subjoin the few books I have ventured to buy for you. I have been induced to do it by the combined circumstances of their utility and cheapness. I wish I had a catalogue of the books you would be willing to buy, because they are often to be met on stalls very cheap, and I would get them as occasion should arise. The subscription for the Encyclopedia is still open. Whenever an opportunity offers of sending you what is published of that work (37 vols.) I shall subscribe for you and send it with the other books purchased for you.

Whatever money I may lay out for you here in books, or in anything else which you may desire, may be replaced crown for crown (without bewildering ourselves in the exchange) in Virginia by making payments.

Colonel Le Maire, whom you know, is the bearer of this; he comes to Virginia to obtain the two thousand acres of land given him for his services in procuring us arms, and what else he may be entitled to as having been an officer in our service; above all things, he wishes to obtain the Cincinnatus eagle, because it will procure him here the order of St. Louis, and of course a pension for life of one thousand livres; he is so extremely poor that another friend and myself furnish him money for his whole expenses from here to Virginia. There I am in hopes the hospitality of the country will be a resource for him till he can convert a part of his lands advantageously into money; but as he will want some small matter of money, if it should be convenient for you to furnish him with as much as ten guineas from time to time on my account, I will invest that sum in books or anything else you may want here by way of payment. He is honest and grateful, and you may be assured that no aid that you can give him in the forwarding his claims will be misplaced.

To James Monroe
Paris, Nov. 11, 1784
Dear Sir,

Your journey to the Westward having prevented my writing to you till now that a letter may probably find you at Congress I shall resume the correspondence discontinued since I left Boston. My passage was remarkably short, being only 19 days from land to land, & I suffered little by sickness. Having very thick weather when we approached the coast of Europe, we fell in with no vessel which could take me & put me on the French coast as I had intended. I therefore went ashore at Portsmouth where I was detained three or four days by a fever which had seized my daughter two days before we landed. As soon as she was clear of it I hired a vessel to carry me over to Havre, from whence I came on to this place, thro' a country than which nothing can be more fertile, better cultivated & more elegantly improved. It was at the time when harvest was beginning, & it is principally a farming country.

I informed you from Boston that before I had received your letters of May 25 & June 1, I had packed up our cipher and therefore could not there make out the passages which were put into cipher. I have tried it here & find that by some

title to western lands might possibly come under the discussion of the ministers," he withdrew himself from the discussion. (Koch 1950, 16-17)

unfortunate mistake, probably in the young gentleman who wrote the cipher, it will not explain a single syllable. He has arranged all the numbers in their regular order, and then placed against each the words, syllables &c in alphabetical order. You can judge whether this was the plan of it. The want of the cipher would have restrained me from mentioning some things were I not assured of the fidelity of the bearer hereof Colo. Le Maire.

I am to acknowledge the receipt of your letter of Aug. 9. from New York, but not of the previous one therein mentioned to be sent by Mr. Short, he being not yet come, nor any tidings of him.

The die is thrown here & has turned up war. Doubts whether an accommodation may not yet take place are still entertained by some, but I hold it impossible.[1] Probably the Emperor will encourage negotiations during the winter, while no warlike operations may go on, in order to amuse his adversary & lessen their preparations. It is believed the campaign will open on the Scheld. How the other nations of Europe will conduct themselves seems very doubtful. The probability is that France, Prussia, & the Porte will take an active part with the Dutch & Russia with the Germans. It is presumed that England will endeavor to keep out of the scrape. 1. Because she cannot borrow money to take part in it. 2. Because Ireland is likely to give her disturbance. 3. Because her disputes with us are not settled by a full execution of the articles of the treaty, and the hatred of her people towards us has arisen to such a height as to prepare their minds for a recommencement of hostilities should their government find this desirable. Supposing we are not involved in a new contest with Great Britain, this war may possibly renew that disposition in the powers of Europe to treat with us on liberal principles, a disposition which blazed out with enthusiasm on the conclusion of peace, but which had subsided as far below the just level in consequence of the anarchy, & depravation of principle which the British papers have constantly held forth as having taken place among us. I think when it shall become certain that war is to take place, that those nations at least who are engaged in it will be glad to ensure our neutrality & friendly dispositions by a just treaty. Such a one, or none is our business. With England nothing will produce a treaty but an enforcement of the resolutions of Congress proposing that there should be no trade where there is no treaty. The infatuation of that nation seems really preternatural. If anything will open their eyes it will be an application to the avarice of the merchants who are the very people who have opposed the treaty first meditated, and who have excited the spirit of hostility at present prevailing against us. Deaf to every principle of common sense, insensible to the feelings of man, they firmly believe they shall be permitted by us to keep all the carrying trade and that we shall attempt no act of retaliation because they are pleased to think it our interest not to do so. A gentleman immediately from England dined

---

[1] Brandt notes that an accommodation did take place. The Hapsburg emperor gained access to the Schelde, which bordered his Belgian possessions, but there was always talk of war in Europe. In a couple of years it would break out to the east, against the Turks, with Russia and the Hapsburgs fighting them on the Black Sea. John Paul Jones would serve on the Russian side, essentially as a mercenary. (Brandt 2006)

the other day at the same house with an American. They happened to sit next each other at table and spoke on the subject of our commerce. He had the air of a man of credibility. He said that just before his departure from England he had a conversation with Mr. Pitt, in which Mr. Pitt assured him the proclamation of which we complain would be passed into an act at the next session of parliament.

In the dispatches we send to Congress you will see a great interval between the Spanish Ambassador's answer to us & our reply to him. The reason of our keeping back was the hope that in the meantime he would get an answer from his Court which would save us the difficulty of answering him. I have had a hint that they may agree to make New Orleans a free port for our vessels coming down the Mississippi but without permission to us to export our produce thence.[1] All the inadequacies of this to our purpose strike me strongly. Yet I would wish you to sound your acquaintances on this subject & to let me know what they think of it; and whether if nothing more can be obtained this or no treaty, that is to say, this or war would be preferred.

Can nothing be done for young Franklin? He is sensible, discreet, polite, & good humored, & fully qualified as a Secretaire d'Ambassade. His grandfather has none annexed to his legation at this Court. He is most sensibly wounded at his grandson's being superseded. Should this war take place it would certainly be acceptable to Congress to receive regular, early, & authentic intelligence of its operations. In this view would it not be worthwhile to continue the agency of Dumas.[2] His intelligence has all these qualities. He is undoubtedly in the confidence of someone who has a part in the Dutch government, & who seems to allow him to communicate to us.

Before my arrival here Mr. Barclay in consequence of the powers given him by his commission had made an appointment or two of Consuls for some of the ports of this country: particularly of Franks for Marseilles. He is very anxious to be continued in it & is now there in the exercise of his office. If I have been rightly informed his services & sacrifices during the war have had their merit and I should suppose Congress would not supersede him but on good grounds. I promised him that I would communicate his wishes to some of my friends that his pretensions might not be set aside for want of being known.

There is an idea here of removing the packets from L'Orient to Havre. This latter may be considered as the port of Paris itself, because the transportation between them is down the Seine in boats & makes scarcely a greater addition to the price than in transportation from a warehouse to the waterside. Paris is the only place at which all the productions & manufactures of France are brought to a point. Mr. Tracy, who is here from Boston has carefully examined into all their manufactures, and finds them of almost every kind, as good as in England, & cheaper generally. This truth once known, & our ships coming hither for those

---

[1] American navigation of the Mississippi remained a contentious issue until the Louisiana Purchase solved the problem in 1804. Ibid.

[2] C. F. W. Dumas, although his position was largely informal, was dedicated to American interests. He lived in a house owned by the United States in The Hague and served as a source of intelligence on Dutch affairs. He was frequently in correspondence with Jefferson and continued in his role for many years. (Ibid.)

articles which England thinks she alone can furnish us will advantage us first in opening to us double markets, & secondly in the shock it will communicate across the Channel. L'Orient is convenient in war & therefore should be left as it is, a free port. But conveyances from hence thither are by land, long, precarious, & expensive. I think our merchants will turn their views on Havre.

There is here some Frenchman from Philadelphia (perhaps Perée) who has drawn up a visionary scheme of a settlement of French emigrants, 500 in number on the Ohio. He supposes Congress, flattered by the prospect of such an addition to our numbers, will give them 400,000 acres of land, & permit them to continue French subjects. My opinion has been asked, & I have given it, that Congress will make bargains with nobody, that they will lay down general rules, to which all applicants must conform themselves by applying to the proper offices & not perplexing Congress with their visions: that they are sufficiently assured that the land office will absorb all their certificates of public debt, beyond which they have no object but to provide that the new governments shall admit an easy & firm union with the old; & that therefore I did not think they would encourage a settlement in so large a body of strangers whose language, manners & principles were so heterogeneous to ours.

I shall subscribe for you to the *Encyclopedia Methodique*. It will be in about 60 vols, & will cost 751 livres equal to 30 English guineas. If you should not chose to take it, it will be only a sacrifice of the subscription money, which is a guinea & half. The subscription is daily expected to be closed. There is about two fifths of the work now ready to be delivered amounting to about 300 livres.

We have taken some pains to find out the sums which the nations of Europe give to the Barbary States to purchase their peace. They will not tell this: yet from some glimmerings it appears to be very considerable: and I do expect that they would tax us at one, two, or perhaps three hundred thousand dollars a year. Surely our people will not give this. Would it not be better to offer them an equal treaty? If they refuse, why not go to war with them? Spain, Portugal, Naples, France & Venice are now at war with them. Every part of the Mediterranean therefore would offer us friendly ports. We ought to begin a naval power, if we mean to carry on our own commerce. Can we begin it on a more honorable occasion, or with a weaker foe? I am of opinion Paul Jones with half a dozen frigates would totally destroy their Commerce: not by attempting bombardments as the Mediterranean states do wherein they act against the whole Barbary force brought to a point, but by constant cruising & cutting them to pieces by piecemeal.

I must say a word on my own affairs because they are likely to be distressed. All the ministers who came to Europe before me, came at a time when all expenses were paid and a sum allowed in addition for their time. Of course they all had their outfit. Afterwards they were put on fixed salaries: but still these were liberal. Congress in the moment of my appointment struck off 500 guineas of the salary, and made no other provision for the outfit but allowing me to call for two quarters' salary in advance. The outfit has cost me near a thousand guineas; for which I am in debt, and which, were I to stay here seven years, I could never make good by savings out of my salary: for be assured we are the lowest & most obscure of the whole diplomatic tribe. When I was in Congress I chose never to intermeddle on the subject of salary, first because I was told the eyes of some were turned on me for this office; & secondly because I was really ignorant what might be its expenses. The latter reason ceases; the former which presents me as an interested person shall still keep me silent with all the world but yourself, to whose secrecy & delicacy I can trust. I live here about as well as we did at Annapolis. I keep a hired carriage & two horses. A riding horse I cannot afford to keep. This still is far below the level. Yet it absorbs the whole allowance, and return when I will to America, I shall be the outfit in debt to Congress. I think I am the first instance in the world where it has not been given. I mention these circumstances to you that if you should think the allowance reasonable and any opportunity should occur while you are in Congress wherein it can be decently obtained, you would be so good as to think of it. I would wish it could be done on some general occasion. The article of house rent in Mr. Adams' account in Holland and in Dr. Franklin's here may perhaps afford an occasion of touching on this article as to myself. Mr. A. lived at the Hague in a house belonging to the U. S. The question is whether you will charge him rent. Dr. F. has lived in a house the rent of which (6000 livres per. ann.) has been always charged to the U.S. The question on that is whether you will reject that & make him pay eight or nine years rent. If these articles pass it will of course add house rent to the salaries, which will be some aid but not an adequate one for the ministers in general. When this matter shall be considered the difference which has taken place between them & me as to the article of outfit may perhaps be mentioned & redressed: otherwise, as I have before mentioned, I shall return that much in debt & be obliged to sell to pay it: a circumstance which I shall think hard. I ask nothing for my time: but I think my expenses should be paid in a stile equal to that of those with whom I am classed.

I must ask the favor of you on behalf of Mr. Adams as well as myself to explain the following transaction to our Commissioners of the treasury. Congress you know directed the financier to advance me two quarters salary. He gave me a letter of credit to Mr. Grand. Relying on the effect of this I had ordered furniture for a small hotel which I rent: & had entered into engagements for paying part of the rent in advance.[1] A little before the parties were to call on me for the money I applied to Mr. Grand: but our funds were out & I found he was not disposed to advance the money. Nothing could equal my distress. In this situation Mr. Adams thought himself justifiable in drawing in my favor on the fund in Holland for 6000 florins: knowing of the order of Congress in my favor, of the failure of the funds here and that it could not be important to Congress from what part the money came. It was unlucky I did not know of the failure here before I had contracted the debt because I could have hired furniture for one third or one half of its worth annually. But this was such miserable economy, amounting to from

---

[1] Ferdinand Grand was the Paris banker who handled U.S. funds in France. (Peterson 1975, 362)

33 1/3 to 50 per cent per ann. for the use of money, as induced me to buy. I wish this to be explained to the Commissioners to save Mr. Adams from censure.

Address your letters "A Monsr. Jefferson Ministre plenipotentiaire des etats unis de l'Amerique a Paris Cul-de-sac Tetebout."

To Charles Thomson[1]
Paris, Nov. 11, 1784
Dear Sir,

There has been a lamp called the cylinder lamp lately invented here. It gives a light equal as is thought, to that of six or eight candles. It requires olive oil, but its consumption is not great. The improvement is produced by forcing the wick into a hollow cylinder so that there is a passage for the air through the hollow. The idea had occurred to Doctor Franklin a year or two before, but he tried his experiment with a rush, which not succeeding he did not prosecute it. The fact was the rush formed too small a cylinder; the one used is of an inch diameter. They make shade candlesticks for studious men, which are excellent for reading; these cost two guineas. I should have sent you a specimen of the phosphoric matches, but that I am told Mr. Rittenhouse has had some of them. They are a beautiful discovery and very useful, especially to heads which like yours and mine cannot at all times be got to sleep. The convenience of lighting a candle without getting out of bed, sealing letters without calling a servant, of kindling a fire without flint, steel, punk, &c., are of value. Will you subscribe for the *Encyclopedie Methodique?* The subscription is as yet open; about two-fifths of the work is published; the whole will cost to subscribers 751 livres. I know of no other work here lately published or now on hand which is interesting. I must pray you send me a complete copy of the journals from Nov. 1, 1783 downwards. The few sheets I had I sent when in Philadelphia to Dunlap to complete, and he never returned them or any others to me. I have the pleasure of seeing Mr. Norris sometimes. I am in hopes he is discreet and that you need not fear the corruption of his morals; he is well at present. There is one danger at his age which some other instances have proved real — that of forming a connection, as is the fashion here, which he might be unwilling to shake off when it shall be proper for him to return to his own country, and which might detain him disadvantageously here. I have not the smallest intimation that he is disposed to do this, but it is difficult for young men to refuse it where beauty is a begging in every street. Indeed, from what I have seen here I know not one good purpose on earth which can be affected by a young gentleman coming here. He may learn indeed to speak the language, but put this in the scale amongst other things he will learn and evils he is sure to acquire and it will be found too light. I have always disapproved of a European education for our youth from theory; I now do it from inspection.

---

[1] Charles Thomson was an Irish émigré and political leader during the American Revolution. He served as secretary of the Continental Congress (1774–89) and is credited as being the moving spirit in the committee that obtained the design for the Great Seal of the United States. (Wood 2009, 555)

To James Madison[1]
Paris, December 8, 1784
Dear Sir,

I thank you very much for the relation of the proceedings of assembly. It is the most grateful of all things to get those details when one is so distant from home. I like to see a disposition increasing to replenish the public coffers, and so far approve of the young stamp act. But would it not be better to simplify the system of taxation rather than to spread it over such a variety of subjects, and pass the money through so many new hands? Taxes should be proportioned to what may be annually spared by the individual, but I do not see that the sale of his land is an evidence of his ability to spare. One of my reasons for wishing to center our commerce at Norfolk was that it might bring to a point the proper subjects of taxation and reduce the army of tax- gatherers almost to a single hand. The simplest system of taxation yet adopted is that of levying on the land and the laborer. But it would be better to levy the same sums on the produce of that labor when collected in the barn of the farmer; because then if through the badness of the year he made little, he would pay little. It would be better yet to levy only on the surplus of this product above his own wants. It would be better too to levy it not in his hands, but in those of the merchant purchaser; because though' the farmer would in fact pay it, as the merchant purchaser would deduct it from the original price of his produce yet the farmer would not be sensible that he paid it. This idea would no doubt meet its difficulties & objections when it should come to be reduced to practice: yet I suspect it would be practical & expedient. Our tax-gatherers in Virginia cost as much as the whole civil list besides. What a comfort to the farmer to be allowed to supply his own wants before he should be liable to pay anything, & then only pay on his surplus.

The proposition for a Convention has had the result I expected. If one could be obtained I do not know whether it would not do more harm than good. While Mr. Henry lives another bad constitution would be formed & forever on us. What we have to do I think is devotedly to 252.746. for his death in the meantime to 203. 925. 243. 719 the 896.755 that the present is but an 851 & to 268. 661. the 872.

---

[1] Providing a large measure of insight into their friendship, in this affectingly cordial letter Jefferson urged Madison to come and spend the approaching summer in France, taking "room, bed, and plate" at Jefferson's commodious abode, where he would "become of the family." Agreeable society, Jefferson reminded Madison, is the first essential for happiness and value in life. Someday, he confided, he looked forward to a friendly community — Madison, Monroe, and [William] short settling in the neighborhood of his own Monticello, where they would form a unique "inestimable society." But first things first. At least Madison should avail himself of the opportunity to spend several months in Europe, at little more cost than his own passage money. Thus could he purchase cheaply "the knowledge of another world," wrote Jefferson. But Madison did not trust his supposedly "inferior health," and he contented himself with the vicarious knowledge afforded by the discriminating reports, purchases, and gifts of his indefatigable and loyal friend. (Koch 1950, 22)

of the 312. 730. 737. I am glad the 1005. 83 953. 735. 380. 945 have again shewn their teeth & fangs. The 777.400 had almost forgotten them.[1]

I still hope something will be done for Paine. He richly deserves it; and it will give a character of littleness to our state if they suffer themselves to be restrained from the compensation due for his services by the paltry consideration that he opposed our right to the western country. Who was there out of Virginia who did not oppose it?

Place this circumstance in one scale, and the effect his writings produced in uniting us in independence in the other, and say which preponderates. Have we gained more by his avocation of independence than we lost by his opposition to our territorial right? Pay him the balance only. I look anxiously to the approaching and improving the navigation of the Potomac and Ohio; the actual junction of the Big Beaver and Cuyahoga by a canal; as also that of Albemarle Sound and Elizabeth through the Dismal. These works will spread the field of our commerce westwardly and southwardly beyond anything ever yet done by man.

I once hinted to you the project of seating yourself in the neighborhood of Monticello, and my sanguine wishes made me look on your answer as not absolutely excluding the hope. Monroe is decided in settling there, and is actually engaged in the endeavor to purchase. Short is the same. Would you but make it a "partie quarrée," I should believe that life had still some happiness in store for me. Agreeable society is the first essential in constituting the happiness, and, of course, the value of our existence. And it is a circumstance worthy great attention when we are making first our choice of a residence. Weigh well the value of this against the difference in pecuniary interest, and ask yourself which will add most to the sum of your felicity through life. I think that, weighing them in this balance, your decision will be favorable to all our prayers. Looking back with fondness to the moment when I am again to be fixed in my own country, I view the prospect of this society as inestimable. I find you thought it worthwhile to pass the last summer in exploring the woods of America, and I think you were right. Do you not think the men and arts of this country would be worth another summer?

You can come in April, pass the months of May, June, July, August, and most of September here, and still be back to the commencement of real business in the assembly following, which I would not have you absent from. You shall find with me a room, bed, and plate, if you will do me the favor to become one of the family; as you would be here only for the summer season, I think your outfit of

---

[1] Paragraph deciphered: *The proposition for a Convention has had the result I expected. If one could be obtained I do not know whether it would not do more harm than good. While Mr. Henry lives, another bad constitution would be formed, and saddled forever on us. What we have to do I think is devoutly to pray for his death, in the meantime to keep alive the idea that the present is but an ordinance and to prepare the minds of the young men. I am glad the Episcopalians have again shewn their teeth and fangs. The dissenters had almost forgotten them.* (Boyd 1990) Note: For the remainder of the annotation in this volume, deciphered text (in italics) will be substituted for numerical encodings and placed within the body of the correspondence.

clothes need not cost you more than 50 guineas, and perhaps the attendance on the theatres and public entertainments, with other small expenses, might be half a guinea or three quarters a day. Your passage backward and forward would, I suppose, be 60 or 70 guineas more. Say that the whole would be 200 guineas. You will for that have purchased the knowledge of another world. I expect Monroe will come in the spring, and return to congress in the fall. If either this object, or the one preceding, for settling you near Monticello, can be at all promoted by the use of the money which the assembly have given me for my share in the revisal, make use of it freely, and be assured it can in no other way be applied so much to my gratification. The return of it may wait your perfect convenience.

To James Monroe[1]
Paris, Dec. 10, 1784
Dear Sir,

I wrote you the 11th. of Nov. by the last packet. Since that I have received by Mr. Short yours of July 20. inclosing the cipher. I hope that the establishment of a port on each river will end in the final success of one or of two only. Actual circumstances will prevent York and Tappahannock from being anything in spite of any encouragement. The accumulation of commodities at Norfolk and Alexandria will be so great as to carry all purchasers there; and York and Tappahannock will find it their interest to send their commodities to the same places in order to have the benefit of a competition among a great mass of purchasers. It is not amiss to encourage Alexandria because it is a rival in the very bosom of Baltimore.

I know of no investigation, at the instance of any nation, of the extent of the clause giving the rights of the most favored nation. But from the import of the words themselves, and from the clause that a privilege granted to any other nation

---

[1] This is a rather significant discussion, as it addresses the subject of the most favored nation principle as applied to the entire extent of treaties to which the United States had bound herself, or was to bind herself. This issue was raised in a July 24, 1784, correspondence from Monroe to Jefferson that contained this query. What, Monroe wondered, were the possibilities of making regulations that will induce reciprocal advantages from other nations? Thus, Virginia had just enacted a law whose operation was suspended for two years, by which foreign vessels were to be restricted to one port on each river in the State. But, he continued, suppose Spain should remove or lighten the duties on American commerce and we should try to reciprocate. "Can we and is it consistent with the usage of nations to give her reciprocal advantages here, the treaties between us and each power being, as that with France, on the principle of the right of the most favored nation?" His question, he asserted, was directed more toward information on actual international practice than on the "usual import of the wards." Here, Jefferson answers that he did not know of any investigation of the extent of the clause giving most favored nations rights; but reasoning from the words themselves, as used to express the idea that a privilege granted to any nation immediately became common, freely where freely given, or upon paying the same compensation, when any compensation was demanded. He did not doubt that if any nation would admit our goods free of duty in consideration of our doing the same, another nation could not claim exemption in our ports without yielding us the same right in theirs. (Wollery 1927, 15)

shall immediately become common, freely where freely granted, or *yielding the compensation*[1] where a compensation is given, I have no doubt that if any one nation will admit our goods duty free in consideration of our doing the same by theirs, no other nation can claim an exemption from duties in our ports without yielding us the same in theirs. The abolition of the *monopoly* of our *tobacco* in the hands of the *Farmers General* will be pushed by *us* with all *our* force. But it is so interwoven with the very foundations of *their* system of *finance* that it is of *doubtful event*.

I could not get my answer to the queries on Virginia printed in Philadelphia; but I am printing it here, and will certainly ask your acceptance of a copy. Can you employ the succeeding summer better than by coming here? Suppose Congress rises in time for you to sail by the first of April, you may pass May, June, July, August, and September here, and still be at the meeting of the ensuing Congress. You shall find with me a room, bed, and plate, with a hearty welcome: and I do not think the other expenses of your passage coming and going, outfit of clothes, attending the theatres and other public places, will exceed 200 guineas. I have recommended the same measure to Mr. Madison. Perhaps you can make the voyage together.

I wrote you in my last that there would probably be war. The common belief is now that matters will be accommodated. Those who are not in the secrets of the cabinet can only judge from external circumstances. Every movement of the two parties indicate war. I found much too on the character of the emperor, whose public acts speak him much above the common level. Those who expect peace say also that they have in view the emperor's character which they represent as whimsical and eccentric, and that he is especially affected in the Dog days. We shall not know what will be done till the spring admits the movements of troops into the field. I see no probable event which may divert the emperor from his object but the health of the empress of Russia, which at present is very precarious. Any accident to her might possibly cripple the projects of Vienna. By this packet Congress will receive the British ambassador's letter to us. It appears extraordinary, when in our letter to him we had informed him that we (three in number) had full powers to treat, that his court should propose in answer as a *previous stipulation*, that Congress should send a *person*[1] with full powers to London. I cannot suppose they have any personal objections; and therefore believe they only want to gain time in order to see how their schemes will work without a treaty. We shall bring them to an issue. I suppose it will probably end in our going to London. I think that after this we shall be obliged to go to Madrid and probably to some of the other more important courts. As it is impossible for us whenever we leave Paris to give up our houses (in which are our furniture and whatever we do not carry with us) and to find others in the instant of our return, and to remove into them, it is visible that during these journeys we are subject to double expenses, for a confidential servant must be left to take care of the house. And as during our travels the daily expenses will be much greater than at Paris where we are settled, *it will shew the reasonableness of Congress allowing houserent* in the cases formerly mentioned to you of *Mr. Adams and Doctor Franklin*

---

[1] These and subsequent words in italics were originally written in cipher and were decoded by Monroe. (Boyd 1990)

and of course *to me. I write on this subject to you alone* and would not *to you were* it not *necessary* from *circumstances explained* in a *former letter. I am like* to be *distressed* in the article of *houserent*. My case will of course *rest* on a common *bottom with* the other *gentlemen*. Indeed theirs being to be previously *settled mine* will *follow* of *course* and I would *not* have the *article* of the *outfit mentioned* if it should be *like* to *excite* an *indelicate* thought as to *me*. It appears to *me* not subject to the *imputation* of *avarice* to desire to have *my expenses paid* or I would have *suppressed* the first *thought* of it.

There are great complaints of the stoppage of letters in New York, as well those which are coming from America to France as those from France to America. If a letter is sent from hence for S. Carolina for instance it is deposited at N. York till the French postage is paid. If one is sent from S. Carolina to France, it is deposited at N.Y. till the American postage is paid. Every person then in France or America, whoever expects to receive a letter by post, must keep an Agent and a little bank in New York. In Europe this matter is so arranged that letters pass from one country to another without the least difficulty. France has a convention for this purpose with almost every country in Europe. She had such a one with England till the late war, and they are now proposing to renew it. Would it not be well for Congress to send us an instruction and power to form conventions to facilitate the passage of letters with those powers with whom we form treaties, or at least with some of them. It is certainly material with France, Holland, Gr. Br. Spain and Portugal and perhaps the Italian states.

Be so good as to present my compliments to your colleagues. I think Mr. Hardy promised to write to me sometimes. I shall take great pleasure in an exchange of information with [him]. I am with great sincerity Dear Sir Your friend & servt.,

P. S. I hope you will not desist from your plan of settlement in Albem. Short will join us, & I hope Mr. Madison. Can you inform me if letters to & from us are free of postage in America?

To Horatio Gates
Paris, Dec. 13, 1784
Dear General,

I duly received the letter you were so good as to write me from New York. We have here under our contemplation the future miseries of human nature, like to be occasioned by the ambition of a young man, who has been taught to view his subjects as his cattle. The pretensions he sets up to the navigation of the Scheld would have been good, if natural right had been left uncontrolled but it is impossible for express compact to have taken away a right more effectually than it has the Emperor's. There are numbers here (but not of the cabinet) who still believe he will retract, but I see no one circumstance on which to found such a belief. Nothing had happened but what he must have foreseen and calculated on. And in fact all his movements indicate war. The Dutch are truly animated and ready to place their existence on the stake now contended for. The spring which brings general happiness to all other beings will probably open the sluices of calamity on our wretched fellow creatures on this side of the Atlantic. France, Holland, Prussia & Turkey against the two empires I think will be an overmatch. England will be neuter from interest as well as importance. The disposition of her inhabitants is very unfriendly to us. It remains to see whether their ministers suffer themselves to be led by passions also. I think it probable we shall go over there for a short time. An American vessel (a Virginia), has been lately taken by a frigate of the emperor of Morocco, who has five of them cruising on the Atlantic. The brig had just left Cadiz. Our trade to Portugal, Spain, & the Mediterranean is annihilated unless we do something decisive. Tribute or war is the usual alternative of these pirates. If we yield the power, it will require sums which our people will feel. Why not begin a navy then & decide on war? We cannot begin in a better cause nor against a weaker foe. You will have heard that the E. of Shelburne is made Marquis of Lansdown & Lord Temple Marquis of Buckingham. There is no appearance however of the former coming into the ministry which seem absolutely firm.[1]

1785

To Nathanael Greene[2]
Paris, Jan. 12, 1785
Sir,

Everything in Europe is quiet, & promises quiet for at least a year to come. We do not find it easy to make commercial arrangements in Europe. There is a want of confidence in us. This country has lately reduced the duties on American

---

[1] Horatio Gates was a retired colonial army general. The Barbary challenge to American merchant shipping sparked a great deal of debate over how to cope with corsair aggression, actual or threatened. Jefferson's early view guided him in future years. He doubted the American people would be willing to pay annual tribute and believed, generally, that it might be better to offer them an equal treaty and, if they refuse, then go to war with them. But when, in December 1784, having learned that a small American brig had been seized by a Moroccan corsair in the Atlantic, as reflected in this letter to Gates, he emphasized the hard line: "Our trade to Portugal, Spain, and the Mediterranean is annihilated unless we do something decisive. Tribute or war is the usual alternative of these pirates. If we yield the former, it will require sums which our people will feel. Why not begin a navy then and decide on war? We cannot begin in a better cause nor against a weaker foe." Jefferson was convinced this solution would be more honorable, more effective, and less expensive than paying tribute. (Thomas Jefferson Foundation, "First Barbary War" 2015)

[2] Some suggest that General Nathanael Greene was, next to George Washington, the greatest American military leader of the War for Independence. In 1775, at age thirty-two, Greene sprang from relative obscurity as a Warwick, Rhode Island, anchorsmith and small merchant to become the youngest general in the Continental Army. Although lacking in military experience, he became successively Washington's ablest brigade and division commander, quartermaster general of the army, and commander of the Southern Department. In that latter position, Greene recaptured in less than a year most of the Carolinas and Georgia after a stunning series of American defeats had given the British virtual control of the area. A brilliant strategist, Greene fought this southern campaign with a small, ill-equipped army, overcoming enormous odds. His early and unexpected death in 1786, at the age of forty-three, may explain why he has never been accorded his rightful place in the pantheon of revolutionary heroes. (Conrad 2015)

whale oil to about a guinea & a half a ton, and I think they will take the greatest part of what we can furnish. I hope therefore that this branch of our commerce will resume its activity. Portugal shews a disposition to court our trade, but this has for some time been discouraged by the hostilities of the piratical states of Barbary. The Emperor of Morocco who had taken one of our vessels, immediately consented to suspend hostilities, & ultimately gave up the vessel, cargo & crew. I think we shall be able to settle matters with him, but I am not sanguine as to the Algerians. They have taken two of our vessels, and I fear will ask such a tribute for the forbearance of their piracies as the U. S. would be unwilling to pay. (When this idea comes across my mind my faculties are absolutely suspended between indignation & impotence.) I think whatever sums we are obliged to pay for freedom of navigation in the European seas, should be levied on European commerce with us, by a separate impost, that these powers may see that they protect these enormities for their own loss.

To The Governor of Virginia (Patrick Henry)
Paris, Jan. 12, 1785
Sir,

The letter of July 20, 1784 with which your Excellency was pleased to honor me & which enclosed the resolution of assembly for the statue of Gen'l Washington came to my hands on the 29th of Nov. by Mr. Short: & a few days afterwards I received a duplicate of it. As it was not practicable to get the business into any train before the sailing of the December packet, I omitted acknowledging its receipt till the packet of this month should sail. There could be no question raised as to the Sculptor who should be employed; the reputation of Monsr. Houdon of this city being unrivalled in Europe.[1] He is resorted to for the statues of most of the sovereigns in Europe. On conversing with him Dr. Franklin & myself became satisfied that no statue could be executed so as to obtain the approbation of those to whom the figure of the original is known, but on an actual view by the artist. Of course no statue of Gen'l. Washington, which might be a true evidence of his figure to posterity, could be made from his picture. Statues are made every day from portraits: but if the person be living, they are always condemned by those who know him for a want of resemblance, and this furnishes a conclusive presumption that similar representations of the dead are equally unfaithful. Monsr. Houdon, whose reputation is such as to make it his

---

[1] Jean-Antoine Houdon was a French neoclassical sculptor. He quickly became famous in Paris for his extraordinarily accurate portrait sculptures and received commissions from all over the world. In 1785, he visited the United States briefly and stayed at Mt. Vernon while making studies for his statue of Washington (the subject of this letter). Among his portrait busts are those of Jefferson, Franklin, Diderot, Rousseau, John Paul Jones, Napoleon, Josephine, Lafayette, Molière, Mirabeau, Buffon, and Prince Henry of Prussia, and he also sculpted a full-length statue of Voltaire. Houdon succeeded not only in creating sculptural documents of his time, but in developing a type of portraiture remarkable for its elegance, measured realism, and depiction of individuality. Houdon exerted a strong influence over European and American sculptors for several generations. (*The Columbia Encyclopedia*, 2015)

principal object, was so anxious to be the person who should hand down the figure of the General to future ages, that without hesitating a moment he offered to abandon his business here, to leave the statues of kings unfinished, & to go to America to take the true figure by actual inspection & mensuration. We believe, from his character, that he will not propose any very considerable sum for making this journey; probably two or three hundred guineas, as he must necessarily be absent three or four months & his expenses will make at least a hundred guineas of the money. When the whole merit of the piece was to depend on this previous expenditure, we could not doubt your approbation of the measure; and that you would think with us that things which are just or handsome should never be done by halves. We shall regulate the article of expense as economically as we can with justice to the wishes of the world. This article, together with the habit, attitude, devices &c. are now under consideration, & till they be decided on, we cannot ultimately contract with

Monsr. Houdon. We are agreed in one circumstance, that the size shall be precisely that of life. Were we to have executed a statue in any other case, we should have preferred making it somewhat larger than life; because as they are generally a little elevated, they appear smaller, but we think it important that some one monument should be preserved of the true size as well as figure, from which all other countries (and our own at any future day when they shall desire it) may take copies, varying them in their dimensions as may suit the particular situation in which they wish to place them. The duty as well as the glory of this presentation we think belongs peculiarly to Virginia. We are sensible that the eye, alone considered, will not be quite as well satisfied; but connecting the consideration that the whole, & every part of it presents the true size of the life, we suppose the beholders will receive a greater leisure on the whole. Should we agree with Monsr. Houdon, he will come over in the April packet & of course may be expected in Virginia about the last of May. His stay with the General will be about a month. This will be employed in forming his bust of plaster. With this he will return to Paris, & will then be between two & three years in executing the whole in marble. I have thought it my duty to detail to your Excellency our ideas on the subject as far as they are settled, that if in any point we are varying from the wishes of the Executive or legislature, we may be set right in time. I conjecture that you will receive this about the latter end of February and as Monsr. Houdon will not set out till about the 12th. or 14th of April there may be time to receive your pleasure in the mean while. We think that the whole expense of the journey & execution of the figure will be within the limits conjectured by your Excellency; but of this we cannot be certain as yet.

To James Monroe
Paris. Feb. 6, 1785
Dear Sir,

You were informed by my letters of Nov. 11. & Jan. 14 that the cipher established between us would not explain a syllable of your letters. Those of Nov. 1. & Dec. 14 having rendered me extremely desirous of deciphering them,

I set to work with a resolution to effect it if possible. I soon found that they were written by your first cipher. To this, therefore, I applied myself and after several days spent on it I was able to set to rights the many errors of your copyist, whose inattention alone had inducted those difficulties. I found the numbers in my copy & yours to correspond as follows.[1]

> From 1–153 was right.
>
> 154 in yours corresponded to 185 in mine.
>
> From 156 to 205 in yours corresponded to from 186 to 235 in mine.
>
> From 206 to 236 in yours corresponded to from 154 to 184 in mine.
>
> From 237 to 248 in yours corresponded to from 236 to 247 in mine.
>
> From 268 to 352 in yours corresponded to from 266 to 350 in mine.
>
> From 359 to 454 in yours corresponded to from 356 to 451 in mine.
>
> From 456 to 551 in yours corresponded to from 452 to 547 in mine.
>
> From 558 to 989 in yours corresponded to from 553 to 984 in mine.
>
> 994 in yours corresponded to 988, 989 in mine.
>
> 996, 997 in yours corresponded to 01. 02 in mine.
>
> 02. 03. 04. 05. 06. 07. 08. 09. in yours corresponded to 06. 07. 08.09. 009. 008. 007. 006. in mine.
>
> 006. 002. 017. 016. 060. 050. 032. 041. 042. in yours corresponds to 002. 017. 013. 012. 020. 021. 036. 045. 046.

The remaining numbers of the cipher either did not enter into your letters at all, or not often enough to detect the errors. I have now therefore completely deciphered your letters of June 1. June 25. Nov. 1 and Dec. 14.

At present my only uneasiness is about my letters which have gone to you in cipher. That of Nov. 11 must have been in the 1st cipher. For this reason I have noted to you the differences in our copies as above that you may translate my numbers into yours. As I received the 2d cipher the 29th of Nov., I think it probable that my letters of Dec. 10. & Jan. 14 were written by that. If they were, I am in hopes you will have understood them. If they were written by the 1st. you will now be able by translating the numbers to understand them also; and thus this comedy of errors will be cleared up. Since writing so far I have made out a

---

[1] Even after the 1783 Treaty of Paris ended the American Revolution and the threat of British dispatch capture, the Virginia Congressional delegates remained obsessed with secrecy. Throughout the 1780s, Madison, Monroe, Jefferson, and the other delegates expanded to 1,500, the initial 600-element "nomenclator" as the fundamental cipher application. This is essentially a list with numbers keyed to the same number of words or parts of words (elements) in a random pattern and then used as their substitutes in an encoded message. When Jefferson served as United States minister to France from 1784 to 1789, he, Monroe and Madison often encoded parts of their letters. When Jefferson returned from France, he and Madison abandoned their ciphers until the heated political animosities of the 1790s led them to resume the use of the one devised in 1785. Fearing that their letters would be read by postmasters of the opposing Federalist Party, they relied on private conversations for most of their political discussions, left letters unsigned, and began to encipher their letters when forced to put pen to paper about a potentially embarrassing or controversial topic. (Library of Congress, "Madison" 2015)

table adjusting the numbers in my copy to those in yours, which will enable you to translate with ease.

Our business goes on very slowly. No answers from Spain or Britain. The backwardness of the latter is not new. Perhaps Mr. Jay or Mr. Laurens who have been at that court since the present ministry has been in place may have been able to account for this on better grounds than we can. The English Parliament, Irish Parliament and Irish Convention sitting together will surely bring their disputes to a crisis. Scotland too seems to be stepping in as a third party with her difficulties, and their affairs in the East Indies are in a wretched situation. The opposition have opened their campaign on the East India regulations, the proceedings with Ireland, & the late taxes. The minister having declared he will propose a plan of parliamentary reform, they have taken the contrary side of course on that question. I am anxious to see whether the parliament will take any and what steps as to our commerce. The effecting treaties with the powers holding positions in the West Indies, I consider as the important part of our business. It is not of great consequence whether the others treat or not. Perhaps trade may go on with them well enough without. But Britain, Spain, Portugal, France are consequent, and Holland, Denmark, Sweden may be of service too. We have hitherto waited for favorable circumstances to press matters with France. We are now about to do it though I cannot say the prospect is good. The merchants of this country are very clamorous against our admission into the West Indies and ministers are afraid for their places. The pamphlet which I sent you is approved by the sensible people here and I am in hopes has been of some service. There are warm ones written against it. Our affairs with the piratical states are distressing. It is impossible I fear to find out what is given by other countries. Either shame or jealousy makes them wish to keep it secret. Several of their ministers to whom we have applied have promised to procure information. These pirates are contemptibly weak. Morocco who has just dared to commit an outrage on us owns only four or five frigates of 18 or 20 guns. There is not a port in their country which has more than 13 feet water. Tunis is not quite so strong (having 3 or 4 frigates only, small and worthless) is more mercantile than predatory, and would easily be led to treat either by money or fear. Tripoli has one frigate only. Algiers alone possesses any power, & they are brave. As far as I have been able to discover she possesses about 16 vessels from 22 up to 52 guns, but the vessels of all these powers are wretched in the last degree, being mostly built of the discordant pieces of other vessels which they take and pull asunder, their cordage & sails are of the same kind, taken from vessels of different sizes & powers, seldom any two guns of the same bore, & all of them light. These States too are divided, & jealous of each other, & especially of Algiers the most powerful. The others would willingly see her reduced. We have two plans to pursue. The one to carry nothing for ourselves, & thereby render ourselves invulnerable to the European states, the other (which our country will be for) is to carry as much as possible. But this will require a protecting force on the sea. Otherwise the smallest power in Europe, every one which possesses a single ship of the line, may dictate to us, and enforce their demands by captures on our commerce.

Some naval force then is necessary if we mean to be commercial. Can we have a better occasion of beginning one? or find a foe more certainly within our dimensions? The motives pleading for war rather than tribute are numerous & honorable, those opposing them are mean & short sighted. However if it be decided that their peace shall be bought it shall engage my most earnest endeavors — it is as uncertain as ever whether we are to have war or peace. The ministers of this country intimate peace and Monsr. de Maillebois who is to command the Dutch army is not set out. I should consider his departure as an indication of war.

I must pray you to send your letters by the French packet. They come by that conveyance with certainty, having first undergone the ceremony of being opened & read in the post office which I am told is done in every country in Europe. Letters by the way of England are sometimes months getting from London here. Give me fully always the Congressional news, & by every letter if you please the journals of Congress.

I would make an additional observation or two as to the piratical states. If we enter into treaty there, a consul must be kept with each to recover our vessels taken in breach of their treaty. For these violations they practice constantly against the strongest nations & the vessels so taken are recovered with trouble & always some loss & considerable delay. The attempts heretofore made to suppress these powers have been to exterminate them at one blow. They are too numerous and powerful by land for that. A small effort, but long continued, seems to be the only method. By suppressing their marine & trade totally and continuing this till the present race of seamen should be pretty well out of the way & the younger people betake themselves to husbandry for which their toil & climate is well fitted, these nests of banditti might be reformed. I am not well enough acquainted with the present disposition of the European courts to say whether a general confederacy might be formed for suppressing these piracies. Such as should refuse would give us a just right to turn pirates also on their West India trade, and to require an annual tribute which might reimburse what we may be obliged to pay to obtain a safe navigation in their seas. Were we possessed even of a small naval force what a bridle would it be in the mouths of the West Indian powers and how respectfully would they demean themselves towards us. Be assured that the present disrespect of the nations of Europe for us will inevitably bring on insults which must involve us in war. A coward is much more exposed to quarrels than a man of spirit.

Be so good as to present one of the pamphlets with my esteem to Mr. Gherry & let him know he is a letter in my debt.

To James Madison
Paris, Mar. 18, 1785
Dear Sir,

My last to you was dated Dec. 8. Since that yours of Feb. 1, has come to hand; and I am in hopes I shall shortly receive from you the history of the last session of our assembly. I will pray you always to send your letters by the French packet which sails from N. York the 15th of every Month. I had made Neill Jamieson my post master general there, who will always take care of my letters and confide them to passengers when there are any worthy of confidence. Since the removal of Congress to that place, you can choose between N. Jamieson & our delegates there, to which you would rather address my letters. The worst conveyances you can possibly find are private hands, or Merchant ships coming from Virginia directly to France. Those letters either come not at all, or like the histories of antient times they detail to us events after their influence is spent.

Your character of the 446. magistrate is precisely agreeable to the idea I had formed of him. I take him to be of unmeasured ambition but that the men he uses are virtuous. He is re. 476. ed fraught with affection to 375. and dispose merchants to render every 1071. service. Of the cause which separated the com. of the states we never have had. 945. 578. 394. 957. 421. 574. 1040. 130. 421 and 360. 561. 164. 400. 597. From newspapers & private letters have excited without satisfying our curiosity. As your cipher is safe pay 792. me a de 13 of it. The navigation of the Scheld had for a great while agitated the politics of Europe & seemed to threaten the involving it in a general war. All of a sudden another subject, infinitely more interesting is brought on the carpet. There is reason to believe that the Emperor has made an exchange of territories with the Elector of Bavaria, & that while the Scheld has been the ostensible, Bavaria has been the real object of his Military preparations. When the proposition was communicated to the King of Prussia it is said he declared qu'il mourroit le cul sur le selle rather than see it take effect. The 895. 421. 1009. it is thought would be secretly 1070. 495. 359. with it. And some think that certain 8 said to be 564. 333. 719. 359. By the Emperor on the 781. 763. 561. of 103. are meant to be given to the latter for her acquiescence. I am attending with anxiety to the part she will act. On this occasion I shall change my opinion of her system. Of policy if it be not executable. If the Dutch escape war, they seem still to be in danger of internal revolution. The Stadholder & aristocracy can carry their differences no further without an appeal to the sword. The people are on the side of the 185. The conduct of the aristocracy in pushing their measures to such extremity is inexplicable but on the supposition that 103. has promised to support them which it is 39. 543. Was 971. 359. to do before they would enter into the late treaty.[1]

---

[1] Paragraph deciphered: Your character of the M. Fayette is precisely agreeable to the idea I had formed of him. I take him to be of unmeasured ambition but that the means he uses are virtuous. He is returned fraught with affection to America and disposed to render every possible service. Of the cause which separated the committee of the states we never have had an explicit account. Hints and dark sentences from newspapers and private letters have excited without satisfying our curiosity. As your cipher is safe pray give me a detail of it. The navigation of the Scheld had for a great while agitated the politics of Europe and seemed to threaten the involving it in a general war. All of a sudden another subject, infinitely more interesting is brought on the carpet. There is reason to believe that the Emperor has made an exchange of territories with the Elector of Bavaria,

We hear nothing from England. This circumstance, with the passage of their N. F. land bill through' the house of commons, & the sending a Consul to America (which we hear they have done) sufficiently prove a perseverance in the system of managing for us as well as for themselves in their connection with us. The administration of that country are governed by the people, & the people by their own interested wishes without calculating whether they are just or capable of being effected. Nothing will bring them to reason but physical obstruction, applied to their bodily senses. We must show that we are capable of foregoing commerce with them, before they will be capable of consenting to an equal commerce. We have all the world besides open to supply us with gew-gaws [baubles or trinkets], and all the world to buy our tobacco, for in such an event England must buy it from Amsterdam, l'Orient or any other place at which we should think proper to deposit it for them. They allow our commodities to be taken from our own ports to the W. Indies in their vessels only. Let us allow their vessels to take them to no port. The transportation of our own produce is worth 750.000 £ sterl. annually, will employ 200.000 tonnage of ships, & 12.000 seamen constantly. It will be no misfortune that Gr. Br. obliges us to exclude her from a participation in this business. Our own shipping will grow fast under the exclusion, & till it is equal to the object the Dutch will supply us. The commerce with the Eng. W. I. is valuable & would be worth a sacrifice to us. But the commerce with the British dominion in Europe is a losing one & deserves no sacrifice. Our tobacco they must have from whatever place we make its deposit, because they can get no other whose quality so well suits the habits of their people. It is not a commodity like wheat, which will not bear a double voyage. Were it so, the privilege of carrying it directly to England might be worth something. I know nothing which would act more powerfully as a sumptuary law with our people than an inhibition of commerce with England. They are habituated to the luxuries of that Country & will have them while they can get them. They are unacquainted with those of other countries, and therefore will not very soon bring them so far into fashion as that it shall be thought disreputable not to have them in one's house or on their table.

It is to be considered how far an exemption of Ireland from this inhibition would embarrass the councils of England, on the one hand, and defeat the

---

and that while the Scheld has been the ostensible, Bavaria has been the real object of his military preparations. When the proposition was communicated to the King of Prussia it is said he declared *qu'il mourroit le cul sur la selle* rather than see it take effect. The Dutch it is thought would be secretly pleased with it. And some think that certain places said to be reserved by the Emperor on the borders of France are meant to be given to the latter for her acquiescence. I am attending with anxiety to the part she will act on this occasion. I shall change my opinion of her system of policy if it be not honorable. If the Dutch escape a war, they seem still to be in danger of internal revolution. The Stadtholder and Aristocracy can carry their differences no further without an appeal to the sword. The people are on the side of the Stadtholder. The conduct of the aristocracy in pushing their measures to such extremity is inexplicable but on the supposition that France has promised to support them which it is thought she was obliged to do before they would enter into the late treaty. (Boyd 1990)

---

regulation itself on the other. I rather believe it would do more harm in the latter way than good in the former. In fact a heavy aristocracy & corruption are two bridles in the mouths of the Irish which will prevent them from making any effectual efforts against their masters.

We shall now 406. 643. call for decisive answer to certain points interesting to the 826. and unconnected with the general treaty which they have a right to decline. I mentioned to you in a former letter a very good dictionary of universal law called the Code d'humanité in 13 vols 4to. Meeting by chance an opportunity of buying a copy, new & well in England costs 15/sterl. a volume. I shall have an opportunity of sending this & what other books I have bought for you in May. But new information throws me all into doubt what to do with them. Late letters tell us you are nominated for the 80. of Spain. I must depend on further intelligence therefore to decide whether to send them or to await your orders. I need not tell you how much I shall be pleased with such an event. Yet it has its displeasing sides also. I sent in the 170. 110. and also in 730. Yet we cannot have 312. 378. 823 485. We must therefore be contented to have 312. 485. 312. 1009. 638.[1]

Adieu, yours affectionately &c.

To James Monroe
Paris, Mar. 18, 1785
Dear Sir,

I wrote you by the packet which sailed from hence in Feb. and then acknowledged the receipt of yours of Dec. 14, which came by the packet arriving here in Jan. That which sailed from N. Y. in Jan. & arrived here in Feb. brings me no letter from anybody except from Mr. Jay to Mr. Adams, Dr. F. & myself jointly. Since my last the rumor of an exchange proposed between the Emperor & El. of Bavaria has proved to have some foundation. What issue it will be permitted to have is doubtful. The K. of Prussia will risk his own annihilation to prevent it. The Dutch would rather be pleased with it; and it is thought by some that it will not be disagreeable to France. It has even been said that certain places are reserved by the emperor on the borders of France to give to this court by way of trust money. I am watching with anxiety the part which this court will act. If

---

[1] Paragraph deciphered: We shall now very soon call for decisive answers to certain points interesting to the United States and unconnected with the general treaty which they have a right to decline. I mentioned to you in a former letter a very good dictionary of universal law called the *Code d'humanité* in 13. vols. Meeting by chance an opportunity of buying a copy, new, and well bound for 104 livres I purchased it for you. It comes to 8 livres a volume which is a fraction over a dollar and a half, and in England costs 15 sterl. a volume. I shall have an opportunity of sending this and what other books I have bought for you in May. But new information throws me all into doubt what to do with them. Late letters tell us you are nominated for the court of Spain. I must depend on further intelligence therefore to decide whether to send them or to await your orders. I need not tell you how much I shall be pleased with such an event. Yet it has its displeasing sides also. I want you in the Virginia Assembly and also in Congress yet we cannot have you everywhere. We must therefore be contented to have you where you chose. (Boyd 1990)

the sordid one suspected by some, I shall renounce all faith in national rectitude, and believe that in public conduct we are not yet emerged from the rascality of the 16th century.

There are great numbers of well enlightened men in this nation. The ministry is such. The King has an honest heart. The line of policy hitherto pursued by them has been such as virtue would dictate and wisdom approve, relying on their wisdom only I think they would not accept the bribe suppose it would be to relinquish that honorable character of disinterestedness and new faith which they have acquired by many sacrifices and which has put in their hands the government as it were of Europe. A wise man, if nature has not formed him honest, will yet act as if he were honest: because he will find it the most advantageous & wise part in the long run. I have believed that this court possesses this high species of wisdom even if it's new faith be ostensible only. If they trip on any occasion it will be warning to us. I do not expect they will, but it is our business to be on the watch. The Dutch seem to be on the brink of some internal revolution, even if they escape being engaged in war, as appearances at present seem to indicate. The division between the Stadholder and the aristocracy cannot be greater & the people are on the side of the former. The fury with which the aristocracy drive their measures is inexplicable but on the supposition that France has promised to support and this I believe she did to induce them to the late treaty. We hear nothing from England. This circumstance, with the passage of their N. F. land bill through the H. of Commons and the sending a Consul to America (which we hear they have done) sufficiently prove a perseverance in the system of managing for both sides in their connection with us.[1]

Our people and merchants must consider their business as not yet settled with England. After exercising the self-denial which was requisite to carry us through' the war, they must push it a little further to obtain proper peace arrangements with them. They can do it the better as all the world is open to them; and it is very extraordinary if the whole world besides cannot supply them with what they may want. I think it essential to exclude them from the carriage of American produce. We wait the arrival of the packet which left you in Feb. in expectation of some instructions on the subject of England. Should none come, we shall immediately press them for an answer on those subjects which were unconnected with a treaty of commerce.

It is to be considered how far an exception in favor of Ireland in our commercial regulations might embarrass the councils of England on the one hand, & on the other how far it might give room to an evasion of the regulations.

Mr. Carmichael has obtained the interference of the court of Madrid for the vessel & crew taken by the Emperor of Morocco: & I understand there

---

[1] Although Jefferson speaks to "wise" and "honest" men, as Combs reminds us, both Jefferson and Madison continued to fear power even when it was concentrated in the hands of virtuous people. They remained convinced that power corrupted and consequently they always sought to balance it with a countervailing power. Jefferson believed that to concentrate all powers in one branch of government — even a popularly elected legislature — was the very definition of a despotic governance. (Combs 1970, 68)

is a prospect of their being restored. A letter on this subject is come to Doctr. Franklin.[1] I have not yet seen it & I doubt whether it will be in time to be copied & communicated by this packet, the post being near it's departure. On the arrival of the packet now expected here, whether she brings us new instructions or not as to those states, we shall proceed to act for the best on the ground before marked out for us. The Marquis Fayette has arrived here in good health, and in the best dispositions towards us. I have had a very bad winter, having been confined the greatest part of it. A seasoning as they call it is the lot of most strangers: & none I believe have experienced a more severe one than myself. The air is extremely damp, and the waters very unwholesome. We have had for three weeks past a warm visit from the sun (my almighty physician) and I find myself almost reestablished. I begin now to be able to walk 4 or 5 miles a day, & find myself much better for it. If the state of our business will permit I wish much to take a tour through the South of France for three or four weeks. The climate & exercise would I think restore my health.

I have used the second cipher in this letter. Either by a gentleman who will go to America in the April packet, or by young Mr. Adams who will go in May, I will send you a new cipher which I have prepared on a large & commodious plan. This young gentleman is I think very promising. To a vast thirst after useful knowledge he adds a facility in acquiring it.[2] What his judgement may be I am not well enough acquainted with him to decide: but I expect it is good, & much hope it, as he may become a valuable & useful citizen.

I sent you by the former packet the pour and contre [pros and cons] for the emancipation of the French W. I. [West Indies] Trade. I now send you the answer to it. The mass of the nation is with the latter. Adieu.

To James Monroe
Paris, Apr. 15, 1785
Dear Sir,

We wrote a public letter to Mr. Jay the day before yesterday. We were induced to hasten it, because young Mr. Chaumont was to set out yesterday for l'Orient to go to N. York in the packet, & a private conveyance is alone to be depended on for secrecy.

---

[1] William Carmichael was then the *chargé d'affaires* at Madrid, (Kimball, 1950, 24)
[2] This "young gentleman" is John Quincy Adams, son of John Adams. In February 1778, at the age of eleven, he had accompanied his father on a brief diplomatic mission to France. In June 1779 they left on a second mission to Europe, John Adams having been commissioned to negotiate a treaty of peace with Great Britain. When John Adams was sent as minister to Holland, John Quincy left the schools of Paris and entered those of Amsterdam. Among the opportunities that came to him during this period was his assignment to St. Petersburg in July 1781, as the fourteen-year-old private secretary to Francis Dana, newly appointed American representative in Russia and where he remained until September 1782. He travelled extensively in Sweden, Denmark and Germany, met his father at The Hague and went with him to Paris where he witnessed the signing of the treaty of peace between Great Britain and the colonies. After spending a few months in England, he returned to study in Paris until May 1785, when he planned to return to America to attend Harvard University. (Lipsky 1950, 8)

I have put off writing any letters as long as I could, expecting the arrival of the packet. She is arrived as the packet of the last month did without bringing a scrip of a pen public or private to any American here. This perplexes us extremely. From your letter of Dec. 14. and from one written at the same time by Mr. Jay to Dr. Franklin we have reason to believe congress have done something in the affairs with England and Spain. We also thought something would be said to us on the subject of the Barbary state. We therefore deferred moving lest we should have to change our move which is always dishonorable. We particularly expected instructions as to the posts still held by the English. We shall do the best we can under our old instructions. The letter from the duke of Dorset will dare say surprise you all. It is a folly above the highest that could have been expected. I know from one who saw his instructions that he softened them much in the letter to us. The following paragraph is from a letter I received from Doctor Price about ten days ago. "There is, I fancy no probability that Britain can be brought to consent to that reciprocity in trade which the United States expect. This is bad policy for Britain but it may turn out to be best for America and should the issue be our exclusion from the American ports we may be ruined but I do not see that trade would suffer in its true interest. The fixed conviction however is that we are able to employ America on so much better terms than any other country that do what we will we must have its trade." It is dated March twenty. He is said to be in great intimacy with Mr. Pitt, and I verily believe this paragraph contains the genuine creed of the nation and ministry. You will observe that the 4th article of our original draught of a treaty transmitted to the several courts was contrary to a right reserved by the states in the confederation. We shall correct it in every instance.

War and peace still doubtful. It rather seems that the peace may continue a while yet but not very long. The Emperor has a head too combustible to be quiet.[1] He is an eccentric character, all enterprise, without calculation, without principle, without feelings. Ambitious in the extreme but too unsteady to surmount difficulties. He had in view at one time to open the Scheld, to get Maestricht from the Dutch, to take a large district from the Turks, to exchange some of his Austrian Dominions for Bavaria, to create a ninth electorate, to make his nephew King of the Romans, and to change totally the Constitution of

---

[1] Joseph II, the Holy Roman Emperor from 1765 to 1790, was the eighteenth century's epitome of political reform as Voltaire was of polemical literature. He was the most significant of the "enlightened despots," the final effort of absolute monarchy to save its existence and prove its usefulness. All the currents of the epoch converged in the revolutionary Joseph, making him an idealist and cynic, a reformer and despot. He conversed about mankind with Rousseau and planned political schemes with Catharine II of Russia; he discussed administration with Turgot and fought a war with Frederick the Great. No ruler of his time was more conscientious than Joseph, but the tasks he set himself were impossible to achieve. He strove to bring wealth to his state, to modernize the administration, to make his empire powerful, to destroy the privileged classes, to free his people from feudal burdens, to give them equality, opportunity, education, and justice. He failed heroically. (Padover 1934, 9)

Hungary. Any one of these was as much as a wise prince would have undertaken at any one time. Quod ault, valde ault, sed non diu ault.

I send you Voltaire's legacy to the K. of Prussia, a libel which will do much more injury to Voltaire than to the King. Many of the traits in the character of the latter to which the former gives a turn satirical & malicious, are real virtues. I should remind you that two packets have now come without bringing me a letter from you, and should scold you soundly, but that I consider it as certain evidence of your being sick. If this be so, you know you have my sincere prayers for better health, but why has nobody else written to me? Is it that one is forgotten as soon as their back is turned? I have a better opinion of men. It must be either that they think that the details known to themselves are known to everybody & so come to us through' a thousand channels, or that we should set no value on them. Nothing can be more erroneous than both those opinions. We value those details little & great, public & private in proportion to our distance from our own country: and so far are they from getting to us through a thousand channels, that we hear no more of them or of our country here than if we were among the dead. I have never received a tittle from any member of Congress but yourself & one letter from Dr. Williamson.

The D. de Rochefoucault is kind enough to communicate to us the intelligence which he receives from Mr. St John, & the M. de la F. what he gets from his correspondents. These have been our only sources of intelligence since the middle of December.[1]

There are particular public papers here which collect and publish with a good deal of accuracy the facts connected with political arithmetic. In one of these I have just read the following table of the proportion between the value of gold and silver in several countries: Germany 1. to 14 11/71; Spain 1. to 14 3/10; England 1. to 15 ½; France 1. to 14 42/100; Russia 1. to 15; Holland 1. to 14 3/4; Savoy 1. to 14 3/5. The average is 1. to 14 ⅝. As Congress were on this subject when I left them and I have not heard of their having finished it, I thought this worth your notice.

Since the warm weather has set in I am almost perfectly re-established. I am able now to walk six or eight miles a day which I do very regularly. This must supply the place of the journey I had meditated into the South of France.

---

[1] François Alexandre Frédéric, Duc de La Rochefoucauld-Liancourt was a French philanthropist, author, and political figure who combined practical interests in technology and agriculture with an impulse for social reform. Liancourt held an honorary position at the court of Louis XVI. As a member of the Estates General he supported both popular liberty and the authority of the crown. Days before the fall of the Bastille, when the king characterized the situation in Paris as "une révolte," Liancourt reputedly answered, "Non, Sire, c'est une révolution." Immediately thereafter, he became the president of the National Assembly, where he proposed the abolition of the death penalty and championed other liberal causes. He fled to England in 1792 after plotting unsuccessfully to transport the king out of Paris to safety. From Britain, where he knew Arthur Young, La Rochefoucauld-Liancourt traveled to Philadelphia in 1794. During the next three years he journeyed from Canada to Georgia. He visited Jefferson at Monticello, and later wrote that he found Jefferson "somewhat cold and reserved" but possessing in general "a mild, easy and obliging temper." (Boyd 1990)

Tho' our business does not afford constant occupation, it is of such a nature one does not know when our presence may be wanted. I need add no signature but wishing you every happiness bid you adieu.

To James Madison
Paris, May 11, 1785
Dear Sir,

Your favor of Jan. 9 came to my hands on the 13th of April. The very full and satisfactory detail of the proceedings of Assembly which it contained, gave me the highest pleasure. The value of these communications cannot be calculated at a shorter distance than the breadth of the Atlantic. Having lately made a cipher on a more convenient plan than the one we have used, I now transmit it to you by a Monsr. Doradour, who goes to settle in Virginia. His family will follow him next year.[1]

Should he have occasion of your patronage I beg leave to solicit it for him. They yesterday finished printing my notes. I had 200 copies printed, but do not put them out of my own hands, except two or three copies here & two which I shall send to America, to yourself & Colo Monroe, if they can be ready this evening, as promised.

In this case you will receive one by Monsr. Doradour. I beg you to peruse it carefully, because I ask your advice on it & ask no body's else. I wish to put it into the hands of the young men at the college, as well on account of the political as physical parts. But there are sentiments on some subjects which I apprehend might be displeasing to the country, perhaps to the assembly or to some who lead it. I do not wish to be exposed to their censure; nor do I know how far their influence, if exerted, might effect a misapplication of law to such a publication were it made. Communicate it then in confidence to those whose judgments & information you would pay respect to, & if you think it will give no offence I will send a copy to each of the students of W. M. C. and some others to my friends & to your disposal, otherwise I shall only send over a very few copies to particular friends in confidence & burn the rest.

Answer me soon & without reserve. Do not view me as an author & attached to what he has written. I am neither. They were at first intended only for Marbois. When I had enlarged them, I thought first of giving copies to three or four friends. I have since supposed they might set our young students into a useful train of thought, and in no event do I propose to admit them to go to the public at large. A variety of accidents have postponed my writing to you till I have no further time to continue my letter. The next packet will sail from Havre. I will then send your books & write more fully. But answer me immediately on the preceding subject.

---

[1] Comte de Doradour had recently lost much of his fortune in a lawsuit, and was planning to settle with his family in Virginia where, he thought, his modest means would be less of a burden than in polite French society. The count planned to sail with John Quincy Adams in the May packet, but at the last minute he delayed his departure for a month, much to Adam's annoyance. Doradour was soon disappointed with Virginia, and returned to France in 1786. (Taylor 2015)

To The Governor of Virginia (Patrick Henry)
Paris, June 16, 1785
Sir,

I had the honor of receiving the day before yesterday the resolution of council of Mar. 10, and your letter of Mar. 30, and shall with great pleasure unite my endeavors with those of the M. de la Fayette and Mr. Barclay for the purpose of procuring the arms desired. Nothing can be more wise than this determination to arm our people as it is impossible to say when our neighbors may think proper to give them exercise. I suppose that the establishing a manufacture of arms to go hand in hand with the purchase of them from hence is at present opposed by good reasons. This alone would make us independent for an article essential to our preservation, and workmen could probably be either got here, or drawn from England to be embarked hence.

In a letter of Jan. 12, to Govr. Harrison I informed him of the necessity that the statuary should see Gen'l. Washington, that we should accordingly send him over unless the Executive disapproved of it, in which case I prayed to receive their pleasure. Mr. Houdon being now re-established in his health, and no countermand received, I hope this measure meet the approbation of the Executive; Mr. Houdon will therefore go over with Dr. Franklin sometime in the next month.

I have the honor of inclosing you the substance of propositions which have been made from London to the Farmers general of this country to furnish them with the tobaccos of Virginia & Maryland which propositions were procured for me by the M. de la Fayette. I take the liberty of troubling you with them on a supposition that it may be possible to have this article furnished from those two states to this country immediately without its passing through the entrepot [port of entry] of London, & the returns for it being made of course in London merchandise. 20,000 hhds of tobō [tobacco] a year delivered here in exchange for the produce and manufactures of this country, many of which are as good, some better, & most of them cheaper than in England, would establish a rivalship for our commerce which would have happy effects in all the three countries.[1] Whether this end will be best effected by giving out these propositions to our merchants, & exciting them to become candidates with the farmers general for this contract or by any other means, your Excellency will best judge on the spot.

---

[1] During the seventeenth and eighteenth century, the primary goods transported in hogsheads (hhds) were sugar, tobacco, molasses, and rum. Tobacco hogsheads were made of white or red oak staves and loops; each measured about 48 inches in height and weighed about 1,000 lbs. Hogsheads could be rolled easing transport via cart or boat. Each grower marked his barrels with a tobacco mark, usually some configuration of stylized initials, so each could be identified in warehouses, on board ships, and by overseas buyers. (Reisz 2013)

To James Monroe[1]
Paris, June 17, 1785
Dear Sir,

I received three days ago your favor of Apr. 12. You therein speak of a former letter to me, but it has not come to hand, nor any other of later date than the 14th of December. My last letter to you was of the 11th of May by Mr. Adams who went in the packet of that month. These conveyances are now becoming deranged. We have had expectations of their coming to Havre which would infinitely facilitate the communication between Paris & Congress: but their deliberations on the subject seem to be taking another turn. They complain of the expense, and that their commerce with us is too small to justify it. They therefore talk of sending a packet every six weeks only. The present one therefore, which should have sailed about this time, will not sail until the 1st of July. However the whole matter is as yet undecided. I have hoped that when Mr. St. John arrives from N. York he will get them replaced on their monthly system. By the bye what is the meaning of a very angry resolution of Congress on this subject? I have it not by me and therefore cannot cite it by date, but you will remember it, and will oblige me by explaining its foundation. This will be handed you by Mr. Otto who comes to America as Chargé des Affaires in the room of Mr. Marbois promoted to the Intendancy of Hispaniola, which office is next to that of Governor. He becomes the head of the civil as the Governor is of the military department. I am much pleased with Otto's appointment. He is good humored, affectionate to America, will see things in a friendly light when they admit of it, in a rational one always, and will not pique himself on writing every trifling circumstance of irritation to his court. I wish you to be acquainted with him, as a friendly intercourse between individuals who do business together produces a mutual spirit of accommodation useful to both parties. It is very much our interest to keep up the affection of this country for us, which is considerable. A court has no affections, but those of the people whom they govern influence their decisions even in the most arbitrary governments.

The negotiations between the Emperor & Dutch are spun out to an amazing length. At present there is no apprehension but that they will terminate in peace. This court seems to press it with ardor and the Dutch are averse considering the terms cruel & unjust as they evidently are. The present delays therefore are imputed to their coldness & to their forms. In the meantime the Turk is delaying the demarcation of limits between him and the emperor, is making the most vigorous preparations for war, and has composed his ministry of war-like

---

[1] The contrast between the Old and New Worlds left Jefferson shaken and disillusioned. As Bernstein (2012) suggests, in 1785, in this letter, he seemingly assures Monroe hat only after experiencing life in Europe did he have any idea of the difference between American innocence, freedom, and virtue and European corruption and decadence. Though he enjoyed his years in Europe, his exposure to European decadence and corruption left him traumatized; long after returning to America he was wary of the least sign that similar corruption might take root at home, and this fear shaped his development as a politician in the early years of the American constitutional system. (Bernstein 2012, 242)

characters deemed personally hostile to the emperor. Thus time seems to be spinning out both by the Dutch & Turks, & time is wanting for France. Every year's delay is a great thing to her. It is not impossible therefore but that she may secretly encourage the delays of the Dutch & hasten the preparations of the Porte while she is recovering vigour herself and, in order to be able to present such a combination to the emperor as may dictate to him to be quiet. But the designs of these courts are inscrutable. It is our interest to pray that this country may have no continental war till our peace with England is perfectly settled. The merchants of this country continue as loud & furious as ever against the Arret of August 1784, permitting our commerce with their islands to a certain degree.[1] Many of them have actually abandoned their trade. The Ministry are disposed to be firm, but there is a point at which they will give way, that is if the clamors should become such as to endanger their places. It is evident that nothing can be done by us, at this time, if we may hope it hereafter. I like your removal to N. York, and hope Congress will continue there and never execute the idea of building their federal town. Before it could be finished a change of Members in Congress or the admission of new states would remove them somewhere else. It is evident that when a sufficient number of the Western states come in they will remove it to Georgetown. In the meantime it is our interest that it should remain where it is, and give no new pretensions to any other place. I am also much pleased with the proposition to the states to invest Congress with the regulation of their trade, reserving its revenue to the states. I think it a happy idea, removing the only objection which could have been justly made to the proposition.

The time too is the present, before the admission of the Western states. I am very differently affected towards the new plan of opening our land office by dividing the lands among the states and selling them at vendue [auction]. It separates still more the interests of the states which ought to be made joint in every possible instance in order to cultivate the idea of our being one nation, and to multiply the instances in which the people shall look up to Congress as their head. And when the states get their portions they will either fool them away, or make a job of it to serve individuals. Proofs of both these practices have been

---

[1] By 1763 the French government had legalized the importation of American products and the exportation of molasses and rum. A few years later two ports were set aside to serve as depots for foreign merchandise: the Mole St. Nicholas in Santo Domingo and the careenage of St. Lucia. French merchants protested in vain. When the treaty of alliance and commerce was made in 1778, French policy was made directly favorable to the Americans. One article provided that the Americans should have one or more free ports in France itself to which they could bring and sell their produce. It was agreed that ports in the French West Indies should be kept open as they had been. Other articles of the treaty granted Americans most favored nation treatment. After the war this policy was extended even further. By an *arrêt* of 30 August 1784, seven ports were declared open and the French West Indies were opened to salt fish and other American products. French merchants wailed, and in 1785 managed to get a bounty placed on dried codfish carried to the French islands in French vessels. In 1787 the bounty was increased and a duty placed on foreign vessels carrying such fish, but it is doubtful that this had much effect, since the Americans were as adept in avoiding rules in the French islands as in the English. (Jensen 1950. 166)

furnished, and by either of them that invaluable fund is lost which ought to pay our public debt. To sell them at vendue, is to give them to the bidders of the day be they many or few. It is ripping up the hen which lays golden eggs. If sold in lots at a fixed price as first proposed, the best lots will be sold first. As these become occupied it gives a value to the interjacent ones, and raises them, though' of inferior quality, to the price of the first.

I send you by Mr. Otto a copy of my book. Be so good as to apologize to Mr., Thomson for my not sending him one by this conveyance. I could not burthen Mr. Otto with more on so long a road as that from here to l'Orient. I will send him one by a Mr. Williams who will go ere long. I have taken measures to prevent its publication.[1] My reason is that I fear the terms in which I speak of slavery and of our constitution may produce an irritation which will revolt the minds of our countrymen against reformation in these two articles, and thus do more harm than good. I have asked of Mr. Madison to sound this matter as far as he can, and if he thinks it will not produce that effect, I have then copies enough printed to give one to each of the young men at the college, and to my friends in the country.

I am sorry to see a possibility of A. L. being put into the Treasury. He has no talents for the office, and what he has will be employed in rummaging old accounts to involve you in eternal war with R. M. and he will in a short time introduce such dissensions into the Commission as to break it up. If he goes on the other appointment to Kaskaskia he will produce a revolt of that settlement from the U. S. I thank you for your attention to my outfit. For the articles of household furniture, clothes, and a carriage, I have already paid 28,000 livres and have still more to pay. For the greatest part of this I have been obliged to anticipate my salary from which however I shall never be able to repay it. I find that by a rigid economy, bordering however on meanness I can save perhaps $500 a month, at least in the summer. The residue goes for expenses so much of course & of necessity that I cannot avoid them without abandoning all respect to my public character. Yet I will pray

---

[1] The book mentioned is Jefferson's own *Notes on the State of Virginia* that, because of its unique circumstances of composition and publication, occupies a transitional place in literary history. It stands at the crossroads of manuscript culture and print culture. With the early version he completed for Marbois, Jefferson had a few manuscript copies made for friends, including Chastellux. Once the work tripled in bulk, Jefferson realized it had become too long to keep having manuscript copies made, so he reluctantly decided to have the work printed. But even with the first edition, he still treated it like a manuscript work. Instead of publishing it, that is, having a publisher undertake the cost of printing the work and assume the tasks of marketing and distribution, Jefferson assumed the cost of printing and distributed the work himself. The first edition of *Notes* was printed, but it was not published in the sense that it was made available to the reading public at large. Jefferson carefully tried to control his readership. Keeping the work private, he had more freedom to speak his mind. Within his text, Jefferson critiqued both the Virginia constitution and the practice of slavery. The passages against slavery, John Adams said, "are worth Diamonds. They will have more effect than Volumes written by mere Philosophers." Jefferson feared that his critiques would offend Virginia readers, but he hoped that his book would eventually influence political and social behavior in the South. In this letter, discussing his reluctance to publish *Notes* in very brief detail and with the first Paris edition, he sent only a few copies to his closest friends in Virginia. (Hayes 2008, 243)

you to touch this *string,* which *I know to be a tender one* with *Congress* with the utmost *delicacy. I* had *rather be ruined* in *my fortune,* than in their *esteem. If they allow me half a year's salary* as an *outfit I* can *get through my debts in time. If they raise* the *salary* to what *it was, or even pay our house rent* & *taxes,* I can *live with more decency.* I *trust* that *Mr. A.'s house* at *the Hague* & *Dr. F.'s at Passy* the *rent* of which had been always *allowed him* will *give just expectations* of the *same allowance* to *me. Mr. Jay* however did not *charge it. But he lived economically* and *laid up money.*[1]

I will take the liberty of hazarding to you some thoughts on the policy of entering into treaties with the European nations, and the nature of them. I am not wedded to these ideas, and therefore shall relinquish them cheerfully when Congress shall adopt others, and zealously endeavor to carry theirs into effect.[2] First as to the policy of making treaties. Congress, by the Confederation have no original and inherent power over the commerce of the states. But by the 9th article they are authorized to enter into treaties of commerce. The moment these treaties are concluded the jurisdiction of Congress over the commerce of the states springs into existence, and that of the particular states is superseded so far as the articles of the treaty may have taken up the subject. There are two restrictions only on the exercise of the power of treaty by Congress. 1st. that they shall not by such treaty restrain the legislatures of the states from imposing such duties on foreigners as their own people are subject to. 2dly nor from prohibiting the exportation or importation of any particular species of goods. Leaving these two points free, Congress may by treaty establish any system of commerce they please. But, as I before observed, it is by treaty alone they can do it. Though they may exercise their other powers by resolution or ordinance, those over commerce can only be exercised by forming a treaty, and this probably by an accidental wording of our Confederation. If therefore it is better for the states that Congress should regulate their commerce, it is proper that they should form treaties with all nations with whom we may possibly trade. You see that my primary object in the formation of treaties is to take the commerce of the states out of the hands of the states, and to place it under the superintendence of Congress, so far as the imperfect provisions of our constitution will admit, and until the states shall by new compact make them more perfect. I would say then to every nation on earth, *by treaty,* your people shall trade freely with us, & ours with you, paying no more than the most favored nation, in order to put an end to the right of individual states acting by fits and starts to interrupt our commerce

---

[1] In this letter, Jefferson employed the new cipher mentioned in the letter of March 18, 1785. All in italic is represented as cipher numbers in the original correspondence. Note: "A.L." is Arthur Lee, while "R.M." is Robert Morris.

[2] The anomalous situation of a central American government, loosely organized and essentially powerless, and thirteen individual states each nursing its own ego and intent upon preserving it, thus making concerted action difficult if not impossible, must indeed have been a spectacle that amazed the Europeans. It likewise gave Jefferson much food for thought. Here, to Monroe written after he had been in Europe some months struggling with the difficulties of treaty making, he sets down at considerable length his own observations on the subject. (Kimball 1950, 20)

or to embroil us with any nation. As to the terms of these treaties, the question becomes more difficult. I will mention three different plans. 1. That no duties shall be laid by either party on the productions of the other. 2. That each may be permitted to equalize their duties to those laid by the other. 3. That each shall pay in the ports of the other such duties only as the most favored nations pay. 1. Were the nations of Europe as free and unembarrassed of established system as we are, I do verily believe they would concur with us in the first plan. But it is impossible. These establishments are fixed upon them, they are interwoven with the body of their laws & the organization of their government & they make a great part of their revenue; they cannot then get rid of them. 2. The plan of equal imposts presents difficulties insurmountable. For how are the equal imposts to be effected? Is it by laying in the ports of A. an equal percent on the goods of B. with that which B. has laid in his ports on the goods of A.? But how are we to find what is that percent? For this is not the usual form of imposts. They generally pay by the ton, by the measure, by the weight, & not by the value. Besides if A. sends a million's worth of goods to B. & takes back but the half of that, and each pays the same percent, it is evident that A. pays the double of what he recovers in the same way with B. This would be our case with Spain. Shall we endeavor to effect equality then by saying A. may levy so much on the sum of B.'s importations into his ports, as B. does on the sum of A's importations into the ports of B.? But how find out that sum? Will either party lay open their custom house books candidly to evince this sum? Does either keep their books so exactly as to be able to do it? This proposition was started in Congress when our institutions were formed, as you may remember, and the impossibility of executing it occasioned it to be disapproved. Besides who should have a right of deciding when the imposts were equal. A. would say to B. my imposts do not raise so much as yours; I raise them therefore. B. would then say you have made them greater than mine, I will raise mine, and thus a kind of auction would be carried on between them, and a mutual imitation, which would end in anything sooner than equality, and right. 3. I confess then to you that I see no alternative left but that which Congress adopted, of each party placing the other on the footing of the most favored nation. If the nations of Europe from their actual establishments are not at liberty to say to America that she shall trade in their ports duty free they may say she may trade there paying no higher duties than the most favored nation. And this is valuable in many of these countries where a very great difference is made between different nations. There is no difficulty in the execution of this contract, because there is not a merchant who does not know, or may not know, the duty paid by every nation on every article. This stipulation leaves each party at liberty to regulate their own commerce by general rules; while it secures the other from partial and oppressive discriminations. The difficulty which arises in our case is, with the nations having American territory. Access to the West Indies is indispensably necessary to us. Yet how to gain it, when it is the established system of these nations to exclude all foreigners from their colonies. The only chance seems to be this, our commerce to the mother countries is valuable to them. We must endeavor then to make this the price of an admission into their West Indies, and to those who refuse the admission we must refuse our commerce or load theirs by odious discriminations in our ports. We have this circumstance in our favor too, that what one grants us in their islands, the others will not find it worth their while to refuse. The misfortune is that with this country we gave this price for their aid in the war, and we have now nothing more to offer. She being withdrawn from the competition leaves Gr. Britain much more at liberty to hold out against us. This is the difficult part of the business of treaty, and I own it does not hold out the most flattering prospect.

I wish you would consider this subject and write me your thoughts on it. Mr. Gherry [*sic*] wrote me on the same subject. Will you give me leave to impose on you the trouble of communicating this to him? It is long, and will save me much labor in copying. I hope he will be so indulgent as to consider it as an answer to that part of his letter, and will give me his further thoughts on it.

Shall I send you so much of the Encyclopedia as is already published or reserve it here till you come? It is about 40 vols. which probably is about half the work. Give yourself no uneasiness about the money. Perhaps I may find it convenient to ask you to pay trifles occasionally for me in America. I sincerely wish you may find it convenient to come here. The pleasure of the trip will be less than you expect but the utility greater. It will make you adore your own country, its soil, its climate, its quality, liberty, laws, people & manners. My God! How little do my country men know what precious blessings they are in possession of, and which no other people on earth enjoy. I confess I had no idea of it myself. While we shall see multiplied instances of Europeans going to live in America, I will venture to say no man now living will ever see an instance of an American removing to settle in Europe & continuing there. Come then & see the proofs of this, and on your return add your testimony to that of every thinking American, in order to satisfy our countrymen how much it is their interest to preserve uninfected by contagion those peculiarities in their government & manners to which they are indebted for these blessings. Adieu, my dear friend. Present me affectionately to your colleagues. If any of them think me worth writing to, they may be assured that in the epistolary account I will keep the debit side against them. Once more adieu.

June 19. Since writing the above we receive the following account. Mons. Pilatre de Rosiere, who has been waiting some months at Boulogne for a fair wind to cross the channel, at length took his ascent with a companion. The wind changed after a while & brought him back on the French coast. Being at a height of about 6000 f. some accident happened to his balloon of inflammable air. It burst, they fell from that height & were crushed to atoms. There was a Montgolfier combined with the balloon of inflammable air. It is suspected the heat of the Montgolfier rarified too much the inflammable air of the other & occasioned it to burst. The Montgolfier came down in good order.

To Mrs. John (Abigail) Adams[1]
Paris, June 21 [1785]
Dear Madam,

I have received duly the honor of your letter and am now to return you thanks for your condescension in having taken the first steps for settling a correspondence which I so much desired; for I now consider it as settled and proceed accordingly. I have always found it best to remove obstacles first. I will do so therefore in the present case by telling you that I consider your boasts of the splendor of your city and of its superb hackney coaches as a flout, and declaring that I would not give the polite, self-denying, feeling, hospitable, good-humored people of this country & their amiability in every point of view, (tho' it must be confessed our streets are somewhat dirty, & our fiacres rather indifferent) for ten such races of rich, proud hectoring, swearing, squibbling, carnivorous animals as those among whom you are; and that I do love this people with all my heart, and think that with a better religion, a better form of Government and their present governors their condition & Country would be most enviable. I pray you to observe that I have used the term "people" and that this is a noun of the masculine as well as feminine gender. I must add too that we are about reforming our fiacres, and that I expect soon an ordinance that all their drivers shall wear breeches unless any difficulty should arise whether this is a subject for the police or for the general legislation of the country to take care of. We have lately had an incident of some consequence, as it shews a spirit of treason, and audaciousness which was hardly thought to exist in this Country. Some eight or ten years ago a Chevalr. was sent on a message of state to the princess of — of — of (before I proceed an inch further I must confess my profound stupidity. For tho' I have heard this story told fifty times in all its circumstances, I declare I am unable to recollect the name of the Ambassador, the name of the Princess & the nation he was sent to; I must therefore proceed to tell you the naked story, shorn of all those precious circumstances) some chevalier or other was sent on some business or other to some princess or other. Not succeeding in his negotiation, he wrote on his return the following song:

Ennivré du brillant poste Que j'occupe récemment, Dans une chaise de poste
  Je me campe fierement;
Et jevais en ambassade

---

[1] Abigail had first met Thomas Jefferson in 1784 in Paris. She had recently arrived in Europe, where John and Benjamin Franklin served as American ministers. Jefferson soon joined the Americans in France. For almost a year — until John's appointment as the first American minister to Great Britain — the Adamses remained in France, and Abigail was unsettled. During the first forty years of her life, she had ventured scarcely twenty miles beyond her home in Braintree, and now in addition to the enormity of her voyage and her general displacement, she did not speak the language. The more urbane Jefferson experienced less cultural displacement, but he too suffered from isolation. Abigail and he immediately formed a warm friendship based not just upon alienation and empathy but upon compatibility of interests and the love of intelligent conversation. Jefferson became a welcome visitor at the Adamses' residence, and together they explored the art, theater, and musical offerings of Paris. (Gelles 1995, 86-87)

Au mon de mon souverain
Dire que je suis malade, Et que lui se porte bien. Avec une joue enflie,
Je debarque tout honteux: La princesse pour soufflée.
Au lieu d'une, en avoit deux: Et son altesse sauvage
Sans doute a trouvé mauvais Que j'eusse sur mon visage La moitié de ses
    attraits. Princesse, le roi mon maitre M'a pris pour Ambassadeur; Je viens
    vous faire connoitre
Quelle est pour vous son Ardeur. Quand vous serier sous le chaume, Il
    donneroit, m'a-t-il dit,
La moitié de son royaume
Pour celle de votre lit.
La princesse à son pupitre Compose un remerciment: Elle me donne une spitre
    Que j'emporte lestement, Et je m'en vais dans la rue Fort satisfait d' ajouter
A l'honneur de l'avoir vue
Le plaisir de la quitter.

This song run through all companies and was known to everybody. A book was afterwards printed with a regular license, called "Les quatres saisons litteraires," which being a collection of little things, contained this also, and all the world bought it or might buy it if they would, the Government taking no notice of it; it being the office of the *Journal de Paris* to give an account and criticism of new publications, this book came in turn to be criticised by the redacteur, and he happened to select and print in his Journal this song as a specimen of what the collection contained. He was seized in his bed that night and has been never since heard of. Our excellent *Journal de Paris* then is suppressed and this bold traitor has been in jail now three weeks, and for ought anybody knows will end his days there. Thus you see, madam, the value of energy in Government; our feeble republic would in such a case have probably been wrapt in the flames of war & desolation for want of a power lodged in a single hand to punish summarily those who write songs. The fate of poor Pilatre de Rosiere will have reached you before this does, and with more certainty than we yet know it. This will damp for a while the ardor of the Phaetons of our race who are endeavoring to learn us the way to heaven on wings of our own. I took a trip yesterday to Saunois and commenced an acquaintance with the old Countess d' Hocquetout. I received much pleasure from it and hope it has opened a door of admission for me to the circle of literati with which she is environed.[1] I heard there the nightingale in all its perfection: and I do not hesitate to pronounce that in America it would be deemed a bird of the third rank only, our mocking bird, & fox-colored thrush being unquestionably superior to it.

---

[1] As Jefferson predicted, his friendship with the Comtesse helped introduce him to other important literary figures. And he would return to Sannois. The Comtesse had a fine garden there and asked his help in obtaining some American plants for cultivation. He also became a frequent visitor to her townhouse. After returning to America, he wrote a heartfelt letter thanking her for the "manifold kindnesses by which you added so much to the happiness of my stay in Paris." (Hayes 2008, 295-296)

The squibs against Mr. Adams are such as I expected from the polished, mild tempered, truth-speaking people he is sent to. It would be ill policy to attempt to answer or refute them, but counter-squibs I think would be good policy. Be pleased to tell him that as I had before ordered his Madeira Frontignac to be forwarded, and had asked his orders to Mr. Garvey as to the residue, which I doubt not he has given, I was afraid to send another order about the Bourdeaux lest it should produce confusion. In stating my accounts with the United States, I am at a loss whether to charge house rent or not. It has always been allowed to Dr. Franklin. Does Mr. Adams mean to charge this for Auteuil & London? Because if he does, I certainly will, being convinced by experience that my expenses here will otherwise exceed my allowance. I ask this information of you Madam, because I think you know better than Mr. Adams what may be necessary & right for him to do in occasions of this class. I will beg the favor of you to present my respects to Miss Adams. I have no secrets to communicate to her in cipher at this moment, what I write to Mr. Adams being mere commonplace stuff, not meriting a communication to the Secretary.

I have the honor to be with the most perfect esteem. Madam, your most obedient & most humble servt.

To James Monroe
Paris, July 5, 1785
Dear Sir,

I wrote you by Mr. Adams, May 11, and by Mr. Otto June 17. The latter acknowledged the receipt of yours of Apr. 12, which is the only one come to hand of later date than Dec. 14. Little new has occurred since my last. Peace seems to shew herself under a more decided form. The emperor is now on a journey to Italy, and the two Dutch plenipotentiaries have set out for Vienna; there to make an apology for their state having dared to fire a gun in defense of their invaded rights; this is insisted on as a preliminary condition. The emperor seems to prefer the glory of terror to that of justice; and to satisfy this tinsel passion, plants a dagger in the heart of every

Dutchman which no time will extract; I enquired lately of a gentleman who lived long at Constantinople, in a public character, and enjoyed the confidence of that government, insomuch as to become well acquainted with its spirit & its powers, what he thought might be the issue of the present affairs between the emperor & the porte. He thinks the latter will not push matters to a war; and if they do they must fail under it. They have lost their warlike spirit, and their troops cannot be induced to adopt the European arms. We have no news yet of Mr. Lambe; of course our Barbary proceedings are still at a stand. *This* will be *handed you by Mr. Franklin.*[1] *He* has a separate *letter* of *introduction* to *you.* I have *never been with him enough* to *unravel his character* with certainty. *It seems* to be *good* in the *main. I see sometimes* an *attempt* to *keep himself unpenetrated* which perhaps is

---

[1] These and subsequent words in italics were originally written in cipher and were decoded by Monroe, who experienced some difficulty in the process. (Boyd 1990)

the *effect* of the *cause* — *lessons* of *his grandfather. His understanding* is *good enough* for *common uses* but not *great enough* for *uncommon* ones. However *you* will have *better opportunities* of *knowing him.* The *doctor* is *extremely wounded by* the *inattention* of *congress* to his *applications* for *him. He expected* something to be done as a *reward for his own services. He* will *preserve* a *determined silence* on this *subject* in *future.* Adieu. Yours affectionately.

P.S. Europe fixes an attentive eye on *your reception of Doctr. Franklin. He* is infinitely *esteemed. Do* not *neglect* any *marks* of *your approbation* which *you think just* or *proper.* It will *honor you* here.

To Mrs. Andrew Sprowle[1]
Paris, July 5, 1785
Madam,

Your letter of the 21st of June has come safely to hand. That which you had done me the honor of writing before has not yet been received. Having gone by Dr. Witherspoon to America, which I had left before his return to it, the delay is easily accounted for.

I wish you may be rightly informed that the property of Mr. Sprowle is yet unsold. It was advertised for sale so long ago as to found a presumption that the sale has taken place. In any event, you may go safely to Virginia. It is in the London newspapers only that exist those mobs and riots which are fabricated to deter strangers from going to America. Your person will be sacredly safe, & free from insult. You can best judge from the character and qualities of your son whether he may be a useful coadjutor to you there. I suppose him to have taken side with the British before our declaration of independence; and if this was the case, I respect the candour of the measure, though I do not its wisdom. A right to take the side which every man's conscience approves in a civil contest is too precious a right and too favorable to the preservation of liberty not to be protected by all its well informed friends. The Assembly of Virginia have given sanction to this right in several of their laws, discriminating honorably those who took side against us before the declaration of independence, from those who remained among us and strove to injure us by their treacheries. I sincerely wish that you & every other to whom this distinction applies favorably, may find in the Assembly of Virginia the good effects of that justice & generosity which have dictated to them this discrimination. It is a sentiment which will gain strength in their breasts in proportion as they can forget the savage cruelties committed on them, and will I hope in the end induce them to restore the property itself wherever it is unsold, and the price received for it where it has been actually sold. I am Madam Your very humble servt,

---

[1] Andrew Sprowle, was an influential shipyard owner who once was one of the wealthiest men in Virginia. Although he had signed the non-importation associations of 1770 and 1774, it was Sprowle whose Gosport shipyard had hosted Lord Dunmore's fleet but who had nevertheless insisted to Norfolk leaders that he was not a Tory. In the end, Sprowle had sailed with Dunmore and died some thirty miles from the shipyard that he had made into one of the greatest in America. (Kranish 2010, 90)

To Mrs. John (Abigail) Adams

Paris, July 7, 1785

Dear Madam,

I had the honor of writing you on the 21st of June, but the letter being full of treason, has waited a private conveyance. Since that date there has been received for you at Auteuil a cask of about 60 gallons of wine. I would have examined its quality, & have ventured to decide on its disposal, but it is in a cask within a cask, and therefore cannot be got at but by operations which would muddy it and disguise its quality. As you probably know what it is, what it cost, &c., be so good as to give me your orders on the subject & they shall be complied with.

Since my last I can add another chapter to the history of the redacteur of the *Journal de Paris*. After the paper had been discontinued about three weeks it appeared again, but announcing in the first sentence a changement de domicile of the redacteur, the English of which, is that the redaction of the paper had been taken from the imprisoned culprit, and given to another. Whether the imprisonment of the former has been made to cease, or what will be the last chapter of his history I cannot tell. I love energy in Government dearly — it is evident it was become necessary on this occasion, & that a very daring spirit has lately appeared in this country, for notwithstanding the several examples lately made of suppressing the London papers, suppressing the Leyden *Gazette*, imprisoning Beaumarchais,[1] & imprisoning the redacteur of the *Journal*, the author of the *Mercure* of the last week has had the presumption, speaking of the German newspapers, to say 'car les journaux de ce pays — la ne sont pas forcés de s'en tenir à juger des hemistiches ou à annoncer des programes academiques.' — Probably he is now suffering in a jail the just punishments of his insolent sneer on this mild Government tho' as yet we do not know the fact.

The settlement of the affairs of the Abbie Mably is likely to detain his friends Arnoud & Chault in Paris the greatest part of the summer. It is a fortunate circumstance for me, as I have much society, with them.

What mischief is this which is brewing anew between Faneuil hall and the nation of God-demmees?[2] Will that focus of sedition be never extinguished? I apprehend the fire will take thro' all the states and involve us again in the displeasure of our Mother Country.

---

[1] Pierre Augustin Caron de Beaumarchais, son of a watchmaker, was a familiar figure in Colonial American foreign policy. He conveyed arms and munitions of war to the American insurgents and made a large fortune by these means. He wrote, *Le Barbier de Seville, Le Marriage de Figaro, Tartare and La Mère Coupable.* (Browning and Dorset 1909, 44)

[2] In April, 1785, Boston merchants, following prewar precedent, held a meeting in Faneuil Hall, where they voted to petition Congress "for laws putting our commerce on an equality," made arrangements to communicate with committees in other colonies, and pledged themselves not only to boycott the British factors but to prevent so far as possible others from doing business with them. They agreed not to lease warehouses to the British and not to employ any person who helped the British. This anti-English feeling was widespread in the Northern states. (Carman and Syrett 1952, 200)

To Richard Henry Lee[1]
Paris, July 12, 1785
Sir,

I was honored two days ago with yours of May 16. and thank you for the intelligence it contained, much of which was new to me. It was the only letter I received by this packet except one from Mr. Hopkinson on philosophical subjects. I generally write about a dozen by every packet, & receive sometimes one, sometimes two, & sometimes n'er a one. You are right in supposing all letters opened which come either through the French or English channel, unless trusted to a passenger. Yours had been evidently opened, and I think I never received one through the post office which had not been. It is generally discoverable by the smokiness of the wax & faintness of the reimpression. Once they sent me a letter open, having forgotten to reseal it. I should be happy to hear that Congress thought of establishing packets of their own between N. York and Havre. To send a packet from each port once in two months, the business might possibly be done by two packets, as will be seen by the following scheme, wherein we will call the two packets A. and B.

Jan. A. sails from New York, B. from Havre. Feb.

Mar. B. New York. A. Havre. Apr.

May A. New York. B. Havre. June.

July B. New York. A. Havre. Aug.

Sep. A. New York. B. Havre. Oct.

Nov. B. New York. A. Havre. Dec.

I am persuaded this government would gladly arrange this matter with us, and send their packets in the intermediate months, as they are tired of the expense. We should then have a safe conveyance every two months, & one for common matters every month. A courier would pass between this & Havre in twenty-four hours. Could not the surplus of the Post office revenue be applied to this? This establishment would look like the commencement of a little Navy, the only kind of force we ought to possess. You mention that Congress is on the subject of requisition. No subject is more interesting to the honor of the states. It is an opinion which prevails much in Europe that our government wants authority to draw money from the states, & that the states want faith to pay their debts. I shall wish much to hear how far the requisitions on the

---

[1] Richard Henry Lee — then president of the Continental Congress — favored strong state rights and believed that the South, through a careful and limited restraint of trade, could avoid major injury to itself. "But it seems to me clearly beyond doubt," he wrote to Madison, "that giving Congress a power to legislate over the trade of the Union would be dangerous in the extreme to the five Southern or Staple States, whose want of ships & Seamen would expose their freightage & their produce to a most pernicious and destructive Monopoly.... In truth it demands most careful circumspection that the Remedy be not worse than the disease, bad as the last may be." Similarly, Lee reported to Jay in September 1785 that he had little confidence in New England carriers who "might fix a ruinous Monopoly upon the trade & productions of the Staple States." Madison observed to Jefferson in January 1786 that the adversaries of centralized restrictions on British trade "were bitter and illiberal against Congress & the Northern States, beyond example." Some even argued that the South might be better positioned encourage the British. (Graebner, Burns and Siracusa 2011, 95).

states are productive of actual cash. Mr. Grand informed me the other day that the Commissioners were dissatisfied with his having paid to this country but 200,000 livres of the 400,000 for which Mr. Adams drew on Holland, reserving the residue to replace his advances & furnish current expenses. They observe that these last objects might have been effected by the residue of the money in Holland which was lying dead. Mr. Grand's observation to me was that Mr. Adams did not like to draw for these purposes, that he himself had no authority, and that the Commissioners had not accompanied their complaint with any draught on that fund, so that the debt still remains unpaid while the money is lying dead in Holland. He did not desire me to mention this circumstance, but should you see the Commissioners it might not be amiss to communicate it to them, that they may take any measures they please, if they think it proper to do anything in it. I am anxious to hear what is done with the states of Vermont & Franklin. I think that the former is the only innovation on the system of Apr. 23, 1784, which ought ever possibly to be admitted. If Congress are not firm on that head, our several states will crumble to atoms by the spirit of establishing every little canton into a separate state. I hope Virginia will concur in that plan as to her territory South of the Ohio & not leave to the Western country to withdraw themselves by force & become our worst enemies instead of our best friends.[1] Europe is likely to be quiet. The departure of the Dutch deputies for Vienna, is a proof that matters are arranged between the Emperor & Dutch. The Turks shew a disposition to rally against the pursuits of the Emperor: but if this country can preserve the peace she will do it. She is not ready for war, and yet could not see peaceably any new accession of power to him. A lover of humanity would wish to see that charming country from which the Turks exclude science & freedom, in any hands rather than theirs, & in those of the native Greeks rather than any others. The recovery of their antient language would not be desperate, could they recover their antient liberty. But those who wish to remove the Turks, wish to put themselves in their places. This would be exchanging one set of Barbarians for another only.

I am sorry to hear your health is not yet established. I was in hopes a change of climate would have effected it. Perhaps the summer of N. York may have produced that good effect.

This will be handed you by Monsr. Houdon. The letter which I give him to our delegation will apprise you of his character and mission, as well as of the object he would propose with Congress. I will here only add my request to you personally to render him such civilities as may be convenient, and to avail him of those opportunities which are in your power of making him acquainted with the members of Congress and of disposing them in his favor. He will well merit their notice.

---

[1] If there was some measure of consensus that some states were too large and that new states should be created on the northern and western frontiers, it was also generally understood that frontier settlers could not be allowed to take the initiative. One of the most popular arguments against the creation of new states was that in the absence of common interests, they would spin out of the American orbit and into the arms of neighboring colonial powers. The argument assumed that the union of the states was powerless and that there was no countervailing national loyalty or patriotism in the West. (Onuf 1893, 36)

To The Virginia Delegates in Congress
Paris, July 12, 1785
Gentlemen,

In consequence of the orders of the Legislative & Executive bodies of Virginia, I have engaged Monsr. Houdon to make the Statue of Gen'l. Washington. For this purpose it is necessary for him to see the General. He therefore goes with Doctor. Franklin, & will have the honor of delivering you this himself. As his journey is at the expense of the State according to our contract, I will pray you to favor him with your patronage & counsels, and to protect him as much as possible from those impositions to which strangers are but too much exposed. I have advised him to proceed in the stages to the General's. I have also agreed, if he can see General Greene & Gates, whose busts he has a desire to make, that he may make a moderate deviation for this purpose, after he is done with General Washington.

But the most important object with him is to be employed to make General Washington's equestrian statue for Congress. Nothing but the expectation of this could have engaged him to have undertaken this voyage. The pedestrian statue for Virginia will not make it worth the business he loses by absenting himself. I was therefore obliged to assure him of my recommendations for this greater work. Having acted in this for the state, you will I hope think yourselves in some measure bound to patronize & urge his being employed by Congress. I would not have done this myself, nor asked you to do it, did I not see that it would be better for Congress to put this business into his hands, than those of any other person living, for these reasons: 1. He is without rivalship the first statuary of this age; as a proof of which he receives orders from every other country for things intended to be capital: 2. he will have seen General Washington, have taken his measures in every part, and of course whatever he does of him will have the merit of being original, from which other workmen can only furnish copies. 3. He is in possession of the house, the furnaces, & all the apparatus provided for making the statue of Louis XV. If any other workman is employed, this will all be to be provided anew and of course to be added to the price of the statue, for no man can ever expect to make two equestrian statues. The addition which this would be to the price will much exceed the expectation of any person who has not seen that apparatus. In truth it is immense. As to the price of the work it will be much greater than Congress is aware of, probably. I have enquired somewhat into this circumstance, and find the prices of those made for two centuries past have been from 120.000 guineas down to 16.000 guineas, according to the size. And as far as I have seen, the smaller they are, the more agreeable. The smallest yet made is infinitely above the size of the life, and they all appear outrée and monstrous. That of Louis XV. is probably the best in the world, and it is the smallest here. Yet it is impossible to find a point of view from which it does not appear a monster, unless you go so far as to lose sight of the features and finer lineaments of the face and body. A statue is not made, like a mountain, to be seen at a great distance. To perceive those minuter circumstances which constitute its beauty you must be near it, and, in that case, it should be so little above the size of the life, as to appear actually of that size from your point of view. I should not therefore fear to propose that the one intended by Congress should be considerably smaller than any of those to be seen here; as I think it will be more beautiful, and also cheaper. I have troubled you with these observations as they have been suggested to me from an actual sight of works in this kind, & supposed they might assist you in making up your minds on this subject. In making a contract with Monsr. Houdon it would not be proper to advance money, but as his disbursements and labour advance. As it is a work of many years, this will render the expense insensible. The pedestrian statue of marble is to take three years. The equestrian of course much more.[1] Therefore the sooner it is begun the better.

To The Governor of Virginia (Patrick Henry)[2]
Paris, July 15, [1785]
Sir,

Mr. Houdon's long & desperate illness has retarded till now his departure for Virginia, and we had hoped from our first conversations with him that it would be easy to make our terms, and that the cost of the statue and expense of sending him would be but about a thousand guineas but when we came to settle this precisely, he thought himself obliged to ask vastly more. Insomuch that at one moment we thought our treaty at an end. But unwilling to commit such a work to an inferior hand, we made him an ultimate proposition on our part. He was as much mortified at the prospect of not being the executor of such a work, as we were, not to have it done by such a hand. He therefore acceded to our terms, though' we are satisfied he will be a considerable loser. We were led to insist on them because in a former letter to the Governor I had given the hope we entertained of bringing the whole within 1000 guineas. The terms are 25,000 livres or 1000 English guineas (the English guinea being worth 25 livres) for the statue & pedestal. Besides this we pay his expenses going & returning, which we expect will be between four and five thousand livres: and if he dies in the voyage we pay his family 10,000 livres. This latter proposition was disagreeable to us. But he has a father, mother & sisters who have no resource but in his labour: and he is himself one of the best men in the world. He therefore made it a sine qua non, without which all would have been off. We have reconciled it to ourselves by determining to get insurance on his life made in London, which we expect can be done for 5 per cent, so that it becomes an additional sum of 500

[1] It should be noted that Taylor indicates that Congress had proposed as early as 1783 "that an equestrian statue be erected to General Washington," although no action had been taken for providing the necessary means. Jefferson, however, had been informed of the project, and he had not failed to call Houdon's attention to the prospect of obtaining the order, for this greater undertaking would "make it worth the business he would lose by absenting himself." (Taylor 1930, xvi)

[2] While a copy of the original agreement with Houdon has not been found, the sculptor references it in a later (8 Sep. 1796) letter Houdon wrote to Virginia Governor Robert Brooke, "The 8th of July, 1785. it was agreed between his Excellency Mr. Jefferson, in the Virginia's State's name, and me, that I should execute in marble the statue of Mr. Washington for the sum of 25,000f French money, to be paid in three times." (Houdon 1796, 396)

livres. I have written to Mr. Adams to know for what per cent the insurance can be had. I enclose you for a more particular detail, a copy of the agreement. Dr. Franklin being on his departure did not become a party to the instrument though it has been concluded with his approbation. He was disposed to give 250 guineas more, which would have split the difference between the actual terms & Mr. Houdon's demand. I wish the state, at the conclusion of the work may agree to give him this much more, because I am persuaded he will be a loser, which I am sure their generosity would not wish. But I have not given him the smallest expectation of it, choosing the proposition should come from the state which will be more honorable. You will perceive by the agreement that I pay him immediately 8333? livres, which is to be employed in getting the marble in Italy, it's transportation &c. The package & transportation of his stucco to make the molds will be about 500 livres. I shall furnish him with money for his expenses in France & I have authorized Dr. Franklin when he arrives in Philadelphia to draw on me for money for his other expenses going, staying & returning. These draughts will have been made probably & will be on their way to me before you receive this, & with the payments made here will amount to about 5000 livres more than the amount of the bill remitted me. Another third, of 8333? will become due at the end of the ensuing year. Dr Franklin leaves Passy this morning. As he travels in a litter, Mr. Houdon will follow him some days hence and will embark with him for Philadelphia. I am in hopes he will not stay in America more than a month.

To N. And J. Van Staphorst[1]
Paris, July 30, 1785
Gentlemen,

I received yesterday your favor of the 25th. Supposing that the funds which are the object of your enquiry are those which constitute what we call our domestic debt, it is my opinion that they are absolutely secure: I have no doubt

---

[1] Jefferson, who was abroad during the discussion and adoption of the Constitution, in general approved of the strengthened national government as being in the commercial interest of the country and, in France, he assumed the task of promoting and developing the commercial interests of the country. This involved commercial intercourse not only with European countries, but especially with their colonies and notably the West Indies at America's own door. In this letter to Dutch banker Nicolaas van Staphorst — and his brother Jacobus — Jefferson notes that if the American government would pay off its war debts to the financially pressed King, American commerce might legally penetrate into the French West Indies. He felt that commercial privileges might be obtained more easily from the European powers if the public credit of the United States were better, because public credit is a barometer of national strength and wealth. Therefore the public debts should be paid in full even though original holders have been forced to sell to speculators at a considerable discount. The proposed import duty to pay the debts is sound, for the funds thus obtained would make the securities desirable for investment by raising their value. Foreign creditors, and thus foreign nations, would be further impressed with the strength of the Confederation if creditors were given instantaneous recovery against debtors on pain of imprisonment. (Dorfman 1961, 260-261)

at all but that they will be paid with their interest at six per cent. But I cannot say that they are as secure and solid as the funds which constitute our foreign debt; because no man in America ever entertained a doubt that our foreign debt is to be paid fully; but some people in America have seriously contended that the certificates & other evidences of our domestic debt ought to be redeemed only at what they have cost the holder; for I must observe to you, that these certificates of Domestic debt having as yet no provision for the payment either of principal or interest, and the original holders being mostly needy, they have been sold at a very great discount. When I left America (July 1784) they sold in different states at from 15/ to 2/6 in the pound, and any amount of them might then have been purchased. Hence some thought that full justice would be done if the public paid the purchasers of them what they actually paid for them, & interest on that. But this is very far from being a general opinion; a very great majority being firmly decided that they shall be paid fully. Were I the holder of any of them, I should not have the least fear of their full payment. There is also a difference between different species of certificates, some of them being receivable in taxes, others having the benefit of particular assurances, &c. Again some of these certificates are for paper money debts. A deception here must be guarded against. Congress ordered all such to be re-settled by the depreciation tables, and a new certificate to be given in exchange for them expressing their value in real money. Yet all have not yet been resettled. In short this is a science in which few in America are expert, and no person in a foreign country can be so. Foreigners should therefore be sure that they are well advised before they meddle with them, or they may suffer. If you will reflect with what degree of success persons actually in America could speculate in the European funds which rise and fall daily, you may judge how far those in Europe may do it in the American funds, which are more variable from a variety of causes.

I am not at all acquainted with Mr. Daniel Parker, but as having once seen him in Philadelphia. He is of Massachusetts (I believe) and I am of Virginia. His circumstances are utterly unknown to me. I think there are few men in America, if there is a single one, who could command a hundred thousand pounds sterling's worth of these notes, at their real value. At their nominal amount this might be done perhaps with 25.000£ sterling, if the market price of them be as low as when I left America.

To John Adams
Paris, July 31, 1785
Dear Sir,

I was honored yesterday with yours of the 24th. instant. When the *1st. article* of *our instructions* of May 7. 1784. was *under debate in Congress*, it was *proposed* that *neither party* should make *the other pay* in *their ports greater duties than* they *paid* in the *ports* of the *other*.[1] One *objection* to this was *its impracticability*, another *that it*

---

[1] These and subsequent words in italics were originally written in cipher and were decoded for Adams by William Stephens Smith, who had been sent to England as a secretary to the U.S. legation in London. (Boyd 1990) While

would *put it* out *of our power to lay* such *duties* on *alien importation* as might *encourage importation* by *natives. Some members* much *attached* to *English policy* thought such a *distinction* should actually be *established. Some* thought the *power* to do it should be *reserved* in *case any* peculiar circumstances should *call for it, tho* under the present or *perhaps any* probable *circumstances they* did not *think* it would be *good policy* ever to *exercise* it. The *footing gentis amicissimi* was therefore *adopted* as you see in the *instruction.* As far as my enquiries enable me to judge *France and Holland* make no *distinction of duties between Aliens and natives.* I also rather believe that the *other states of Europe* make none, *England* excepted, to whom this *policy,* as that of her *navigation act, seems peculiar.* The question then *is, Should* we *disarm ourselves* of the *power to* make this *distinction against all nations* in order to *purchase an exemption* from the *Alien duties in England* only; for if we *put her importations* on the *footing of native,* all other *nations with whom we treat will* have a *right to claim the same.* I think we *should, because against other nations* who make no *distinction* in their *ports between us* and their *own subjects,* we ought *not to* make a *distinction in ours.* And *if the English* will *agree in like manner to* make none, *we should with equal reason abandon* the *right* as against *them.* I think all the *world would gain by setting commerce* at perfect *liberty.* I remember that when we were *digesting* the *general form* of *our treaty* this *proposition* to *put foreigners* and *natives on the same footing* was *considered:* and we were *all three* (Dr. *F.*) as *well as you* and *myself* in *favor of it. We* finally however *did not admit* it partly from the *objection* you *mention, but* more *still* on account of *our instructions.* But tho' the *English proclamation* had *appeared* in *America* at the time of *framing these instructions* I think its *effect as to alien duties* had *not yet been experienced* and therefore was *not attended* to. *If it* had been *noted* in the *debate I am* sure that the *annihilation of our whale trade* would have been *thought too great a price to pay* for the *reservation* of a *barren power* which a *majority of the members* did not propose *ever to exercise tho* they were willing to *retain it. Stipulating equal rights* for *foreigners and natives* we obtain more in *foreign ports than our instructions required,* and *we* only *part* with, in *our own ports,* a *power* of which *sound policy* would *probably* forever *forbid* the *exercise.* Add to this that *our treaty will be* for a very *short term,* and *if any evil be experienced under it,* a *reformation will soon* be in *our power. I am therefore for putting* this among *our original propositions* to the *court of London. If* it should *prove an insuperable obstacle with them, or if* it should *stand* in the *way of a greater advantage, we* can *but abandon* it in the *course* of the *negotiation.*

In my copy of the cipher, on the Alphabetical side, numbers are wanting from 'Denmark' to 'disc' inclusive, and from 'gone' to 'governor' inclusive. I suppose them to have been omitted in copying. Will you be so good as to send them to me from yours by the first safe conveyance? Compliments to the ladies and to Colo. Smith from Dr. Sir Your friend & servant,

---

in London Smith courted and married John Adams' daughter, Abigail "Nabby" Adams. (Massachusetts Historical Society 2015)

To Dr. Richard Price[1]
Paris, Aug. 7, 1785
Sir,

Your favor of July 2. came duly to hand. The concern you therein express as to the effect of your pamphlet in America, induces me to trouble you with some observations on that subject. From my acquaintance with that country I think I am able to judge with some degree of certainty of the manner in which it will have been received. Southward of the Chesapeak it will find but few readers concurring with it in sentiment on the subject of slavery. From the mouth to the head of the Chesapeak, the bulk of the people will approve it in theory, and it will find a respectable minority ready to adopt it in practice, a minority which for weight & worth of character preponderates against the greater number, who have not the courage to divest their families of a property which however keeps their conscience inquiet. Northward of the Chesapeak you may find here & there an opponent to your doctrine as you may find here & there a robber & a murderer, but in no greater number. In that part of America, there being but few slaves, they can easily disencumber themselves of them, and emancipation is put into such a train that in a few years there will be no slaves northward of Maryland. In Maryland I do not find such a disposition to begin the redress of this enormity as in Virginia. This is the next state to which we may turn our eyes for the interesting spectacle of justice in conflict with avarice & oppression: a conflict wherein the sacred side is gaining daily recruits, from the influx into office of young men grown & growing up. These have sucked in the principles of liberty as it were with their mother's milk; and it is to them I look with anxiety to turn the fate of this question. Be not therefore discouraged. What you have written will do a great deal of good: and could you still trouble yourself with our welfare, no man is more able to give aid to the labouring side. The college of William & Mary in Williamsburg, since the remodeling of its plan, is the place where are collected together all the young men (of Virginia) under preparation for public life. They are there under the direction (most of them) of a Mr. Wythe one of the most virtuous of characters, and whose sentiments on the subject of slavery are unequivocal. I am satisfied if you could resolve to address an exhortation to those young men, with all that eloquence of which you are master, that its influence on the future decision of this important question would be great, perhaps decisive. Thus you see that, so far from thinking you have cause to repent of what you have done, I wish you to do more, and wish it on an assurance

---

[1] Richard Price was a British moral philosopher and economic theorist who was staunch in defending the American and French Revolutions. Abolitionists had made a point of seeing to it that copies of Price's pamphlet, *Observations on the Importance of the American Revolution, and the Means of Making It a Benefit to the World* (published in 1784 in London), reached men who wielded power in the new government in America. Richard Henry Lee sent a copy to George Washington and several copies to the president of the Congress, to be distributed among the members, while Price himself forwarded several to Chief Justice John Jay, explaining that his purpose was to promote measures for gradual abolition of both slavery and the slave trade. (Fladeland, 1972, 42.)

of its effect. The information I have received from America of the reception of your pamphlet in the different states agrees with the expectations I had formed. Our country is getting into a ferment against yours, or rather has caught it from yours. God knows how this will end; but assuredly in one extreme or the other. There can be no medium between those who have loved so much. I think the decision is in your power as yet, but will not be so long. I pray you to be assured of the sincerity of the esteem & respect with which I have the honor to be Sir your most obedt humble servt.

To John Jay[1]
Paris Aug 23, 1785
Dear Sir,

I shall sometimes ask your permission to write you letters, not official but private. The present is of this kind, and is occasioned by the question proposed in yours of June 14. "Whether it would be useful to us to carry all our own productions, or none?" Were we perfectly free to decide this question, I should reason as follows. We have now lands enough to employ an infinite number of people in their cultivation. Cultivators of the earth are the most valuable citizens. They are the most vigorous, the most independent, the most virtuous, & they are tied to their country & wedded to its liberty & interests by the most lasting bonds. As long therefore as they can find employment in this line, I would not convert them into mariners, artisans or anything else. But our citizens will find employment in this line till their numbers, & of course their productions, become too great for the demand both internal & foreign. This is not the case as yet, & probably will not be for a considerable time. As soon as it is, the surplus of hands must be turned to something else. I should then perhaps wish to turn them to the sea in preference to manufactures, because comparing the characters of the two classes I find the former the most valuable citizens. I consider the class of artificers as the panders of vice & the instruments by which the liberties of a country are generally overturned. However we are not free to

---

[1] John Jay was born in New York City December 12, 1745; was graduated from King's College in 1764; was admitted to the bar in 1768 and practiced law; married Sarah Van Brugh Livingston in 1774; was a member of the Continental Congress 1774–1779; aided in obtaining approval of the Declaration of Independence and in drafting the State constitution; served as Chief Justice of New York State 1777–1778; was president of the Continental Congress 1778–1779; was Minister to Spain 1779–1782; was one of the Commissioners named in 1781 to negotiate peace with Great Britain and signed the treaties of 1782 and 1783; took office as Secretary of Foreign Affairs under the Continental Congress December 21, 1784 — his office at the time of this letter — and where he continued until the establishment of Government under the Constitution, only to unofficially superintend the Department until Jefferson took office as Secretary of State on March 22, 1790. During his tenure of office, treatise of commerce with Prussia and Morocco and a consular convention with France were negotiated. He later served as Chief Justice of the United States 1789–1795; Minister to Great Britain 1794–1795 and negotiated and signed Jay's Treaty; Governor of New York 1795–1801. After retiring to his farm at Bedford, New York City, he died May 17, 1829. (Patterson 1956, 2)

decide this question on principles of theory only. Our people are decided in the opinion that it is necessary for us to take a share in the occupation of the ocean, & their established habits induce them to require that the sea be kept open to them, and that that line of policy be pursued which will render the use of that element as great as possible to them. I think it a duty in those entrusted with the administration of their affairs to conform themselves to the decided choice of their constituents: and that therefore we should in every instance preserve an equality of right to them in the transportation of commodities, in the right of fishing, & in the other uses of the sea. But what will be the consequence? Frequent wars without a doubt. Their property will be violated on the sea, & in foreign ports, their persons will be insulted, imprisoned &c. for pretended debts, contracts, crimes, contraband, &c., &c. These insults must be resented, even if we had no feelings, yet to prevent their eternal repetition, or in other words, our commerce on the ocean & in other countries must be paid for by frequent war. The justest dispositions possible in ourselves will not secure us against it. It would be necessary that all other nations were just also. Justice indeed on our part will save us from those wars which would have been produced by a contrary disposition. But to prevent those produced by the wrongs of other nations? By putting ourselves in a condition to punish them. Weakness provokes insult & injury, while a condition to punish it often prevents it. This reasoning leads to the necessity of some naval force, that being the only weapon with which we can reach an enemy. I think it to our interest to punish the first insult; because an insult unpunished is the parent of many others. We are not at this moment in a condition to do it, but we should put ourselves into it as soon as possible. If a war with England should take place, it seems to me that the first thing necessary would be a resolution to abandon the carrying trade because we cannot protect it. Foreign nations must in that case be invited to bring us what we want & to take our productions in their own bottoms. This alone could prevent the loss of those productions to us & the acquisition of them to our enemy. Our seamen might be employed in depredations on their trade. But how dreadfully we shall suffer on our coasts, if we have no force on the water, former experience has taught us. Indeed I look forward with horror to the very possible case of war with an European power, & think there is no protection against them but from the possession of some force on the sea. Our vicinity to their West India possessions & to the fisheries is a bridle which a small naval force on our part would hold in the mouths of the most powerful of these countries. I hope our land office will rid us of our debts, & that our first attention then will be to the beginning a naval force of some sort. This alone can countenance our people as carriers on the water, & I suppose them to be determined to continue such.

I wrote you two public letters on the 14th inst., since which I have received yours of July 13. I shall always be pleased to receive from you in a private way such communications as you might not chose to put into a public letter.

To James Monroe
Paris Aug. 28, 1785

Dear Sir,

I wrote you on the 5th of July by Mr. Franklin & on the 12th of the same month by Monsr. Houdon. Since that date yours of June 16. by Mr. Mazzei is received. Everything looks like peace here. The settlement between the Emperor & Dutch is not yet published, but it is believed to be agreed. Nothing is done as yet between him & the Porte. He is much wounded by the Confederation of several of the Germanic body at the head of which is the King of Prussia, & to which the King of England as elector of Hanover is believed to accede. The object is to preserve the constitution of that empire. It shews that these princes entertain serious jealousies of the ambition of the Emperor, and this will very much endanger the election of his nephew as King of the Romans. A late arret of this court against the admission of British Manufactures produces a great sensation in England. I wish it may produce a disposition there to receive our commerce in all their dominions on advantageous terms. *This is* the *only balm* which can *heal* the *wound* that it has *received.*[1] It is but *too true* that that *country furnishes market, three fourths* of the *exports* of the *eight northern most states. A truth* not *proper* to be *spoken* of, but which should *influence our proceedings* with *them. How that negotiation advances* you are probably better informed than I am. The infidelity of the post offices rendering the communication *between Master Adams* and *myself difficult.* The improvement of our commerce *with France will be advanced more* by *negotiation at Saint James* than at *Versailles.*

The July French packet being arrived without bringing any news of Mr Lambe. If the English one of the same month be also arrived without news of him, I expect Mr Adams will concur with me in sending some other person to treat with the Barbary states.[2] Mr. Barclay is willing to go, & I have proposed him to Mr. Adams but have not yet received his answer. The peace expected between Spain & Algiers will probably not take place. It is said the former was to have given a million of dollars. Would it not be prudent to *send a minister to Portugal?* Our commerce with *that country* is very important. Perhaps *more so than* with *any other* country *in Europe.* It is possible too that they might *permit our*

---

[1] These and subsequent words in italics were originally written in cipher. (Ford 1904)

[2] To pursue peace negotiations, American consul Thomas Barclay had been sent to Morocco and Connecticut sea captain John Lamb to Algiers. In Morocco the draft treaty Barclay carried with him was accepted with only minor changes. Jefferson, Adams and Congress were very satisfied; the Morocco treaty made American vessels safe from Moroccan corsairs and there was no call for future tribute. The offer of an equal treaty did not work elsewhere in Barbary. Algiers was much more dependent than Morocco on the fruits of corsairing — captured goods, slaves, the ransoms they brought, and tribute — and less amenable to a peace treaty with the United States. While planning the Barbary missions the American Commissioners had learned that two American ships — the *Maria* and the *Dauphin* — had been captured by Algerine corsairs. As a result, Lamb was instructed to negotiate ransom for the captives in Algiers as well as a peace treaty to prevent further attacks on American vessels. This proved impossible with the limited budget Congress had approved. (Thomas Jefferson Foundation 2015)

whaling vessels to *refresh* in *Brazil or* give some other indulgence in *South America.* The lethargic character of *their ambassador here* gives a very *unhopeful aspect* to a *treaty* on this *ground.* I lately spoke with *him on the subject and he* has promised to interest him*self* in obtaining *an answer from his court.* I have waited to see what was the pleasure of Congress as to the secretaryship of my office here; that is, to see whether they proposed to appoint a secretary of legation, or leave me to appoint a private secretary. Colo. Humphrey's occupation in the dispatches & record of the matters which relate to the general commissions does not afford him leisure to aid me in my office, were I entitled to ask that aid. In the meantime the lengthy papers which often accompany the communications between the ministers here & myself, & the other business of the office absolutely require a scribe. I shall therefore on Mr. Short's return from the Hague appoint him my private secretary till Congress shall think proper to signify their pleasure.[1] The salary allowed Mr. Franklin in the same office was 1000 Dollars a year. I shall presume that Mr Short may draw the same allowance from the funds of the N. T. here as soon as I shall have made this appointment. I shall give official notice of it to Mr. Jay, that Congress may, if they disapprove of it, say so.

I am much pleased with your land ordinance, & think it improved from the first in the most material circumstances. I had mistaken the object of the division of the lands among the states. I am sanguine in my expectations of lessening our debts by this fund, and have expressed my expectations to the Minister & others here. I see by the public papers you have adopted the dollar as your money unit. In the arrangement of coins I had proposed, I ought to have inserted a gold coin of 5. dollars, which being within 2/ of the value of a guinea will be very convenient.

The English papers are incessantly repeating their lies about the tumults, the anarchy, the bankruptcies & distresses of America, these ideas prevail very generally in Europe. At a large table where I dined the other day, a gentleman from Switzerland expressed his apprehensions for the fate of Doctr. Franklin as he said he had been informed he would be received with stones by the people, who were generally dissatisfied with the revolution & incensed against all those who had assisted in bringing it about. I told him his apprehensions were just, & that the People of America would probably salute Dr. Franklin with the same stones they had thrown at the Marquis Fayette. The reception of the Doctor is an object of very general attention, and will weigh in Europe as an evidence of the satisfaction or dissatisfaction of America with their revolution. As you are to be in Williamsburgh early in November, this is the last letter I shall write you till about that time; I am with very sincere esteem Dr. Sir Your friend and servt.

To David Hartley[2]

---

[1] William Short, described as being "modest and soft in his manners," was Jefferson's protégé and private secretary. (Kimball 1950, 11)

[2] After some years a Whig pamphleteer, outspoken in his attacks on the ministry, and especially on Grenville, David Hartley entered Parliament in 1774 and spent the greater part of his time in opposition to the American war. Maintaining throughout the war a correspondence with Franklin, and being

Paris, Sep 5, 1785
Dear Sir,

Your favor of Apr 15, happened to be put into my hands at the same time with a large parcel of letters from America, which contained a variety of intelligence. It was then put where I usually place my unanswered letters, & I from time to time put off acknowledging the receipt of it till I should be able to furnish you American intelligence worth communicating. A favorable opportunity, by a courier, of writing to you occurring this morning, what has been my astonishment & chagrin on reading your letter again to find there was a case in it which required an immediate answer, but which, by the variety of matters which happened to be presented to my mind at the same time had utterly escaped my recollection. I pray you to be assured that nothing but this slip of memory would have prevented my immediate answer, & no other circumstance would have prevented it's making such an impression on my mind as that it could not have escaped. I hope you will therefore obliterate the imputation of want of respect, which under actual appearances must have arisen in your mind, but which would refer to an untrue cause the occasion of my silence. I am not sufficiently acquainted with the proceedings of the New York Assembly to say with certainty in what predicament the lands of Mr. Upton may stand. But on conferring with Colo Humphreys, who being from the neighboring state was more in the way of knowing what passed in New York, he thinks that the descriptions in their confiscation laws were such as not to include a case of this nature. The first thing to be done by Mr. Upton is to state his case to some intelligent lawyer of the country, that he may know with certainty whether they be confiscated, or not; & if not confiscated, to know what measures are necessary for completing & securing his grant. But if confiscated, there is then no other tribunal of redress but their general assembly. If he is unacquainted there, I would advise him to apply to Colo Hamilton (who was aid to Gen'l. Washington) and is now very eminent at the bar, and much to be relied on. Your letter in his favor to Mr. Jay will also procure him the benefit of his council.

With respect to America I will rather give you a general view of its situation, than merely relate recent events. The impost is still unpassed by the two states of New York & Rhode Island; for the manner in which the latter has passed it does not appear to me to answer the principal object, of establishing a fund, which, by

---

also on friendly terms with Lord North, he occupied an unusual, and at times an ambiguous, position between ministry and opposition. In 1780, as a result of his criticism, circulated in a series of published letters two years previously, he lost his seat at the general election, but he regained it in time to play some part in the ministerial changes of 1782 and 1783; and in the latter year he was appointed plenipotentiary to sign the final treaty with America. After vainly seeking some continued connection between England and the United States, by a commercial treaty or by a common nationalization, he retired from politics and can be remembered as the minister who signed the first treaty of peace between England and America, and for having introduced the first Parliamentary motion for the abolition of the slave trade. (Toth 1989, 140)

being subject to Congress alone, may give such credit to the certificates of public debt as will make them negotiable. This matter then is still suspended.

Congress have lately purchased the Indian right to nearly the whole of the land lying in the new state bounded by Lake Erie, Pennsylvania & the Ohio. The northwestern corner alone is reserved to the Delawares & Wiandots. I expect a purchase is also concluded with other tribes for a considerable proportion of the state next to this on the north side of the Ohio. They have passed an ordinance establishing a land office, considerably improved I think on the plan of which I had the honor of giving you a copy. The lands are to be offered for sale to the highest bidder. For this purpose portions of them are to be proposed in each state, that each may have the means of purchase carried equally to their doors, & that the purchasers may be a proper mixture of the citizens from all the different states. But such lots as cannot be sold for a dollar an acre are not to be parted with. They will receive as money the certificates of public debt. I flatter myself that this arrangement will very soon absorb the whole of these certificates, & thus rid us of our domestic debt, which is four fifths of our whole debt. Our foreign debt will then be a bagatelle.

I think it probable that Vermont will be made independent, as I am told the state of New York is likely to agree to it. Le-Maine will probably in time be also permitted to separate from Massachusetts. As yet they only begin to think of it. Whenever the people of Kentucky shall have agreed among themselves, my friends write me word that Virginia will consent to their separation. They will constitute the new state on the South side of Ohio, joining Virginia. North Carolina, by an act of their assembly, ceded to Congress all their lands Westward of the Alleghany. The people inhabiting that territory thereon declared themselves independent, called their state by the name of Franklin, & solicited Congress to be received into the Union. But before Congress met, N. Carolina (for what reasons I could never learn) resumed their cession. The people however persist; Congress recommended to the state to desist from their opposition, & I have no doubt they will do it. It will therefore result from the act of Congress laying off the Western country into new states. that these states will come into the union in the manner therein provided, & without any disputes as to their boundaries.

I am told that some hostile transaction by our people at the Natchez against the Spaniards has taken place. If it be fact Congress will certainly not protect them, but leave them to be chastised by the Spaniards, saving the right to the territory. A Spanish minister being now with Congress, & both parties interested in keeping the peace I think, if such an event has happened, it will be easily arranged.

I told you when here of the propositions made by Congress to the States to be authorized to make certain regulations in their commerce; & that from the disposition to strengthen the hands of Congress, which was then growing fast, I thought they would consent to it. Most of them did so, & I suppose all of them would have done it, if they have not actually done it, but that events proved a much more extensive power would be requisite. Congress have therefore desired to be invested with the whole regulation of their trade, & forever: & to prevent all temptations to abuse & all fears of it, they propose that whatever monies shall be levied on commerce, either for the purpose of revenue or by way of forfeitures or penalty, shall go directly into the coffers of the state wherein it is levied without being touched by Congress. From the present temper of the states & the conviction which your country has carried home to their minds that there is no other method of defeating the greedy attempts of other countries to trade with them on equal terms, I think they will add an article for this purpose to their confederation. But the present powers of Congress over the commerce of the states under the Confederation seems not at all understood by your ministry. They say that body has no power to enter into a treaty of commerce; why then make one? This is a mistake. By the 6th art. of the confederation the states renounce individually all power to make any treaty of whatever nature with a foreign nation. By the 9th article they give the power of making treaties wholly to Congress, with two reservations only. 1. That no treaty of commerce shall be made which shall restrain the legislatures from making foreigners pay the same imposts with their own people: nor 2, from prohibiting the exportation or importation of any species of merchandize which they might think proper. Were any treaty to be made which should violate either of these two reservations, it would be so far void. In the treaties therefore made with France, Holland, &c. this has been cautiously avoided. But are these treaties of no advantage to those nations? Besides the advantages expressly given by them, there results another of great value. The commerce of those nations with the U. S. is thereby under the protection of Congress, & no particular state, acting by fits & starts, can harass the trade of France, Holland, &c. by such measures as several of them have practiced against England by loading her merchandize with partial impost, refusing admittance to it altogether, excluding her merchants, &c. &c. For you will observe that tho by the 2d. reservation before-mentioned they can prohibit the importation of any *species* of merchandize, as for instance tho' they may prohibit the importation of wines in general, yet they cannot prohibit that of *French* wines in particular. Another advantage is that the nations having treaties with Congress can & do provide in such treaties for the admission of their consuls, a kind of officer very necessary for the regulation & protection of commerce. You know that a Consul is the creature of treaty. No nation, without an agreement, can place an officer in another country with any powers or jurisdiction whatever. But as the states have renounced the separate power of making treaties with foreign nations, they cannot separately receive a consul; & as Congress have by the Confederation no immediate jurisdiction over commerce, as they have only a power bringing that jurisdiction into existence by entering into a treaty, till such treaty be entered into Congress themselves cannot receive a Consul. Till a treaty then there exists no power in any part of our government, federal or particular, to admit a Consul among us; & if it be true as the papers say that you have lately sent one over, he cannot be admitted by any power in existence to an exercise of any function. Nothing less than a new article to be agreed to by all the states would enable Congress or the particular states to receive him. You must not be surprised then if he be not received.

I think I have by this time tired you with American politics & will therefore only add assurances of the sincere regard & esteem with which I have the honor to be dr Sir your most obedient humble servt.

To Mary Jefferson
Paris, Sept. 20, 1785
My Dear Polly,

I have not received a letter from you since I came to France If you knew how much I love you and what pleasure the receipt of your letters gave me at Philadelphia, you would have written to me, or at least have told your aunt what to write, and her goodness would have induced her to take the trouble of writing it I wish so much to see you, that I have desired your uncle and aunt to send you to me. I know, my dear Polly, how sorry you will be, and ought to be, to leave them and your cousins; but your sister and myself cannot live without you, and after a while we will carry you back again to see your friends in Virginia. In the meantime you shall be taught here to play on the harpsichord, to draw, to read and talk French, and such other things as will make you more worthy of the love of your friends; but above all things by our care and love of you, we will teach you to love us more than you will do if you stay so far from us I had no opportunity since Colonel Le Maire went, to send you anything; but when you come here you shall have as many dolls and playthings as you want for yourself, or to send to your cousins whenever you shall have opportunities. I hope you are a very good girl, that you love your uncle and aunt very much, and are very thankful to them all for their goodness to you; that you never suffer yourself to be angry with anybody, that you give your playthings to those who want them, that you do whatever anybody desires of you that is right, that you never tell stories, never beg for anything, mind your books and your work when your aunt tells you, never play but when she permits you, nor go where she forbids you; remember, too, as a constant charge, not to go out without your bonnet, because it will make you very ugly, and then we shall not love you so much. If you always practice these lessons we shall continue to love you as we do now, and it is impossible to love you anymore. We shall hope to have you with us next summer, to find you a very good girl, and to assure you of the truth of our affection for you.[1] Adieu, my dear child. Yours affectionately.

---

[1] Jefferson asked Francis Eppes, his brother-in-law, to send his daughter Polly in care of a responsible friend, with "a careful negro woman, Isabel, for instance, if she has had the small pox." She need not, he said, "come farther than Havre, l'Orient, Nantes, or whatever port she should land at, because I could go there for the child myself, and the person could return to Virginia directly." Francis and Elizabeth Eppes, who had fought with pleas and procrastination against Polly's going, who had even encouraged their fourteen-year-old son Jack (whom

To Mrs. John (Abigail) Adams
Paris Sep. 25. 1785
Dear Madam,

Mr. Short's return the night before last availed me of your favor of Aug. 12. I immediately ordered the shoes you desired which will be ready tomorrow. I am not certain whether this will be in time for the departure of Mr. Barclay or of Col. Franks, for it is not yet decided which of them goes to London. I have also procured for you three plateaux de dessert with a silvered ballustrade round them, and four figures. Of Biscuit the former cost 192#, the latter 12# each, making together 240. livres or 10. Louis. The merchant undertakes to send them by the way of Rouen through the hands of Mr. Garvey & to have them delivered in London. There will be some additional expenses of packing, transportation & duties here. Those in England I imagine you can save. When I know the amount I will inform you of it, but there will be no occasion to remit it here. With respect to the figures I could only find three of those you named, matched in size. These were Minerva, Diana, and Apollo, I was obliged to add a fourth, unguided by your choice. They offered me a fine Venus; but I thought it out of taste to have two at table at the same time. Paris & Helen were represented. I conceived it would be cruel to remove them from their peculiar shrine. When they shall pass the Atlantic, it will be to sing a requiem over our freedom & happiness. At length a fine Mars was offered, calm, bold, his faulchion not drawn but ready to be drawn. This will do, thinks I, for the table of the American Minister in London, where those whom it may concern may look and learn that though Wisdom is our guide, and the Song and Chase our supreme delight, yet we offer adoration to that tutelar God also who rocked the cradle of our birth, who has accepted our infant offerings & has shown himself the patron of our rights & avenger of our wrongs. The group then was closed, and your party formed. Envy & malice will never be quiet. I hear it already whispered to you that in admitting Minerva to your table I have departed from the principle which made me reject Venus: in plain English that I have paid a just respect to the daughter but failed to the mother. No Madam, my respect to both is sincere. Wisdom, I know, is social. She seeks her fellows, but Beauty is jealous, and illy bears the presence of a rival.

But, Allons, let us turn over another leaf, & begin the next chapter, I receive by Mr. Short a budget of London papers, they teem with every horror of which human nature is capable, assassinations, suicides, thefts, robberies, &, what is worse than assassination, theft, suicide, or robbery, the blackest slanders! indeed the man must be of rock, who can stand all this; to Mr Adams it will be but one victory the more. It would have illy suited me. I do not love difficulties. I am fond of quiet, willing to do my duty, but irritable by slander & apt to be forced by it to abandon my post. These are weaknesses from which reason & your

---

Polly later married) to write telling Jefferson that she would not come without being forced, had capitulated in the spring of 1787, arranging to put her on a British vessel sailing from Norfolk to London in the care of the captain, John Ramsay. But instead of the slave Isabel that Jefferson had specified, Eppes sent a substitute, Sally [Hemings]. (Brodie 1974, 216)

counsels will preserve Mr. Adams. I fancy it must be the quantity of animal food eaten by the English which renders their character insusceptible of civilization. I suspect it is in their kitchens & not in their churches that their reformation must be worked, & that Missionaries of that description from hence would avail more than those who should endeavor to tame them by precepts of religion or philosophy. But what do the foolish printers of America mean by retailing all this stuff in our papers? As if it was not enough to be slandered by one's enemies without circulating the slanders among his friends also.[1]

To show you how willingly, I shall ever receive & execute your commissions, I venture to impose one on you. From what I recollect of the diaper & damask we used to import from England I think they were better & cheaper than here, you are well acquainted with those of both countries, if you are of the same opinion I would trouble you to send me two sets of tablecloths & napkins for 20 covers each, by Col. Franks or Mr. Barclay who will bring them to me, but if you think they can be better got here I would rather avoid the trouble this commission will give. I enclose you a specimen of what is offered me at 100 livres for the tablecloth & 12 napkins. I suppose that, of the same quality, a table cloth. 2 aunes wide &. 4 aunes long & 20 napkins of 1 aune each, would cost 7. guineas.

I shall certainly charge the publick my houserent & court taxes. I shall do more. I shall charge my outfit. Without this I can never get out of debt. I think it will be allowed. Congress is too reasonable to expect, where no imprudent expenses are incurred, none but those which are required by a decent respect for the mantle with which they cover the public servants that such expenses should be left as a burthen on our private fortunes.

But when writing to you I fancy myself at Auteuil, and chatter on till the last page of my paper awakes me from my reverie, & tells me it is time to assure you of the sincere respect & esteem with which I have the honor to be Dear Madam, Your Most Obedient & Most Humble Servt.

P.S. The cask of wine at Auteuil, I take cheerfully. I suppose the seller will apply to me for the price. Otherwise, as I do not know who he is, I shall not be able to find him out.

To Hogendorp (Count Gysbert Charles Van) [2]

---

[1] After the first formal welcomes were over, the London press, government-inspired, entered upon a campaign of unremitting abuse against John Adams and the country which he represented. Jefferson commiserated herein, but thought Adams could stand it. As for himself, he was thinner-skinned. "I do not love difficulties," he confessed candidly. "I am fond of quiet, willing to do my duty, but irritable by slander & apt to be forced by it to abandon my post." It was an honest self-appraisal. Jefferson knew his own failings as a political figure. He had quit under fire as Governor; he was to quit again as Secretary of State, though only after long steeling of his nerves; and every time the storm of abuse rose too high during his Presidency, he began to think of Monticello with longing. (Schachner 1957, 299)

[2] Count Gysbert Charles Van Hogendorp was born at Rotterdam, in 1762; and, having lost his father by shipwreck in 1773, he went to Berlin with his elder brother Dyrk, who afterwards distinguished himself in the service of Napoleon, and entered the cadet school. He then became a page of Prince Henry and

Paris, Oct. 13, 1785

Dear Sir,

Having been much engaged lately, I have been unable sooner to acknowledge the receipt of your favor of Sep. 8. What you are pleased to say on the subject of my Notes is more than they deserve. The condition in which you first saw them would prove to you how hastily they had been originally written; as you may remember the numerous insertions I had made in them from time to time, when I could find a moment for turning to them from other occupations. I have never yet seen Monsr. de Buffon. He has been in the country all the summer. I sent him a copy of the book, & have only heard his sentiments on one particular of it, that of the identity of the Mammoth & Elephant. As to this he retains his opinion that they are the same. If you had formed any considerable expectations from our Revised code of laws you will be much disappointed. It contains not more than three of four laws which could strike the attention of the foreigner. Had it been a digest of all our laws, it would not have been comprehensible or instructive but to a native. But it is still less so, as it digests only the British statutes & our own acts of assembly, which are but a supplementary part of our law. The great basis of it is anterior to the date of the Magna Charta, which is the oldest statute extant. The only merit of this work is that it may remove from our book shelves about twenty folio volumes of our statutes, retaining all the parts of them which either their own merit or the established system of laws required.

You ask me what are those operations of the British nation which are likely to befriend us, and how they will produce this effect? The British government as you may naturally suppose have it much at heart to reconcile their nation to the loss of America. This is essential to the repose, perhaps even to the safety of the King & his ministers. The most effectual engines for this purpose are the public papers. You know well that that government always kept a kind of standing army of news writers who without any regard to truth, or to what should be like truth, invented & put into the papers whatever might serve the minister. This suffices with the mass of the people who have no means of distinguishing the false from the true paragraphs of a newspaper. When forced to acknowledge our independence they were forced to redouble their efforts to keep the nation quiet. Instead of a few of the papers formerly engaged, they now engaged every one. No paper therefore comes out without a dose of paragraphs against America. These are calculated for a secondary purpose also, that of preventing the emigrations of their people to America. They dwell very much on American bankruptcies. To

---

followed him, as ensign, in the war of the Bavarian succession. After the peace, he returned to his country, and the stadtholder, the provincial executive officer in the Netherlands, William V, gave him a place among his guards in 1782. In the following year he went to America, where he was received with kindness by Benjamin Franklin. After passing seven months in Philadelphia, he returned, in 1784, to his own country, and attended the lectures at Leyden, where he received the degree of doctor. Through attachment to the house of Orange, he left the military service when the patriots obtained the superiority. After the restoration of the stadtholder, he was named grand-pensioner of Rotterdam, but he gave up his place when (1795) the French conquered Holland, and the stadtholder fled to England. (Lieber, 1835, 384)

explain these would require a long detail, but would shew you that nine tenths of these bankruptcies are truly English bankruptcies in no wise chargeable on America. However they have produced effects the most desirable of all others for us. They have destroyed our credit & thus checked our disposition to luxury; & forcing our merchants to buy no more than they have ready money to pay for, they force them to go to those markets where that ready money will buy most. Thus you see they check our luxury, they force us to connect ourselves with all the world, & they prevent foreign emigrations to our country all of which I consider as advantageous to us. They are doing us another good turn. They attempt without disguise to possess themselves of the carriage of our produce, & to prohibit our own vessels from participating of it. This has raised a general indignation in America. The states see however that their constitutions have provided no means of counteracting it. They are therefore beginning to invest Congress with the absolute power of regulating their commerce, only reserving all revenue arising from it to the state in which it is levied. This will consolidate our federal building very much, and for this we shall be indebted to the British.

You ask what I think on the expediency of encouraging our states to be commercial? Were I to indulge my own theory, I should wish them to practice neither commerce nor navigation, but to stand with respect to Europe precisely on the footing of China. We should thus avoid wars, and all our citizens would be husbandmen. Whenever indeed our numbers should so increase as that our produce would overstock the markets of those nations who should come to seek it, the farmers must either employ the surplus of their time in manufactures, or the surplus of our hands must be employed in manufactures, or in navigation. But that day would, I think be distant, and we should long keep our workmen in Europe, while Europe should be drawing rough materials & even subsistence from America. But this is theory only, & a theory which the servants of America are not at liberty to follow. Our people have a decided taste for navigation & commerce. They take this from their mother country: & their servants are in duty bound to calculate all their measures on this datum: we wish to do it by throwing open all the doors of commerce & knocking off its shackles. But as this cannot be done for others, unless they will do it for us, & there is no great probability that Europe will do this, I suppose we shall be obliged to adopt a system which may shackle them in our ports as they do us in theirs.[1]

---

[1] Jefferson, in this section, seems to be referring to the concept of "embargo," not altogether a new policy for Jefferson. To some degree it was the realization of an old dream that he shared with other Founding Fathers: the isolation of the United States from the evils of the Old World. As such, it was a measure that fitted easily into a pattern of behavior which he periodically had advocated for the "common herd" when endangered by the jungle world of international politics. Inasmuch as Britain and France had virtually banned American commerce from the seas, the embargo could be a face-saving means of giving their decrees the force of American law, and thus remove a source of conflict with the belligerents. This conception of the embargo was more in consonance with the ideal role of a small nation than were other considerations that motivated the President and the Secretary of State at this time: territorial and pecuniary advantages that might be derived from Britain's vulnerability to commercial retaliation. (Kaplan 1967, 123)

With respect to the sale of our lands, that cannot begin till a considerable portion shall have been surveyed. They cannot begin to survey till the fall of the leaf of this year, nor to sell probably till the ensuing spring. So that it will be yet a twelve-month before we shall be able to judge of the efficacy of our land office to sink our national debt. It is made a fundamental that the proceeds shall be solely & sacredly applied as a sinking fund to discharge the capital only of the debt. It is true that the tobaccos of Virginia go almost entirely to England. The reason is that they owe a great debt there which they are paying as fast as they can.

I think I have now answered your several queries, & shall be happy to receive your reflections on the same subjects, & at all times to hear of your welfare & to give you assurances of the esteem with which I have the honor to be Dear Sir your most obedient & most humble servant.

To N. And J. Van Staphorst[1]
Paris, Oct. 25, 1785
Gentlemen,

I received yesterday your favor of the 20th. inst. In order to give you the information you desire on the subject of the liquidated debts of the United States, and the comparative footing on which they stand, I must observe to you that the first and great division of our federal debt is into 1. Foreign, and 2. Domestic. The Foreign debt comprehends 1. The loan from the government of Spain. 2. The loans from the government of France and from the Farmers general. 3. The loans negotiated in Holland by order of Congress. This branch of our debt stands absolutely singular: no man in the United states having ever supposed that Congress or their legislatures can in any wise modify or alter it. They justly view the United states as the one party and the lenders as the other and that the consent of both would be requisite were any modification to be proposed. But with respect to the Domestic debt, they consider Congress as representing both the borrowers and lenders, and that the modifications which have taken place in this, have been necessary to do justice between the two parties, and that they flowed properly from Congress as their mutual umpire. The Domestic debt comprehends 1. The army debt. 2. The Loan office debt. 3. The liquidated debt, and 4. the unliquidated debt. The 1st. term includes debts to the officers and soldiers for pay, bounty and subsistence. The 2d. term means monies put into the loan office of the United states. The 3d. comprehends all debts contracted by Quartermasters, Commissaries, and others duly authorized to procure supplies

---

[1] A scattering of American public securities had been held in Europe since the Revolution, but in everything but price they were a poor investment for Europeans in the immediate postwar years. This was so obvious that American merchants hardly tried to interest their European counterparts in the speculations they themselves were carrying on. Foreign capitalists were properly dubious about risking money in the United States and the brothers Nicolaas and Jacobus Van Staphorst were employed to sell shares in American government loans to Dutch investors. As an aside, it is probably worth mentioning that as long as Jefferson remained in France, he tried to discourage the transfer of American domestic securities to foreigners. (Ferguson 1961, 260-261)

for the army, and which have been liquidated (that is, settled) by Commissioners appointed under the resolution of Congress of June 12. 1780. or by the officer who made the contract. The 4th. comprehends the whole mass of debts described in the preceding article which have not yet been liquidated. These are in a course of liquidation, and are passing over daily into the 3d. class. The debts of this 3d. class, that is the liquidated debt is the object of your enquiry. No time is fixed for the payment of it, no fund as yet determined, nor any firm provision for the interest in the meantime. The consequence is that the certificates of these debts sell greatly below par. When I left America they could be bought for from 2/6 to 15/ in the pound: this difference proceeding from the circumstance of some states having provided for paying the interest on those due in their own state, which others had not. Hence an opinion had arisen with some, and propositions had even been made in the legislatures for paying off the principal of these debts with what they had cost the holder and interest on that. This opinion is far from being general, and I am of opinion will not prevail. But it is among possible events. I have been thus particular that you might be able to judge not only in the present case, but also in others, should any attempts be made to speculate in your city on these papers. It is a business in which foreigners will be in great danger of being duped. It is a science which bids defiance to the powers of reason. To understand it, a man must not only be on the spot and be perfectly possessed of all the circumstances relative to every species of these papers, but he must have that dexterity which the habit of buying and selling them alone gives. The brokers of these certificates are few in number, and any other person venturing to deal with them engages in a very unequal contest.

I have the honor to be with the highest respect, Gentlemen. Your most obedient humble servant,

To Philip Mazzei
Paris, Nov. 28, 1785
Dear Sir,

You desire me to give you an idea of the Origin and Object of our court of Chancery, the Limits of its jurisdiction, and it's Tendency to render property and liberty more or less secure in a country where that security is infinitely valued. The purpose for which you require this obliges me to be concise, as indeed does my situation here, where, as you know, I am without books which might enable me to enter into details. I shall confine myself therefore to general description only. The terms of this, if presented to professors of the law, would furnish matter for abundant exceptions. But these should be suppressed by the reflection that we mean only to sketch for foreigners a general idea of this court.[1]

---

[1] For Jefferson, the Constitution remained primarily a political document, and judges had no monopoly in interpreting it. In this letter to his friend, the Italian merchant, surgeon, and horticulturist Philip Mazzei, he speaks to the fact that, indeed, he believed that judges' ability to interpret any law ought to be strictly limited. Statutes ought to be precisely drawn, and judges ought to be bound by the letter of these statutes. "Relieve the judges from the rigour of text law, and permit them to wander into its equity," he said, "and the whole

The system of law in most of the United States, in imitation of that of England, is divided into two departments, the Common law and the Chancery.

The Common law is a written law the text of which is preserved from the beginning of the 13th. century downwards, but what preceded that is lost. It's substance however has been retained in the memory of the people and committed to writing from time to time in the decisions of the judges and treatises of the jurists, insomuch that it is still considered as a lex scripta, the letter of which is sufficiently known to guide the decisions of the courts. In this department the courts restrain themselves to the letter of the law. Antiently indeed, before the improvement or perhaps the existence of the court of Chancery, they allowed themselves greater latitude, extending the provisions of every law not only to the cases within its letter, but to those also which came within the spirit and reason of it. This was called the equity of the law. But it is now very long since certainty in the law has become so highly valued by the nation that the judges have ceased to extend the operation of laws beyond those cases which are clearly within the intention of the legislators. This intention is to be collected principally from the words of the law: only where these are ambiguous they are permitted to gather further evidence from the history of the times when the law was made and the circumstances which produced it. In antient times, when contracts and transfers of property were more rare, and their objects more simple, the imperfections of this administration of justice according to the letter of the law were less felt. But when commerce began to make progress, when the transfer of property came into daily use, when the modifications of these transfers were infinitely diversified, when with the improvement of other faculties that of the moral sense became also improved, and learnt to respect justice in a variety of cases which it had not formerly discriminated, the instances of injustice left without remedy by courts adhering to the letter of the law, would be so numerous as to produce a general desire that a power should be found somewhere which would redress them. History renders it probable that appeals were made to the king himself in these cases, and that he exercised this power sometimes in person, but more generally by his Chancellor, to whom he referred the case. This was most commonly an Ecclesiastic, learning being rare in any other class at that time. Roman learning, and a prejudice in favor of Roman institutions are known to have been a leading feature in the ecclesiastical character. Hence it happened that the forms of proceeding in the court of Chancery and the rules of

---

legal system becomes uncertain." Jefferson rejected out of hand the eighteenth-century "revolution" in jurisprudence that Blackstone and Mansfield had created in England, dismissing their efforts to construe the common law equitably and to broaden judicial discretion as dangerous to liberty. The goal of judges was supposed to be "to render the law more & more certain." The goal of Mansfield and Blackstone, according to Jefferson, had been the exact opposite. They intended "to render it more uncertain under pretense of rendering it more reasonable." Jefferson realized that these English advocates of judicial flexibility had a powerful influence on American judicial thinking and practice. Jefferson never ceased complaining that "the honeyed Mansfieldism of Blackstone" had forced young Americans to slide into "toryism" to the point where they "no longer know what whigism or republicanism means." (Wood 2009, 449)

its decisions were assimilated to those of the Roman law. The distinction in that system between the jus praetorium, or discretion of the Praetor, and the general law is well known. Among the Romans and in most modern nations these were and are exercised by the same person. But the Chancellors of England, finding the ordinary courts in possession of the administration of general law, and confined to that, assumed to themselves by degrees that of the jus praetorium, and made theirs be considered as a court of conscience, or of equity. The history of the struggles between the ordinary, or common law courts, and the court of equity or Chancery would be beyond our purpose. It is sufficient to say that the interpositions of the Chancellor were at first very rare, that they increased insensibly, and were rather tolerated from their necessity, than authorized by the laws in the earlier periods of history. Ld. Bacon first introduced regularity into their proceedings and Finch, Earl of Nottingham, in the reign of Charles the 2d. opened to view that system which has been improving from that time to this. The power of that court as acknowledged at this day, is to relieve

~ where the Common law gives no remedy.

~ where it's remedy is imperfect.

~ where it would do injustice by comprehending within its letter cases not within its reason, nor intended to have been comprehended.

But this court whilst developing and systematizing its powers, has found, in the jealousy of the nation and it's attachment to certain and impartial law, an obstacle insuperable beyond that line. It has been obliged therefore to establish for itself certain barriers as the limitations of its power, which, whenever it transcends, the general judicature, which superintends all the courts and receives appeals from them, corrects it's encroachments and reverses it's decisions. This is the House of Lords in England, and the Court of Appeals in Virginia. These limitations are 1. That it cannot take cognizance of any case wherein the Common law can give complete remedy. 2. That it cannot interpose in any case against the express letter and intention of the legislature. If the legislature means to enact an injustice, however palpable, the court of Chancery is not the body with whom a correcting power is lodged. 3. That it shall not interpose in any case which does not come within a general description and admit of redress by a general and practicable rule: this is to prevent partiality. When a Chancellor pretends that a case is distinguished from all others, it is thought better that that singular case should go without remedy, than that he should be at liberty to cover partial decisions under pretense of singular circumstances, which ingenious men can always invent. Hence all the cases remediable in chancery are reduced to certain classes. When a new case presents itself, not found in any of these classes it is dismissed as irremediable. If in the progress of commerce, and of the developments of moral duties the same case is presented so often that the Chancellor can seize certain leading features which submit it to a general description, and shew that it is a proper object for the application of some moral rule, here is a new class of cases formed, and brought within the regular relief of the court of Chancery, which thus continues the administration of justice progressive almost in equal pace with the progress of commerce and refinement of morality. One practice only is wanting to render this court completely valuable. That is that when a class of cases has been formed, and has been the subject of so many decisions in the court of Chancery as to have been seen there under all circumstances, and in all its combinations, and the rules for its decision are modified accordingly and thoroughly digested, the legislatures should reduce these rules to a text and transplant them into the department of the common law, which is competent then to the application of them, and is a safer depository for the general administration of justice. This would be to make the Chancery a nursery only for the forming new plants for the department of the common law. Much of the business of Chancery is now actually in a state of perfect preparation for removal into the Common law.

It has often been predicted in England that the Chancery would swallow up the Common law. During many centuries however that these two courts have gone on together, the jurisdiction of the Common law has not been narrowed in a single article; on the contrary it has been enlarged from time to time by acts of the legislature. But jealousy uncorrected by reason or experience, sees certainty wherever there is a possibility, and sensible men still think that the danger from this court overweighs its utility. Even some of the states in our Union have chosen to do without this court, and it has been proposed to others to follow their example. In this case, one of two consequences must follow. Either 1. The cases now remediable in Chancery must be left without remedy, in which event the clamours for justice which originally begat this court, would produce its re-institution; or 2. the courts of Common law must be permitted to perform the discretionary functions of the Chancery. This will be either by adopting at once all the rules of the Chancery, with the consent of the legislature, or, if that is withheld, these courts will be led, by the desire of doing justice, to extend the text of the law according to its equity as was done in England before the Chancery took a regular form. This will be worse than running on Scylla to avoid Charybdis. For at present nine tenths of our legal contestations are perfectly remedied by the Common law, and can be carried before that judicature only. This proportion then of our rights is placed on sure ground. Relieve the judges from the rigour of text law, and permit them, with pretorian discretion, to wander into its equity, and the whole legal system becomes uncertain. This has been its fate in every country where the fixed, and the discretionary law have been committed into the same hands. It is probable that the singular certainty with which justice has been administered in England, has been the consequence of their distribution into two distinct departments. Unhappily for that country, however, a very unexpected revolution is working in their laws of late years. Ld. Mansfeild, a man of the clearest head and most seducing eloquence, coming from a country where the powers of the common law and chancery are united in the same court, has been able since his admission to the bench of judges in England, to persuade the courts of Common law to revive the practice of construing their text equitably. The object of former judges has been to render the law more and more certain, that of this personage to render it more uncertain under pretense of rendering it more reasonable: no period of the English law, of whatever length it be taken, can be produced wherein so many of its settled rules have been reversed as during the time of this judge. His decisions will be precious in those states where no Chancery is established: but his accession to the bench should form the epoch, after which all recurrence to English decisions should be proscribed in those states which have separated the two courts. His plan of rendering the Chancery useless by administering justice in the same way in the courts of Common law has been admirably seconded by the celebrated Dr. Blackstone, a judge in the same department, who has endeavored seriously to prove that the jurisdiction of the Chancery is a chaos, irreducible to system, insusceptible of fixed rules, and incapable of definition or explanation. Were this true it would be a monster whose existence should not be suffered one moment in a free country wherein every power is dangerous which is not bound up by general rules.

Before I end my letter I will further observe to guard still more effectually against the dangers apprehended from a court of Chancery, the legislature of Virginia have very wisely introduced into it the trial by jury for all matters of fact.

I have thus gone over, with much rapidity, the subject of your enquiries; yet I fear I have been more lengthy than you wished. You can, however, extract such of these details as will fulfill your object, neglecting those which go beyond it. I shall close therefore with assurances of the sincere esteem with which I am Dear Sir Your friend & servant,

1786

To The Governor Of Virginia (Patrick Henry)
Paris, January 24, 1786
Sir,

I have been honored with your Excellency's two letters of Sept. 10th, and that of Oct. 14th, 1785. The former were brought me by Mr. Houdon, who is returned with the necessary moulds and measures for General Washington's Statue. I fear the expenses of his journey have been considerably increased by the unlucky accident of his tools, materials, clothes, &c., not arriving at Havre in time to go with him to America, so that he had to supply himself there. The money which you were so kind as to send by Captain Littlepage, for the purpose of this statue, he found himself obliged to deposit in New York, to satisfy a demand made upon him there.[1] This was a debt which he owed to Mr. Jay. He assures me that

---

[1] Lewis Littlepage, a ward of John Jay, had evolved not into the studious prospective lawyer that Jay assumed he would be but into a world-class soldier of fortune and friend of royalty. He did so after having broken from Jay's tutelage, and, against Jay's advice, entered into the service of the Spanish military, starting June 1781, as an unpaid aide-de-camp to the Duc de Crillon, the general who commanded, first, the successful combined Spanish–French assault on Minorca in the winter of 1781–82, and then the failed one on Gibraltar in September 1782. (Brecher 2003, 155)

in a settlement with his guardian the latter took credit for this debt, so as to be answerable to Mr. Jay for it, and of course to the State, now that Mr. Jay is paid with the State's money. I mention this circumstance, that your Excellency may be enabled to take the earliest measures for recovering this money and indemnifying the State.

Mr. Little page, to satisfy me, had obtained from the M. de la Fayette his engagement to stand bound as Mr. Little page's security for the payment of this money, but knowing the punctuality and responsibility of his guardian, I did not suppose a security necessary. Besides, if a loss were to be incurred, I know too well the sentiments of the State of Virginia towards M. de la Fayette to suppose they would be willing to throw that loss on him. I therefore acted as I thought your Excellency and the Council would have directed me to act could you have been consulted. I waited on the Marquis, and in his presence cancelled his name from the obligation which had been given me, leaving only that of Mr. Little page. I have now the honor to enclose you one of those instruments, duplicates of which had been given me by Mr. Little page. The first of the Marquis's busts will be finished next month. I shall present that one to the City of Paris, because the delay has been noticed by some. I hope to be able to send another to Virginia in the course of the summer. These are to cost three thousand livres each.

The agreement for the arms has been at length concluded by Mr. Barclay. He was so much better acquainted with this business than the Marquis Fayette or myself, that we left it altogether with him. We were sensible that they might have been got cheaper, but not so good. However, I suppose he has given you the details of his proceedings, so as to render them unnecessary from me. It will be eight months before they will be ready. The cause of this, too, Mr. Barclay told me he would explain to you. It is principally to ensure their goodness. The bills remitted to pay for them have been honored, and the money is lodged in Mr. Grand's hands who is willing to allow a small interest for it.

An improvement is made here in the construction of the musket, which may be worthy of attention. It consists in making every part of them so exactly alike that every part of every one may be used for the same part in any other musket made by the same hand. The government here has examined and approved the method, and is establishing a large manufactory for the purpose. As yet the inventor has only completed the lock of the musket on this plan. He will proceed immediately to have the barrel, stock and their parts executed in the same way. I visited the workman. He presented me the parts of 50 locks taken to pieces and arranged in compartments. I put several together myself, taking the pieces at hazard as they came to hand, and found them to fit interchangeably in the most perfect manner. The tools by which he effects this have, at the same time, so abridged the labour that he thinks he shall be able to furnish the musket two livres cheaper than the King's price. But it will be two or three years before he will be able to finish any quantity.

I have duly received the propositions of Messrs. Ross, Pleasants & Co. for furnishing tobacco to the farmers general; but Mr. Morris had, in the meantime, obtained the contract. I have been fully sensible of the baneful influence on the commerce of France and America which this double monopoly will have. I have struck at its root here, and spared no pains to have the farm itself demolished, but it has been in vain. The persons interested in it are too powerful to be opposed, even by the interest of the whole country. I mention this matter in confidence, as a knowledge of it might injure any future endeavors to attain the same object.

Everything is quiet here, and will certainly remain so another year. Mr. Barclay left Paris a few days ago, and will be absent from France for some time. I shall spare no endeavors to fulfill the several objects with which he was charged in the best manner I can.

To John Jay[1]
Paris, 25 Jan. 1786
Dear Sir,

I received on the 18th instant your private favor of Dec. 9 and thank you for the confidence you are so good as to repose in me, of which that communication is a proof. As such it is a gratification to me, because it meets the esteem I have ever borne you. But nothing was needed to keep my mind right on that subject, and I believe I may say the public mind here. The sentiments entertained of you in this place are too respectful to be easily shaken. The person of whom you speak in your letter arrived here on the 19th and departed for Warsaw on the 22d. It is really to be lamented that after a public servant has passed a life in important and faithful services, after having given the most plenary satisfaction in every station, it should yet be in the power of every individual to disturb his quiet, by arraigning him in a gazette and by obliging him to act as if he needed a defence, an obligation imposed on him by unthinking minds which never give themselves the trouble of seeking a reflection unless it be presented to them. However it is a part of the price we pay for our liberty, which cannot be guarded but by the freedom of the press, nor that be limited without danger of losing

---

[1] This letter is in response to Jay's 9 December letter to Jefferson in which Jay explained the troubled relationship with his former ward, Lewis Littlepage. In that correspondence, Jay stated, "From the public papers which will go by the packet, you will perceive that a very indecent attack has been made upon me by a Mr. Littlepage, who was formerly in my family, and from whom I merit better things. It has so happened, that among the few enemies I have, the far greater part are men on whom I have conferred essential benefits. This young man does not stand single. I have no reason to suspect that he is supported by more than one single American. It has been remarked to me from many quarters, that the persons who have stood behind him in this business are Frenchmen. What could have been their views can only be a matter of conjecture. Whatever may be the sentiments of their court respecting me, I am persuaded that such conduct will not recommend them to their minister, of whose good sense and respect for propriety I entertain too good an opinion, to suppose that such exertions of zeal can meet with his approbation." (Jay 1833, 224-225)

it. To the loss of time, of labour, of money, then, must be added that of quiet, to which those must offer themselves who are capable of serving the public, and all this is better than European bondage. Your quiet may have suffered for a moment on this occasion, but you have the strongest of all supports that of the public esteem. It is unnecessary to add assurances of that with which I have the honor to be Dear Sir, Your most obedient and most humble Servt.

To Archibald Stuart[1]
Paris, Jan. 25, 1786
Dear Sir,

I have received your favor of the 17th. of October, which though you mention as the third you have written me, is the first which has come to hand. I sincerely thank you for the communications it contains. Nothing is so grateful to me at this distance as details both great and small of what is passing in my own country. Of the latter we receive little here, because they either escape my correspondents or are thought unworthy notice. This however is a very mistaken opinion, as every one may observe by recollecting that when he has been long absent from his neighborhood the small news of that is the most pleasing and occupies his first attention either when he meets with a person from thence, or returns thither himself. I still hope therefore that the letter in which you have been so good as to give me the minute occurrences in the neighborhood of Monticello may yet come to hand, and I venture to rely on the many proofs of friendship I have received from you, for a continuance of your favors. This will be the more meritorious as I have nothing to give you in exchange. The quiet of Europe at this moment furnishes little which can attract your notice, nor will that quiet be soon disturbed, at least for the current year. Perhaps it hangs on the life of the K. of Prussia, and that hangs by a very slender thread. American reputation in Europe is not such as to be flattering to its citizens. Two circumstances are particularly objected to us, the nonpayment of our debts, and the want of energy in our government. These discourage a connection with us. I own it to be my opinion that good will arise from the destruction of our credit. I see nothing else which can restrain our disposition to luxury, and the loss of those manners which alone can preserve republican government. As it is impossible to prevent credit, the best way would be to cure its ill effects by giving an instantaneous recovery to the creditor. This would be reducing purchases on credit to purchases for ready

---

[1] Archibald Stuart (March 19, 1757–July 11, 1832), lawyer and judge, read law under Thomas Jefferson. The relations between Stuart and Jefferson were friendly, although Stuart was years younger. After Stuart become a lawyer, he looked after Jefferson's interests on "the other side of the mountain," which included collecting debts owed for the sale of Monticello nails and paying taxes on the Natural Bridge. Stuart and Jefferson exchanged nearly a hundred letters between the early 1780s and Jefferson's death in 1826. (Thomas Jefferson Foundation, "Archibald Stuart" 2015)

money. A man would then see a prison painted on everything he wished but had not ready money to pay for.

I fear from an expression in your letter that the people of Kentucky think of separating not only from Virginia (in which they are right) but also from the confederacy. I own I should think this a most calamitous event, and such a one as every good citizen on both sides should set himself against. Our present federal limits are not too large for good government, nor will the increase of votes in Congress produce any ill effect. On the contrary it will drown the little divisions at present existing there. Our confederacy must be viewed as the nest from which all America, North and South is to be peopled. We should take care too not to think it for the interest of that great continent to press too soon on the Spaniards. Those countries cannot be in better hands. My fear is that they are too feeble to hold them till our population can be sufficiently advanced to gain it from them piece by piece. The navigation of the Mississippi we must have. This is all we are as yet ready to receive. I have made acquaintance with a very sensible candid gentleman here who was in South America during the revolt which took place there while our revolution was working. He says that those disturbances (of which we scarcely heard anything) cost on both sides an hundred thousand lives.

I have made a particular acquaintance here with Monsieur de Buffon, and have a great desire to give him the best idea I can of our elk. Perhaps your situation may enable you to aid me in this. Were it possible, you could not oblige me more than by sending me the horns, skeleton, and skin of an elk. The most desirable form of receiving them would be to have the skin slit from the under jaw along the belly to the tail, and down the thighs to the knee, to take the animal out, leaving the legs and hoofs, the bones of the head, and the horns attached to the skin. By sewing up the belly &c. and stuffing the skin it would present the form of the animal. However as an opportunity of doing this is scarcely to be expected, I shall be glad to receive them detached, packed in a box, and sent to Richmond to the care of Doctor Currie. Everything of this kind is precious here, and to prevent my adding to your trouble I must close my letter with assurances of the esteem and attachment with which I am Dr. Sir your friend & servt.,

P.S. I must add a prayer for some Paccan [pecan] nuts, 100, if possible, to be packed in a box of sand and sent me. They might come either directly or viâ N. York.

To Dr. James Currie[1]

---

[1] Jefferson was a staunch advocate of freedom of the press, asserting in this letter to James Currie, a Virginia physician and frequent correspondent during Jefferson's residence in France: "our liberty depends on the freedom of the press, and that cannot be limited without being lost." This letter rather typifies the notion that many eighteenth-century political philosophers concerned themselves with the balance between the restrictions needed to make a government function and the individual liberties guaranteed by that government. Jefferson's efforts to protect

Paris, Jan. 28, 1786
Dear Sir,

Your favor of Oct. 17. with a P.S. of Oct. 20. came to hand a few days ago and I am now to thank you for the intelligence it contains. It is more difficult here to get small than great news because most of our correspondents in writing letters to cross the Atlantic, think they must always tread in buskins, so that half one's friends might be dead without it's being ever spoken of here. Your letter was handed me by Mr. Little page whom I have never seen before and who set out from home for Warsaw after two or three days stay. I observe by the public papers that he has brought on a very disagreeable altercation with Mr. Jay, in which he has given to the character of the latter a coloring which does not belong to it. These altercations, little thought of in America, make a great impression here, in truth it is afflicting that a man who has past his life in serving the public, who has served them in every the highest stations with universal approbation, and with a purity of conduct which has silenced even party opprobrium, who tho' poor, has never permitted himself to make a shilling in the public employ, should yet be liable to have his peace of mind so much disturbed by any individual who shall think proper to arraign him in a newspaper. It is however an evil for which there is no remedy, our liberty depends on the freedom of the press, and that cannot be limited without being lost. To the sacrifice of time, labor, fortune, a public servant must count upon adding that of peace of mind and even reputation.

And all this is preferable to European bondage, he who doubts it need only be placed for one week on any part of the Continent of Europe. Your desire of possessing the new Encyclopedie was expressed so problematically in a former letter that I doubted whether you did not merely render yourself thro' complaisance to my proposition. Your last letter, however, is more explicit, wherefore I have immediately subscribed for you. And have obtained an abatement of two guineas in the price. It will be brought to me to-day and as there are now 29. vols complete, and binding is done so much better and cheaper here (about 3 livres a volume) I will have them bound and send them by the first conveyance. The medical part has not yet begun to appear, that author having chosen to publish the whole at once. I do not expect it will be the most valuable part of the work, for that science was demolished here by the blows of Moliere, and in a nation so addicted to ridicule, I question if ever it rises under the weight while his comedies continue to be acted. It furnished the most striking proof I have ever seen in my life of the injury which ridicule is capable of doing. I send by this conveyance designs for the Capitol. They are simple & sublime, more cannot be said, they are not the brat of a whimsical conception never before brought to light, but copied from the most precious, the most perfect model of antient architecture remaining on earth; one which has received the approbation of near 2000 years, which is sufficiently remarkable to have been visited by all travelers. It will be less expensive, too, than the one begun. For some time past

individual rights including freedom of the press were persistent and pivotal, although not always successful. (Library of Congress, "Jefferson" 2015)

nothing has come out here worth sending you. Whenever there does you shall receive it. The Abbé Rochon (who had discovered that all the natural crystals were composed of two different substances of different refracting powers, and those powers actually uncombined tho' the substance seem perfectly combined.) has lately applied the metal called Platina to the purpose of making the specula of telescopes. It is susceptible of as high a polish as the metallic composition heretofore used, and as insusceptible of rust as gold; it yields like that to no acid but the aqua vegra. One Hoffman practices here a pleasing method of engraving, such as would be useful to any Gentleman. He gives you a plate of copper, write on it with his ink, letters, designs of animals, landscapes, architecture, music, geography, or what you please, and in an hour the plate is ready to strike off what number of copies you please.

I charge you always with my affectionate respects to the families at Tuckaho & Ampthill & to McLurg whose indolence is the only bar to our correspondence without an intermediate. I have taken the liberty of desiring A. Stuart to send some objects of natural history for me to your care, relying you will be so good as to contrive them to me, always remembering that Havre is the most convenient port, & next to that l'Orient, and that packages for me must be directed to the American Consul at the port. I am with sincere esteem Dear Sir, Your friend & servt.

To C. W. F. Dumas[1]
Paris, Feb. 2, 1786
Sir,

I was honored some time ago with a letter from you of Dec. 6 inclosing two for America which I forwarded by the first occasion. On the 18th of this month I received a letter from his Excellency the Count de Vergennes expressing the interest which he takes in your welfare and recommending you to Congress. This I had an opportunity of forwarding from hence on the 27th of Jan. under cover to Mr. Jay. Yesterday I was gratified with the receipt of your favor of Jan. 27 containing a copy of the resolution of Congress of Oct. 14 in your favor, and which I wish had been more so. With respect to the payment of the arrearages, two things are necessary, first an order from the treasury and secondly money to comply with it. Mr. Grand wrote to me this morning that he had not now as much left to pay a bill of Mr. Carmichael's for 4500 livres just presented. I shall forward your letter to Mr. Jay the next week with a request that the necessary measures may be taken for the payment of your arrearages and interest. In the meantime I think you would do well to write a line for the same purpose to Mr.

---

[1] Charles W. F. Dumas was the second agent — the first being Arthur Lee — to be recruited abroad by the Committee of Secret Correspondence. He was a Swiss journalist at The Hague and was briefed personally by Thomas Story, a courier of the Committee, and instructed on the use of cover names and letter drops to be used for his reports to the Committee and for communication with Dr. Lee in London. Dumas, a and friend of Benjamin Franklin, planted stories in a Dutch newspaper, *Gazette de Leide*, intended to give the United States a favorable rating in Dutch credit markets. (Central Intelligence Agency, 2015)

Jay, or to the Commissioners of the Treasury. I do not mean that what I have said above should prevent your drawing in due time for the salary of the current quarter. I will honor that draught from a private fund with which I can take that liberty. I thank you for what you say of the Notes on Virginia. It is much more than they deserve: tho the various matters they touch on would have been beyond the information of any one person whatever to have treated fully, and infinitely beyond mine, yet had I, at the time of writing them, had anything more in view than the satisfying a single individual, they should have been more attended to both in form and matter. Poor as they are, they have been thought worthy of a surreptitious translation here, with the appearance of which very soon I have been threatened. This has induced me to yield to a friendly proposition from the Abbé Morellet to translate and publish them himself submitting the sheets previously to my inspection.[1] As a translation by so able a hand will lessen the faults of the original instead of their being multiplied by a hireling translator, I shall add to it a map, and such other advantages as may prevent the mortification of my seeing it appear in the injurious form threatened. I shall with great pleasure send a copy of the original to you by the first opportunity, praying your acceptance of it.

To James Madison[2]
Paris, Feb. 8, 1786
Dear Sir,

My last letters have been of the 1st & 20th of Sept. and the 28th of Oct. Yours unacknowledged are of Aug. 20, Oct. 3, & Nov. 15. I take this the first safe opportunity of enclosing to you the bills of lading for your books, & two others for your namesake of Williamsburgh & for the attorney which I will pray you to forward. I thank you for the communication of the remonstrance against the assessment. Mazzei who is now in Holland promised me to have it published in the Leyden gazette. It will do us great honor. I wish it may be as much approved by our assembly as by the wisest part of Europe. I have heard with great pleasure that our assembly have come to the resolution of giving the regulation of their commerce to the federal head. I will venture to assert that there is not one of its opposers who, placed on this ground, would not see the wisdom of this measure.

---

[1] Abbé André Morellet was a liberal French economist and philosopher who had originally befriended Benjamin Franklin in 1771 during a visit at the home of Lord Shelburne. Morellet shared Franklin's love for wine, invention, and economic theory. (Isaacson 2003, 252-53, 364)

[2] An important piece of correspondence, Jefferson crafted this letter to Madison after hearing of the final action of the Legislature of Virginia in favor of the proposed grant to Congress of the power over commerce. He states in very emphatic terms: "I have heard, with great pleasure, that our Assembly have come to the resolution of giving the regulation of their commerce to the Federal head. I will venture to assert, that there is not one of its opposers who, placed on this ground, would not see the wisdom of this measure. The politics of Europe render it indispensably necessary, that, with respect to everything external, we be one nation, firmly hooped together. Interior government is what each State should keep to itself." (Rives 1870, 34)

The politics of Europe render it indispensably necessary that with respect to everything external we be one nation only, firmly hooped together. Interior government is what each state should keep to itself. If it could be seen in Europe that all our states could be brought to concur in what the Virginia assembly has done, it would produce a total revolution in their opinion of us, and respect for us. And it should ever be held in mind that insult & war are the consequences of a want of respectability in the national character. As long as the states exercise separately those acts of power which respect foreign nations, so long will there continue to be irregularities committing by some one or other of them which will constantly keep us on an ill footing with foreign nations.

I thank you for your information as to my Notes. The copies I have remaining shall be sent over to be given to some of my friends and to select subjects in the college. I have been unfortunate here with this trifle. I gave out a few copies only, & to confidential persons, writing in every copy a restraint against its publication. Among others I gave a copy to a Mr. Williams. He died. I immediately took every precaution I could to recover this copy. But by some means or other a bookseller had got hold of it. He employed a hireling translator and was about publishing it in the most injurious form possible. An Abbé Morellet, a man of letters here to whom I had given a copy, got notice of this. He had translated some passages for a particular purpose: and he compounded with the bookseller to translate & give him the whole, on his declining the first publication. I found it necessary to confirm this, and it will be published in French, still mutilated however in its freest parts. I am now at a loss what to do as to England. Everything, good or bad, is thought worth publishing there; and I apprehend a translation back from the French, and a publication there. I rather believe it will be most eligible to let the original come out in that country; but am not yet decided.

I have purchased little for you in the book way, since I sent the catalogue of my former purchases. I wish first to have your answer to that, and your information what parts of those purchases went out of your plan. You can easily say buy more of this kind, less of that &c. My wish is to conform myself to yours. I can get for you the original Paris edition in folio of the Encyclopedie for 620 livres, 35. vols.; a good edn in 39 vols, 4to, for 380#; and a good one in 39 vols 8vo, for 280#. The new one will be superior in far the greater number of articles: but not in all. And the possession of the ancient one has moreover the advantage of supplying present use. I have bought one for myself, but wait your orders as to you. I remember your purchase of a watch in Philadelphia. If it should not have proved good, you can probably sell her. In that case I can get for you here, one made as perfect as human art can make it for about 24 louis. I have had such a one made by the best & most faithful hand in Paris. It has a second hand, but no repeating, no day of the month, nor other useless thing to impede and injure the movements which are necessary. For 12 louis more you can have in the same cover, but on the back side & absolutely unconnected with the movements of the watch, a pedometer which shall render you an exact account of the distances you walk. Your pleasure hereon shall be awaited.

Houdon is returned. He called on me the other day to remonstrate against the inscription proposed for Gen'l W.'s statue. He says it is too long to be put on the pedestal. I told him I was not at liberty to permit any alteration, but I would represent his objection to a friend who could judge of its validity, and whether a change could be authorized. This has been the subject of conversations here, and various devices & inscriptions have been suggested. The one which has appeared best to me may be translated as follows: "Behold, Reader, the form of George Washington. For his worth, ask History: that will tell it, when this stone shall have yielded to the decays of time. His country erects this monument: Houdon makes it." This for one side. On the 2d represent the evacuation of Boston with the motto "Hostibus primum fugatis." On the 3d the capture of the Hessians with "Hostibus iterum devictis." On the 4th the surrender of York, with "Hostibus ultimum debellatis." This is seizing the three most brilliant actions of his military life. By giving out here a wish of receiving mottos for this statue, we might have thousands offered, of which still better might be chosen. The artist made the same objection of length to the inscription for the bust of the M. de la Fayette. An alteration of that might come in time still, if an alteration was wished. However I am not certain that it is desirable in either case. The state of Georgia has given 20.000 acres of land to the Count d' Estaing. This gift is considered here as very honorable to him, and it has gratified him much. I am persuaded that a gift of lands by the state of Virginia to the Marquis de la Fayette would give a good opinion here of our character, and would reflect honor on the Marquis. Nor am I sure that the day will not come when it might be a useful asylum to him. The time of life at which he visited America was too well adapted to receive good & lasting impressions to permit him ever to accommodate himself to the principles of monarchical government; and it will need all his own prudence & that of his friends to make this country a safe residence for him. How glorious, how comfortable in reflection will it be to have prepared a refuge for him in case of a reverse. In the meantime he could settle it with tenants from the freest part of this country, Bretagny. I have never suggested the smallest idea of this kind to him: because the execution of it should convey the first notice. If the state has not a right to give him lands with their own officers, they could buy up at cheap prices the shares of others. I am not certain however whether in the public or private opinion, a similar gift to Count Rochambeau could be dispensed with. If the state could give to both, it would be better: but in any event, I think they should to the Marquis. C. Rochambeau too has really deserved more attention than he has received. Why not set up his bust, that of Gates, Green, Franklin in your new capitol? A propos of the Capitol. Do my dear friend exert yourself to get the plan begun on set aside, & that adopted which was drawn here. It was taken from a model which has been the admiration of 16. centuries, which has been the object of as many pilgrimages as the tomb of Mahomet: which will give unrivalled honor to our state, and furnish a model whereon to form the taste of our young men. It will cost much less too than the one begun, because it does not cover one half the Area. Ask if you please, a sight of my letter of Jan. 26 to Messrs. Buchanan & Hay, which will spare me repeating its substance here.

Everything is quiet in Europe. I recollect but one new invention in the arts which is worth mentioning. It is a mixture of the arts of engraving & printing, rendering both cheaper. Write or draw anything on a plate of brass with the ink of the inventor, and in half an hour he gives you engraved copies of it so perfectly like the original that they could not be suspected to be copies. His types for printing a whole page are all in one solid piece. An author therefore only prints a few copies of his work from time to time as they are called for. This saves the loss of printing more copies than may possibly be sold, and prevents an edition from being ever exhausted.

I am with a lively esteem Dear Sir, your sincere friend & servant.

P. S. Could you procure & send me an hundred or two nuts of the peccan? they would enable me to oblige some characters here whom I should be much gratified to oblige. They should come packed in sand. The seeds of the sugar maple too would be a great present.

To The Marquis De La Fayette[1]
Paris, Feb. 10, 1786
Dear Sir,

I forgot last night a very material circumstance in my calculation. The Farmers general are, by their bail, obliged to keep a certain provision of tobacco and snuff always on hand. I believe it is three years consumption. However for fear of error I will call it two years; because were the bail silent on this head they would certainly have always on hand one year's stock ready for manufacture, and one year's stock manufactured. There is no extensive manufacture which does not find that it has on hand generally two years' stock of goods. As the Farmers buy their tobacco for ready money (and I know they even advance money) they lay out of their money two years. This interest must therefore be added, and the estimate will stand thus

22 millions of pounds weight of tobacco at 6 sous cost 11,600,000 livre tournois
the cost of manufacture is 1. sol the pound 692,500
guards &c. to prevent contraband 5,000,000
revenue paid annually to the king 28,000,000
interest on the whole for 2. years @ 5. pr. cent 4,529,500l
whole cost of annual purchase of tobacco then is 49,821,750²
they sell annually but 13,850,000 . which at 3 livre tournois–10s brings them 45,705,000
they lose annually then by the farm of tobacco 4,116,750.

Thus, according to their own shewing, the king should in favor to them, discontinue the bail; and they cannot ask its continuance without acknowledging they have given in a false state of quantities and sums. I am Dear Sir your's affectionately,

[1] The "last night" calculations that were revised in the present letter were intended to assist Lafayette in his effort as a member of the American committee to abolish the tobacco monopoly of the farmers-general. (Boyd 1990)

To The Secretary for Foreign Affairs (John Jay)
London, Mar. 12, 1786
Dear Sir,

The date of a letter from London will doubtless be as unexpected to you as it was unforeseen by myself a few days ago. On the 27th of the last month Col. [William Stephens] Smith arrived in Paris with a letter from Mr. Adams informing me that there was at this place a minister from Tripoli having general powers to enter into treaties on behalf of his state, and with whom it was possible we might do something in our Commission to that power and that he gave reason to believe he could also take arrangements with us for Tunis: he further added that the minister of Portugal here had received ultimate instructions from his court, and that probably that treaty might be concluded in the space of three weeks were we all on the spot together. He therefore pressed me to come over immediately.[1] The first of these objects had some weight in my mind, because as we had sent no person to Tripoli or Tunis I thought if we could meet a minister from them on this ground our arrangements would be settled much sooner & at less expense. But what principally decided with me was the desire of bringing matters to a conclusion with Portugal before the term of our commission should expire or any new turn in the negotiations of France & England should abate their willingness to fix a connection with us. A third motive had also its weight. I hoped that my attendance here, and the necessity of shortening it, might be made use of to force a decisive answer from this court. I therefore concluded to comply with Mr. Adams's request. I went immediately to Versailles and apprised the Count de Vergennes that circumstances of public duty called me hither for three or four weeks, arranged with him some matters, and set out with Col°. Smith for this place where we arrived last night, which was as early as the excessive rigour of the weather admitted. I saw Mr. Adams immediately, & again to-day. He informs me that the minister of Portugal was

---

[1] Though any further efforts in this regard had seemed fruitless, new and unexpected opportunities for negotiating treaties with Portugal, Tripoli, and possibly other nations of the Barbary Coast arose that winter. In recent weeks, Adams had been meeting with Abdrahaman, the envoy of the Sultan of Tripoli. Adams went so far to endear himself to the Tripoline ambassador that he actually began smoking a hookah in his presence. After three such meetings, Adams remained hopeful that a diplomatic agreement between the United States and Tripoli could be hammered out, provided he and Jefferson acted quickly. From Adams's view, a treaty would prevent a grim alternative, "a universal and horrible War with these Barbary States, which will continue for many Years." He felt quite strongly about the matter and conveyed his feelings in an urgent letter to Jefferson. "I am so impressed and distressed with this affair," Adams wrote, "that I will go to New York or to Algiers or first to one and then to the other, if you think it necessary, rather than it should not be brought to a Conclusion." Jefferson was more skeptical than his fellow commissioner when it came to negotiating with Tripoli. He suspected that the nation wanted money before it would sign a treaty, and more money than the United States could or should pay. From Jefferson's perspective, the situation with Portugal was more promising, and this, more than Adams's fervent remarks about Tripoli, motivated him to go to London. (Hayes 2008, 309-310)

taken ill five or six days ago, has been very much so, but is now somewhat better. It would be very mortifying indeed should this accident, with the shortness of the term to which I limit my stay here, defeat what was the principal object of my journey, and that without which I should hardly have undertaken it. With respect to this country, I had no doubt but that every consideration had been urged by Mr. Adams which was proper to be urged. Nothing remains undone in this way. But we shall avail ourselves of our journey here as if made on purpose, just before the expiration of our commission, to form our report to Congress on the execution, of that Commission, which report they may be given to know cannot be formed without decisive information of the ultimate determination of their court. There is no doubt what that determination will be; but it will be useful to have it: as it may put an end to all further expectations on our side of the water, and shew that the time is come for doing whatever is to be done by us for counteracting the unjust & greedy designs of this country. We shall have the honor, before I leave this place to inform you of the result of the several matters which have brought me to it.

A day or two before my departure from Paris I received your letter of Jan. The question therein proposed How far France considers herself as bound to insist on the delivery of the posts, would infallibly produce another, How far we consider ourselves as guarantees of their American possessions & bound to enter into any future war in which these may be attacked? The words of the treaty of alliance seems to be without ambiguity on either head, yet I should be afraid to commit Congress by answering without authority. I will endeavor on my return to sound the opinion of the minister if possible without exposing myself to the other question. Should anything forcible be meditated on those posts, it would possibly be thought prudent previously to ask the good offices of France to obtain their delivery. In this case they would probably say we must first execute the treaty on our part by repealing all acts which have contravened it. Now this measure, if there be any candour in the court of London, would suffice to obtain a delivery of the posts from them, without the mediation of any third power. However if this mediation should be finally needed I see no reason to doubt our obtaining it, and still less to question its omnipotent influence on the British court.

I have the honor to be with sentiments of the highest respect & esteem Sir Your most obedient & most humble servt.,

To Alexander McCaul[1]

---

[1] Jefferson's own private debts were largely held by two firms: the Scottish Alexander McCaul and the English Farrell and Jones. They had refused his tender of Virginia currency during the war as a dishonorable attempt to pay in almost valueless paper and were pressing him for payment now. The ethics of some of the original transactions, particularly between Farrell and Jones and Jefferson's father-in-law, John Wayles, relating as they did to a trade in human flesh, might be considered equally doubtful in modern eyes; but it was perfectly legitimate at the time this occurred. In this letter, Jefferson explains his position. Given

London, Apr. 19, 1786

Dear Sir,

Your favor of Mar. 30 came to hand some days ago, and renewed the recollection of a friendship among the earliest I formed in life, and which neither time nor events have weakened at any moment since. I wish it were in my power to inform you that arrangements were at length taken between the two nations for carrying into complete execution the late treaty of peace, and for settling those conditions which are essential to the continuance of a commerce between them. I suppose all arrangement is thought unnecessary here, as the subject has not been deemed worthy of a conference. Both nations are left to pursue their own measures and it is not easy to foresee what these will be. Each has complaints on the subject of the late treaty. We, that but one post out of six or eight within our limits has yet been evacuated by the British troops; and that a great number slaves were brought away contrary to stipulation, on the other part it is urged that we have thrown obstructions in the way of the recovery of the debts due to the merchants of this country. There are two circumstances of difficulty in the payment of these debts. To speak of the particular state with which you & I are best acquainted, we know that its debt is ten times the amount of its circulating cash. To pay that debt at once then is a physical impossibility. Time is requisite. Were all the creditors to rush to judgment together, a mass of two millions of property would be brought to market where there is but the tenth of that sum of money in circulation to purchase it. Both debtor and creditor would be ruined, as debts would be thus rendered desperate which are in themselves good. Of this truth I find the merchants here sufficiently sensible, & I have no doubt we should have arranged the article of time to mutual satisfaction, allowing judgment to pass immediately, & dividing the execution into instalments. There was another point on which we should have differed. It is a general sentiment in America that the principal of these debts should be paid, & that that alone is stipulated by the treaty. But they think the interest also which arose before & since the war, is justly due. They think it would be as unjust to demand interest during the war. They urge that during that time they could not pay the debt, for that of the remittances attempted, two thirds on an average were taken by the nation to whom they were due: that during that period they had no use of the money, as from the same circumstance of capturing their produce on the sea, tobacco sold at 5/ the hundred, which was not sufficient to bear the expenses of the estate, that they paid the taxes and other charges on the property during that period, and stood it's insurers in the ultimate event of the war. They admit indeed that such individual creditors as were not engaged in privateering against them have lost this interest; but that it was the fault of their own nation and that

---

time, he would pay off what he owed him, with interest for the years preceding and subsequent to the war. With some bitterness he delved into the history of the transaction. In 1776, he had sold land for £4,200 to pay McCaul and Jones. "I did not receive the money till it was not worth Oak leaves." Then Cornwallis had devastated his lands, all to his damage in the sum of three or four thousand pounds. Nevertheless, he intended to be honorable. He had left instructions in Virginia to apply all the profits of his estates to the payments; nor would he draw one shilling personally from them until the debts were fully paid. But again, he would pay no interest for the war years. (Schachner 1957, 303-304)

this is the case where both parties having lost, each may justifiably endeavor to save himself. Setting aside this portion of the interest I am persuaded the debts in America are generally good, and that there is an honest intention to pay them. The improvident and indolent may delay the commencement of that duty, but they do not think certainly to avoid it. After the war ceased the first profits of their plantations would be applied to get supplies of clothing, to rebuild their houses, fences, barns, &c. where they were burned, or decayed, and to repair the other ravages of the war. This might reasonably take two or three years: but it is now time that they should begin the payment of their old debts.

With respect to myself I acknowledge to you that I do not think an interest justly demandeable during the war. Whatever I owed, with interest previous & subsequent to the war, I have taken measures for paying as speedily as possible. My chief debts are to yourself & to Mr. Jones of Bristol. In the year 1776 before there was a shilling of paper money issued, I sold land for £4200 to pay these two debts. I did not receive the money till it was not worth Oak leaves. I have lost the principal and interest of these debts once then in attempting to pay them. Besides this L^d. Cornwallis' army took off 30 of my slaves, burnt one year's crop of tobacco in my houses & destroyed another in the fields with other damages to the amount of three or four thousand pounds. Still I am renewing my efforts to pay what I justly ought; and I hope these will be more successful. My whole estate is left in the hands of Mr. Lewis of Albemarle and Mr. Eppes of Chesterfield to apply it's whole profits to the payment of my debts. Some had been necessarily contracted during the war. They write me word that these will be cleared off this year. There will remain then only yours & Mr. Jones's, toward which the labour of 100 slaves will be annually applied till the payment is effected, for till that I shall not draw one shilling from the estate nor resume its possession. I do not know the exact amount of either of these debts, but I propose that the profits of my estate shall be annually divided in proportion to them. I think it very possible that you will not concur with me in opinion as to the intermediate interest: and that so far I shall meet your censure. Both parties are liable to feel too strongly the arguments which tend to justify their endeavors to avoid this loss. Yet after making allowances for this prejudice, it seems to me impossible but that the hardships are infinitely greater on our side than on yours. You have lost the interest but it is not we who have gained it. We deem your nation the aggressors. They took those profits which arose from your property in our hands, and inflicted on us immeasurable losses besides. I urge these considerations because while they decide my own opinion, I wish them to weigh so much as to preserve me yours, which I highly esteem, and should be afflicted were I to lose it. I have thus stated to you my views of things both public & private, according to the wish expressed in your letters, and I rely on your justice that you make use of the information for your own purposes only, without committing me. I shall at all times be happy to hear from you, being with sincere esteem, Dear Sir, Your friend and servt.

To Richard Henry Lee[1]
London, Apr. 22, 1786
Dear Sir,

In your letter of October the 29th, you desired me to send you one of the new lamps. I tried at every probable place in Paris, and could not get a tolerable one. I have been glad of it since I came here, as I find them much better made here. I now deliver one with this letter into the hands of Mr. Fulwar Skipwith, a merchant from Virginia settled here, who promises to send it to you, with one for Mr. C. Thomson. Of this be pleased to accept from me. It is now found that they may be used with almost any oil,

I expect to leave this place in about three days. Our public letters, joint and separate, will inform you what has been done, and what could not be done here. With respect to a commercial treaty with this country, be assured that the government not only has it not in contemplation at present to make any, but that they do not conceive that any circumstances will arise which shall render it expedient for them to have any political connection with us. They think we shall be glad of their commerce on their own terms. There is no party in our favor here, either in power or out of power. Even the opposition concur with the ministry & the nation in this. I can scarcely consider as a party the Marquis of Lansdowne, and a half dozen characters about him, such as Dr. Price &c. who are impressed with the utility of a friendly connection with us. The former does not venture this sentiment in parliament, and the latter are not in situations to be heard. The Marquis of Lansdowne spoke to me affectionately of your brother, Doct[r]. Lee, and desired his respects to him, which I beg leave to communicate through you. Were he to come into the ministry (of which there is not the most distant prospect) he must adopt the King's system, or go out again, as he did before, for daring to depart from it. When we see that through all the changes of ministry which have taken place during the present reign, there has never been a change of system with respect to America, we cannot reasonably doubt that

---

[1] Richard Henry Lee had been appointed delegate to the Continental Congress in 1775 and was one of the signers of the Declaration of Independence in 1776. He served next in the Virginia House of Delegates in 1777, 1780, and 1785. His brother, Dr. Arthur Lee, was well-known to Jefferson. Earlier, on September 26, 1776, the Congress' Committee of Secret Correspondence — which had been created for the purpose of procuring arms and ammunition — elected and appointed a joint commission consisting of three members to represent the new nation at the court of France. In the order they were elected, the commissioners were Benjamin Franklin, Silas Deane, and Thomas Jefferson. These three were the first full-fledged diplomatic representatives to be appointed by the U.S. Government. Jefferson declined, however, on account of his wife's health; and on October 22, 1776, the Congress elected Arthur Lee in his stead. While Franklin was in Philadelphia, Deane, of Connecticut, and Lee, of Virginia, were already in Europe, serving in their capacity as secret agents "for the purpose of ascertaining sentiment there toward the Colonies and obtaining any other information that might be useful in the Colonies' contest with England." While the commissioners were to pursue a treaty with the British, Congress stipulated two nonnegotiable conditions: acknowledgment of America's independence and the continuation of the treaty with France. The rest was left to the discretion of the commissioners (Brands 2000, 599)

this is the system of the King himself. His obstinacy of character we know; his hostility we have known, and it is embittered by ill success. If ever this nation, during his life, enters into arrangements with us, it must be in consequence of events of which they do not at present see a possibility. The object of the present ministry is to buoy up the nation with flattering calculations of their present prosperity, and to make them believe they are better without us than with us. This they seriously believe; for what is it men cannot be made to believe! I dined the other day in a company of the ministerial party. A General Clark sat next to me, a Scotchman & ministerialist. He introduced the subject of American affairs, and in the course of the conversation told me that were America to petition Parliament to be again received on their former footing, the petition would be very generally rejected. He was serious in this, & I think it was the sentiment of the company, and is the sentiment perhaps of the nation. In this they are wise, but for a foolish reason. They think they lost more by suffering us to participate of their commercial privileges at home & abroad, than they lose by our political severance. The true reason however why such an application should be rejected, is that in a very short time we should oblige them to add another hundred millions to their debt in unsuccessful attempts to retain the subjection offered to them. They are at present in a frenzy, and will not be recovered from it till they shall have leaped the precipice they are now so boldly advancing to. Writing from England, I write you nothing but English news. The continent at present furnishes nothing interesting. I shall hope the favor of your letters at times. The proceedings & views of Congress, & of the assemblies, the opinions and dispositions of our people in general, which in governments like ours must be the foundation of measures, will always be interesting to me, as will whatever respects your own health & happiness, being with great esteem Dear Sir your most obedient, and most humble servant.

To Anna Scott Randolph Jefferson[1]
London, April 22, 1786
My Dear Nancy,

Being called here for a short time, and finding that I could get some articles on terms here of which I thought you might be in want, I have purchased them for you. They are two pieces of linen, three gowns, and some ribbon. They are done up in paper, sealed, and packed in a trunk, in which I have put some other things for Colonel Nicholas Lewis. They will of course go to him, and he will contrive them to you. I heard from Patsy a few days ago; she is well. I left her in France, as my stay here was to be short. I hope my dear Polly is on her way to me. I desired you always to apply to Mr. Lewis for what you should want; but should you at any time wish anything particular from France, write to me and I will send it to you. Doctor Currie can always forward your letters. Pray remember me

---

[1] Anna Scott Randolph Jefferson, Thomas' younger sister — and the twin of Randolph Jefferson — was born in 1755. In her memoir, Jefferson's great grand-daughter Sarah suggests that this letter "…proves him to have been as devoted and thoughtful as a brother as a father." (Randolph 1871, 81)

to my sisters Carr and Bolling, to Mr. Bolling and their families, and be assured of the sincerity with which I am, my dear Nancy, your affectionate brother.

To The Secretary For Foreign Affairs (John Jay)[1]
London, Apr. 23, 1786
Sir,

In another letter of this day I stated to you what had passed with public characters, since my arrival here. Conversations with private individuals I thought it best not to mingle with the contents of that letter. Yet as some have taken place which relate to matters within our instructions, and with persons whose opinions deserve to have some weight, I will take the liberty of stating them. In a conversation with an antient and respectable merchant of this place such a view of the true state of the commercial connection of America & Great Britain was presented to him, as induced him to acknowledge they had been mistaken in their opinions, and to ask that Mr. Adams and myself would permit the chairman of the committee of American merchants to call on us. He observed that the same person happened to be chairman of the committee of

---

[1] The lack of a sufficient treaty with Great Britain prevented the United States from having a true foundation for her foreign relations in the first ten years of her independence. Three-fourths of her trade was subject to the regulation of a foreign legislative body, and several trials at meeting that regulation with reciprocal discriminations met with failure. Only the favoring accident that the American nation became a strong commercial neutral in a critical war amended the unsatisfactory relationship. If legal control of Anglo–American commerce was one-sided, all classes in England were content to believe that the economic advantages also rested with them. While Adams was in London he noted that no group, not even the opposition, favored a change. In fact, the English complaints on nonexecution of the treaty of 1783 by the United States bore the appearance of a defense against the American insistence that commercial relations be adjusted by a treaty; and so long as this emphasis could be maintained, no other reason was required for avoiding a commercial agreement. It was complete protection so long as Adams had no powerful friend at court, as Lafayette was in France. There was, it is true, a committee of American merchants, formed to make protests, but their voice was drowned in the noise made by the whole body of British merchants. Through the spokesman mentioned here, Duncan Campbell, Jefferson and Adams had made an attempt to open discussion with the ministry on the treaty of 1783, but without success. The deep enmity that Jefferson had toward the English government began in his experience as war governor in Virginia and remained with him while he was in Europe. He preferred to divorce the tastes of his countrymen from the luxuries that he thought they indulged in by trading with England, but he realized that the advantages of longer credit would perpetuate that trade. While Americans were thus always in debt to British merchants, it was difficult to remove the shackles from commerce, and so long as British regulations succeeded in holding American trade it seemed to Jefferson that independence was not realized. A letter to W. T. Franklin summed up his view: "They think their commerce indispensable to us. I think that if we are excluded from their W. Indies we shall be better without the commerce to Great Britain than with it. The luxuries of that country are familiar to us and will always tempt us to be in debt. They think we cannot unite to retaliate upon them. I hope we can, and that we shall exclude them from carrying our produce, if not suppress their commerce altogether. They think our whole people would be glad to return to their former dependence on them." (Woolery 1927, 85-86)

the whole body of British merchants; and that such was the respect paid to his person & office that we might consider what came from him as coming from the committees themselves. He called on us at an appointed hour. He was a Mr. Duncan Campbell, formerly much concerned in the American trade. We entered on the subject of the non-execution of the late treaty of peace alleged on both sides. We observed that the refusal to deliver the Western posts, and the withdrawing American property contrary to express stipulation, having preceded what they considered as breaches on our part, were to be considered as the causes of our proceedings. The obstructions thrown by our legislatures in the way of recovery of their debts were insisted on by him. We observed to him that the great amount of the debt from America to Great Britain, and the little circulating coin in the former country, rendered an immediate payment impossible, that time was necessary, that we had been authorized to enter into explanatory arrangements on this subject; that we had made overtures for the purpose which had not been attended to, and that the states had therefore been obliged to modify the article for themselves. He acknowledged the impossibility of immediate payment, the propriety of an explanatory convention, and said that they were disposed to allow a reasonable time. We mentioned the term of five years, including the present, but that judgments might be allowed immediately, only dividing the execution into equal & annual parts so that the last should be levied by the close of the year 1790. This seemed to be quite agreeable to him, and to be as short a term as would be insisted on by them. Proceeding to the sum to be demanded, we agreed that the principal with the interest incurring before and after the war should be paid; but as to that incurring during the war, we differed from him. He urged it's justice with respect to themselves who had laid out of the use of their money during that period. This was his only topic. We opposed to it all those which circumstances both public & private gave rise to. He appeared to feel their weight but said the renunciation of this interest was a bitter pill, and such an one as the merchants here could not swallow. He wished that no declaration should be made as to this article: but we observed that if we entered into explanatory declarations of the points unfavorable to us, we should expect, as a consideration for this, corresponding declarations on the parts in our favor. In fact we supposed his view to be to leave this part of the interest to stand on the general expressions of the treaty, that they might avail themselves in individual cases of the favorable dispositions of debtors or of juries. We proceeded to the necessity of arrangements of our future commerce, were it only as a means of enabling our country to pay its debts. That they had been contracted while certain modes of remittance had existed here, and had been an inducement to us to contract these debts. He said he was not authorized to speak on the subject of the future commerce. He appeared really & feelingly anxious that arrangements should be stipulated as to the payment of the old debts; said he would proceed in that moment to Lord Caermarthen's, and discuss the subject with him, and that we might expect to hear from him. He took leave; and we never since heard from him or any other person on the subject. Congress will judge how far these conversations should influence their future proceedings, or those of the states.

I have the honor to be with the highest respect & esteem, Sir, your most obedient humble serv.

To John Page[1]
Paris, May 4, 1786
Dear Sir,

Your two favors of Mar 15 and Aug 23, 1785, by Monsieur de la Croix came to hand on the 15th of November. His return gives me an opportunity of sending you a copy of the nautical almanacs for 1786, 7, 8, 9. There is no late and interesting publication here, or I would send it by the same conveyance. With these almanacs I pack a copy of some Notes I wrote for Monsr de Marbois in the year 1781, of which I had a few printed here. They were written in haste & for his private inspection. A few friends having asked copies I found it cheaper to print than to write them. They will offer nothing new to you, not even as an oblation of my friendship for you which is as old almost as we are ourselves. Mazzei brought me your favor of Apr 28. I thank you much for your communications. Nothing can be more grateful at such a distance. It is unfortunate that most people think the occurrences passing daily under their eyes, are either known to all the world, or not worth being known. They therefore do not give them place in their letters. I hope you will be so good as to continue your friendly information. The proceedings of our public bodies, the progress of the public mind on interesting questions, the casualties which happen among our private friends, and whatever is interesting to yourself and family will always be anxiously received by me. There is one circumstance in the work you were concerned in which has not yet come to my knowledge, to wit how far Westward from Fort Pitt does the Western boundary of Pennsylvania pass, and where does it strike the Ohio? The proposition you mention from Mr. Anderson on the purchase of tobacco, I would have made use of, but that I have engaged the abuses of the tobacco trade on a more general scale. I confess their redress does not appear with any certainty: but till I see all hope of removing the evil by the roots, I cannot propose to prune it's branches.

I returned but three or four days ago from a two months trip to England. I traversed that country much, and own both town & country fell short of my expectations. Comparing it with this, I found a much greater proportion of barrens, a soil in other parts not naturally so good as this, not better cultivated, but better manured, & therefore more productive. This proceeds from the practice of long leases there, and short ones here. The laboring people here

---

[1] John Page was a particular friend and close associate whom Jefferson had first encountered at William and Mary. While this letter generally discusses gardening, farming, life in France, and religion, it was to John Page that Jefferson, when possible, often confided his inmost thoughts and engaged in philosophical speculations. (Kimball 1943, 140)

are poorer than in England. They pay about one half their produce in rent, the English in general about a third. The gardening in that country is the article in which it surpasses all the earth. I mean their pleasure gardening. This indeed went far beyond my ideas. The city of London, tho' handsomer than Paris, is not so handsome as Philadelphia. Their architecture is in the most wretched stile I ever saw, not meaning to except America where it is bad, nor even Virginia where it is worse than in any other part of America, which I have seen. The mechanical arts in London are carried to a wonderful perfection. But of these I need not speak, because of them my countrymen have unfortunately too many samples before their eyes. I consider the extravagance which has seized them as a more baneful evil than toryism was during the war. It is the more so as the example is set by the best and most amiable characters among us. Would that a missionary appear who would make frugality the basis of his religious system, and go thro the land preaching it up as the only road to salvation, I would join his school tho' not generally disposed to seek my religion out of the dictates of my own reason & feelings of my own heart. These things have been more deeply impressed on my mind by what I have heard & seen in England. That nation hates us, their ministers hate us, and their King more than all other men. They have the impudence to avow this, tho' they acknowledge our trade important to them. But they say we cannot prevent our countrymen from bringing that into their laps. A conviction of this determines them to make no terms of commerce with us. They say they will pocket our carrying trade as well as their own. Our overtures of commercial arrangement have been treated with a derision which shows their firm persuasion that we shall never unite to suppress their commerce or even to impede it. I think their hostility towards us is much more deeply rooted at present than during the war. In the arts the most striking thing I saw there, new, was the application of the principle of the steam-engine to grist mills. I saw 8 pr. of stones which are worked by steam, and they are to set up 30 pair in the same house. A hundred bushels of coal a day are consumed at present. I do not know in what proportion the consumption will be increased by the additional geer.

Be so good as to present my respects to Mrs. Page & your family, to W. Lewis, F. Willis & their families and to accept yourself assurances of the sincere regard with which I am Dr Sir your affectionate friend & servt.

P.S. Mazzei is still here and will publish soon a book on the subject of America.

To James Ross[1]

---

[1] The issue of tobacco continued to press Jefferson. As he had earlier mentioned to Vergennes, tobacco was the big crop that the United States could furnish France and, with the money received in payment, buy French products in return. However, Vergennes had never been struck with Jefferson's "good idea" before, repeated his old argument of the King's revenue and the long-standing arrangements, and ended the interview with the remark that no promises could

Paris, May 8, 1786
Dear Sir,

I have duly received your favor of Octob 22, and am much gratified by the communications therein made. It has given me details which do not enter into the views of my ordinary correspondents, and which are very entertaining. I experience great satisfaction at seeing my country proceed to facilitate the intercommunications of its several parts by opening rivers, canals & roads. How much more rational is this disposal of public money, than that of waging war.

Before the receipt of your letter, Morris's contract for 60,000 hhds of tob [tobacco] was concluded with the Farmers general. I have been for some time occupied in endeavoring to destroy the root of the evils which the tobacco trade encounters in this country; by making the ministers sensible that merchants will not bring a commodity to a market where but one person is allowed to buy it: and that so long as that single purchaser is obliged to go to foreign markets for it, he must pay for it in coin & not in commodities. These truths have made their way to the minds of the ministry, insomuch as to have delayed the execution of the new lease of the farms six months. It is renewed however for three years, but so as not to render impossible a reformation of this great evil. They are sensible of the evil, but it is so interwoven with their fiscal system that they find it hazardous to disentangle. The temporary distress too of the revenue they are not prepared to meet. My hopes therefore are weak, though not quite desperate. When they become so, it will remain to look about for the best palliative this monopoly can bear. My present idea is that it will be found in a prohibition to the farmers general to purchase tobacco anywhere but in France. You will perceive by this that my object is to strengthen the connection between this country & my own in all useful points. I am of opinion that 23,000 hhds of tobacco, the annual consumption of this country, do not exceed the amount of those commodities which it is more advantageous to us to buy here than in England, or elsewhere, and such a commerce would powerfully reinforce the motives for a friendship from this country towards ours. This friendship we ought to cultivate closely, considering the present dispositions of England towards us. I am lately returned from a visit to that country. It appears to me to be more hostile than during the war; this spirit of hostility has always existed in the mind of the King, but it has now extended itself thro' the whole mass of people, and the majority in the public councils. In a country where the voice of the people influences so much the measures of administration and where it coincides with the private temper

---

be made. This was most discouraging for Jefferson. As indicated in this letter to Federalist James Ross — soon the be a senator from Pennsylvania — what particularly infuriated him was the fact that Robert Morris, a Pennsylvanian, not a Virginian, had been able by appropriate means to obtain a monopolistic contract from the farmers-general, whereby he could ship 60,000 hogsheads of American tobacco to France, and no other Americans need apply. What the "double monopoly" meant to Virginia tobacco Jefferson was only too well aware. Morris could compel her merchants to sell to him at his own figure — since the excess that normally would have gone to France had now no other outlet, and the commerce of that article would be thrown "in agonies," while Morris made enormous profits. (Schachner 1957, 280)

of the King, there is no pronouncing on future events. It is true they have nothing to gain & much to lose by a war with us. But interest is not the strongest passion in the human breast. There are difficult points too still unsettled between us. They have not withdrawn their armies out of our country nor given satisfaction for the property they brought off. On our part we have not paid our debts, and it will take time to pay them. In conferences with some distinguished mercantile characters, I found them sensible of the impossibility of our paying these debts at once, and that an endeavor to force universal & immediate payment would render debts desperate, which are good in themselves. I think we should not have differed in the term necessary. We differed essentially in the article of interest. For while the principal and interest preceding & subsequent to the war seems justly due from us, that which incurred during the war does not. Interest is a compensation for the use of money. Their money in our hands was in the form of lands & negroes. Tobacco, the produce of these lands and negroes (or as I may call it, the interest of them) being almost impossible of conveyance to the markets of consumption, because taken by themselves in its way there, sold during the war at 5/ or 6/ the hundred. This did not pay tools, taxes, & other plantation charges. A man who should have attempted to remit to his creditor tobacco for either principal or interest, must have remitted it three times before one would have arrived safe: and this from the depredations of their own nation, and often of the creditor himself, for some of the merchants entered deeply into the privateering business. The individuals who did not, say they have lost this interest: the debtor replies that he has not gained, & that it is a case where a loss having incurred, everyone tries to shift it from himself. The known bias of the human mind from motives of interest, should lessen the confidence of each party in the justice of their reasoning; but it is difficult to say which of them should make the sacrifice both of reason & interest. Our conferences were intended as preparatory to some arrangement. It is uncertain how far we should have been able to accommodate our opinions. But the absolute aversion of the government to enter into any arrangement prevented the object from being pursued. Each country is left to do justice to itself & to the other according to its own ideas, as to what is past, and to scramble for the future as well as they can: to regulate their commerce by duties and prohibitions, and perhaps by cannons & mortars; in which event we must abandon the ocean where we are weak, leaving to neutral nations the carriage of our commodities: & measure with them on land where they alone can lose. Farewell then all our useful improvements of canals, roads, reformations of laws & other rational employments. I really doubt whether there is temper enough on either side to prevent this issue of our present hatred. Europe is at this moment without the appearance of a cloud. The death of the K of Prussia, daily expected, may raise one. My paper admonishes me that after asking a continuance of your favors, it is time for me to conclude with assurances of the esteem with which I am Dr Sir, your friend & servt.

To James Monroe[1]
Paris, May 10, 1786
Dear Sir,

My last to you was of Jan. 27. Since that I have received yours of Jan. 19. Information from other quarters gives me reasons to suspect you have in negotiation a very important change in your situation. You will carry into the execution all my wishes for your happiness. I hope it will not detach you from a settlement in your own country. I had even entertained hopes of your settling in my neighborhood: but these were determined by your desiring a plan of a house for Richmond. However reluctantly I relinquish this prospect, I shall not the less readily obey your commands by sending you a plan. Having been much engaged since my return from England in answering the letters & dispatching other business which had accumulated during my absence & being still much engaged, perhaps I may not be able to send the plan by this conveyance. If I do not send it now, I will surely by the first conveyance after this. Your Encyclopedia, containing 18 livraisons, went off last night for Havre, from whence it will go in a vessel bound to N. York. It will be under the care of M. la Croix a passenger, who, if he does not find you in N. York will carry it to Virginia. I send it to Richmond. Another copy in a separate box, goes for Currie. I pay here all charges to N. York. What may occur afterwards I desire him to ask either of you or Currie, as either will pay for the other, or to draw on me for them. My letters to Mr. Jay will inform you of the objects which carried me to England: and that the principal one, the treaty with Portugal has been accomplished. Tho' we were unable to procure any special advantages in that, yet we thought it of consequence to insure our trade against those particular checks and discouragements which it has heretofore met with there. The information as to the Barbary states, which we obtained from Abdrahaman the Tripoline ambassador was also given to Mr. Jay. If it be right, & the scale of proportion between those nations which we had settled be also right, eight times the sum required by Tripoli will be necessary to accomplish a peace with the whole, that is to say about *two hundred and fifty thousand guineas*.[2] The continuance of this peace will depend on their idea

---

[1] The financial debts owed by the United States to European creditors, in Jefferson's mind, involved two problems. One was interest during the war, and the other was prejudice in court action on recovery. His own debt to Alexander McCaul seemingly caused Jefferson to hold a conviction regarding interest payments, the same, in fact, as he held at the time of instructing the envoys in Europe in the early part of 1784: that it was unallowable for the period of the war. But he was equally positive that the courts should be opened to British creditors. The judgments they obtained could be divided into equal annual installments, the last due in 1790. As Jefferson opines in this letter to Monroe, "Since it is left for each nation to pursue their own measures in the execution of the late treaty, may not Congress with propriety recommend a mode of executing that article respecting the debts, and send it to each state to be passed into law. Whether England gives up the posts or not, these debts must be paid, or our character stained with infamy among all nations & to all times. As to the satisfaction for slaves carried off, it is a bagatelle which if not made good before the last instalment becomes due, may be secured out of that." (Woolery 1927, 86-87)
[2] All italics were originally written in cipher. (Boyd 1990)

of our power to enforce it, and on the life of the particular Dey or other head of the government, with whom it is contracted. Congress will no doubt weigh these circumstances against the expense & probable success of compelling a peace by arms. Count d'Estaing having communicated to me verbally some information as to an experiment formerly made by this country, I shall get him to put it into writing and I will forward it to Congress, as it will aid them in their choice of measures. According to this a force, which after the first outfit, might cost about *three thousand guineas a month* sufficed in a short time. However, which plan is eligible can only be known to ourselves who are on the spot & have under your view all the difficulties of both. There is a third measure: that of abandoning the Mediterranean carriage to other nations. With respect to England no arrangements can be taken. The merchants were certainly disposed to have consented to accommodation as to the article of debts. I was not certain when I left England that they would relinquish the interest during the war. A letter received since from the first character among the American merchants in Scotland satisfies me they would have relinquished it to insure the capital & residue of interest. Would to heaven all the states therefore would settle on a uniform plan. To open the courts to them so that they might obtain judgments, to divide the executions into so many equal annual instalments as that the last might be paid in the year 1790, to have the payments in actual money, and to include the capital & interest preceding & subsequent to the war, would give satisfaction to the world, and to the merchants in general. Since it is left for each nation to pursue their own measures in the execution of the late treaty, may not Congress with propriety recommend a mode of executing that article respecting the debts, and send it to each state to be passed into law. Whether England gives up the posts or not, these debts must be paid, or our character stained with infamy among all nations & to all times. As to the satisfaction for slaves carried off, it is a bagatelle which if not made good before the last instalment becomes due, may be secured out of that.

I formerly communicated the overtures for a treaty which had been made by the Imperial ambassador. The instructions from Congress being in their favor, and Mr. Adams's opinion also, I encouraged them. He expected his full powers when I went to England. Yet I did not think, nor did Mr. Adams, that this was of importance enough to weigh against the objects of that journey. He received them soon after my departure, & communicated it to me on my return, asking a copy of our propositions. I gave him one, but observed our commission had then but a few days to run. He desired I would propose to Congress the giving new powers to go on with this, and said that in the meantime he would arrange with us the plan. In a commercial view, no great good is to be gained by this, but in a political one it may be expedient. Our national respect needs strengthening in Europe. It will certainly receive reinforcement by our being received into alliance by the second power & what will shortly be the first character in Europe. He is at the head too of the other great European confederacy, and may serve us with all the powers in that scale. As the treaty would of course be in the terms of those of Prussia & Portugal, it will give us but little additional embarrassment in any commercial regulations we may wish to establish. The exceptions from these which the other treaties will require, may take in the treaty with the Emperor. I should be glad to communicate some answer as soon as Congress shall have made up their minds on it. My information to Congress on the subject of our commercial articles with this country has only come down to Jan 27. Whether I shall say anything on it in my letter to Mr. Jay by this conveyance, depends on it's not being too early for an appointment. I expect hourly word from the Count de Vergennes to meet him on this & other subjects. My last information was that the lease was too far advanced to withdraw from it the article of tobacco, but that a clause is inserted in it empowering the King to discontinue it at any time. A discontinuance is therefore the only remaining object, and as even this cannot be effected till the expiration of the old lease, which is about the end of the present year, I have wished only to stir the subject from time to time so as to keep it alive. This idea led me into a measure proposed by the M. de la Fayette whose return from Berlin found the matter in that point to which my former report to Congress had conducted it. I communicated to him what I had been engaged on, what were my prospects, and my purpose of keeping the subject just open. He offered his services with that zeal which commands them on every occasion respecting America. He suggested to me the meeting two or three gentlemen well acquainted with this business. We met. They urged me to propose to the Ct de Vergennes the appointing a committee to take this matter into consideration. I told them that decency would not permit me to point out to the Ct de Vergennes the mode by which he should conduct a negotiation, but that I would press again the necessity of an arrangement, if whilst that should be operating on his mind they would suggest the appointment of a committee. The Marquis offered his service for this purpose. The consequence was the appointment of a committee, & the Marquis as a member of it. I communicated to him my papers. He collected other lights wherever he could, & particularly from the gentlemen with whom he had before concerted, and who had a good acquaintance with the subject. The Marquis became our champion in the committee and two of its members, who were of the corps of Farmers general entered the lists on the other side. Each gave in memorials. The lease indeed was signed while I was gone to England, but the discussions were & still are continued in the Committee from which we derive two advantages, 1, that of shewing that the object is not to be relinquished and 2, to enlighten government as to it's true interest. The Ct de Vergennes is absolutely for it; but it is not in his department. Calonnes is his friend, and in this instance his principle seems so be *America veritas sed magis amicus Plato.* An additional hope is founded in the expectation of a change of the minister of finance. The present one is under the absolute control of the farmers general. The committee's views have been somewhat different from mine. They despair of a suppression of the farm, and therefore wish to obtain palliatives which would coincide with the particular good of this country. I think that so long as the monopoly in the sale is kept up, it is of no consequence to us how they modify the pill for their own internal relief: but on the contrary the worse it remains, the more necessary it will render a reformation. Any palliative would take from us all those arguments & friends who would be satisfied with accommodation. The Marquis, tho differing in opinion from me in this point, has however adhered to my principle of absolute liberty or nothing. In this condition is the matter at this moment. Whether I say anything on the subject to Mr. Jay will depend on my interview with Ct de Vergennes. I doubt whether that will furnish anything worth communicating & whether it will be in time. I therefore state this much to you, that you may see the matter is not laid aside.

I must beg leave to recommend Colo Humphreys to your acquaintance & good offices. He is an excellent man, an able one, & in need of some provision. Besides former applications to me in favor of Dumas, the Rhingrave of Salm (the effective minister of the government of Holland, while their two ambassadors here are ostensible, and) who is conducting secret arrangements for them with this court, presses his interests on us. It is evident the two governments make a point of it. You ask why they do not provide for him themselves? I am not able to answer the question but by a conjecture that Dumas's particular ambition prefers an appointment from us. I know all the difficulty about this application which Congress has to encounter. I see the reasons against giving him the primary appointment at that court, and the difficulty of his accommodating himself to a subordinate one. Yet I think something must be done in it to gratify this court, of which we must be always asking favors. In these countries personal favors weigh more than public interest. The minister who has asked a gratification for Dumas, has embarked his own feelings & reputation in that demand. I do not think it was discreet by any means. But this reflection might perhaps aggravate a disappointment. I know not really what you can do: but yet hope something will be done. Adieu my dear Sir & believe me to be yours affectionately.

To The Secretary for Foreign Affairs (John Jay)[1]
Paris, May 23, 1786
Sir,

Letters received from both Madrid & Algiers while I was in London having suggested that treaties with the states of Barbary would be much facilitated by a previous one with the Ottoman porte, it was agreed between Mr. Adams and myself that on my return I should consult on this subject the Count de Vergennes, whose long residence at Constantinople rendered him the best judge of its expediency. Various circumstances have put it out of my power to consult him till to-day. I stated to him the difficulties we were likely to meet

---

[1] The purpose of insisting on a treaty with the Ottoman Porte was to prevent Spain from interceding for Portugal and Naples since they had no such treaties. But this political dodge was much less important than the amount of money the dey [ruler] and his council demanded. Vergennes, who had been ambassador from France to Turkey from 1754 to 1768, disagreed with D'Espilly, the Spanish Ambassador, and scoffed at the Turkish treaty: "The Barbary States," as Jefferson recalls Vergennes' opinion to Jay, "acknowledged a sort of vassalage to the Porte, and availed themselves of that relation when anything was to be gained by it; but, that whenever it subjected them to a demand from the Porte, they totally disregarded it; that money was the sole agent at Algiers, except so far as fear could be induced also." (Woolery 1927, 26)

with at Algiers and asked his opinion what would be the probable expense of a diplomatic mission to Constantinople, & what it's effect at Algiers. He said that the expense would be very great, for that presents must be made at that court, and every one would be gaping after them; and that it would not procure us a peace at Algiers one penny the cheaper. He observed that the Barbary states acknowledged a sort of vassalage to the Porte, & availed themselves of that relation when anything was to be gained by it: but that whenever it subjected them to a demand from the Porte they totally disregarded it: that money was the sole agent at Algiers, except so far as fear could be induced also. He cited the present example of Spain, which tho' having a treaty with the Porte, would probably be obliged to buy a peace at Algiers at the expense of upwards of six millions of livres. I told him we had calculated from the demands & information of the Tripoline ambassador at London that to make peace with the four Barbary states would cost us between two & three hundred thousand guineas, if bought with money. The sum did not seem to exceed his expectations. I mentioned to him that, considering the uncertainty of a peace when bought, perhaps Congress might think it more eligible to establish a cruise of frigates in the Mediterranean & even to blockade Algiers. He supposed it would require ten vessels great & small. I observed to him that Monsr. de Massiac had formerly done it with five; he said it was true, but that vessels of relief would be necessary. I hinted to him that I thought the English capable of administering aid to the Algerines. He seemed to think it impossible, on account of the scandal it would bring on them. I asked him what had occasioned the blockade by Mr. de Massiac: he said, an infraction of their treaty by the Algerines. I had a good deal of conversation with him also on the situation of affairs between England & the United States: & particularly on their refusal to deliver up our posts. I observed to him that the obstructions thrown in the way of the recovery of their debts were the effect & not the cause, as they pretended, of their refusal to deliver up the posts: that the merchants interested in these debts shewed a great disposition to make arrangements with us, that the article of time we could certainly have settled, & probably that of the interest during the war: but that the minister shewing no disposition to have these matters arranged, I thought it a sufficient proof that this was not the true cause of their retaining the posts. He concurred as to the justice of our requiring time for the payment of our debts; said nothing which shewed a difference of opinion as to the article of interest, and seemed to believe fully that their object was to divert the channel of the fur trade before they delivered up the posts, and expressed a strong sense of the importance of that commerce to us. I told him I really could not foresee what would be the event of this detention, that the situation of the British funds, & desire of their minister to begin to reduce the national debt seemed to indicate that they could not wish a war. He thought so, but that neither were we in a condition to go to war. I told him I was yet uninformed what Congress proposed to do on this subject, but that we should certainly always count on the good offices of France, and I was sure that the offer of them would suffice to induce Gr. Britain to do us justice. He said that surely we might always count on the friendship of France. I added that by the treaty of alliance, she was bound to guarantee our limits to us, as they should be established at the moment of peace. He said they were so "mais qu'il nous etoit necessaire de les constater." I told him there was no question what our boundaries were, that the English themselves admitted they were clear beyond all question. I feared however to press this any further lest a reciprocal question should be put to me, & therefore diverted the conversation to another object. This is a sketch only of a conference which was lengthy. I have endeavored to give the substance, & sometimes the expressions where they were material. I supposed it would be agreeable to Congress to have it communicated to them, in the present undecided state in which these subjects are. I should add that an explanation of the transaction of Monsieur de Massaic with the Algerines, before hinted at, will be found in the enclosed letter from the Count d'Estaing to me, wherein he gives also his own opinion. The whole is submitted to Congress, as I conceive it my duty to furnish them with whatever information I can gather which may throw any light on the subjects depending before them. I have the honor to be with the most perfect esteem & respect Sir your most obedient and most humble servt.

To The Swedish Ambassador at Paris (Baron Stahe)[1]
Paris, June 12, 1786
Sir,

In compliance with your Excellency's desire I will throw on paper such considerations as occur to me on the question "How may the island of St. Bartholomews be rendered instrumental for promoting commerce between Sweden and the United States." They will be rapid, undigested & incomplete: but a desire of contributing to bind the two Countries together in interest, and a respect for your commands will induce me to hazard them. I shall make the interests of Sweden the basis of my theory because we have no right to expect her to depart from them in order to promote ours.

Antient nations considered Colonies principally as Receptacles for a too numerous population, and as natural & useful allies in times of war: but modern nations, viewing commerce as an object of first importance, value Colonies chiefly as Instruments for the increase of that. This is principally effected by their taking commodities from the mother State, whether raised within herself, or obtained elsewhere in the course of her trade & furnishing in return Colonial productions necessary for her consumption or for her commerce of exchange with other nations. In this way the colonies of Spain, Portugal, France and England have been chiefly subservient to the advantages of their Mother Country. In this way too in a smaller degree has Denmark derived utility from her American Colonies and so also Holland, except as to the Island of St. Eustatius. This is by nature a rock, barren and unproductive in itself, but its owners became sensible that what Nature had denied it, Policy could more than supply. It was conveniently situated for carrying on contraband trade with both the continents & with the islands of America. They made it therefore an entrepot for all nations. Hither

[1] Erik Magnus Staël von Holstein.

are brought the productions of every other part of America and the Dutch give in exchange such articles as in the course of their commerce they can most advantageously gather up. And it is a question, on which they will not enable us to decide, whether by furnishing American productions to the commerce of Holland & by finding vent for such productions of the old world as the Dutch merchants obtain to advantage, the barren rock of saint Eustatius does not give more activity to their commerce & leave with them greater profits, than their more fertile possessions on the continent of South America. The Danes finding that their islands were capable of yielding but moderate advantages by their native productions, have also laid them open to foreign commerce, in order to draw thro' them articles which they do not produce in themselves, or not in great quantities. But these nations, only half emancipated from the fetters of commercial prejudices, have taken only half a step towards placing these institutions on their best footing. Both the Dutch & Danish free ports are under restrictions which discourage very much the operations of exchange in them.

The island of St. Bartholomew, lately ceded to Sweden, is, if I am rightly informed, capable of furnishing little of its own productions to that country. It remains then to make it the instrument for obtaining through its intermediation such American productions as Sweden can consume or dispose of, and for finding in return a vent for the native productions of Sweden. Let us suppose it then made a free port without a single restriction. These consequences will follow: 1. It will draw to itself that tide of commerce which at present sets towards the Dutch and Danish islands, because vessels going to these are often obliged to negotiate a part of their cargoes at saint Eustatius, and to go to saint Thomas's to negotiate the residue, whereas when they shall know that there is a port where all articles are free both for importation and exportation, they will go to that port which enables them to perform by one voyage the exchanges which hitherto they could only effect by two. 2. Every species of American produce, whether of the precious metals or commodities, which Sweden may want for its own consumption or as aliment for its own commerce with other nations, will be collected either fairly or by contraband into the magazines of Saint Bartholomew. 3. All the productions which Sweden can furnish from within itself or obtain to advantage from other nations, will in like manner be deposited in the magazines of S^t. Bartholomew, and will be carried to the several ports of America in payment for what shall be taken from them.

If it be objected that this unrestrained license will give opportunity to the subjects of other nations to carry on exchanges there in which Sweden will be no ways interested: I say, 1. That there will be few of these operations into which the Swedish merchants will not be taken in the beginning or in the long run. 2. That there will be few of these exchanges into which Swedish productions will not enter, when productions of that nature are wanted in return. 3. But suppose neither Swedish merchants nor productions enter into the operation, what objections can Sweden have to other people's meeting in one of her ports to carry on their commercial exchanges? On the contrary, would not every enlightened nation be glad if all others would come to her as a common center for commercial operations? If all the merchants who make the exchanges of commerce in Amsterdam, London, Lisbon, Leghorn, etc would go by common consent to perform these operations in Stockholm, would that wise Government obstruct such an assembly? If all the exchanges now made in the several parts of the two continents, & of the islands, of America, in Philadelphia for instance, Charlestown, S^t. Eustatius, Porto-bello, Rio Janeiro, were proposed to be transferred to the island of S^t. Bartholomew would that island be rendered thereby less able to promote the commerce of the mother country?

These general observations have anticipated the answer to our question, How may the island of S^t. Bartholomew be rendered instrumental to the particular commerce between Sweden and the United States? The United States have much occasion for the productions of Sweden, particularly for its iron. For a part of this they can furnish indigo, rice, tobacco: and so far the exchange may be effected by the merchants of the two countries in the ports of the United States or of Sweden. The surplus of the want they cannot take at all unless Sweden will administer to them the means of paying for it. This she may do by receiving at S^t. Bartholomew whatever productions they will bring. They will of course send their flour, saltfish, & other things wanting in the other ports of America, which by the Swedish merchants at S^t. Bartholomew, will run into those ports and exchanged for precious metals or commercial commodities: or the American merchant taking on himself those operations will run his flour or salt fish into those ports himself, take cash or such commercial articles as suit Sweden, & go with these to S^t. Bartholomew to pay for the iron he wants.

The interest of the United States then is that St. Bartholomew be made a port of unlimited freedom, & such too is evidently the interest of Sweden. If it be freed by halves, the freeports of other nations, at present in possession of the commerce, will retain it against any new port offering no superior advantages. The situation of St. Bartholomew is very favorable to these views, as it is among the most Windward, and therefore the most accessible, of the West Indian Islands. How far they may be seconded by the character of its port, the government of Sweden will best know, as they have taken the necessary informations on that point.

Unacquainted with the details of commerce I am able to present only general views of this subject, they are such however as experience seems to have approved. They may appear founded on a want of attention to the laws of society, inconsistent with sound morality — but first let the line be drawn between the just and equal regulations of associated states, and the partial and oppressive rescripts of Metropolitan cupidity, & we shall see whether the Interloper, or the Legislator of Chili & Peru is on the right side of that line. They will need apology for another cause where it will be more difficult to be found; that is as they offer nothing but what would have occurred, & in a better form, to yourself. Nobody is more sensible of this than myself: and I can expect your indulgence only by praying you to consider them, not as pretending to any information which you do not already possess, but as the offerings of that perfect esteem & respect with which I have the honor to be your hble servt.

To William Carmichael[1]
Paris, June 20, 1786

I find that all the states had come into the impost except N. York whose assembly were then sitting & it was thought would adopt it. N. Hampshire, Massachusetts, Rho. isld. New Jersey, Delaware & Virginia have agreed to confer on Congress the regulation of their trade, & lest this disjointed method of proceeding should fail of its effect, the latter has appointed commissioners & invited the other states to do the same to meet & settle an article of Confederation for this purpose. Virginia has declared Kentucky an independent state, provided its inhabitants consent to it, & Congress will receive them into a union. Massachusetts has repealed so much of her navigation act as respected any foreign nation except Gr. Britain. Contributions of money come slowly to the public treasury. A committee of Congress have drawn a strong report on that subject, which has produced a good effect in the states.

In a letter of Mar. 20, from Dr. Franklin to me is this passage: "As to public affairs the Congress has not been able to assemble more than 7 or 8 states during the whole winter, so the treaty with Prussia remains still unratified, tho' there is no doubt of its being done so soon as a full Congress assembles which is expected next month. The disposition to furnish Congress with ample powers augments daily, as people become more enlightened, & I do not remember ever to have seen, during my long life, more signs of public felicity than appear at present throughout these states; the cultivators of the earth who make the bulk of our nation, have made good crops, which are paid for at high prices, with ready money; the artisans too receive high wages, & the value of all real estates is augmented greatly. Merchants & shopkeepers indeed complain that there is not business enough. But this is evidently not owing to the fewness of buyers, but to the too great number of sellers; for the consumption of goods was never greater, as appears by the dress, furniture & manner of living of all ranks of the people." His health is good, except as to the stone which does not grow worse. I thank

---

[1] At this time, Carmichael was the Chargé d'Affaires at the Spanish royal court. As background, the subsequent actions of and proposals by Virginia (and the other southern states) sustain the contention that, by the mid-1780s, southern statesmen were interested primarily in increasing their relative decision-making capacities within the national government. In January 1786, for example, the Virginia legislature reversed its previous indifference toward Kentucky statehood petitions and enacted legislation promoting the separation of the Kentucky District and its admission into the Union.[14] Later the same year, Virginia delegate James Monroe won congressional approval for a reduction in the number of new western states to be formed north of the Ohio River.[15] The proposed admission of Kentucky was intended to add another vote to the southern state bloc in Congress and the latter policy change orchestrated by Monroe was intended (over the short term) to strengthen the southern state bloc by accelerating the admission of yet another noncommercial state into the Union. The reduced number of western states also strengthened Virginia's congressional representation (over the long term) because, as Monroe suggested to Jefferson in 1785, it effectively prevented them from "outnumber[ing] us in congress." (Kromkowski 2002, 243-244)

you for your attention to my request about the books which Mr. Barclay writes me he has forwarded from Cadiz.

I have the honor to be,

To James Monroe[1]
Paris, July 9, 1786
Dear Sir,

I wrote you last on the 10th of May, since which your favor of May 11 has come to hand. The political world enjoys great quiet here. The King of Prussia is still living, but like the snuff of a candle which sometimes seems out, & then blazes up again. Some think that his death will not produce any immediate effect in Europe. His kingdom, like a machine will go on for some time with the winding up he has given it. The King's visit to Cherbourg has made a great sensation in England & here. It proves to the world that it is a serious object to this country, and that the King commits himself for the accomplishment of it. Indeed so many cones have been sunk that no doubt remains of the practicability of it. It will contain, as is said, 80 ships of the line, be one of the best harbors in the world, & by means of two entrances on different sides will admit vessels to come in and go out with every wind. The effect of this in another war with England defies calculation. Having no news to communicate I will recur to the subjects of your letter of May 11.

With respect to the new states were the question to stand simply in this form: How may the ultramontane territory be disposed of so as to produce the greatest & most immediate benefit to the inhabitants of the maritime states of the union? the plan would be more plausible of laying it off into two or three states only. Even on this view however there would still be something to be said against it which might render it at least doubtful. But it is a question which good faith forbids us to receive into discussion. This requires us to state the question in its just form, How may the territories of the Union be disposed of so as to

---

[1] In this letter, Jefferson offers Monroe his opinions on the states' fundamental structure. After the federal government, next in the descending scale come the states; and these are, historically, the starting point of Jefferson's system. He was satisfied with the various distinct colonial administrations, until the necessity of presenting an united front in the war for independence led him to conceive them as organized under a federal head; and it was only considerably later that he realized the possibilities of the further subdivision of the states into counties, and finally into wards or townships. The size of the states cannot, of course, be precisely determined; but Jefferson suggests that new territory be divided into sections of moderate size, say 30,000 square miles. Larger divisions he feels will eventually crumble into smaller, and will at the same time be opposed to the wishes of the people. When Congress adopted a different plan, proposing to make the western states fewer and larger, he objected that this "is reversing the natural order of things. A tractable people may be governed in large bodies; but, in proportion as they depart from this character, the extent of their government must be less. We see into what small divisions the Indians are obliged to reduce their societies." He does not offer a population unit: to do so would mean progressive dissection of the states, which could only result in confusion and disorder. (Wiltse 1935, 228-129)

produce the greatest degree of happiness to their inhabitants? With respect to the maritime states nothing or little remains to be done. With respect then to the ultramontane states, will their inhabitants be happiest divided into states of 30,000 square miles, not quite as large as Pennsylvania, or into states of 160,000 square miles each, that is to say three times as large as Virginia within the Alleghany? They will not only be happier in states of a moderate size, but it is the only way in which they can exist as a regular society. Considering the American character in general, that of those people particularly, and the energetic nature of our governments, a state of such extent as 160,000 square miles would soon crumble into little ones. These are the circumstances which reduce the Indians to such small societies. They would produce an effect on our people similar to this. They would not be broken into such small pieces because they are more habituated to subordination, & value more a government of regular law. But you would surely reverse the nature of things in making small states on the ocean & large ones beyond the mountains. If we could in our consciences say that great states beyond the mountains will make the people happiest, we must still ask whether they will be contented to be laid off into large states? They certainly will not; and if they decide to divide themselves, we are not able to restrain them. They will end by separating from our confederacy & becoming it's enemies. We had better then look forward & see what will be the probable course of things. This will surely be a division of that country into states of a small, or at most of a moderate size. If we lay them off into such, they will acquiesce, and we shall have the advantage of arranging them so as to produce the best combinations of interest. What Congress has already done in this matter is an argument the more in favor of the revolt of those states against a different arrangement, and of their acquiescence under a continuance of that. Upon this plan, we treat them as fellow citizens, they will have a just share in their own government, they will love us, & pride themselves in an union with us. Upon the other we treat them as subjects, we govern them, & not they themselves, they will abhor us as masters, & break off from us in defiance. I confess to you that I can see no other turn that these two plans would take. But I respect your opinion, and your knowledge of the country too much, to be ever confident in my own.

I thank you sincerely for your communication, that my not having sooner given notice of the Arrets relative to fish gave discontent to some persons. These are the most friendly offices you can do me, because they enable me to justify myself if I am right, or correct myself if wrong. If those who thought I might have been remiss would have written to me on the subject, I should have loved them for their candor & thanked them for it: for I have no jealousies nor resentments at things of this kind where I have no reason to believe they have been excited by a hostile spirit, & I suspect no such spirit in a single member of Congress. You know there were two Arrets the first of Aug. 30, 1784, the 2d. of the 18th & 25th of September, 1785. As to the first it would be a sufficient justification of myself to say that it was in the time of my predecessor, nine months before I came into office, & that there was no more reason for my giving information of it when I did come into office than of all the other transactions which preceded that period. But this would seem to lay a blame on Dr. Franklin for not communicating it which I am conscious he did not deserve. This government affects a secrecy in all its transactions whatsoever, tho they be of a nature not to admit a perfect secrecy. Their Arrets respecting the islands go to those islands and are unpublished & unknown in France except in the bureau where they are formed. That of Aug. 1784, would probably be communicated to the merchants of the seaport towns also But Paris having no commercial connections with them, if anything makes its way from a seaport town to Paris, it must be by accident. We have indeed agents in these seaports: but they value their offices so little that they do not trouble themselves to inform us of what is passing there. As a proof that these things do not transpire here, nor are easily got at, recollect that Mr. Adams, Dr Franklin and myself were all here on the spot together from Aug. 1784. to June 1785. that is to say 10. months, and yet not one of us knew of the Arret of Aug. 1784. September 18 & 25 1785. the second was passed. & here alone I became responsible. I think it was about 6 weeks before I got notice of it, that is in November. On the 20th of that month writing to Count de Vergennes on another subject I took occasion to remonstrate to him on that. But from early in November when the Fitzhughs went to America, I had never a confidential opportunity of writing to Mr. Jay from hence directly for several months. In a letter of Dec. 14 to Mr. Jay I mentioned to him the want of opportunity to write to him confidentially, which obliged me at that moment to write by post via London & on such things only as both post offices were welcome to see. On the 2d January Mr. Bingham setting out for London, I wrote to Mr. Jay, sending him a copy of my letter to Ct. de Vergennes, and stating something which had passed in conversation on the same subject. I prayed Mr. Bingham to take charge of the letter, & either to send it by a safe hand or carry it himself as circumstances should render most advisable. I believe he kept it to carry himself. He did not sail from London till about the 12th of March, nor arrived in America till about the middle of May. Thus you see what causes had prevented a letter which I had written on the 20th of November from getting to America till the month of May. No wonder then if notice of this Arret came first to you by way of the W. Indies; and in general, I am confident that you will receive notice of the regulations of this country respecting their islands by the way of those islands before you will from hence. Nor can this be remedied but by a system of bribery which would end in the corruption of your own ministers, & produce no good adequate to the expense. Be so good as to communicate these circumstances to the persons who you think may have supposed me guilty of remissness on this occasion.

I will turn to a subject more pleasing to both, and give you my sincere congratulations on your marriage. Your own dispositions and the inherent comforts of that state will insure you a great addition of happiness. Long may you live to enjoy it, & enjoy it in full measure. The interest I feel in everyone connected with you will justify my presenting my earliest respects to the lady, and of tendering her the homage of my friendship. I shall be happy at all times to be useful to either of you & to receive your commands. I enclose you the bill of lading of your *Encyclopedie*. With respect to the remittance for it, of which you make mention, I beg you not to think of it. I know by experience that proceeding to make a settlement in life, a man has need of all his resources, and I should be unhappy were you to lessen them by an attention to this trifle. Let it lie till you have nothing else to do with your money. Adieu my dear Sir and be assured of the esteem with which I am, your friend & servt.

To John Adams[1]
Paris, July 9. 1786
Dear Sir,

Have you no news yet of the treaty with Portugal? does it hang with that court? My letters from N York of the 11th of May inform me that there were then 11. states present & that they should ratify the Prussian treaty immediately. As the time for exchange of ratifications is drawing to a close, tell me what is to be done, and how this exchange is to be made. We may as well have this settled between us before the arrival of the ratification, that no time may be lost after that. I learn through the Marechal de Castries that he has information of New York's having ceded the impost in the form desired by Congress, so as to close this business. Corrections in the acts of Maryland, Pennsylvania &c. will come of course. We have taken up again the affair of whale oil that they may know in time in America what is to be done in it. I fear we shall not obtain any farther abatement of duties; but the last abatement will be continued for three years. The whole duties payable here are nearly 102 livres on the English ton, which is an atom more than four guineas according to the present exchange.

The monopoly of the purchase of tobacco for this country which had been obtained by Robert Morris had thrown the commerce of that article in agonies. He had been able to reduce the price in America from 40/ to 22/6. lawful the hundred weight, and all other merchants being deprived of that medium of remittance the commerce between America & that country, so far as it depended on that article, which was very capitally too, was absolutely ceasing. An order

---

[1] The articles of the proposed treaty with Portugal were drawn up, as Jefferson later declared, "almost in the precise terms of those of Prussia." It is true that the project was based on the "General Form" of a treaty as prepared in 1784,but the draft that Adams caused his secretary of legation, William Stephens Smith, to draw up for use in the negotiations had been in part modified in the light of suggestions made by Jefferson however, did not incorporate some of the more important suggestions such as the idea of a joint force to be employed against the Algerines and the admission of American trade to the Portuguese possessions outside of Europe, particularly those in America. Jefferson in later life declared that "the only article of difficulty between us was a stipulation that our bread stuff should be received in Portugal in the form of flour as well as of grain." He added that De Pinto [Portuguese *Minister* in London] "approved of it himself, but observed that several Nobles of great influence at their court were the owners of windmills in the neighborhood of Lisbon which depended much for their profits on manufacturing our wheat, and that this stipulation would endanger the whole treaty. He signed it, however, and its fate was what he had candidly portended." However, the Commissioners' observations upon alterations proposed by De Pinto show that the article dealing with contraband goods was also one that involved serious differences. There were other minor differences as well. (Boyd "Editorial Note,"1990)

has been obtained obliging the farmers general to purchase from such other merchants as shall offer, 15,000 hogsheads of tobacco at 34. 36. & 38. livres the hundred according to the quality, and to grant to the sellers in other respects the same terms as they had granted to Robert Morris. As this agreement with Morris is the basis of this order I send you some copies of it which I will thank you to give to any American (not British) merchants in London who may be in that line. During the year this contract has subsisted, Virginia & Maryland have lost 400,000£ by the reduction of the price of their tobacco.

I am meditating what step to take to provoke a letter from Mrs. Adams, from whom my files inform me I have not received one these hundred years. In the meantime present my affectionate respects to her, and be assured of the friendship & esteem with which I have the honor to be Dear Sir your most obedient, and most humble servt.

To Hector St. John Crevecoeur[1]
Paris, July 11, 1786
Sir,

I have been honored with a letter from M. Delisle Lt. Gl. au bailliage de Caën, to which is annexed a postscript from yourself. Being unable to write in French so as to be sure of conveying my true meaning, or perhaps any meaning at all, I will beg of you to interpret what I have now the honor to write.

It is true that the United States, generally, and most of the separate states in particular, are endeavoring to establish means to pay the interest of their public debt regularly, and to sink its principal by degrees. But as yet their efforts have been confined to that part of their debts which is evidenced by certificates. I do not think that any state has yet taken measures for paying their paper money debt. The principle on which it shall be paid I take to be settled, tho' not directly yet virtually, by the resolution of Congress of June 3. 1784., that is that they will pay the holder or his representatives what the money was worth at the time he received it, with an interest from that time of 6. per centum per annum. It is not said in the letter whether the money received by Barboutin was Continental money, or Virginia money; nor is it said at what time it was received. But that M. Delisle may be enabled to judge what the 5398 dollars were worth in hard money when Barboutin received them, I will state to you what was the worth of one hard dollar both in Continental and Virginia money through the whole of the years 1779. and 1780. within some part of which it was probably received.

---

[1] J. Hector St. John de Crèvecoeur lived a cosmopolitan life as a French soldier in Canada, farmer in New York's Hudson Valley, author and salon favorite in Paris, and Consul of France in New York City. He was an American farmer and writer who became a French diplomat and who had his illusions shattered about the coalescence of the Atlantic World in the wake of the American Revolution — where the practice of transnational cosmopolitanism destroyed its myth. He is an important figure in the history of American literature for his 1782 work, *Letters from an American Farmer*. In particular, the chapter entitled, "What is an American?" is often cited by American history and literature professors alike for its definition of American identity at the time when the new nation was being born. (Moore 2011, 133)

Continental money			Virginia money		
1779.	Jan. 9	7 72/100	1779	Jan. 8	1780 Jan. 42
	24	8 30/100		Feb. 10	Feb. 48
	Feb. 11	9 13/100		Mar. 10	Mar. 50
	Mar. 2	10		Apr. 16	Apr. 60
	Apr. 3	11 12/100		May 20	May 60
	May 10	12 31/100		June 20	June 65
	June 23	14 3/10		July 22	July 65
	Aug. 8	16 60/100		Aug. 22	Aug. 70
	Sep. 28	20		Sep. 24	Sep. 72
	Nov. 22	25 6/100		Oct. 28	Oct. 73
1780.	Feb. 2	33 44/100		Nov. 36	Nov. 74
	Mar. 18	40.		Dec. 40	Dec. 75

Thus you see that in Jan. 1779. 7 dollars and 72 hundredths of a dollar of Continental paper were worth one dollar of silver, and at the same time 8. dollars of Virginia paper were worth one dollar of silver: &c. After Mar. 18. 1780. Continental paper received in Virginia will be estimated by the table of Virginia paper.

I advise all the foreign holders of paper money to lodge it in the office of their Consul for the state where it was received, that he may dispose of it for their benefit the first moment that payment shall be provided by the state or Continent.

I had lately the pleasure of seeing the Coun[tess] d'Houditot well at Sanois, and have now that of assuring you of the perfect esteem and respect with which I have the honor to be Dear Sir your most obedient humble servt.,

To The Marquis De La Fayette[1]
Paris, July 17, 1786

[1] As background to this note, despite the leadership of the able Vergennes, France's political policy was almost as confused as her economic policy. At one and the same time France wanted the United States to be strong enough to serve as a foil to Britain and weak enough to remain dependent upon French economic and political support. Although France wanted payment for American debts, she would rather forgo it than accept the money from too strong and independent a central government. Such motives tended to be self-defeating because they blinded statesmen of both nations to the fundamental fact that the United States and France were working toward the same end: the transference of the American economy from the British orbit to that of the French. Their flexible foreign policy made no sense when combined with an antiquated and inflexible economic one. French policy makers failed to recognize that if France loosened her commercial regulations in favor of American trade, as Jefferson advocated, she would gain a far tighter control over American commerce and even American politics. Confusion of purpose exhibited by the framers of French policy assumed even greater proportions as it spread among members of the discontented merchant class, which had been so long abused by the regime that it did not know how to direct its anger into the proper channels. The merchants — who would have been the

Dear Sir,

I have now the honor of inclosing to you an estimate of the Exports & Imports of the United States. Calculations of this kind cannot pretend to accuracy, where inattention and fraud combine to suppress their objects. Approximation is all that they can aim at. Neither care nor candor have been wanting on my part to bring them as near the truth as my skill and materials would enable me to do. I have availed myself of the best documents from the custom houses which have been given to the public: and have been able to rectify these in many instances by information collected by myself on the spot in many of the states. Still remember however that I call them but approximations and that they must present some errors as considerable as they were unavoidable. Our commerce divides itself into European & West Indian. I have conformed my statement to this division.

On running over the Catalogue of American imports, France will naturally mark out those articles with which she could supply us to advantage: & she may safely calculate that after a little time shall have enabled us to get rid of our present encumbrances, and of some remains of attachment to the particular forms of manufacture to which we have been habituated we shall take those articles which she can furnish on as good terms as other nations, to whatever extent she will enable us to pay for them. It is her interest therefore, as well as ours, to multiply the means of payment. These must be found in the catalogue of our Exports, & among these will be seen neither gold nor silver. We have no mines of either of these metals. Produce therefore is all we can offer. Some articles of our produce will be found very convenient to this country for her own consumption. Others will be convenient, as being more commerciable in her hands than those she will give in exchange for them. If there be any which she can neither consume, nor dispose of by exchange, she will not buy them of us, and of course we shall not bring them to her. If American produce can be brought into the ports of France, the articles of exchange for it will be taken in those ports: & the only means of drawing it hither is to let the merchant see that he can dispose of it on better terms here than anywhere else. If the market price of this country does not in itself offer this superiority, it may be worthy of consideration whether it should be obtained by such abatements of duties, and even by such other encouragements as the importance of the article may justify. Should some loss attend this in the beginning, it can be discontinued when the trade shall be well established in this channel.

With respect to the West India commerce, I must apprise you that this estimate does not present its present face. No materials have enabled us to say how it stands since the war. We can only shew what it was before that period. New regulations have changed our situation there much for the worse.

---

first to profit from a free exchange of American tobacco, whale oil, and rice, and the products of France and her colonies — resented the free trade movement out of fear of foreign competition. Inured by habit and prejudice to the ways of mercantilism, they saw in free trade only an opportunity for Britain to inundate France with manufactured goods that would undersell the products of French manufacturers. Hence they were not prepared to distinguish between the doctrinaire spirit of the physiocrats, which looked to free trade on principle, and the enlightened imperialism of Lafayette, which sought commercial privileges for the United States as a powerful weapon against British interests. (Kaplan 1967, 31-31)

This is most sensibly felt in the Exports of fish, and flour. The surplus of the former, which these regulations throw back on us, is forced to Europe, where, by increasing the quantity, it lessens the price: the surplus of the latter is sunk: and to what other objects this portion of industry is turned, or turning, I am not able to discover. The Imports too of Sugar & Coffee are thrown under great difficulties. These increase the price: and being articles of food for the poorer class (as you may be sensible on observing the quantities consumed) a small increase of price places them above the reach of this class, which being very numerous, must occasion a great diminution of consumption. It remains to see whether the American will endeavor to baffle these new restrictions in order to indulge his habits; or will adapt his habits to other objects which may furnish employment to the surplus of industry formerly occupied in raising that bread which no longer finds a vent in the West Indian market. If, instead of either of these measures, he should resolve to come to Europe for coffee & sugar, he must lessen equivalently his consumption of some other European articles in order to pay for his coffee & sugar, the bread with which he formerly paid for them in the West Indies not being demanded in the European market. In fact the catalogue of Imports offers several articles more dispensable than coffee & sugar. Of all these subjects, the committee and yourself are the more competent judges. To you therefore I trust them with every wish for their improvement, & with sentiments of that perfect esteem & respect with which I have the honor to be, Dear Sir, your most obedient, & most humble servt.

To The Marquis De St. Lambert[1]
Paris, Aug. 8, 1786

---

[1] Jefferson first encountered Jean-François, Marquis de Saint-Lambert in June 1785 when visiting the Comtesse d'Houdetot, who was considered one of the great romantic figures of her era, despite the defects in her personal appearance. With crossed eyes and a sallow, pock-marked complexion, she hardly had the physical beauty to sustain her reputation, but the Comtesse nonetheless had a sexual appeal men found irresistible. Pierre Choderlos de Laclos, the author of *Les Liaisons Dangereuses* said of her, "She knew that the great affair of life is love." But the Comtesse also had a keen mind, which accounts for her particular appeal among the philosophers. For decades she had a steady lover in the poet-soldier-philosopher the Marquis de Saint-Lambert, who was fixture in her salon. Known to have shared mistresses with Jean-Jacques Rousseau and Voltaire, Saint-Lambert had published a volume of verse and contributed various articles to Diderot's *Encyclopédie*. Jefferson joined the Comtesse's literary circle during a period of transition: Franklin was soon leaving France, and Diderot had left the year before. Jefferson had great respect for Saint-Lambert, who would translate his *Act for Establishing Religious Freedom* into French and publish it in a parallel French/English edition. Asserting that Saint-Lambert wrote his books on the basis of what he heard from Diderot and D'Alembert in the salon of Comtesse d'Houdetot, Jefferson was not criticizing him. Rather, he was emphasizing how important conversation within the salons was to French literary culture. As his later remarks to Webster suggest, Jefferson realized that some of the finest literature produced in France during the eighteenth century was inspired by and could be traced to conversations that occurred within its salons. (Hayes 2008, 295-297)

Mr. Jefferson has the honor of presenting his compliments to Monsieur le Marquis de St. Lambert, and of thanking him for his very excellent translation of the act of the Virginia Assembly. An opportunity having occurred, before the receipt of it of forwarding the act to some foreign courts where it was thought it would be well received Mr. Jefferson had been obliged to print copies from a translation prepared for the Encyclopedie. He shall endeavor as soon as possible to avail the public of the better one of M. de St. Lambert. He begs leave to present to him and also through him to Madame la Comtesse d'Houditat the homage of his respects.

To Mrs. John (Abigail) Adams[1]
Paris, Aug. 9, 1786
Dear Madam,

It is an age since I have had the honor of a letter from you, and an age and a half since I presumed to address one to you. I think my last was dated in the reign of King Amri, but under which of his successors you wrote, I cannot recollect, Ocharias Zoachar, Manahem or some such hard name. At length it is resumed; I am honored with your favor of July 23, and I am at this moment writing an answer to it. And first we will dispatch business. The shoes you ordered, will be ready this day and will accompany the present letter, but why send money for them? You know the balance of trade was always against me. You will observe by the enclosed account that it is I who am to export cash always, tho' the sum has been lessened by the bad bargains I have made for you & the good ones you have

---

[1] Jefferson had not lacked for female society in France, and Abigail Adams had become his firm friend. It was a thoroughly American type of friendship; comfortable, solid, without any of the overtones that usually accompanied male-and-female friendship among the French. The acquaintance, begun during the stay of the Adamses in France, had ripened when Jefferson came to England. Some two months after his return to Paris, he wrote with graceful exaggeration to John: "I am meditating what step to take to provoke a letter from Mrs. Adams, from whom my files inform me I have not received one these hundred years." The whimsical appeal brought results. She sent her reply along with Mr. Trumble and told of keeping Jefferson's portrait (for which, during his London stay, he had sat to Mather Brown, an American painter) in their room; though, she politely added, "it is but a poor substitute for those pleasures which we enjoyed some months past." More seriously, in this letter he notes that he had heard of an attempt to assassinate the English king. "No man on earth," he declared with bitter irony, "has my prayers for his continuance in life more sincerely than him.... Twenty long years has he been labouring to drive us to our good and he labours and will labour still for it if he can be spared." In France, there were no such plots. "Here we have singing, dancing, laugh & merriment, no assassinations, no treasons, rebellions nor other dark deeds. When our king goes out, they fall down and kiss the earth where he has trodden." In retrospect, it seems that if Jefferson was writing this seriously, then he promptly heads the list of the world's poorest prophets. He misread the times completely, and noted none of the premonitory quivers which amplified to later convulsions and upheavals, the like of which the world had not witnessed to that time. And he was serious; for, in all his letters of this period, he stressed the utter peace and calm of Europe. He foresaw the possibility of trouble ahead only in the event that the elderly King of Prussia, then quite ill, might die. (Schachner 1957, 314-315)

made for me. This is a gaining trade, and therefore I shall continue it, begging you will send no more money here. Be so good as to correct the enclosed that the errors of that may not add to your losses in this commerce.

You were right in conjecturing that both the gentlemen might forget to communicate to me the intelligence about Captn. Stanhope. Mr. Adams' head was full of whale oil, and Col^o. Smith's of German politics. (but don't tell them this) so they left it to you to give me the news. De tout mon coeur, I had rather receive it from you than them. This proposition about the exchange of a son for my daughter puzzles me. I should be very glad to have your son, but I cannot part with my daughter. Thus you see I have such a habit of gaining in trade with you that I always expect it. We have a blind story here of somebody attempting to assassinate your King. No man upon earth has my prayers for his continuance in life more sincerely than him. He is truly the American Messias, the most precious life that ever god gave. And may god continue it. Twenty long years has he been laboring to drive us to our good and he labors and will labor still for it if he can be spared. We shall have need of him for twenty more. The Prince of Wales on the Throne, Lansdown & Fox in the Ministry & we are undone! We become chained by our habits to the tails of those who hate & despise us. I repeat it then that my anxieties are all alive for the health and long life of the King. He has not a friend on earth who would lament his loss as much & so long as I should.

Here we have singing, dancing, laugh & merriment, no assassinations, no treasons, rebellions nor other dark deeds. When our King goes out, they fall down and kiss the earth where he has trodden; and then they go to kissing one another, and this is the truest wisdom, they have as much happiness in one year as an Englishman in ten. The presence of the Queen's Sister enlivens the Court, still more the birth of the princess, there are some little bickerings between the King & his parliament, but they end with a sic volo, sic jubes. The bottom of my page tells me it is time for me to end with assurances of the affectionate esteem with which I have the honor to be, Dear Madam, Your most obedient & most humble servant.

To James Monroe[1]
Paris, Aug. 11, 1786

---

[1] Although Jefferson could indeed prosecute a war with vigor when it could not be avoided, he was tireless in his efforts to make it at least less frequent, and when it had become inevitable, to render it as humane as possible. "Of my disposition to maintain peace," he wrote in 1817, "until its condition shall be made less tolerable than that of war itself, the world has had proofs.... I hope it is practicable, by improving the mind and morals of society, to lessen the disposition to war; but of its abolition I despair. Still, on the axiom that a less degree of evil is preferable to a greater, no means should be neglected which may add weight to the better scale." War is a terrible thing, and it must not be waged for petty causes. Jefferson offers a *reductio ad absurdum* in opposing the use of force to restrain the *Little Sarah*, a French prize fitted as a privateer in Philadelphia, "Because I would not gratify the combination of kings with the spectacle of the two only republics on earth destroying each other for two cannon." He went the length, also, in this letter, of proposing a union of powers for the preservation of peace — "Were only two or three to begin a confederacy of this kind...." —

Dear Sir,

I wrote you last on the 9th of July & since that have received yours of the 16th of June with the interesting intelligence it contained. I was entirely in the dark as to the progress of that negotiation, and concur entirely in the views you have taken of it. The difficulty on which it hangs is a sine qua non with us. It would be to deceive them & ourselves to suppose that an amity can be preserved while this right is withheld. Such a supposition would argue not only an ignorance of the people to whom this is most interesting, but an ignorance of the nature of man, or an inattention to it. Those who see but half way into our true interest will think that that concurs with the views of the other party. But those who see it in all its extent will be sensible that our true interest will be best promoted by making all the just claims of our fellow citizens, wherever situated, our own, by urging & enforcing them with the weight of our whole influence, & by exercising in this as in every other instance a just government in their concerns & making common cause even where our separate interest would seem opposed to theirs. No other conduct can attach us together; & on this attachment depends our happiness. The King of Prussia still lives, and is even said to be better. Europe is very quiet at present. The only germ of dissension which shews itself at present is in the quarter of Turkey. The Emperor, the Empress, & the Venetians seem all to be pecking at the Turks. It is not probable however that either of the two first will do anything to bring on an open rupture while the K of Prussia lives. You will perceive, by the letters I enclose to Mr. Jay that Lambed, under the pretext of ill health, declines returning either to Congress, Mr. Adams or myself. This circumstance makes me fear some malversation. The money appropriated to this object being in Holland, & having been always under the care of Mr. Adams, it was concerted between us that all the draughts should be on him. I know not therefore what sums may have been advanced to Lambe. I hope however nothing great. I am persuaded that an angel sent on this business, & so much limited in his terms, could have done nothing. But should Congress propose to try the line of negotiation again, I think they will perceive that Lambe is not a proper agent. I have written to Mr. Adams on the subject of a settlement with Lambe. There is little prospect of accommodation between the Algerines & the Portuguese & Neapolitans. A very valuable capture too, lately made by them on the Empress of Russia, bids fair to draw her on them. The probability is therefore that these three nations will be at war with them, & the possibility that could we furnish a couple of frigates, a convention might be formed with those powers, establishing a perpetual cruise on the coast of Algiers which would bring them to reason. Such a convention being left open to all powers willing to come into it, should have for its object a general peace, to be guaranteed to each by the

---

when he suggested concerted action on the part of the states whose commerce suffered at the hands of the Barbary pirates, to maintain a police force in the Mediterranean. World opinion, however, was not prepared for that form of coöperation, and the question was only settled by a series of wars, carried on individually by the interested nations. (Wiltse 1935. 197-198)

whole. Were only two or three to begin a confederacy of this kind, I think every power in Europe would soon fall into it except France, England, & perhaps Spain & Holland. Of these, there is only England who would give any real aid to the Algerines. Morocco, you perceive, will be at peace with us. Were the honor & advantage of establishing such a confederacy out of the question, yet the necessity that the US should have some marine force, & the happiness of this as the ostensible cause for beginning it, would decide on its propriety. It will be said there is no money in the treasury. There never will be money in the treasury till the confederacy shows it's teeth. The states must see the rod; perhaps it must be felt by some one of them. I am persuaded all of them would rejoice to see every one obliged to furnish it's contributions. It is not the difficulty of furnishing them which beggars the treasury, but the fear that others will not furnish as much. Every rational citizen must wish to see an effective instrument of coercion, & should fear to see it on any other element but the water. A naval force can never endanger our liberties, nor occasion bloodshed: a land force would do both. It is not in the choice of the states whether they will pay money to cover their trade against the Algerines. If they obtain a peace by negotiation they must pay a great sum of money for it; if they do nothing they must pay a great sum of money in the form of insurance; and in either way as great a one & probably less effectual than in the way of force. I look forward with anxiety to the approaching moment of your departure from Congress. Besides the interest of the Confederacy & of the State I have a personal interest in it. I know not to whom I may venture confidential communications after you are gone. *Lee I scarcely know. Grayson is lazy. Carrington is industrious but not always as discreet as well-meaning, yet* on the whole I believe *he would be the best* if you find him *disposed to the correspondence. Engage him to begin* it.[1] I take the liberty of placing here my respects to Mrs. Monroe and assurances of the sincere esteem with which I am Dear Sir your friend & servant.

To George Wythe[2]

---

[1] These words in italics were originally written in cipher and were decoded by Monroe. (Boyd 1990)

[2] After college, from 1762 to 1767, he apprenticed law — and a new kind of classicism — with George Wythe. In an age that cherished the intellectual generalist, Wythe was known not just as a foremost legal scholar but also as one of the most learned classicists in Virginia. The English traveler Andrew Burnaby said Wythe possessed "a perfect knowledge of the Greek language, which was taught him by his mother in the back woods." Late in life Jefferson called the morally upright Wythe "the Cato of his country," fondly remembering his years under Wythe as "my classical days." He joined Wythe and William Small, another teacher, for evenings of intellectual conversation and music at the elegant Georgian-style mansion of Virginia's lieutenant governor, Francis Fauquier. It was from these conversations, what he later called "truly Attic societies," that Jefferson was exposed to the humanist ideal of classicism as something that was fully lived, a component of a life dedicated to intellectual cultivation and public service. The experience of youthful classical learning affected Jefferson profoundly over the course of his life, for he continued to think deeply about which kinds of classical education were appropriate for which people. He

Paris, August 13, 1786
Dear Sir,

Your favors of Jan. 10 & Feb. 10, came to hand on the 20th & 2d of May. I availed myself of the first opportunity which occurred, by a gentleman going to England, of sending to Mr. Joddrel a copy of the Notes on our country, with a line informing him that it was you who had emboldened me to take that liberty. Madison, no doubt, informed you of the reason why I had sent only a single copy to Virginia. Being assured by him that they will not do the harm I had apprehended, but on the contrary may do some good, I propose to send thither the copies remaining on hand, which are fewer than I had intended. But of the numerous corrections they need, there are one or two so essential that I must have them made, by printing a few new leaves & substituting them for the old. This will be done while they are engraving a map which I have constructed of the country from Albemarle sound to Lake Erie, & which will be inserted in the book. A bad French translation which is getting out here, will probably oblige me to publish the original more freely, which it neither deserved nor was ever intended. Your wishes, which are laws to me, will justify my destining a copy for you, otherwise I should as soon have thought of sending you a hornbook; for there is no truth there that which is not familiar to you, and it's errors I should hardly have proposed to treat you with.

Immediately on the receipt of your letter, I wrote to a correspondent at Florence to inquire after the family of Tagliaferro as you desired. I received his answer two days ago, a copy of which I now enclose. The original shall be sent by some other occasion. I will have the copper-plate immediately engraved. This may be ready within a few days, but the probability is that I shall be long getting an opportunity of sending it to you, as these rarely occur. You do not mention the size of the plate but, presuming it is intended for labels for the inside of books, I shall have it made of a proper size for that. I shall omit the word "agisos" according to the license you allow me, because I think the beauty of a motto is to condense much matter in as few words as possible. The word omitted will be supplied by every reader. The European papers have announced that the assembly of Virginia were occupied on the revisal of their code of laws. This, with some other similar intelligence, has contributed much to convince the people of Europe, that what the English papers are constantly publishing of our anarchy, is false; as they are sensible that such a work is that of a people only who are in perfect tranquility. Our act for freedom of religion is extremely applauded. The ambassadors & ministers of the several nations of Europe resident at this court have asked of me copies of it to send to their sovereigns, and it is inserted at full length in several books now in the press; among others, in the new Encyclopedie. I think it will produce considerable good even in these countries where ignorance, superstition, poverty, & oppression of body & mind in every form, are so firmly settled on the mass of the people, that their redemption from them can never be hoped. If the

advocated a thorough classical education for boys that included languages and history; this education should prepare them for the useful employments awaiting them in public life as lawyers, politicians, or jurists. (Winterer 2012, 381-382)

Almighty had begotten a thousand sons, instead of one, they would not have sufficed for this task. If all the sovereigns of Europe were to set themselves to work to emancipate the minds of their subjects from their present ignorance & prejudices, & that as zealously as they now endeavor the contrary, a thousand years would not place them on that high ground on which our common people are now setting out. Ours could not have been so fairly put into the hands of their own common sense had they not been separated from their parent stock & kept from contamination, either from them, or the other people of the old world, by the intervention of so wide an ocean. To know the worth of this, one must see the want of it here. I think by far the most important bill in our whole code is that for the diffusion of knowledge among the people. No other sure foundation can be devised, for the preservation of freedom and happiness. If anybody thinks that kings, nobles, or priests are good conservators of the public happiness send them here. It is the best school in the universe to cure them of that folly. They will see here with their own eyes that these descriptions of men are an abandoned confederacy against the happiness of the mass of the people. The omnipotence of their effect cannot be better proved than in this country particularly, where notwithstanding the finest soil upon earth, the finest climate under heaven, and a people of the most benevolent, the most gay and amiable character of which the human form is susceptible, where such a people I say, surrounded by so many blessings from nature, are yet loaded with misery by kings, nobles and priests, and by them alone. Preach, my dear Sir, a crusade against ignorance; establish & improve the law for educating the common people. Let our countrymen know that the people alone can protect us against these evils, and that the tax which will be paid for this purpose is not more than the thousandth part of what will be paid to kings, priests & nobles who will rise up among us if we leave the people in ignorance. The people of England, I think, are less oppressed than here. But it needs but half an eye to see, when among them, that the foundation is laid in their dispositions for the establishment of a despotism. Nobility, wealth & pomp are the objects of their adoration. They are by no means the free-minded people we suppose them in America. Their learned men too are few in number, and are less learned and infinitely less emancipated from prejudice than those of this country. An event too seems to be preparing, in the order of things, which will probably decide the fate of that country. It is no longer doubtful that the harbor of Cherburg will be complete, that it will be a most excellent one, & capacious enough to hold the whole navy of France. Nothing has ever been wanting to enable this country to invade that, but a naval force conveniently stationed to protect the transports. This change of situation must oblige the English to keep up a great standing army, and there is no King, who, with sufficient force, is not always ready to make himself absolute. My paper warns me it is time to recommend myself to the friendly recollection of Mrs. Wythe, of Colo. Tagliaferro & his family & particularly of Mr. R. T.; and to assure you of the affectionate esteem with which I am Dear Sir your friend and servt.

To Francis Hopkinson[1]
Paris, Aug. 14, 1786
Dear Sir,

After the present then I shall still be a letter in your debt. One would think that this balance did not justify a scold. The manner of curing the Essence d'Orient is, as you are apprised, kept secret here. There is no getting at it therefore openly. A friend has undertaken to try whether it can be obtained either by proposing the partnership you mention, or by finding out the process. You shall have the result of these endeavors. I think I sent you in January the 5th & 6th volumes of the Bibliotheque physico-ecconomique, which are the last published. I have for yourself and Dr. Franklin the 17th & 18th livraisons of the Encyclopedie, & expect the 19th will come out very soon. These will form a respectable package & shall then be forwarded.

I will send as you propose, copies of my Notes to the Philosophical society and the City library as soon as I shall have received a map which I have constructed for them, & which is now engraving. This will be a map of the Country from Albemarle Sound to Lake Erie, as exact as the materials hitherto published would enable me to make it, & brought into a single sheet. I have with great impatience hoped to receive from some of my friends a particular description of the Southern & Western limits of Pennsylvania. Perhaps it might still come in time, if you could send it to me in the moment almost of your receiving this. Indeed it would be very desirable if you could only write me an answer to these two queries, viz. How far Westward of F. Pitt does the Western line of Pennsylvania pass? At what point of the river Ohio does that line strike it? Should this arrive even after they shall have begun to strike off the map, I can have the plate altered so as that the latter copies shall give that line right. Mr. Rittenhouse will have the goodness to furnish you answers to these queries. Could you prevail on him to answer this also. When will the Lunarium be done?

I envy your Wednesday evenings entertainments with him & Dr. Franklin. They would be more valued by me than the whole week at Paris.

Will you be so good as to send me a copy of a Botanical book published by some person in the Country not far from Philadelphia, whose name I have not heard? It is a description of the plants of Pennsylvania. I have nothing new to Communicate to you either in the Arts or sciences. Our countryman Trumbul is here, a young painter of the most promising talents. He brought with him his Battle of Bunker's hill & Death of Montgomery to have them engraved here, & we may add, to have them sold; for like Dr. Ramsey's history, they are too true to suit the English palate. He returned last night from examining the king's collection of paintings at Versailles, and acknowledges it surpassed not only everything he had seen, but every idea he had ever formed of this art. I persuade

---

[1] Francis Hopkinson of Pennsylvania, 1737–1791, a signer of the Declaration of Independence, a distinguished lawyer, and a writer of some note, he was also one of the most accomplished litterateurs and musicians in early America. Jefferson had known him since they had served together in the Continental Congress. He called Hopkinson "a man of genius, gentility, and great merit." (Jefferson 1926, 47; Hayes 2008, 266)

him to fix himself here awhile, & then proceed to Rome. My daughter is well and joins me in respects to her & your common mother, to your lady & family also, as well as to our friends of the other house, meaning Mr. Rittenhouse's. Be assured yourself of the perfect esteem with which I am, Dear Sir, your friend and servant.

To Jean Pierre Brissot De Warville[1]
Paris, Aug. 16, 1786

[1] As background to this letter, it is fair to say that Jefferson's relationship with Jacques-Pierre Brissot de Warville was conflicted. Brissot was a leader of the Girondins, a moderate bourgeois faction that later opposed the radical-democratic Jacobins during the French Revolution. The son of an eating-house keeper, Brissot began to work as a clerk in lawyers' offices, first at Chartres, then in Paris. He had literary ambitions, which, in 1783, led him to go to London where he published literary articles and founded two periodicals, which failed. Returning to France, he was imprisoned in the Bastille for pamphlets against the queen and the government but was released in September 1784. From his perspective, Jefferson's appreciation of the differences in the political environments of France and America was, by this writing, reasonably well established. The people, he noted in his travels, had little in common with American yeomen; they were so incredibly poverty-stricken that he would later observe: "Of twenty millions of people supposed to be in France I am of opinion there are nineteen millions more wretched, more accursed in every circumstance of human existence, than the most conspicuously wretched individual of the whole United States." The ignorance and passivity of the peasants which facilitated their exploitation by their government and their landlords were almost incomprehensible to him. Here was no material for self-government. Granted that his disgust was primarily for the government of the *Ancien Régime*, it must necessarily have extended to people who would permit themselves to be so misgoverned. Not only are the French not the free-minded people we in America think they are, he previously suggested in his August 13, 1786, letter to George Wythe, but it would take them a thousand years to achieve America's political accomplishments. And even the intelligentsia did not escape this judgment, despite Jefferson's reliance upon their connections at Versailles. The idealization of America in the writings of Brissot and Hector Saint John de Crèvecoeur (see letter of July 11, 1786) disturbed as well as flattered him; as he well knew that reality would never satisfy those Frenchmen nurtured on a Utopian myth. Two of his disciples precipitated an embarrassing controversy over the question whether François Jean de Beauvoir, Marquis de Chastellux — a well-respected French major-general who had served in the America during the Revolutionary War — had slurred the United States by accusing the Quakers of indifference to the public welfare in their behavior during the American Revolution; Chastellux's comments suggested, furthermore, that Americans in general were somewhat less than perfect. Jefferson was thereby placed in the uncomfortable position of knowing that Chastellux's account of American life was too mild rather than too harsh, and yet of being unable to express this idea to the aroused opponent Brissot. He tried to temper subtly some of the enthusiasm he had generated in France by declining Brissot's invitation to join his abolitionist society and by privately urging other friends making the journey to America not to expect too much from the New World. He had learned from his French experience that although admiration in France for America might be sincere, it would be shallow if not based upon a true understanding. France and her Revolution may have lessened Jefferson's objectivity in interpreting the course of America's development during his absence from home, but his experience as an American prevented his confusing the American Revolution with the French Revolution. (*Encyclopædia Britannica* 2016; Kaplan 1967, 28-29)

Sir,

I have read with very great satisfaction the sheets of your work on the commerce of France & the United States which you were so good as to put into my hands. I think you treat the subject, as far as these sheets go, in an excellent manner. Were I to select any particular passages as giving me particular satisfaction, it would be those wherein you prove to the United States that they will be more virtuous, more free & more happy, employed in agriculture, than as carriers or manufacturers. It is a truth, and a precious one for them, if they could be persuaded of it. I am also particularly pleased with your introduction. You have properly observed that we can no longer be called Anglo-Americans. That appellation now describes only the inhabitants of Nova Scotia, Canada, &c. I had applied that of Federo-Americans to our citizens, as it would not be so decent for us to assume to ourselves the flattering appellation of Free-Americans. There are two passages in this work on which I am able to give information. The first is in page 62; "ils auront le coton quand ils voudront se livrer à ce genre de culture," and in the note "l'on voit dans la baie de Massachusetts, &c." The four Southernmost states make a great deal of cotton. Their poor are almost entirely clothed in it in winter & summer. In winter they wear shirts of it, & outer clothing of cotton & wool mixed. In summer their shirts are linen but the outer clothing cotton. The dress of the women is almost entirely of cotton manufactured by themselves, except the richer class, and even many of these wear a good deal of home-spun cotton. It is as well manufactured as the calicoes of Europe. These 4 states furnish a great deal of cotton to the states north of them, who cannot make it, as being too cold. There is no neighborhood in any part of the United States without a water-grist-mill for grinding the corn of the neighborhood. Virginia, Maryland, Delaware, Pennsylvania, New Jersey, New York, abound with large manufacturing mills for the exportation of flour. There are abundance of saw-mills in all the states. Furnaces and forges of iron, I believe, in every state, I know they are in the nine Northernmost. There are many mills for plating & slitting iron. And I think there are many distilleries of rum from Norfolk in Virginia to Portsmouth in New Hampshire. I mention these circumstances because your note seems to imply that these things are only in the particular states you mention.

The second passage is pages 101 & 102 where you speak of the "ravages causés par l'abus des eaux de vie," which seems, by the note in page 101, to be taken on authority of Smith. Nothing can be less true than what that author says on this subject; and we may say in general that there are as many falsehoods as facts in his work. I think drunkenness is much more common in all the American States than in France. But it is less common there than in England. You may form an idea from this of the state of it in America. Smith saw everything thro' the medium of strong prejudice. Besides this, he does not hesitate to write palpable lies, which he was conscious were such. When you proceed to form your table of American exports & imports, I make no doubt you will consult the American traveller,1 the estimates in which are nearer the truth than those of Ld Sheffield & Deane, as far as my knowledge of the facts enables me to judge. I must beg your pardon for having so long detained these sheets. I did not finish my American dispatches till the night before last, & was obliged yesterday to go to Versailles. I have the honor to be with very great respect, Sir, your most obedient & most humble servant.

To Honoré Gabriel Requetti, Comte De Mirabeau[1]
Paris, Aug. 20, 1786

> "Il n'est pas un pays sur la terre, je n'en excepte pas les nouvelles republiques Americaines, ou il suffise à un homme de pratiquer les vertus sociales pour participer a tous les avantages de la société." Lettre de M. le comte de Mirabeau sur M. de Cagliostro, pa. 48.

A person who esteems highly the writings and talents of the Count de Mirabeau, and his disposition to exert them for the good of mankind, takes the liberty of inclosing him the original and a translation of an act of one of the legislatures of the American republics, with which the Count de Mirabeau was probably not acquainted when he wrote the above paragraph. It is part of that general reformation of their laws on which those republics have been occupied since the establishment of peace and independence among them. The Count de Mirabeau will perhaps be able on some occasion to avail mankind of this example of emancipating human reason.

To Charles Gysbert, Count Van Hogendorp[2]
Paris, August 25, 1786
Sir,

---

[1] Although Jefferson was well known to numerous members of the French literati, an individual that he certainly did not favor was a man he later described as one of the most powerful in France at the approach of the Revolution, Gabriel-Jean-Honoré de Riquetti, Comte de Mirabeau. A tempestuous French noble with a penchant for political intrigue, Jefferson thought Mirabeau to be unscrupulous adventurer, calling him "this glittering monster." Translated literally, the passage from this note that compelled Jefferson to respond was one in which Mirabeau asserted that there was "not a country on earth, I except not the new American Republics, where it suffices that a man practice the social virtues to participate in all the advantages of society." (Peterson 1975, 335; Jefferson 1943, 41)

[2] Jefferson's practical role in the popular French occupation of "encyclopaedism" was shown by his connection with the *Encyclopédie méthodique*, which, in Jefferson's description "relates to economy politique and diplomatique." His act for Freedom of Religion, passed by the Virginia Legislature in 1786, was reprinted in this encyclopedia as were additional articles and other pieces of information. As he advises in this letter to the conservative Dutch statesman Gysbert Karel van Hogendorp, "The author of the part of the new 'Encyclopédie,' which relates to political economy, having asked of me materials for the article 'Etat Unis' [*sic*], stating a number of questions relative to them. I answered them as minutely and exactly as was in my power. He has from these compiled the greater part of that article." Jefferson also purchased sets of the books for himself and other sets for friends such as Wythe, Madison, Edmund Randolph, Dr. Styles, and a few others. (Koch 1957, 47-48)

Your favor of the 2d. instant has been duly received, and I employ the first moment which has been at my disposal to answer it. The author of the part of the new Encyclopedie which relates to political economy having asked of me materials for the article Etats-unis, and stated a great number of questions relative to them, I answered them as minutely and exactly as was in my power. He has from these compiled the greatest part of that article. I take the liberty of inclosing you one of these as it will give you all the details to which your letter leads, as exactly as it is in my power to furnish them. I can even refer you to the passages which answer your several questions.

What is the extent of the Congress's power in managing the interests of the U. States? The 6th. and 9th. articles of the Confederation define their powers. Those which it is thought they still need you will find indicated in this pamphlet pa. 29. 30. and in page 31.b. their powers of coercion?

Qu. Which are the expenses of Congress?

Ans. pages 42.b. and 43.b.

Qu. Which the revenues?

Ans. As yet they have no standing revenues; they have asked standing revenues as shall be noted under a subsequent question. In the mean time they call annually for the sums necessary for the federal government. See pages 43. 44.

Qu. In which way do the particular states contribute to the general expenses?

Ans. Congress once a year calculate the sum necessary the succeeding year to pay the interest of their debt, and to defray the expenses of the federal government. This sum they then apportion on the several states according to the table page 44.a. and the states thereon raise each it's part by such taxes as they think proper.

Qu. Are general duties, to be levied by Congress, still expected to be acquiesced to by the states?

Ans. See page 30.a. New York the only state which had not granted the impost of 5. per cent, has done it at a late session; but has reserved to herself the appointment of the collectors. Congress will not receive it upon that condition. It is believed that New York will recede from the condition. Still a difficulty will remain. The impost of 5. per cent not being deemed sufficient to pay the interest of our whole debt foreign and domestic, Congress asked at the same time (that is in 1783) supplementary funds to make good the deficiency. Several of the states have not yet provided those supplementary funds. Some of those which have provided them have declared that the Impost and Supplementary fund shall commence only when all the states shall have granted both. Congress have desired those states to uncouple the grants, so that each may come into force separately as soon as it is given by all the states. Pennsylvania has declined this, saying that if the impost be granted alone, as that will do little more than pay the interest of the foreign debt, the other states will be less urgent to provide for the interest of the domestic debt. She wishes therefore to avail herself of the general desire to provide for foreign creditors in order to enforce a just attention to the domestic ones. The question is whether it will be more easy to prevail on Pennsylvania to recede from this condition or the other states to comply with it. The treaties with the Indians have experienced a greater delay than was expected. They are however completed, and the Surveyors are gone into that country to lay out the land in lots. As soon as some progress is made in this, the sale of lands will commence, and I have a firm faith that they will in short time absorb the whole of the certificates of the domestic debt.

The Philadelphia bank was incorporated by Congress. This is perhaps the only instance of their having done that, which they had no power to do. Necessity obliged them to give this institution the appearance of their countenance, because in that moment they were without any other resource for money. The legislature of Pennsylvania however passed an act of incorporation for the bank, & declared that the holders of stock should be responsible only to the amount of their stock. Lately that legislature has repealed their act. The consequence is that the bank is now altogether a private institution and every holder is liable for its engagements in his whole property. This has had a curious effect. It has given those who deposit money in the bank a greater faith in it, while it has rendered the holders very discontented, as being more exposed to risk, and has induced many to sell out, so that I have heard (I know not how truly) that bank stock sells somewhat below par, it has been said 7½ per cent; but as the publication was from the enemies of the bank, I do not give implicit faith to it. With respect to the article "Etats Unis" of the Encyclopedie now enclosed, I am far from making myself responsible for the whole of the article. The two first sections are taken chiefly from the Abbé Raynal & they are therefore wrong exactly in the same proportion; the other sections are generally right. Even in them however there is here & there an error. But on the whole it is good; and the only thing as yet printed which gives a just idea of the American constitutions. There will be another good work, a very good one, published here soon by Mr. Mazzei who has been many years a resident of Virginia, is well informed, and possessed of a masculine understanding. I should rather have said it will be published in Holland, for I believe it cannot be printed here. I should be happy indeed in an opportunity of visiting Holland; but I know not when it will occur. In the meantime it would give me great pleasure to see you here. I think you would find both pleasure & use in such a trip. I feel a sincere interest in the fate of your country, and am disposed to wish well to either party only as I can see in their measures a tendency to bring on an amelioration of the condition of the people, an increase in the mass of happiness. But this is a subject for conversation. My paper warns me that it is time to assure you of the esteem & respect with which I have the honor to be Dear Sir your most obedient humble servant.

To Mrs. Paradise[1]

---

[1] Lucy Ludwell Paradise (1751–1814) and her husband John were close friends of Thomas Jefferson, and of John and Abigail Adams. She was the youngest daughter of Frances Grymes Ludwell and Philip Ludwell III of Green Spring, near Williamsburg, Virginia. In 1760 she sailed for England with her family and did not return permanently to Virginia until 1805. In London in 1769 she married John Paradise of Rathbone-place, the son of an English father who became esteemed in London literary circles, and a Greek-English mother. Known in

Paris, Aug. 27, 1786

Dear Madam,

I am honored with your letter of the 15th inst. by Mr. Voss. I concur with you in opinion that it is for Mr. Paradise's interest to go as soon as possible to America and also to turn all his debts into one, which may be to Mr. Gist or any other: upon condition that the person giving him this credit shall be satisfied to receive annually his interest in money, and shall not require consignments of tobacco. This is the usual condition of the tobacco merchants. No other law can be more oppressive to the mind or fortune, and long experience has proved to us that there never was an instance of a man's getting out of debt who was once in the hands of a tobacco merchant & bound to consign his tobacco to him. It is the most delusive of all snares. The merchant feeds the inclination of his customer to be credited till he gets the burthen of debt so increased that he cannot throw it off at once, he then begins to give him less for his tobacco & ends with giving him what he pleases for it, which is always so little that though the demands of the customer for necessaries be reduced ever so low in order to get himself out of debt, the merchant lowers his price in the same proportion so as always to keep such a balance against his customer as will oblige him to continue his consignments of tobacco. Tobacco always sells better in Virginia than in the hands of a London merchant. The confidence which you have been pleased to place in me induces me to take the liberty of advising you to submit to anything rather than to an obligation to ship your tobacco. A mortgage of property, the most usurious interest, or anything else will be preferable to this. If Mr. Paradise can get no single money lender to pay his debts, perhaps those to whom he owes might be willing to wait, on his placing in the hands of trustees in London whom they should approve, certain parts of his property, the profits of which should suffice to pay them within a reasonable time. Mr. Voss gives me hopes of seeing Mr. Paradise here. I shall not fail to give him such information as my knowledge of the country to which he is going may render useful: nor of availing myself of every occasion of rendering him, yourself & family every service in my power, having the honor to be with sentiments of the most perfect esteem & respect, Madam, &c.

To Thomas Mann Randolph, Jr.[1]

Virginia circles as "Madam Paradise," Lucy Ludwell Paradise was renowned for her pride, stubbornness, personality, charm, and sometimes violent temper. The litigation over Lucy Ludwell Paradise's estate lasted twenty-three years. (Boyd 1990)

[1] As documented by his personal choices, Jefferson had started to steep himself in European literature from his boyhood years through his education at William and Mary College until his time as a young lawyer in the 1770s. His reading had included ancient Greek and Roman authors, early modern jurists and historians, the French Encyclopedists, Scottish moral sense philosophers, and recent *belles lettres*, like Edward Young's poetry, James MacPherson's *Ossian*, and Laurence Sterne's novels. While his interest in modern works of fiction was somewhat reduced in his later years, he remained an avid reader and book collector throughout his life. He assembled extensive libraries, the largest of which he

Paris, Aug. 27, 1786

Dear Sir,

I am honored with your favor of the 16th instant, and desirous, without delay, of manifesting my wishes to be useful to you I shall venture to you some thoughts on the course of your studies, which must be submitted to the better choice with which you are surrounded. A longer race through life may have entitled me to seize some truths which have not yet been presented to your observation & more intimate knowledge of the country in which you are to live & of the circumstances in which you will be placed, may enable me to point your attention to the branches of science which will administer the most to your happiness there. The foundations which you have laid in languages and mathematics are proper for every superstructure. The former exercises our memory while that and no other faculty is yet matured & prevents our acquiring habits of idleness. The latter gives exercise to our reason, as soon as that has acquired a certain degree of strength, and stores the mind with truths which are useful in other branches of science. At this moment then a second order of preparation is to commence. I shall propose to you that it be extensive, comprehending Astronomy, Natural Philosophy (or Physics), Natural History, Anatomy, Botany & Chemistry. No inquisitive mind will be content to be ignorant of any of these branches. But I would advise you to be contented with a course of lectures in most of them, without attempting to make yourself master of the whole. This is more than any genius joined to any length of life is equal to. You will find among them some one study to which your mind will more particularly attach itself. This then I would pursue & propose to attain eminence in. Your own country furnishes the most aliment for Natural History, Botany & Physics & as you express a fondness for the former you might make it your principal object, endeavoring however to make yourself more acquainted with the two latter than with other branches likely to be less useful. In fact you will find botany offering its charms to you at every step during summer & Physics in every season. All these branches of science will be better attained by attending courses of lectures in them. You are now in a place where the best courses upon earth are within your reach and being delivered in your native language — you lose no part of their benefit. Such an opportunity you will never again have. I would therefore strongly press on you to fix no other limit to your stay in Edinborough than your having got through this whole course. The omission of any one part of it will be an affliction & loss to you as long as you live. Beside the comfort of knowledge, every science is auxiliary to every other. While you are attending these courses you can proceed by yourself in a regular series of historical reading. It would be a waste of time to attend a professor of this. It is to be acquired from books and

---

offered for sale to the United States in 1814, making it the foundation of the Library of Congress. Modeled on his own bibliophile education, Jefferson also advised his daughters, grandchildren, and several young men in his family on their reading, drawing up elaborate lists of books, as reflected in this letter to his future son-in-law Thomas Mann Randolph, Jr.; a planter, soldier, and politician from Virginia, who would soon marry his daughter Martha Washington Jefferson. (Spahn 2012, 368)

if you pursue it by yourself you can accommodate it to your other reading so as to fill up those chasms of time not otherwise appropriated. There are portions of the day too when the mind should be eased, particularly after dinner it should be applied to lighter occupation: history is of this kind. It exercises principally the memory. Reflection also indeed is necessary but not generally in a laborious degree. To conduct yourself in this branch of science you have only to consider what areas of it merit a grasp & what a particular attention, & in each area also to distinguish between the countries the knowledge of whose history will be useful & those where it suffices only to be not altogether ignorant. Having laid down your plan as to the branches of history you would pursue, the order of time will be your sufficient guide. After what you have read in antient history I should suppose Millot's digest would be useful & sufficient. The histories of Greece and Rome are worthy a good degree of attention, they should be read in the original authors. The transition from antient to modern history will be best effected by reading Gibbon's. Then a general history of the principal states of Europe, but particular ones of England. Here too the original writers are to be preferred. Kennet published a considerable collection of these in 3 vols. folio, but there are some others not in his collection well worth being read. After the history of England that of America will claim your attention. Here too original authors & not compilers are best. An author who writes of his own times or of times near his own presents in his own ideas & manner the best picture of the moment of which he writes. History need not be hurried but may give way to the other sciences because history can be pursued after you shall have left your present situation as well as while you remain in it. When you shall have got through this second order of preparation the study of the law is to be begun. This like history is to be acquired from books. All the aid you will want will be a catalogue of the books to be read & the order in which they are to be read. It being absolutely indifferent in what place you carry on this reading I should propose your doing it in France. The advantages of this will be that you will at the same time acquire the habit of speaking French which is the object of a year or two. You may be giving attention to such of the fine arts as your turn may lead you to & you will be forming an acquaintance with the individuals & characters of a nation with whom we must long remain in the closest intimacy & to whom we are bound by the strong ties of gratitude and policy. A nation in short of the most amiable dispositions on earth, the whole mass of which is penetrated with an affection for us. You might before you return to your own country make a visit to Italy also.

I should have performed the office of but half a friend were I to confine myself to the improvement of the mind only. Knowledge indeed is a desirable, a lovely possession, but I do not scruple to say that health is more so. It is of little consequence to store the mind with science if the body be permitted to become debilitated. If the body be feeble, the mind will not be strong — the sovereign invigorator of the body is exercise, and of all exercises walking is best. A horse gives but a kind of half exercise, and a carriage is no better than a cradle. No one knows, till he tries, how easily a habit of walking is acquired. A person who never walked three miles will in the course of a month become able to walk

15 or 20 without fatigue. I have known some great walkers & had particular accounts of many more: and I never knew or heard of one who was not healthy & long lived. This species of exercise therefore is much to be advised. Should you be disposed to try it, as your health has been feeble, it will be necessary for you to begin with a little, & to increase it by degrees. For the same reason you must probably at first ascribe to it the hours most precious for study, I mean those about the middle of the day. But when you shall find yourself strong you may venture to take your walks in the evening after the digestion of the dinner is pretty well over. This is making a compromise between health & study. The latter would be too much interrupted were you to take from it the early hours of the day and habit will soon render the evening's exercise as salutary as that of the morning. I speak this from my own experience having, from an attachment to study, very early in life, made this arrangement of my time, having ever observed it, & still observing it, & always with perfect success. Not less than two hours a day should be devoted to exercise, and the weather should be little regarded. A person not sick will not be injured by getting wet. It is but taking a cold bath which never gives a cold to anyone. Brute animals are the most healthy, & they are exposed to all weather and, of men, those are healthiest who are the most exposed. The recipe of those two descriptions of beings is simple diet, exercise and the open air, be its state what it will; and we may venture to say that this recipe will give health & vigor to every other description.

By this time I am sure you will think I have sermonized enough. I have given you indeed a lengthy lecture. I have been led through it by my zeal to serve you; if in the whole you find one useful counsel, that will be my reward, & a sufficient one. Few persons in your own country have started from as advantageous ground as that whereon you will be placed. Nature and fortune have been liberal to you. Everything honorable or profitable there is placed within your own reach, and will depend on your own efforts. If these are exerted with assiduity, and guided by unswerving honesty, your success is infallible: and that it may be as great as you wish is the sincere desire of Dear Sir, your most affectionate humble servant.

P. S. Be so good as to present me affectionately to your brother & cousin.

To John Adams[1]

---

[1] By 1786, the impotence of Congress to protect the general interests of the American people abroad — especially obtaining a commercial treaty with Britain — drove the nation's conservative leadership toward the demand for a new frame of government. The perceived failure of the Confederation to maintain internal order, to meet its financial obligations, to defend its frontiers, and to control interstate commerce contributed to the unrest of American leaders. Granting the urgency of domestic problems, those leaders responsible for the conduct of foreign relations, primarily Jay in New York as secretary for foreign relations and the two principal envoys in Europe — John Adams in the Hague and London, and Thomas Jefferson in Paris — were even more upset with state of America's relations with Europe. The scenario was succinctly expressed in a letter to Adams from his friend Samuel Osgood, an American merchant and from back home in Massachusetts: "The federal government seems to be as near a crisis as it is possible for it to be....The State governments are weak and selfish enough, and they will of course annihilate the first. Their stubborn dignity will never permit

Paris, Aug. 27, 1786
Dear Sir,

Your favor of July 31. was lately delivered me. The papers inform me you are at the Hague, and, uncertain what stay you may make there I send this by Mr. Voss who is returned to London by the way of Amsterdam. I enclose you the last letters from Mr. Barclay & Mr. Carmichael by which we may hope our Peace with Morocco is signed, thanks to the good offices of a nation which is honest if it is not wise. This event with the naval cruises of Portugal will I hope quiet the Atlantic for us. I am informed by authority to be depended on, that insurance is made at L'Orient, on American vessels sailing under their own flag, against every event at the price usually paid for risks of the sea alone. Still however the most important of our Marts, the Mediterranean, is shut. I wrote you a proposition to accept Mr. Barclay's offer of going to Algiers. I have no hope of its making peace; but it may add to our information, abate the ardor of those pirates against us, and shut the mouths of those who might impute our success at Morocco & failure at Algiers to a judicious appointment to the one place & an injudicious one at the other. Let me hear from you as soon as possible on this & if you accede to it send me all the necessary papers ready signed. I enclose you the article "Etats Unis" of one of the volumes of the Encyclopedie, lately published. The author, M. de Meusnier, was introduced to me by the D. de la Rochefoucault. He asked of me information on the subject of our states, & left with me a number of queries to answer. Knowing the importance of setting to rights a book so universally diffused & which will go down to late ages, I answered his queries as fully as I was able, went into a great many calculations for him, and offered to give further explanations when necessary. He then put his work into my hands. I read it, and was led by that into a still greater number of details by way of correcting what he had at first written, which was indeed a mass of errors and misconceptions from beginning to end. I returned him his work & dry details, but he did not communicate it to me after he had corrected it. It has therefore come out with many errors which I would have advised him to correct, & the rather as he was very well disposed. He has still left in a great deal of the Abbé Raynal, that is to say a great deal of falsehood, and he has stated other things on bad information. I am sorry I had not another correction of it. He has paid me for my trouble in the true coin of the country, most unmerciful compliment. This, with his other errors I should surely have struck out had he sent me the work, as I expected, before it went to the press. I find in fact that he is happiest of whom the world sais least, good or bad.

I think if I had had a little more warning, my desire to see Holland, as well as to meet again Mrs. Adams & yourself, would have tempted me to take a flying trip there. I wish you may be tempted to take Paris in your return. You will find many very happy to see you here, & none more so than, Dear Sir, your friend and servant.

a federal government to exist." This would continue to be a particularly thorny issue for both Jefferson and Adams. (Graebner, Burns, and Siracusa 2011, 96)

To Ezra Stiles[1]
Paris, Sep. 1, 1786
Sir,

I am honored with your letter of May 8. That which you mention to have written in the winter preceding never came to hand. I return you my thanks for the communications relative to the Western country. When we reflect how long we have inhabited those parts of America which lie between the Alleghany & the ocean, that no monument has ever been found in them which indicated the use of iron among its' aboriginal inhabitants, that they were as far advanced in arts, at least, as the inhabitants on the other side the Alleghany, a good degree of infidelity may be excused as to the new discoveries which suppose regular fortifications of brickwork to have been in use among the Indians on the waters of the Ohio. Entrenchments of earth they might indeed make: but brick is more difficult. The art of making it may have preceded the use of iron, but it would suppose a greater degree of industry than men in the hunter state usually possess. I should like to know whether General Parsons himself saw actual bricks among the remains of fortifications. I suppose the settlement of our continent is of the most remote antiquity. The similitude between its' inhabitants & those of Eastern parts of Asia renders it probable that ours are descended from them

---

[1]   This letter is concerns a scientific argument drawn from the news of western antiquities located on an ancient mound builder site overlooking the Muskingum River near its junction with the Ohio. Soon afterward the nature and origin of these works was made the subject of an extended debate between Noah Webster and Ezra Stiles, president of Yale. Webster had opened the discussion by adopting the hypothesis, which he attributed to Benjamin Franklin that the mounds at were built by Ferdinand De Soto and his men. In Franklin's library, Webster declared, there was an account of De Soto's expedition that seemed to show he had penetrated as far north as the Muskingum River. Webster concluded that only military earthworks had been constructed by De Soto; and that the ceremonial and burial mounds were probably the work of the present Indian tribes. Stiles countered that the monuments of the western country were too numerous, too large, and too far north to be the work of Spaniards. The Spaniards had constructed no massive forts in Mexico or Peru and would certainly have needed none in their conflicts with the Indians of the Ohio and Mississippi valleys. Stiles gave short shrift to those "flighty geniuses" who imagined that the world had existed for three or four hundred thousand ages and that the inhabitants of America had passed through all the stages of society and subsequently fallen into decline. The similarity between the religious practices of the Indians and those of the peoples of Asia shortly after Noah's flood was proof, he said, that the Indians came to America shortly after that great catastrophe. To Jefferson, Stiles sent a drawing of the Muskingum earthworks, adding: "This, with Bricks, and even pieces of Earthen Ware dug up in the Kentucky Country, shew that there have been European or Asiatic Inhabitants there in antient ages, altho' long extirpated." Jefferson, who was convinced that the Muskingum earthworks were constructed by Indians, was skeptical about reference to brick work, stating in this letter to Stiles, "The art of making it [bricks] may have preceded the use of iron, but it would suppose a greater degree of industry than men in the hunter state usually possess. I should like to know whether General Parsons himself saw actual bricks among the remains of fortifications." As usual, Jefferson had little use for speculation uninformed by careful research. (Greene 1984, 344-345)

or they from ours. The latter is my opinion, founded on this single fact. Among the red inhabitants of Asia there are but a few languages radically different, but among our Indians the number of languages is infinite which are so radically different as to exhibit at present no appearance of their having been derived from a common source. The time necessary for the generation of so many languages must be immense. A countryman of yours, a Mr. Lediard, who was with Capt. Cook on his last voyage, proposes either to go to Kamschatka, cross from thence to the Western side of America, and penetrate through the Continent to our side of it, or to go to Kentucky, & thence penetrate Westwardly to the South sea, the vent from hence lately to London, where if he finds a passage to Kamschatka or the Western coast of America he would avail himself of it: otherwise he proposes to return to our side of America to attempt that route. I think him well calculated for such an enterprise, & wish he may undertake it. Another countryman of yours Mr. Trumbul has paid us a visit here & brought with him two pictures which are the admiration of the Connoisseurs. His natural talents for this art seem almost unparalleled. I send you the 5th & 6th vols. of the Bibliotheque physico-ecconomie erroneously lettered as the 7th & 8th, which are not yet come out. I enclose with them the article "Etats Unis" of the new Encyclopedie. This article is recently published, & a few copies have been printed separate. For this twelvemonth past little new & excellent has appeared either in literature or the arts. An Abbé Rochon has applied the metal called platina to the telescope instead of the mixed metal of which the specula were formerly composed. It is insusceptible of rust, as gold is, and he thinks it's reflective power equal to that of the mixed metal. He has observed a very curious effect of the natural crystals, & especially of those of Iceland; which is that lenses made of them have two distinct focuses, and present you the object distinctly at two different distances. This I have seen myself. A new method of copying has been invented here. I called on the inventor, & he presented me a plate of copper, a pen & ink. I wrote a note on the plate, and in about three quarters of an hour he brought me an hundred copies, as perfect as the imagination can conceive. Had I written my name, he could have put it to so many bonds, so that I should have acknowledged the Signature to be my own. The copying of paintings in England is very conceivable. Any number may be taken, which shall give you the true lineaments & coloring of the original without injuring that. This is so like creation, that had I not seen it, I should have doubted it.

The death of the K. of Prussia, which happened on the 17th inst. will probably employ the pens, if not the swords of politicians. We had exchanged the ratifications of our treaty with him. The articles of this which were intended to prevent or mitigate wars, by lessening their aliment are so much applauded in Europe that I think the example will be followed. I have the honor to be with very sincere esteem, Dear Sir, your most obedt. humble servant.

To François Soulés[1]

---

[1] That Jefferson sought to correct some misconceptions is beyond dispute. But the assistance that Jefferson gave to the French historian François Soulés for

Paris Septemb. 13. 1786

Sir,

Before the receipt of your favor of the 11th. inst. I had written the enclosed short notes on such parts of your work as I have yet been able to go over. You will perceive that the corrections are very trifling. Such as they are I will continue them, and forward them to you from time to time as I get along. I will endeavor also to answer such of the queries you propose in your letter as my memory will enable me to do with certainty. Some of them I shall be unable to answer, having left in America all my notes, memorandums &c. which might have enabled me to give you the information you desire. I have the honor to be with the most perfect esteem & respect Sir Your most obedient humble servt.,

[Enclosure: Answers to Soulés' Queries (13–18 September 1786)]

I am unable to say what was the number of Americans engaged in the affair of Bunker's hill. I am able however to set right a gross falsehood of Andrews. He says that the Americans who were engaged were constantly relieved by fresh hands. This is entirely untrue. Bunker's hill (or rather Brede's hill whereon the action was) is a peninsula, joined to the main land by a neck of land almost level with the water, a few paces wide, and between one and two hundred toises long.[1] On one side of this neck lay a vessel of war, and on the other several gun-boats. The body of our army was on the main land; and only a detachment had been sent into the peninsula. When the enemy determined to make the attack, they sent the vessel of war and gun-boats to take the position before mentioned to cut off all reinforcements, which they effectually did. Not so much as a company could venture in to the relief of the men engaged, who therefore fought through the whole action and at length were obliged to retire across the neck thro' the cross fire of the vessels before mentioned. Single persons passed along the neck during the engagement, particularly General Putnam.

On the fall of Montgomery and his aids at Quebec, there were present Colo. Campbell and Major Dubois. Campbell, tho' having the rank of Colonel was only of the staff; Dubois was of the line. The usage of all nations therefore authorized the latter to take the command. But it was a case for which Congress had not yet provided. Campbell availed himself of this, and believing, on the sight of blood, that all was lost, ordered a retreat.

The speech to the Indians in Andrews page 357 is a little altered and abridged. You will find the genuine one in the Journal of Congress of July 1775.

I do not distinctly enough recollect the anecdote of the Old man's company related by Andrews, to affirm it in all its parts. I think I recollect in general that there was such a company.

---

his oeuvre *Histoire des troubles de l'Amérique anglaise* has, by some, been assumed to have been based on the manuscript or proof-sheets which Soulés submitted to Jefferson. Boyd, however, suggests that there is no evidence that Soulés requested Jefferson to make corrections. To the opposite, there is strong probability that these comments and corrections were undertaken by Jefferson on his own initiative; and it is certain that, in drafting them, he employed neither manuscript nor page-proofs but a previous edition of Soulés' work. (Boyd 1990)

[1] In pre-revolutionary France one toise was approximately six feet.

The questions relative to General Thomas I could only have answered indistinctly from my own memory; but fortunately there came to Paris a few days ago, and will yet continue there a few days, a Colonel Blackden, an American officer of good understanding of truth, and who was at the latter part of the affair of Quebec. He was at the surprise of Ticonderoga by Allen, and continued with the army till 1781. I have spoken with him on this subject, and find he possesses treasures of details which will be precious to M. Soulés. Any day that Mr. Soulés will do me the honor to come and take a family soupe with me (after the 16th. inst.) if he will give me notice in the morning, I will ask Colo. Blackden to meet him here, and will make them acquainted. He is perfectly disposed to give all the information in his power to Mr. Soulés, and whatever he gives may be relied on. To him then I shall refer Mr. Soulés for answers to his military questions, and will wait his orders, recommending dispatch as Colo. Blackden has not long to stay.

The Stamp act was passed in Feb. 1765.

What powers the Parliament might rightfully exercise over us, and whether any, had never been declared either by them or us. They had very early taken the gigantic step of passing the navigation act. The colonies remonstrated violently against it, and one of them, Virginia, when she capitulated to the Commonwealth of England, expressly capitulated for a free trade. See the articles in the Notes on Virginia pa. 201. This capitulation however was as little regarded as the original right, restored by it, had been. The navigation act was re-enacted by Charles 2 and was enforced, and we had been so long in the habit of seeing them consider us merely as objects for the extension of their commerce, and of submitting to every duty or regulation imposed with that view, that we had ceased to complain of them. But when they proposed to consider us as objects of taxation, all the states took the alarm. Yet so little had we attended to this subject that our advocates did not at first know on what ground to take their stand. Mr. Dickinson, a lawyer of more ingenuity than sound judgment, and still more timid than ingenious, not daring to question the authority to regulate commerce so as best to answer their own purposes, to which we had so long submitted, admitted that authority in its utmost extent. He acknowledged in his Farmer's [Let]ters th[at th]ey could put down [rolling or sli]tt[ing mil]l[s] and other [in]st[rumen]t[s] of manufacture, that they could levy duties internal or external, payable in Great Britain or in the States. He only required that these duties should be bonâ fide for the regulation of commerce, and not to raise a solid revenue. He admitted therefore that they might control our commerce, but not tax us. This mysterious system took for a moment in America as well as in Europe. But sounder heads saw in the first moment that he who could put down the loom, could stop the spinning wheel, and he who could stop the spinning wheel could tie the hands which turned it. They saw that this flimsy fabric could not be supported. Who were to be judges whether duties were imposed with a view to burthen and suppress a branch of manufacture, or to raise a revenue? If either party, exclusively of the other, it was plain where that would end. If both parties, it was plain where that would end also. They saw therefore no sure clue to lead them out of their difficulties but reason and right. They dared to follow them, assured that they alone could lead them to defensible ground. The first elements of reason shewed that the members of parliament could have no power which the people of the several counties had not. That these had naturally a power over their own farms, and collectively over all England. That if they had any power over countries out of England it must be founded on compact or force. No compact could be shewn, and neither party chose to bottom their pretensions on force. It was objected that this annihilated the navigation act. True, it does. The navigation act therefore becomes a proper subject of treaty between the two nations. Or if Gr. Britain does not choose to have its basis questioned, let us go on as we have done. Let no new shackles be imposed and we will continue to submit to the old. We will consider the restrictions on our commerce now actually existing as compensations yielded by us for the protection and privileges we actually enjoy, only trusting that if Great Britain, on a revisal of these restrictions, is sensible that some of them are useless to her and oppressive to us, she will repeal them. But on this she shall be free. Place us in the condition we were when the King came to the throne, let us rest so, and we will be satisfied. This was the ground on which all the states very soon found themselves rallied, and that there was no other which could be defended.

I will now proceed with remarks on the history.

I do not find that M. Soules mentions the affair of the Cedars which happened in April 1776. This was an affair of considerable importance. A committee was appointed by Congress to institute enquiries concerning it, as may be seen by the journals of June 15 1776. The report of that committee is inserted in the journals of July 10. and I can assure Mr. Soulés that the facts therein stated were proved incontestably to the committee by witnesses present at the transaction, and who were on watch. I have the originals of that enquiry in my possession in America. The Captn. Foster therein mentioned was afterwards taken with Burgoyne's army; tho permitted to go at large on his parole, he was not received into any American company, nor did the British officers, his fellow prisoners, choose to be seen in company with him, so notorious and so detestable had been this transaction.

Vol. 1. pa. 324. I have been very well informed that during all the latter part of this defense, the garrison were obliged to return the cannon balls of the enemy, with which indeed the ground was covered, having none of their own left.

pa. 325. 'Il y eut un Serjent &c. This particular truly related in Andrews.

Vol. 2. pa. 5. 'Ils en vinrent le 10. de Juin à cette resolution que ces Colonies &c. See the Journ. of Congr. that it was on that day put off to the 1st. of July. This was done at the instance of the members opposed to it. The friends of the resolution objected that if it were not agreed to till the 1st. of July they would after that have to frame a Declaration of Independence and that more time would thus be lost. It was therefore agreed between the two that the resolution should be put off till the 1st of July, and that a committee should be immediately appointed to draw a declaration of Independence conformable to the resolution, should it be adopted. A committee was accordingly appointed the next day. On the 1st of July the resolution was proposed, and when ready for a vote, a state required it to be put off till the next day. It was done, and was passed the next day, 2d. of July. The declaration of Independence was debated during the 2d. 3d. and 4th. days of July and on the last of these was passed and signed.

Pa. 6. a 'Se retirerent ensuite du Congrés.' I do not remember that the delegates of Maryland retired from Congress, and I think I could not have forgotten such a fact. On the contrary I find by the Journals of Congress that they were present and acting on the 11th. 12th. 17th. 18th. and 24th. of June.

Pa. 7. a. 'La plus grande partie.' It should rather be 'the most important parts.'

Pa. 7. b. 'Les etats unis feroient encore aujourdhui partie de l'empire Britannique.' M. Soulés may be assured that the submission of the states could not have been effected but by a long series of disasters, and such too as were irreparable in their nature. Their resources were great, and their determination so rooted, that they would have tried the last of them. I am as satisfied, as I can be of any thing, that the conjectures here stated would not have been verified by the event.

Pa. 14. 'provinces unis.' Should not this always be 'etats-unis.'

Pa. 15. 'Mais qu'on pouvoit aussi les interpreter &c.' His exact answer was that 'it was true the &c. might include anything, but that they might also include nothing.'

Pa. 16. 'Tant de confiance &c. Their main confidence was in their own resources. They considered foreign aid as probable and desirable, but not essential. I believe myself, from the whole of what I have seen of our resources and perseverance 1. that had we never received any foreign aid, we should not have obtained our independence, but that we should have made a peace with Great Britain on any terms we pleased, short of that, which would have been a subjection to the same king, an union of force in war &c. 2. that had France supplied us plentifully with money, suppose about 4. millions of guineas a year, without entering into the war herself at all, we should have established our Independence, but it would have cost more time, and blood, but less money. 3. that France, aiding us as she did, with money and forces, shortened much the time, lessened the expense of blood, but at a greater expense of money to her than would otherwise have been requisite.

Pa. 18. 'l'extremité septentrionale &c. I think the word 'cote' would be better adapted than 'extremité' to the form of the island.

Pa. 21. '3000 hommes'. Enquire of Colo. Blackden.

Perhaps the propositions of Congress to the Hessians may be worth mentioning. See their Journals 1776. Aug. 14.

I will make a general observation here on the events of Long island, New York &c. at this time. The maxim laid down by Congress to their Generals was that not a foot of territory was to be ceded to their enemies where there was a possibility of defending it. In consequence of these views, and against his own judgment, Genl. Washington was obliged to fortify and attempt to defend the city of New York. But that could not be defended without occupying the heights in Long island which commanded the city of New York. He was therefore obliged to establish a strong detachment in Long island [to] defend those heights. The moment that detachment was routed, which he had much expected, his first object was to withdraw them, and his 2d. to evacuate New York. He did this therefore immediately, and without waiting any movement of the enemy. He brought off his whole baggage, stores, and other implements, without leaving a single article except the very heaviest of his cannon and things of little value. I well remember his letter to Congress wherein he expresses his wonder that the enemy had given him this leisure, as, from the heights they had got possession of, they might have compelled him to a very precipitate retreat. This was one of the instances where our commanding officers were obliged to conform to popular views tho' they foresaw certain loss from it. Had he proposed at first to abandon New York, he might have been abandoned himself. An obedience to popular will cost us an army in Charlestown in the year 1779.

Pa. 30. 'Une fuite precipitée.' It was a leisurely retreat as I have before observed.

Pa. 41. 'Que je n'ai pu obtenir que d'un Anglois.' Colo. Blackden can probably give M. Soulés good intelligence on this affair. I think I recollect the slaughter on Kniphausen's side to have been very great.

To Mrs. Maria Cosway[1]
Paris, October 12, 1786
My Dear Madam,

Having performed the last sad office of handing you into your carriage at the pavillon de St. Denis, and seen the wheels get actually into motion, I turned on my heel & walked, more dead than alive, to the opposite door, where my own was awaiting me. Mr. Danquerville was missing. He was sought for, found, & dragged down stairs. We were crammed into the carriage, like recruits for the Bastille, & not having soul enough to give orders to the coachman, he presumed Paris our destination, & drove off. After a considerable interval, silence was broke with a "Je suis vraiment afflige du depart de ces bons gens." This was a signal for a mutual confession of distress. We began immediately to talk of Mr. & Mrs. Cosway, of their goodness, their talents, their amiability; & tho we spoke of nothing else, we seemed hardly to have entered into matter [*sic*]

---

[1] Just as music had played a part in Jefferson's youthful flirtations and in his courtship of his wife, so it was not absent from the romantic interlude in Paris with Maria Cosway. She was a talented musician as well as painter. Here, in this *Dialogue Between my Head and my Heart* he reveals under a pseudo-philosophic calm his suffering at her departure, and writes: "Head..... I often told you, during its course, that you were imprudently engaging your affections, under circumstances that must have cost you a great deal of pain; that the persons, indeed, were of the greatest merit, possessing good sense, good humor, honest hearts, honest manners, and eminence in a lovely art; that the lady had, moreover, qualities and accomplishments belonging to her sex, which might form a chapter apart for her; such as music, modesty, beauty, and that softness of disposition, which is the ornament of her sex and the charm of ours." Kimball offers a somewhat different view suggesting that, in a note to Jefferson, Cosway, "...reveals herself for what she essentially was, a spoiled, egocentric young woman, with a very limited emotional capacity."(Berman 1947, 182; Kimball 1950, 168)

when the coachman announced the rue St. Denis, & that we were opposite Mr. Danquerville's. He insisted on descending there & traversing a short passage to his lodgings. I was carried home. Seated by my fireside, solitary & sad, the following dialogue took place between my Head & my Heart:

Head. Well, friend, you seem to be in a pretty trim.

Heart. I am indeed the most wretched of all earthly beings. Overwhelmed with grief, every fiber of my frame distended beyond its natural powers to bear, I would willingly meet whatever catastrophe should leave me no more to feel or to fear.

Head. These are the eternal consequences of your warmth & precipitation. This is one of the scrapes into which you are ever leading us. You confess your follies indeed; but still you hug & cherish them; & no reformation can be hoped, where there is no repentance.

Heart. Oh, my friend! this is no moment to upbraid my foibles. I am rent into fragments by the force of my grief! If you have any balm, pour it into my wounds; if none, do not harrow them by new torments. Spare me in this awful moment! At any other I will attend with patience to your admonitions.

Head. On the contrary I never found that the moment of triumph with you was the moment of attention to my admonitions. While suffering under your follies, you may perhaps be made sensible of them, but, the paroxysm over, you fancy it can never return. Harsh therefore as the medicine may be, it is my office to administer it. You will be pleased to remember that when our friend Trumbull used to be telling us of the merits & talents of these good people, I never ceased whispering to you that we had no occasion for new acquaintance; that the greater their merits & talents, the more dangerous their friendship to our tranquility, because the regret at parting would be greater.

Heart. Accordingly, Sir, this acquaintance was not the consequence of my doings. It was one of your projects which threw us in the way of it. It was you, remember, & not I, who desired the meeting at Legrand & Molinos. I never trouble myself with domes nor arches. The Halle aux bleds might have rotted down before I should have gone to see it. But you, forsooth, who are eternally getting us to sleep with your diagrams & crotchets, must go & examine this wonderful piece of architecture. And when you had seen it, oh! it was the most superb thing on earth! What you had seen there was worth all you had yet seen in Paris! I thought so too. But I meant it of the lady & gentleman to whom we had been presented; & not of a parcel of sticks & chips put together in pens. You then, Sir, & not I, have been the cause of the present distress.

Head. It would have been happy for you if my diagrams & crotchets had gotten you to sleep on that day, as you are pleased to say they eternally do. My visit to Legrand & Molinos had public utility for its object. A market is to be built in Richmond. What a commodious plan is that of Legrand & Molinos; especially if we put on it the noble dome of the Halle aux bleds. If such a bridge as they shewed us can be thrown across the Schuylkill at Philadelphia, the floating bridges taken up & the navigation of that river opened, what a copious resource will be added, of wood & provisions, to warm & feed the poor of that city? While I was occupied with these objects, you were dilating with your new acquaintances, & contriving how to prevent a separation from them. Every soul of you had an engagement for the day. Yet all these were to be sacrificed, that you might dine together. Lying messengers were to be dispatched into every quarter of the city, with apologies for your breach of engagement. You particularly had the effrontery to send word to the Duchess Danville that, on the moment we were setting out to dine with her, dispatches came to hand which required immediate attention. You wanted me to invent a more ingenious excuse; but I knew you were getting into a scrape, & I would have nothing to do with it. Well, after dinner to St. Cloud, from St. Cloud to Ruggieri's, from Ruggieri to Krumfoltz, & if the day had been as long as a Lapland summer day, you would still have contrived means among you to have filled it.

Heart. Oh! my dear friend, how you have revived me by recalling to my mind the transactions of that day! How well I remember them all, & that when I came home at night & looked back to the morning, it seemed to have been a month agone. Go on then, like a kind comforter & paint to me the day we went to St. Germains. How beautiful was every object! the Port de Reuilly, the hills along the Seine, the rainbows of the machine of Marly, the terrace of St. Germains, the chateaux, the gardens, the statues of Marly, the pavillon of Lucienne. Recollect too Madrid, Bagatelle, the King's garden, the Dessert. How grand the idea excited by the remains of such a column! The spiral staircase too was beautiful. Every moment was filled with something agreeable. The wheels of time moved on with a rapidity of which those of our carriage gave but a faint idea. And yet in the evening when one took a retrospect of the day, what a mass of happiness had we travelled over! Retrace all those scenes to me, my good companion, & I will forgive the unkindness with which you were chiding me. The day we went to St. Germains was a little too warm, I think; was it not?

Head. Thou art the most incorrigible of all the beings that ever sinned! I reminded you of the follies of the first day, intending to deduce from thence some useful lessons for you, but instead of listening to these, you kindle at the recollection, you retrace the whole series with a fondness which shews you want nothing but the opportunity to act it over again. I often told you during its course that you were imprudently engaging your affections under circumstances that must have cost you a great deal of pain: that the persons indeed were of the greatest merit, possessing good sense, good humor, honest hearts, honest manners, & eminence in a lovely art; that the lady had moreover qualities & accomplishments belonging to her sex, which might form a chapter apart for her: such as music, modesty, beauty, & that softness of disposition which is the ornament of her sex & charm of ours, but that all these considerations would increase the pang of separation: that their stay here was to be short: that you rack our whole system when you are parted from those you love, complaining that such a separation is worse than death, inasmuch as this ends our sufferings, whereas that only begins them: & that the separation would in this instance be the more severe as you would probably never see them again.

Heart. But they told me they would come back again the next year.

Head. But in the meantime see what you suffer: & their return too depends on so many circumstances that if you had a grain of prudence you would not count upon it. Upon the whole it is improbable & therefore you should abandon the idea of ever seeing them again.

Heart. May heaven abandon me if I do!

Head. Very well. Suppose then they come back. They are to stay two months, & when these are expired, what is to follow? Perhaps you flatter yourself they may come to America?

Heart. God only knows what is to happen. I see nothing impossible in that supposition. And I see things wonderfully contrived sometimes to make us happy. Where could they find such objects as in America for the exercise of their enchanting art? especially the lady, who paints landscapes so inimitably. She wants only subjects worthy of immortality to render her pencil immortal. The Falling Spring, the Cascade of Niagara, the Passage of the Potomac through the Blue Mountains, the Natural bridge. It is worth a voyage across the Atlantic to see these objects; much more to paint, and make them, & thereby ourselves, known to all ages. And our own dear Monticello, where has nature spread so rich a mantle under the eye? mountains, forests, rocks, rivers. With what majesty do we there ride above the storms! How sublime to look down into the workhouse of nature, to see her clouds, hail, snow, rain, thunder, all fabricated at our feet! and the glorious sun when rising as if out of a distant water, just gilding the tops of the mountains, & giving life to all nature! I hope in God no circumstance may ever make either seek an asylum from grief! With what sincere sympathy I would open every cell of my composition to receive the effusion of their woes! I would pour my tears into their wounds: & if a drop of balm could be found on the top of the Cordilleras, or at the remotest sources of the Missouri, I would go thither myself to seek & to bring it. Deeply practiced in the school of affliction, the human heart knows no joy which I have not lost, no sorrow of which I have not drunk! Fortune can present no grief of unknown form to me! Who then can so softly bind up the wound of another as he who has felt the same wound himself? But Heaven forbid they should ever know a sorrow! Let us turn over another leaf, for this has distracted me.

Head. Well. Let us put this possibility to trial then on another point. When you consider the character which is given of our country by the lying newspapers of London, & their credulous copyers in other countries; when you reflect that all Europe is made to believe we are a lawless banditti, in a state of absolute anarchy, cutting one another's throats, & plundering without distinction, how can you expect that any reasonable creature would venture among us?

Heart. But you & I know that all this is false: that there is not a country on earth where there is greater tranquility, where the laws are milder, or better obeyed: where everyone is more attentive to his own business, or meddles less with that of others: where strangers are better received, more hospitably treated, & with a more sacred respect.

Head. True, you & I know this, but your friends do not know it.

Heart. But they are sensible people who think for themselves. They will ask of impartial foreigners who have been among us, whether they saw or heard on the spot any instances of anarchy. They will judge too that a people occupied as we are in opening rivers, digging navigable canals, making roads, building public schools, establishing academies, erecting busts & statues to our great men, protecting religious freedom, abolishing sanguinary punishments, reforming & improving our laws in general, they will judge I say for themselves whether these are not the occupations of a people at their ease, whether this is not better evidence of our true state than a London newspaper, hired to lie, & from which no truth can ever be extracted but by reversing everything it says.

Head. I did not begin this lecture my friend with a view to learn from you what America is doing. Let us return then to our point. I wished to make you sensible how imprudent it is to place your affections, without reserve, on objects you must so soon lose, & whose loss when it comes must cost you such severe pangs. Remember the last night. You knew your friends were to leave Paris to-day. This was enough to throw you into agonies. All night you tossed us from one side of the bed to the other. No sleep, no rest. The poor crippled wrist too, never left one moment in the same position, now up, now down, now here, now there; was it to be wondered at if it's pains returned? The Surgeon then was to be called, & to be rated as an ignoramus because he could not divine the cause of this extraordinary change. In fine, my friend, you must mend your manners. This is not a world to live at random in as you do. To avoid those eternal distresses, to which you are forever exposing us, you must learn to look forward before you take a step which may interest our peace. Everything in this world is a matter of calculation. Advance then with caution, the balance in your hand. Put into one scale the pleasures which any object may offer; but put fairly into the other the pains which are to follow, & see which preponderates. The making an acquaintance is not a matter of indifference. When a new one is proposed to you, view it all round. Consider what advantages it presents, & to what inconveniences it may expose you. Do not bite at the bait of pleasure till you know there is no hook beneath it. The art of life is the art of avoiding pain: & he is the best pilot who steers clearest of the rocks & shoals with which he is beset. Pleasure is always before us; but misfortune is at our side: while running after that, this arrests us. The most effectual means of being secure against pain is to retire within ourselves, & to suffice for our own happiness. Those, which depend on ourselves, are the only pleasures a wise man will count on: for nothing is ours which another may deprive us of. Hence the inestimable value of intellectual pleasures. Even in our power, always leading us to something new, never cloying, we ride serene & sublime above the concerns of this mortal world, contemplating truth & nature, matter & motion, the laws which bind up their existence, & that eternal being who made & bound them up by those laws. Let this be our employ. Leave the bustle & tumult of society to those who have not talents to occupy themselves without them. Friendship is but another name for an alliance with the follies & the misfortunes of others. Our own share of miseries is sufficient: why enter then as volunteers into those of another? Is there so little gall poured into our cup that we must needs help to drink that of our neighbor? A friend dies or leaves us: we feel as if a limb was cut off. He is sick: we must watch over him, & participate of his pains. His fortune is shipwrecked; ours must be laid under contribution. He loses a child, a parent, or a partner: we must mourn the loss as if it were our own.

Heart. And what more sublime delight than to mingle tears with one whom the hand of heaven hath smitten! to watch over the bed of sickness, & to beguile it's tedious & it's painful moments! to share our bread with one to whom misfortune has left none! This world abounds indeed with misery: to lighten it's burthen we must divide it with one another. But let us now try the virtues of your mathematical balance, & as you have put into one scale the burthen of friendship, let me put it's comforts into the other. When languishing then under disease, how grateful is the solace of our friends! how are we penetrated with their assiduities & attentions! how much are we supported by their encouragements & kind offices! When heaven has taken from us some object of our love, how sweet is it to have a bosom whereon to recline our heads, & into which we may pour the torrent of our tears! Grief, with such a comfort, is almost a luxury! In a life where we are perpetually exposed to want & accident, yours is a wonderful proposition, to insulate ourselves, to retire from all aid, & to wrap ourselves in the mantle of self-sufficiency! For assuredly nobody will care for him who cares for nobody. But friendship is precious, not only in the shade but in the sunshine of life; & thanks to a benevolent arrangement of things, the greater part of life is sunshine. I will recur for proof to the days we have lately passed. On these indeed the sun shone brightly. How gay did the face of nature appear! Hills, valleys, chateaux, gardens, rivers, every object wore it's liveliest hue! Whence did they borrow it? From the presence of our charming companion. They were pleasing, because she seemed pleased. Alone, the scene would have been dull & insipid: the participation of it with her gave it relish. Let the gloomy monk, sequestered from the world, seek unsocial pleasures in the bottom of his cell! Let the sublimated philosopher grasp visionary happiness while pursuing phantoms dressed in the garb of truth! Their supreme wisdom is supreme folly; & they mistake for happiness the mere absence of pain. Had they ever felt the solid pleasure of one generous spasm of the heart, they would exchange for it all the frigid speculations of their lives, which you have been vaunting in such elevated terms. Believe me then my friend, that there is a miserable arithmetic which could estimate friendship at nothing, or at less than nothing. Respect for you has induced me to enter into this discussion, & to hear principles uttered which I detest & abjure. Respect for myself now obliges me to recall you into the proper limits of your office. When nature assigned us the same habitation, she gave us over it a divided empire. To you she allotted the field of science; to me that of morals.

When the circle is to be squared, or the orbit of a comet to be traced; when the arch of greatest strength, or the solid of least resistance is to be investigated, take up the problem; it is yours; nature has given me no cognizance of it. In like manner, in denying to you the feelings of sympathy, of benevolence, of gratitude, of justice, of love, of friendship, she has excluded you from their control. To these she has adapted the mechanism of the heart. Morals were too essential to the happiness of man to be risked on the uncertain combinations of the head. She laid their foundation therefore in sentiment, not in science. That she gave to all, as necessary to all: this to a few only, as sufficing with a few. I know indeed that you pretend authority to the sovereign control of our conduct in all its parts: & a respect for your grave saws & maxims, a desire to do what is right, has sometimes induced me to conform to your counsels. A few facts however which I can readily recall to your memory, will suffice to prove to you that nature has not organized you for our moral direction. When the poor wearied soldier whom we overtook at Chickahomony with his pack on his back, begged us to let him get up behind our chariot, you began to calculate that the road was full of soldiers, & that if all should be taken up our horses would fail in their journey. We drove on therefore. But soon becoming sensible you had made me do wrong, that tho we cannot relieve all the distressed we should relieve as many as we can, I turned about to take up the soldier; but he had entered a bye path, & was no more to be found; & from that moment to this I could never find him out to ask his forgiveness. Again, when the poor woman came to ask a charity in Philadelphia, you whispered that she looked like a drunkard, & that half a dollar was enough to give her for the ale-house. Those who want the dispositions to give, easily find reasons why they ought not to give. When I sought her out afterwards, & did what I should have done at first, you know that she employed the money immediately towards placing her child at school. If our country, when pressed with wrongs at the point of the bayonet, had been governed by its heads instead of its hearts, where should we have been now? Hanging on a gallows as high as Haman's. You began to calculate & to compare wealth and numbers: we threw up a few pulsations of our warmest blood; we supplied enthusiasm against wealth and numbers; we put our existence to the hazard when the hazard seemed against us, and we saved our country: justifying at the same time the ways of Providence, whose precept is to do always what is right, and leave the issue to him. In short, my friend, as far as my recollection serves me, I do not know that I ever did a good thing on your suggestion, or a dirty one without it. I do forever then disclaim your interference in my province. Fill papers as you please with triangles & squares: try how many ways you can hang & combine them together. I shall never envy nor control your sublime delights. But leave me to decide when & where friendships are to be contracted. You say I contract them at random. So you said the woman at Philadelphia was a drunkard. I receive no one into my esteem till I know they are worthy of it. Wealth, title, office, are no recommendations to my friendship. On the contrary great good qualities are requisite to make amends for their having wealth, title, & office. You confess that in the present case I could not have made a worthier choice. You only object that I was so soon to lose them. We are not immortal ourselves, my friend; how can we expect our enjoyments to be so? We have no rose without it's thorn; no pleasure without alloy. It is the law of our existence; & we must acquiesce. It is the condition annexed to all our pleasures, not by us who receive, but by him who gives them. True, this condition is pressing cruelly on me at this moment. I feel more fit for death than life. But when I look back on the pleasures of which it is the consequence, I am conscious they were worth the price I am paying. Notwithstanding your endeavors too to damp my hopes, I comfort myself with expectations of their promised return. Hope is sweeter than despair, & they were too good to mean to deceive me. In the summer, said the gentleman; but in the spring, said the lady: & I should love her forever, were it only for that! Know then, my friend, that I have taken these good people into my bosom; that I have lodged them in the warmest cell I could find: that I love them, & will continue to love them through life: that if fortune should dispose them on one side the globe, & me on the other, my affections shall pervade it's whole mass to reach them. Knowing then my determination, attempt not to disturb it. If you can at any time furnish matter for their amusement, it will be the office of a good neighbor to do it. I will in like manner seize any occasion which may offer to do the like good turn for you with Condorcet, Rittenhouse, Madison, La Cretelle, or any other of those worthy sons of science whom you so justly prize.

I thought this a favorable proposition whereon to rest the issue of the dialogue. So I put an end to it by calling for my night-cap. Methinks I hear you wish to heaven I had called a little sooner, & so spared you the ennui of such a sermon. I did not interrupt them sooner because I was in a mood for hearing sermons. You too were the subject; & on such a thesis I never think the theme long; not even if I am to write it, and that slowly & awkwardly, as now, with the left hand. But that you may not be discouraged from a correspondence which begins so formidably, I promise you on my honor that my future letters shall be of a reasonable length. I will even agree to express but half my esteem for you, for fear of cloying you with too full a dose. But, on your part, no curtailing. If your letters are as long as the bible, they will appear short to me. Only let them be brimful of affection. I shall read them with the dispositions with which Arlequin, in Les deux billets spelt the words "je t'aime," and wished that the whole alphabet had entered into their composition.

We have had incessant rains since your departure. These make me fear for your health, as well as that you had an uncomfortable journey. The same cause has prevented me from being able to give you any account of your friends here. This voyage to Fontainebleau will probably send the Count de Moustier & the Marquise de Brehan to America. Danquerville promised to visit me, but has not done it as yet. De la Tude comes sometimes to take family soup with me, & entertains me with anecdotes of his five & thirty years imprisonment. How fertile is the mind of man which can make the Bastille & Dungeon of Vincennes yield interesting anecdotes! You know this was for making four verses on Mme de Pompadour. But I think you told me you did not know the verses. They were these: "Sans esprit, sans sentiment, Sans etre belle, ni neuve, En France on peut avoir le premier amant: Pompadour en est l' epreuve." I have read the memoir of his three escapes. As to myself my health is good, except my wrist which mends slowly, & my mind which mends not at all, but broods constantly over your departure. The lateness of the season obliges me to decline my journey into the south of France. Present me in the most friendly terms to Mr. Cosway, & receive me into your own recollection with a partiality & a warmth, proportioned, not to my own poor merit, but to the sentiments of sincere affection & esteem with which I have the honor to be, my dear Madam, your most obedient humble servant.

To Mrs. Maria Cosway[1]
Paris, Octob. 13, 1786
My Dear Madam,

Just as I had sealed the enclosed I received a letter of a good length, dated Antwerp with your name at the bottom. I prepared myself for a feast. I read two or three sentences; looked again at the signature to see if I had not mistaken it. It was visibly yours. Read a sentence or two more. Diable! Spelt your name distinctly. There was not a letter of it omitted. Began to read again. In fine after reading a little & examining the signature, alternately, half a dozen times, I found that your name was to four lines only, instead of four pages. I thank you for the four lines however because they prove you think of me little indeed, but better a little than none. To shew how much I think of you I send you the enclosed letter of three sheets of paper, being a history of the evening I parted with you. But how expect you should read a letter of three mortal sheets of paper? I will tell you. Divide it into six doses of half a sheet each, and every day, when the toilette begins, take a dose, that is to say, read half a sheet. By this means it will have the only merit its length & dullness can aspire to, that of assisting your coiffeuse to procure you six good naps of sleep. I will even allow you twelve days to get through it, holding you rigorously to one condition only, that is, that at whatever hour you receive this, you do not break the seal of the enclosed till the next toilette. Of this injunction I require a sacred execution. I rest it on your friendship, & that in your first letter you tell me honestly whether you have honestly performed it. I send you the song I promised. Bring me in return it's subject, Jours heureux! Were I a songster I should sing it all to these words 'Dans ces lieux qu'elle tarde a se rendre!' Learn it I pray you, & sing it with feeling.

---

[1] In this postscript to the *Dialogue* Jefferson says: "I send you the song I promised. Bring me in return the subject, *Jours heureux!* Were I a songster, I should sing it all to these words '*Dans ces lieux qu'elle tarde a se rendre!*' Learn it, I pray you, and sing it with feeling." Maria Cosway had presented him with the duet *Tacit Ombre*, one of a number of Italian songs and duets with harp accompaniment which she had composed. When Jefferson received the collection — the title page carried an engraving she made after a drawing by her husband Richard Cosway, a vignette of a Cupid charming a savage lion with his piping — he wrote to John Trumbull: "Kneel to Mrs. Cosway for me and lay my soul in her lap." (Berman 1947, 182)

My right hand presents its devoirs to, and sees with great indignation the left supplanting it in a correspondence so much valued. You will know the first moment it can resume its rights. The first exercise of them shall be addressed to you, as you had the first essay of its rival. It will yet, however, be many a day. Present my esteem to Mr. Cosway, & believe me to be yours very affectionately.[1]

To William Stephens Smith[2]
Paris, Oct. 22, 1786
Dear Sir,

How the right hand became disabled would be a long story for the left to tell. It was by one of those follies from which good cannot come, but ill may. As yet I have no use of that hand, & as the other is an awkward scribe, I must be sententious & not waste words. Yours of Sep. 18. & 22. & Oct. 1. & 4. have been duly received, as have been also the books from Lackington & Stockdale, & the second parcel from Dilly. The harness is at the Douane of Paris, not yet delivered to me. Dilly's first parcel of books, & the first copying press are arrived at Rouen. You see how much reason I have to say 'well done, thou good and faithful servant.' With Chastellux's voyages & Latré's map I took a great deal more trouble than was necessary, such as going myself to the book shop when a servant might as well have gone etc. merely from a desire to do something in return for you, & that I might feel as if I have done something. You desire to know whether the 2d. order for copying paper & ink was meant to be additional to the former? It was, but I had now rather not receive the paper because I have found a better kind

---

[1] With respect to the nature of Jefferson's relationship with Maria Cosway, only Dumas Malone, of all the male biographers and historians, has been willing to concede that he "fell deeply in love during that golden September" and to suggest that if ever as a widower he engaged in "illicit love-making...this was the time." Helen Bullock, who edited the Cosway-Jefferson letters in 1945 (with great discretion), let the correspondence speak for itself, but one of her chapters is called 'Peep into Elysium.' Finally, Maria Kimball described the romance as "one of the most momentous experiences of Jefferson's life." (Brodie 1974, 207)

[2] On September 18, 1786, about six weeks after their original meeting, Jefferson and Maria Cosway were walking along the Seine westward from the Place Louis XV. In attempting to jump over a fence — whether to retrieve a blowing scarf in the wind or simply in sheer exuberant good spirits one can only guess — he fell very hard and dislocated his right wrist. This at least was the diagnosis of the French surgeons who ineptly treated it, though it would seem from his subsequent agony to recover that he certainly broke a bone, as his daughter Martha believed. "How the right hand became disabled," as Jefferson, in this note, wrote cryptically to Smith, "would be a long story for the left to tell. It was by one of those follies from which good cannot come but ill may." In later years, Jefferson's daughter described the accident as if her father had been walking with a man: He frequently walked as far as seven miles in the country. Returning from one of those rambles, he was joined by some friend, and being earnestly engaged in conversation he fell and fractured his wrist. He said nothing at the moment, but holding his suffering limb with the other hand, he continued the conversation till he arrived near to his own house, when, informing his companion of the accident, he left him to send for the surgeon. The fracture was a compound one, and probably much swollen before the arrival of the surgeon; it was not *set*, and remained ever after weak and stiff. (Ibid. 207-208)

---

here. The ink I shall be glad of. The twelve sheet map I shall send by the first good opportunity, & hope ere long to receive the plate of mine from Mr. Neele. I will trouble you to have the enclosed note to Jones delivered. Will you undertake to prevail on Mr. Adams to set for his picture & on Mr. Brown to draw it for me? I wish to add to those of other principal American characters which I have or shall have: & I had rather it should be original than a copy. We saw a picture of Sr. W. Raleigh at Birmingham, & I do not know whether it was of Mr. Adams or yourself I asked the favor to get it for me. I must pray your tailor to send me a buff casimir waistcoat & breeches with those of cotton, & of my shoemaker to send me two pr. of thin waxed leather slippers. Things of this kind come better by private hands if any such should be coming within any reasonable time. The accident to my wrist has defected my views of visiting the South of France this fall. Present me very affectionately to Mrs. Adams and Mrs. Smith. I hope the former is very well, & that the latter is, or has been very sick, otherwise I would observe to you that it is high time. Adieu.

To George Washington[1]
Paris, Nov. 14, 1786
Sir,

The house of Le Coulteux, which for some centuries has been the wealthiest of this place, has it in contemplation to establish a great company for the fur trade. They propose that partners interested one half in the establishment should be American citizens, born & residing in the U. S. Yet if I understood them rightly they expect that half of the company which resides here should make the greatest part, or perhaps the whole of the advances, while those on our side of the water should superintend the details. They had at first thought

---

[1] Jefferson was very supportive of a plan for engaging a wealthy French mercantile company, the house of Le Coulteux, in the fur trade of the Pacific coast, and he secured from this house a promise that they would consider the advantages of Alexandria, on the Potomac, for their depot of supply. Jefferson's interest in canals connecting the Potomac and the Ohio was partly due to this project. After the failure of company's Parisian plans, Jefferson proposed to the company to cross Russia to Kamchatka, take ship to Nootka Sound, and thence return to the United States by way of the Missouri. But this failed through Russian opposition. The Society of Cincinnati was an elite society of retired revolutionary officers. Because of his leadership in the society, Washington had initially resisted attending the Constitutional Convention — scheduled for the second Monday in May 1787 — because of conflicting loyalties he felt as a leader in the society. Jefferson's letter evidently arrived at Mount Vernon on 25 Apr. 1787, adding to the acute embarrassment Washington was experiencing over the question of attendance at the forthcoming general meeting of the Cincinnati scheduled for the first Monday in May. In the end, Washington came to the convention only at the insistence of Edmund Randolph, Alexander Hamilton, and James Madison, who recognized Washington's importance and prominence among his political peers. Once there, he was appointed by his colleagues to preside over the convention, despite his initial hesitation. While he said very little in the debates and discussions and made a point of giving up his position whenever the convention broke into a "committee of the whole," his mere presence was extremely important, as he became the acknowledged model for what an exemplary president might become. (Turner 1898, 672; Daynes 2000, 3; Boyd 1990)

of Baltimore as the center of their American transactions. I pointed out to them the advantages of Alexandria for this purpose. They have concluded to take information as to Baltimore, Philadelphia, & N. York for a principal deposit, & having no correspondent at Alexandria have asked me to procure a state of the advantages of that place, as also to get a recommendation of the best merchant there to be adopted as partner & head of the business there. Skill, punctuality & integrity are the requisites in such a character. They will decide on their whole information as to the place for their principal factory. Being unwilling that Alexandria should lose its pretensions, I have undertaken to procure them information as to that place. If they undertake this trade at all, it will be on so great a scale as to decide the current of the Indian trade to the place they adopt. I have no acquaintance at Alexandria or in its neighborhood, but believing you would feel an interest in it, from the same motives which I do, I venture to ask the favor of you to recommend to me a proper merchant for their purpose, & to engage some well-informed person to send to me a representation of the advantages of Alexandria as the principal deposit of the fur trade.

The author of the Political part of the Encyclopedie Methodique desired me to examine his article "Etats unis." I did so. I found it a tissue of errors, for in truth they know nothing about us here. Particularly however the article "Cincinnati" was a mere Philippic against that institution; in which it appears that there was an utter ignorance of facts & motives. I gave him notes on it. He reformed it as he supposed & sent it again to me to revise. In this reformed state Colo. Humphreys saw it. I found it necessary to write that article for him. Before I gave it to him I showed it to the Marq. de la Fayette who made a correction or two. I then sent it to the author. He used the materials, mixing a great deal of his own with them. In a work which is sure of going down to the latest posterity I thought it material to set facts to rights as much as possible. The author was well disposed: but could not entirely get the better of his original bias. I send you the article as ultimately published. If you find any material errors in it & will be so good as to inform me of them, I shall probably have opportunities of setting this author to rights. What has heretofore passed between us on this institution, makes it my duty to mention to you that I have never heard a person in Europe, learned or unlearned, express his thoughts on this institution, who did not consider it as dishonorable & destructive to our governments, and that every writing which has come out since my arrival here, in which it is mentioned, considers it, even as now reformed, as the germ whose development is one day to destroy the fabric we have reared. I did not apprehend this while I had American ideas only. But I confess that what I have seen in Europe has brought me over to that opinion; & that tho' the day may be at some distance, beyond the reach of our lives perhaps, yet it will certainly come, when a single fiber left of this institution will produce an hereditary aristocracy which will change the form of our governments from the best to the worst in the world. To know the mass of evil which flows from this fatal source, a person must be in France, he must see the finest soil, the finest climate, the most compact state, the most benevolent character of people, & every earthly advantage combined, insufficient to prevent this scourge from rendering existence a curse to 24 out of 25 parts of the inhabitants of this country. With us the branches of this institution cover all the states. The Southern ones at this time are aristocratical in their disposition; and that that spirit should grow & extend itself, is within the natural order of things. I do not flatter myself with the immortality of our governments: but I shall think little also of their longevity unless this germ of destruction be taken out. When the society themselves shall weigh the possibility of evil against the impossibility of any good to proceed from this institution, I cannot help hoping they will eradicate it. I know they wish the permanence of our governments as much as any individuals composing them. An interruption here & the departure of the gentleman by whom I send this obliges me to conclude it, with assurances of the sincere respect & esteem with which I have the honor to be Dear Sir your most obedt. & most humble servt.

To Mrs. Elizabeth Trist[1]
Paris, Dec. 15, 1786
Dear Madam,

I have duly received your friendly letter of July 24 & received it with great pleasure as I do all those you do me the favor to write me. If I have been long in acknowledging the receipt, the last cause to which it should be ascribed would be want of inclination. Unable to converse with my friends in person, I am happy when I do it in black & white. The true cause of the delay has been an unlucky dislocation of my wrist which has disabled me from writing three months. I only begin to write a little now, but with pain. I wish, while in Virginia, your curiosity had led you on to James river. At Richmond you would have seen your old friends Mr. & Mrs. Randolph, and a little further you would have become acquainted with my friend, Mrs. Eppes, whom you would have found among the most amiable women on earth. I doubt whether you would ever have got away from her. This trip would have made you better acquainted too with my lazy & hospitable countrymen, & you would have found that their character has some

---

[1] Elizabeth House Trist was the daughter of Mary Stretch House and Samuel House, and the grandmother of Nicholas Philip Trist, who married Thomas Jefferson's granddaughter Virginia Jefferson Randolph at Monticello in 1824. Jefferson formed an enduring friendship with her when he stayed at her mother's Philadelphia boardinghouse during service in the Continental Congress, 1782–84. He advised her in recurring financial difficulties, wrote her regularly, persuaded her to move her family to Albemarle County in 1798, and appointed her only child, Hore Browse Trist, port collector for the lower Mississippi River in 1803, upon which she moved with him to New Orleans. Hore Trist died in 1804, and Elizabeth Trist returned to Virginia in 1808. She spent some of her remaining years as an itinerant houseguest at a variety of Albemarle County estates, including Monticello, where she died and is believed to have been buried. The interesting aspect of this letter is that it clearly indicates that Jefferson did not shy from expressing his emotional state to another woman he had known for many years. "I am burning the candle of life without present pleasure, or future object." He wrote, with his still pained wrist and a note of ennui. "A dozen or twenty years ago this scene would have amused me." He recalled those sorrowful days of Martha's decline and death in 1782: "Laid up in port for life, as I thought myself at one time, I am thrown out to sea....By so slender a thread do all our plans of life hang!....The happiest moments [my heart] knows are those in which it is pouring forth it's affections to a few esteemed characters." (Thomas Jefferson Foundation, "Elizabeth House Trist" 2016; Wayson 2012, 308)

good traits mixed with some feeble ones. I often wish myself among them, as I am here burning the candle of life without present pleasure, or future object. A dozen or twenty years ago this scene would have amused me, but I am past the age for changing habits. I take all the fault on myself, and it is impossible to be among a people who wish more to make one happy, a people of the very best character it is possible for one to have. We have no idea in America of the real French character, with some true samples we have had many false ones. I am very, very sorry I did not receive your letter three or four months sooner. It would have been absolutely convenient for me while in England to have seen Browse's relations, and I should have done it with infinite pleasure. At present I have no particular expectation of returning there yet it is among possible events, and the desire of being useful to him would render it a pleasing one. The former journey thither was made at a week's warning, without the least previous expectation. Living from day to day, without a plan for four & twenty hours to come, I form no catalogue of impossible events. Laid up in port, for life, as I thought myself at one time, I am thrown out to sea, and an unknown one to me. By so slender a thread do all our plans of life hang.

My hand itself further, every letter admonishing me, by a pain, that it is time to finish, but my heart would go on in expressing to you all its friendship. The happiest moments it knows are those in which it is pouring forth its affections to a few esteemed characters. I will pray you to write me often. I wish to know that you enjoy health and that you are happy. Present me in the most friendly terms to your mother & brother, & be assured of the sincerity of the esteem with which I am, dear Madam, your affectionate friend & humble servant.

To James Madison[1]
Paris, Dec. 16, 1786
Dear Sir,

After a very long silence, I am at length able to write to you. An unlucky dislocation of my right wrist has disabled me from using my pen for three

---

[1] When Madison introduced the "Bill for Establishing Religious Freedom" bill to the House in 1785, it underwent much debate and amendment but was ultimately approved. In early 1786, it passed both the House of Delegates and the Virginia Senate and became law. Living in France when the bill became law, Jefferson, needless to say, received the news with elation, as he had originally drafted the legislation in 1777 and ultimately ranked this bill with the *Declaration of Independence* among his proudest accomplishments. Considered as a single Act passed in the legislature of the State of Virginia, the bill seems fairly modest, but in terms of philosophical, social, and political significance, its implications were vast. News of the bill spread throughout Europe, and it was widely reprinted as an example of American enlightenment. This letter to Madison shows how much the bill meant to Jefferson" "The Virginia act for religious freedom has been received with infinite approbation in Europe and propagated with enthusiasm...." Not only, in Jefferson's opinion, did it represent the triumph of reason over tyranny, prejudice, and superstition, it also represented the United States and, specifically, Virginia, it also personally represented the Thomas Jefferson and demonstrated his will, his perseverance, and his desire to work toward the freedom of all men. (Hayes 2008, 205)

months. I now begin to use it a little, but with great pain; so that this letter must be taken up at such intervals as the state of my hand will permit, & will probably be the work of some days. Tho' the joint seems to well set, the swelling does not abate, nor the use of it return. I am now therefore on the point of setting out to the South of France to try the use of some mineral waters there, by immersion. This journey will be of 2 or 3 months. My last letters to you were of Apr. 25. & May 20. the latter only a letter of recommendation. Yours of Jan. 22. Mar. 18. May 12. June 19. & Aug. 12. remain unacknowledged.

I enclose you herein a copy of the letter from the minister of finance to me making several advantageous regulations for our commerce. The obtaining this has occupied us a twelvemonth. I say us because I find the M. de la Fayette so useful an auxiliary that acknowledgments for his cooperation are always due. There remains still something to do for the articles of rice, turpentine, & ship duties. What can be done for tobacco when the late regulation expires is very uncertain. The commerce between the U. S. and this country being put on a good footing, we may afterwards proceed to try if anything can be done to favor our intercourse with their colonies. Admission into them for our fish & flour, is very desirable: but unfortunately those articles would raise a competition against their own.

I find by the public papers that your Commercial Convention failed in point of representation. If it should produce a full meeting in May and a broader reformation, it will still be well. To make us one nation as to foreign concerns, & keep us distinct in Domestic ones, gives the outline of the proper division of power between the general & particular governments. But to enable the Federal head to exercise the power given it, to best advantage, it should be organized, as the particular ones are into Legislative Executive & Judiciary. The 1st & last are already separated. The 2d should also be. When last with Congress I often proposed to members to do this by making of the Committee of the states, an Executive committee during the recess of Congress and during its sessions to appoint a Committee to receive & dispatch all executive business, so that Congress itself should meddle only with what should be legislative. But I question if any Congress (much less all successively) can have self-denial enough to go through with this distribution. The distribution should be imposed on them then. I find Congress have reversed their division of the Western states & proposed to make them fewer & larger. This is reversing the natural order of things. A tractable people may be governed in large bodies but in proportion as they depart from this character the extent of their government must be less. We see into what small divisions the Indians are obliged to reduce their societies. This measure, with the disposition to shut up the Mississippi give me serious apprehensions of the severance of the Eastern & Western parts of our confederacy. It might have been made the interest of the Western states to remain united with us, by managing their interests honestly & for their own good. But the moment we sacrifice their interests to our own, they will see it is better to govern themselves. The moment they resolve to do this, the point is settled. A forced connection is neither our interest nor within our power. The Virginia act for religious freedom has been received with infinite approbation in Europe & propagated with enthusiasm. I do not mean by the governments, but by the individuals which compose them. It has been translated into French & Italian, has been sent to most of the courts of Europe, & has been the best evidence of the falsehood of those reports which stated us to be in anarchy. It is inserted in the new Encyclopedie, & is appearing in most of the publications respecting America. In fact it is comfortable to see the standard of reason at length erected, after so many ages during which the human mind has been held in vassalage by kings, priests & nobles: and it is honorable for us to have produced the first legislature who had the courage to declare that the reason of man may be trusted with the formation of his own opinions.

I shall be glad when the revisal shall be got thro'. In the criminal law, the principle of retaliation is much criticized here, particularly in the case of Rape. They think the punishment indecent & unjustifiable. I should be for altering it, but for a different reason: that is on account of the temptation women would be under to make it the instrument of vengeance against an inconstant lord, & of disappointment to a rival. Are our courts of justice open for the recovery of British debts according to the Septennial Act? the principles of that act can be justified: but the total stoppage of justice cannot. The removal of the negroes from New York would duly give cause for stopping some of the last payments, if the British government should refuse satisfaction, which however I think they will not do.

I thank you for your communications in Natural history. The several instances of trees &c found far below the surface of the earth, as in the case of Mr. Hay's well, seem to set the reason of man at defiance.

Another Theory of the earth has been contrived by one Whitford, not absolutely reasonable, but somewhat more so than any that has yet appeared. It is full of interesting facts, which however being inadequate to his theory, he is obliged to supply them from time to time by begging questions. It is worth your getting from London. If I can be useful to you in ordering books from London you know you may command me. You had better send me the duplicate volume of the Encyclopedie. I will take care to send you the proper one. I have many more livraisons for you, & have made some other inconsiderable purchases for you in this way. But I shall not send them till the spring, as a winter passage is bad for books.

I reserve myself till that time therefore to give you an account of the execution of your several commissions, only observing that the watch will not be finished till the spring & that it will be necessary for me to detain her some time on trial, because it often happens that a watch, looking well to the eye, & faithfully made, goes badly at first on account of some little circumstance which escapes the eye of the workman when he puts her together, & which he could easily rectify.

With respect to the proposition about the purchase of lands, I had just before made the experiment desired. It was to borrow money for aiding the opening of the Potomac, which was proposed to me by Gen'l. Washington. I had the benefit of his name, & the foundation of a special Act of Assembly. I lodged the papers in the hands of Mr. Grand to try to obtain Money on loan at 6. per cent, assuring him that the securities should be made completely satisfactory to the lenders. After long trial he told me it could not be done. That this government has always occasion to borrow more money than can be lent in this country: that they pay 6. percent per annum in quarterly payments, & with a religious punctuality: that besides this they give very considerable douceurs to the lenders: that everyone therefore would prefer having his money here rather than on the other side the Atlantic, where distance, want of punctuality, & a habitual protection of the debtor would be against them. There is therefore but one way in which I see any chance of executing your views. Monied men sometimes talk of investing money in American lands. Some such might be willing to ensure an advantageous investiture by interesting trust-worthy characters in the purchase, & to do this, might be willing to advance the whole Money, being properly secured. On this head no satisfaction should be wanting which I could give them: and as persons with these views sometimes advise with me, I shall be attentive to propose to them this plan. I consider its success however as only possible, not probable.

To Charles Thomson[1]
Paris, Dec. 17th, 1786
Dear Sir,

A dislocation of my right wrist has for three or four months past disabled me from writing except with my left hand, which was too slow and awkward to be employed but in cases of necessity. I begin to have so much use of my wrist as to be able to write, but it is slowly and in pain. I take the first moment I can, however, to acknowledge the receipt of your letters of Aug. 6, July 8, and 30. In one of these you say you have not been able to learn whether in the new mills in London, steam is the immediate mover of the machinery or raises water to move it. It is the immediate mover. The power of this agent, tho' long known, is but now beginning to be applied to the various purposes of which it is susceptible. You observe that Whitford supposes it to have been the agent which, bursting the earth, threw it up into mountains and valleys. You ask me what I think of his book. I find in it many interesting facts brought together, and many ingenious commentaries on them, but there are great chasms in his facts, and consequently in his reasoning; these he fills up with suppositions which may be as reasonably denied as granted. A skeptical reader, therefore, like myself, is left in the lurch. I acknowledge, however, he makes more use of fact than any other writer of a theory of the earth. But I give one answer to all theorists, That is as follows: they all suppose the earth a created existence; they must suppose a Creator, then, and that he possessed power and wisdom to a great degree. As he intended the earth for the habitation of animals and vegetables, is it reasonable to suppose he

---

[1] As previously indicated, Charles Thomson was an Irish émigré and political leader during the American Revolution. He served as secretary of the Continental Congress (1774–89) and is credited as being the moving spirit in the committee that obtained the design for the Great Seal of the United States. (Wood 2009, 555)

made two jobs of his Creation? That he first made a chaotic lump and set it into motion, and then, waiting ages necessary to form itself, that when it had done this he stepped in a second time to create the animals and plants which were to inhabit it? As a hand of a Creator is to be called in it may as well be called in at one stage of the process as another. We may as well suppose he created the earth at once nearly in the state in which we see it — fit for the preservation of the beings he placed on it. But it is said we have a proof that he did not create it in its solid form, but in a state of fluidity, because its present shape of an oblate spheroid is precisely that which a fluid mass revolving on its axis would assume; but I suppose the same equilibrium between gravity and centrifugal force which would determine a fluid mass into the form of an oblate spheroid would determine the wise Creator of that mass if he made it in a solid state, to give it the same spherical form. A revolving fluid will continue to change its shape till it attains that in which its principles of contrary motion are balanced; for if you suppose them not balanced it will change its form. Now the balanced form is necessary for the preservation of a revolving solid. The Creator, therefore, of a revolving solid would make it an oblate spheroid, that figure alone admitting a perfect equilibrium. He would make it in that form for another reason; that is, to prevent a shifting of the axis of rotation. Had he created the earth perfectly spherical its axis might have been perpetually shifting by the influence of the other bodies of the system, and by placing the inhabitants of the earth successively under its poles it might have been depopulated; whereas being spheroidal it has but one axis on which it can revolve in equilibrio. Suppose the axis of the earth to shift 45°, then cut it into 180 slices, making every section in the plane of a circle of latitude perpendicular to the axis: every one of these slices except the equatorial one would be unbalanced, as there would be more matter on one side of its axis than on the other. There would be but one diameter drawn through such a slice which would divide it into two equal parts; on every other possible diameter the parts would hang unequal; this would produce an irregularity in the diurnal rotation. We may therefore conclude it impossible for the poles of the earth to shift if it was made spheroidically, and that it would be made spheroidal, tho' solid to obtain this end. I use this reasoning only on the supposition that the earth has had a beginning. I am sure I shall read your conjectures on this subject with great pleasure, tho' I bespeak beforehand a right to indulge my natural incredulity and skepticism. The pain in which I write awakens me here from my reverie and obliges me to conclude with compliments to Mrs. Thomson and assurances to yourself of the esteem and affection with which I am, Dear Sir, your friend and servant.

P. S. Since writing the preceding I have had a conversation on the subject of the steam mills with the famous Bolton, to whom those of London belong, and who is here at this time. He compares the effect of steam with that of horses in the following manner: 6 horses, aided with the most advantageous combination of the mechanical powers hitherto tried will grind 6 bushels of flour in an hour, at the end of which time they are all in a foam and must rest. They can work thus 6 horses in the 24, grinding 36 bushels of flour which is six to each horse for the 24 hours. His steam mill in London consumes 120 bushels of coal in 24 hours, turns 10 pairs of stones which grind 8 bushels of flour an hour each, which is 1920 bushels in the 24 hours. This makes a peck and a half of coal perform exactly as much as a horse in one day can perform.

To Nicholas Lewis[1]
Paris, 19 Dec., 1786
Dear Sir,

I have duly received your favors of March 14 & July 16. My last to you was of Apr. 22, from London. I am obliged to you for the particular account you give me of my affairs, and the state of the cash account made out by the steward. His articles however were generally so shortly expressed as to be quite unintelligible to me. Of this kind are the following.

>To James Foster and Benjamin Harris pr. Carter Braxton. £131.10
>To Richard James and Wm. Clark for cash. 20.
>To Joseph Ashlin and C. Stone for cash at different times. 74.10.2
>To Vincent Markham and Richd. James pr. Doctr. Gilmer. 385.0
>To Tandy Rice and Charles Rice for cash. 69.18.8½
>To David Mullings and Henry Mullings for cash. 31.15
>To Carter Braxton pr. settlement by Colo. Lewis. 119.12.8
>To do. for cash. 11.17.

The steward intended this account for my information, but mentioning only names & sums without saying in some general way why those sums were paid to those names, leaves me uninformed. However the account having passed under your eye leaves me also without a doubt that the articles are right. I suppose, in the 1st article for instance, that Carter Braxton (to whom I was indebted for a doz. bottles of oil only) stands in the place of some person to whom I owed £131.10, and so of the rest, as you give me reason to hope that all other debts will now be paid off. I am in hopes the shoulder can be laid solidly to those of Farrell & Jones, & Kippen & Co. to these objects. I would wish to apply the whole profits of the estate, except the maintenance & education of my sister Carr's two sons, & the interest of my sister Nancy's debt. I shall propose therefore to Jones & McCaul the paying them an annual sum till their debts shall be discharged, & I have asked the favor of Mr. Eppes, to consult with you & let me know what

---

[1] Nicholas Lewis, whom he had left in charge of his affairs at home, had sent him a gloomy accounting which disclosed that the entire profits, after expenses, concluding that the profits "would be no more than the hire of the few Negroes hired out would amount to." Would it not be better, Jefferson asks Lewis in despair, for him to hire out more of his slaves, provided good masters could be found? Perhaps, even, to rent out "the plantations & all, if proper assurance can be provided for the good usage of everything? I am miserable," he burst forth, "till I owe not a shilling: the moment that shall be the case I shall feel myself at liberty to do something for the comfort of my slaves." Jefferson was eventually compelled to ask his chief creditors for additional time. He had sold some of his slaves to put himself in a position to take care of them, he said; if they agreed to take installments-without interest for the war years, however-he would commence payments on an annual basis. (Schachner 1957, 327)

sum you think I may engage to pay them on an average of one year with another? and that you will be so good as to let me know this as soon as possible that I may arrange the matter by agreement with them. You mention that the price of tobo [tobacco] is at 22/6. I can always be sure of receiving for it delivered at Havre 36/ Virginia money for the Virginia hundred weight. Whenever therefore the price with you is less than this after deducting freight, insurance, commission & port charges, if a conveyance can be obtained for it to Havre it would be better to ship it to me. You may at the same time draw bills on me for the whole amount taking care that they shall not be presented till the tobacco is arrived at Havre, & that there be such an usence in them as will give me time to sell it & receive the money, or, for so much of the tobacco as can be destined to Jones & McCaul, no bills need be drawn, as I can remit them the proceeds. In all this however you will act according to your own judgment which is much better than mine. I cannot help thinking however that it might be worth the experiment to ship me at any rate a small adventure to see how it will turn out, but Havre is the only port at which I could manage it.

I observe in your letter of March 14. after stating the amount of the crop & deducting Overseer's & steward's parts, transportation, negroes clothes, tools, medicine & taxes, the profits of the whole estate would be no more than the hire of the few negroes hired out would amount to. Would it be better to hire more where good masters could be got? Would it be better to hire plantations & all, if proper assurance can be provided for the good usage of everything? I am miserable till I owe not a shilling: the moment that shall be the case I shall feel myself at liberty to do something for the comfort of my slaves. * * * I am much obliged to you for your attention to my trees & grass. The latter is one of the principal pillars on which I shall rely for subsistence when I shall be at liberty to try projects without injury to anybody. The negro girl which I sent to Nancy Bolling was not sent as a gift from me. I understood she was claimed under a supposed gift from my mother, which tho' I thought ill-founded I did not choose to enter into disagreeable discussions about. I meant therefore to abandon my right to her and I have no further pretensions to her. With my letter from London, I send under the care of Mr. Fulwar Skipwith a trunk containing some little matters for Mr. Lewis & my sister Nancy. I hope it got safe to hand. I have long had (as I once wrote you) a pretty little piece of furniture, a clock, which I meant for Mrs. Lewis. Tho it is so small that it might almost be put into a pocket, I have as yet found it impossible to get a safe conveyance for it. The case being of marble, & very slender, it cannot bear transportation but by water. I am obliged therefore to wait till some person shall be going from Havre to Richmond. Monsr. Doradour was to have carried it, but he was not able. He is safely returned to his family & in good humor with our country. He made a considerable tramontane purchase. His trip upon the whole turned out better than I had expected. I am glad on account of Madame de Doradour who is a lady of great merit. I have never seen her since the departure of her husband; but I suppose she will decline further views on America. I shall endeavor to send with this a packet of the seeds of trees which I would wish Anthony to sow in a large nursery noting well their names. There will be a little Spanish St. Foin, represented to me as a very precious grass in a hot country. I would have it sowed in one of the vacant lots of my grass ground. I have but just room to render you a thousand thanks for your goodness, to make as many apologies for the details I trouble you with, to recommend myself to the friendly remembrance of Mrs. Lewis & to assure you of the sincere esteem with which I am, Sir &c.

To William Carmichael[1]
Paris, Decr. 26, 1786
Dear Sir,

My *Notes on Virginia*, having been hastily written, need abundance of corrections. Two or three of these are so material that I am reprinting a few leaves to substitute for the old. As soon as these shall be ready, I will beg your acceptance of a copy. I shall be proud to be permitted to send a copy, also, to the Count de Campomanes as a tribute to his science & his virtues. You will find in them that the Natural bridge had found an admirer in me also. I should be happy to make with you a tour of the curiosities you will find therein mentioned. That kind of pleasure surpasses much in my estimation whatever I find on this side the Atlantic. I sometimes think of building a little hermitage at the Natural bridge (for it is my property) and of passing there a part of the year at least. I have received American papers to the 1st of November. Some tumultuous meetings of the people have taken place in the Eastern states, i.e. one in Massachusetts, one in Connecticut, & one in N Hampsh. Their principal demand was a respite in the judiciary proceedings. No injury was done however in a single instance to the person or property of any one, nor did the tumult continue 24 hours in any one instance. In Massachusetts this was owing to the discretion which the malcontents still preserved, in Connecticut & N Hampshire, the body of the

---

[1] Jefferson realized that there were serious problems in the United States that detracted from his presentation of America's achievements. His European friends saw the negative as well as the positive features of the new republic. Economic dislocation and social unrest which followed in the wake of the Revolution tempered the examples of progress he had so proudly cited. The government of the Confederation lacked the necessary powers to cope with the management of thirteen autonomous states. The result of its structural weakness was the possibility that democratic rebellion on the one hand and monarchical reaction on the other would destroy the fruits of the Revolution. Jefferson understood this situation, but fearful of alienating America's liberal supporters in Europe, hesitated between favoring a movement for stronger central government that might provoke the charge of betrayal from the doctrinaire reformers, and advocating the continuation of a powerless government that only invited chaos at home and contempt abroad. Here, in this letter, Jefferson's reaction to incipient civil war in Massachusetts revealed the conflict he saw between America's need to promote an image of stability in order to establish financial credit in Europe and her equally great need to demonstrate that in the New World the European example of curtailing the liberties of citizens would not be followed. He regarded Shays' Rebellion with mixed feelings, calling the rebels malcontents and recognizing the dangers awaiting American institutions at the hands of mobs and demagogues, yet understanding the farmers' reasons for rebellion. (Kaplan 1967, 24)

people rose in support of government & obliged the malcontents to go to their homes. In the last mentioned state they seized about 40, who were in jail for trial. It is believed this incident will strengthen our government. Those people are not entirely without excuse. Before the war those states depended on their whale oil & fish. The former was consumed in England, & much of the latter in the Mediterranean. The heavy duties on American whale oil now required in England exclude it from that market; & the Algerines exclude them from bringing their fish into the Mediterranean. France is opening her port for their oil, but in the meanwhile their antient debts are pressing them & they have nothing to pay with. The Massachusetts assembly too, in their zeal for paying their public debt had laid a tax too heavy to be paid in the circumstances of their state. The Indians seem disposed to make war on us. These complicated causes determined Congress to increase their force to 2000 men. The latter was the sole object avowed, yet the former entered for something into the measure. However I am satisfied the good sense of the people is the strongest army our government can ever have, & that it will not fail them. The Commercial convention at Annapolis was not full enough to do business. They found too their appointments too narrow, being confined to the article of commerce. They have proposed a meeting in Philadelphia in May, and that it may be authorized to propose amendments of whatever is defective in the federal constitution.

Congress have at length determined on a coinage. Their money unit is a dollar & the pieces above & below that are in decimal proportion. You will see their scheme in all the papers, except that the proportion they established between gold & silver is misstated at upwards of 20. to 1. instead of about 15¼ to 1.

It is believed that this court has patched up an accommodation for the moment between Russia & the Porte. In Holland they find greater difficulties. The present King of Prussia is zealous for the Stadholder, & the fear is of driving him into the Austrian scale of the European balance. Such a weight as this, shifted, would destroy all equilibriums and the preponderance once in favor of the restless powers of the north, the peace would soon be disturbed.

When I was in England I formed a portable copying press on the principle of the large one they make there for copying letters. I had a model made there & it has answered perfectly. A workman here has made several from that model. The itinerant temper of your court will, I think, render one of these useful to you. You must therefore do me the favor to accept of one. I have it now in readiness, & shall send it by the way of Bayonne to the care of Mr. Alexander there, unless Don Miguel de Lardizabal can carry it with him.

My hand admonishes me it is time to stop, & that I must defer writing to Mr. Barclay till to-morrow.

1787

To Alexander McCaul[1]
Paris, Jan. 4, 1787
Dear Sir,

In the letter which I had the honor of addressing you from London on the 19th of April 1786, I informed you that I had left my estate in the hands of a Mr. Eppes & a Mr. Lewis, who were first to clear off some debts which had been necessarily contracted during the war, & afterwards to apply the whole profits to the payment of my debt to you (by which I mean that to the several firms with which you were connected) and of my part of a debt due from Mr. Wayles's estate to Farrell & Jones of Bristol. Being anxious to begin the paiment of these two debts, & finding that it would be too long postponed if the residuary one's were to be paid merely from the annual profits of the estate, a number of slaves have been sold, & I have lately received information from Messrs. Eppes & Lewis that the proceeds of that sale with the profits of the estate to the end of 1786 would pay off the whole of the residuary debts. As we are now therefore clear of embarrassments to pursue our principal object, I am desirous of arranging with you such just & practicable conditions as will ascertain to you the receipt of your debt, & give me the satisfaction of knowing that you are contented. What the laws of Virginia are or may be, will in no wise influence my conduct. Substantial justice is my object, as decided by reason, & not by authority or compulsion.

The article of interest may make a difficulty. I had the honor of observing to you, in my former letter that I thought it just I should pay it for all the time preceding the war, & all the time subsequent to it, but that for the time during the war I did not consider myself as bound in justice to pay. This includes the period from the commencement of hostilities Apr. 19, 1775, to their cessation April 19, 1783, being exactly eight years. To the reasons against this paiment which apply in favor of the whole mass of American debtors, I added the peculiar circumstance of having already lost the debt, principal & interest, by endeavoring to pay it by the sale of lands, & by the depreciation of their price; & also a second loss of an equal sum by Ld. Cornwallis's barbarous & useless depredations. I will therefore refer you to that letter, to save the repetition here of those reasons which absolve me in justice from the paiment of this portion of interest. In law, our courts have uniformly decided that the treaty of peace stipulates the paiment of the principal only & not of any interest whatever.

---

[1] Jefferson was compelled to ask his chief creditors (McCaul included) for additional time. He had sold some of his slaves to put himself in a position to take care of them, he said; if they agreed to take installments — without interest for the war years, however — he would commence payments on an annual basis. With the best intentions in the world, Jefferson did not find it easy to rid himself of the incubus of these prewar debts. In the first place, the English firms were unwilling to give up their claim for war-years interest; in the second, Jefferson always overestimated the net income of his lands. It never lived up to expectations. Nor was it the fault of his managers back home; even when he returned and took over personal control, no year yielded what, at the beginning of that year, he was certain it would. (Schachner 1957, 327)

This article being once settled, I would propose to divide the clear proceeds of my estate (in which there are from 80 to 100 laboring slaves) between yourself & Farrell & Jones, one third to you and two thirds to them: & that the crop of this present year 1787 shall constitute the first payment. That crop you know cannot be got to the warehouse completely till May of the next year, & I presume, that three months more will be little enough to send it to Europe or to sell it in Virginia & remit the money. So that I could not safely answer for placing the proceeds in your hands till the month of August, & so annually every August afterwards till the debt shall be paid. It will always be both my interest and my wish to get it to you as much sooner as possible & probably a part of it may always be paid some months sooner. If the assigning the profits in general terms may seem to you too vague, I am willing to fix the annual paiment at a sum certain. But that I may not fall short of my engagement, I shall name it somewhat less than I suppose may be counted on. I shall fix your part at two hundred pounds sterling annually, and as you know our crops of tobacco to be uncertain, I should reserve a right, if they should fall short one year, to make it up the ensuing one, without being supposed to have failed in my engagement, but I would be obliged every second year to pay any arrearages of the preceding one together with the full sum for the current year: so that once in every two years the annual paiment should be fully paid up.

I do not know what the balance is: having for a long time before the war had no settlement, yet there can be no difficulty in making that settlement, & in the mean while the paiments may proceed without affecting the right of either party to have a just settlement.

If you think proper to accede to these propositions, be so good as to say so at the foot of a copy of this letter, on my receipt of that, I will send you an acknowledgement of it, which shall render this present letter obligatory on me for the paiment of the debt before mentioned & interest at the epochs & in the proportions before mentioned excepting always the interest during the war. This done, you may count on my faithful execution of it.

I avail myself of this, as of every other occasion of recalling myself to your friendly recollection, & of assuring you of the sentiments of perfect esteem and attachment with which I am, &c.

To William Jones[1]

---

[1] Jefferson, who was himself never able to live within his means, was in no position to perceive that the merchants were as dependent on the planters — many of whom had in effect been supported by them for ten or fifteen years prior to the Revolution — as the planters were upon them, since a merchant who tried to limit one man's credit risked alienating all his other customers, most of whom were related. But there is no way of settling the final "justice" of a whole society's view of its own experience. What is certain is that for a Virginian, the ideological consequences of this particular experience went very deep. Debt and the very idea of debt, merchants and the very idea of a mercantile way of life, were inseparable from the Anglophobia of the Revolution. Some historians believe Jefferson overestimated the number of fleeing slaves by a factor of five, with one study suggesting that the number of Virginia blacks who fled was less

Paris, Jan. 5, 1787

Sir,

When I had the pleasure of seeing you in London, I mentioned to you that the Affairs of Mr. Wayles's estate were left to be ultimately settled by Mr. Eppes, the only acting executor; that I had left in his hands also & in those of a Mr. Lewis the part of Mr. Wayles's estate which came to me, together with my own: that they were first to clear off some debts which had been necessarily contracted during the war, & would after that apply the whole profits to the paiment of my part of Mr. Wayles's debt to you, & to a debt of mine to Kippen & Co., of Glasgow. Being anxious to begin the paiment of these two debts & finding that it would be too long postponed if the residuary ones were to be paid merely from the annual profits of the estate, a number of slaves have been sold, & I have lately received information from Messrs. Eppes & Lewis that the proceeds of that sale, with the profits of the estate to the end of 1786 would pay off the whole of the residuary debts. As we are now therefore clear of embarrassment to pursue our principal object, I am desirous of arranging with you, such just & practicable conditions as will ascertain to you the terms at which you will receive my part of your debt, & give me the satisfaction of knowing that you are contented. What the laws of Virginia are, or may be, will in no wise influence my conduct. Substantial justice is my object, as decided by reason, & not by authority or compulsion.

The first question which arises is as to the article of interest. For all the time preceding the war, & all subsequent to it, I think it reasonable that interest should be paid; but equally unreasonable during the war. Interest is a compensation for the use of money. Your money in my hands is in the form of lands & negroes, from these, during the war, no use, no profits could be derived, tobacco is the article they produce. That can only be turned into money at a foreign market. But the moment it went out of our ports for that purpose, it was captured either by the king's ships or by those of individuals. The consequence was that tobacco, worth from twenty to thirty shillings the hundred, sold generally in Virginia during the War for five shillings. This price it is known will not maintain the laborer & pay his taxes. There was no surplus of profit then to pay an interest, in the mean while we stood insurers of the lives of the laborers & of the ultimate issue of the war. He who attempted during the war to remit either his principal or interest, must have expected to remit three times to make one paiment; because

---

than six thousand and that the total throughout the United States during the Revolutionary War was closer to twenty thousand. In this letter to William Jones, an English maker of optical and other scientific instruments, who had Thomas Jefferson among his customers, Jefferson may have exaggerated the number of slaves taken from all plantations in Virginia to bolster the complaints of Virginians who had difficulty paying debts to the British stemming from prewar agreements. Indeed, in referring to a debt he owed to British merchants, Jefferson wrote six years after Cornwallis laid waste to Elk Hill that "the useless and barbarous injury he did me in that instance was more than would have paid your debt, principal and interest." At the least, Jefferson argued, he shouldn't be charged interest for an eight-year wartime period. (Elkins and McKitrick 1995, 92; Kranish 2010, 293)

it is supposed that two out of three parts of the shipments were taken. It was not possible then for the debtor to derive any profit from the money which might enable him to pay an interest, nor yet to get rid of the principal by remitting it to his creditor. With respect to the Creditors in Great Britain they mostly turned their attention to privateering, and arming the vessels they had before employed in trading with us. They captured on the seas, not only the produce of the farms of their debtors, but of those of the whole state. They thus paid themselves by capture more than their annual interest, and we lost more. Some merchants indeed did not engage in privateering. These lost their interest. But we did not gain it. It fell into the hands of their countrymen. It cannot therefore be demanded of us. As between these merchants & their debtors it is a case where, a loss being incurred, each party may justifiably endeavor to shift it from himself, each has an equal right to avoid it, one party can never expect the other to yield a thing to which he has as good a right as the demander, we even think he has a better right than the demander in the present instance. This loss has been occasioned by the fault of the nation which was Creditor. Our right to avoid it then stands on less exceptionable ground than theirs, but it will be said that each party thought the other the aggressor. In these disputes there is but one umpire & that has decided the question where the world in general thought the right laid.

Besides these reasons in favor of the general mass of debtors, I have some peculiar to my own case. In the year 1776, before a shilling of paper money was issued I sold lands to the amount of £4200. In order to pay these two debts I offered the bonds of the purchasers to your agent Mr. Evans, if he would acquit me, & accept of the purchasers as debtors in my place. They were as sure as myself had he done it. These debts, being turned over to you, would have been saved to you by the treaty of peace, but he declined it. Great sums of paper money were afterwards issued. This depreciated, and paiment was made me in this money when it was but a shadow. Our laws do not entitle their own citizens to require repayment in these cases, tho' the treaty authorizes the British creditor to do it. Here then I lost the principal and interest once. Again, Ld. Cornwallis encamped 10 days on an estate of mine at Elk Island, having his headquarters in my house he burned all the tobacco houses and barns on the farm. With the produce of the former year in them, he burnt all the enclosures, & wasted the fields in which the crop of that year was growing: (it was the month of June) he killed or carried off every living animal, cutting the throats of those which were too young for service. Of the slaves he carried away thirty. The useless & barbarous injury he did me in that instance was more than would have paid your debt, principal & interest. Thus I lost it a second time. Still I lay my shoulder assiduously to the paiment of it a third time. In doing this however I think yourself will be of opinion I am authorized in justice to clear it of every article not demandable in strict right: of this nature I consider interest during the war.

Another question is, as to the paper money I deposited in the treasury of Virginia towards the discharge of this debt. I before observed that I had sold lands to the amount of £4200 before a shilling of paper money was emitted, with a view to pay this debt. I received this money in depreciated paper. The state was then calling on those who owed money to British subjects to bring it into the treasury engaging to pay a like sum to the creditor at the end of the war. I carried the identical money therefore to the Treasury, where it was applied, as all the money of the same description was, to the support of the war. Subsequent events have been such that the state cannot, & ought not to pay the same nominal sum in gold or silver which they received in paper, nor is it certain what they will do. My intention being & having always been, that, whatever the state decides, you shall receive my part of the debt fully, I am ready to remove all difficulty arising from this deposit, to take back to myself the demand against the state, & to consider the deposit as originally made for myself & not for you.

These two articles of interest & paper money being thus settled, I would propose to divide the clear proceeds of the estate (in which there are from 80 to 100 laboring slaves) between yourself & Kippen & Co, two thirds to you and one third to them, & that the crop of this present year 1787 shall constitute the first paiment. That crop you know cannot be got to the warehouse completely till May of the next year, & I suppose that three months more will be little enough to send it to Europe, or to sell it in Virginia & remit the money, so that I could not safely answer for placing the proceeds in your hands till the month of August, and so annually every August afterwards till the debt shall be paid. It will always be both my interest & my wish to get it to you as much sooner as possible, & probably a part of it may always be paid some months sooner. If the assigning of the profits in general terms may seem to you too vague, I am willing to fix the annual paiment at a sum certain, but that I may not fall short of my engagement, I shall name it somewhat less than I suppose may be counted on. I shall fix your part at four hundred pounds sterling annually, and as you know our crops of tobacco to be uncertain, I should reserve a right if they fall short one year to make it up the ensuing one, without being supposed to have failed in my engagement. But every other year at least all arrearages shall be fully paid up.

My part of this debt of Mr. Wayles's estate being one third, I should require that in proportion as I pay my third, I shall stand discharged as to the other two thirds. So that the paiment of every hundred pounds shall discharge me as to three hundred pounds of the undivided debt. The other gentlemen have equal means of paying, equal desires, and more skill in affairs. Their parts of the debt therefore are at least as sure as mine: & my great object is, in case of any accident to myself, to leave my family uninvolved with any matters whatever.

I do not know what the balance of this debt is. The last acct. current I saw was before the war, making the whole balance, principal & interest somewhere about nine thousand pounds: & after this there were upwards of four hundred hogshead of tobacco & some paiments in money to be credited. However this settlement can admit of no difficulty: & in the meantime the payments may proceed without affecting the right of either party to have a just settlement.

Upon the whole then I propose that on your part you relinquish the claim to interest during the war, say from the commencement of hostilities, April 19, 1775 to their cessation April 19, 1783. being exactly eight years; and that in proportion as I pay my third I shall be acquitted as to the other two thirds. On my part, I take on myself the loss of the paper money deposited in the Treasury, I agree to pay interest previous & subsequent to the war, and oblige myself to remit to you for that & the principal four hundred pounds sterling annually till my third of the whole debt shall be fully paid; & I will begin these paiments in August of the next year.

If you think proper to accede to these propositions, be so good as to say so at the foot of a copy of this letter. On my receipt of that I will send you an acknowledgement of it, which shall render this present letter obligatory on me. In which case you may count on my faithful execution of this undertaking.

To Edward Carrington[1]
Paris, Jan. 16, 1787
Dear Sir,

Uncertain whether you might be at New York at the moment of Colo. Franks' arrival, I have enclosed my private letters for Virginia under cover to our delegation in general, which otherwise I would have taken the liberty to enclose particularly to you, as best acquainted with the situation of the persons to whom they are addressed. Should this find you at New York, I will still ask your attention to them. The two large packages addressed to Colo. N. Lewis contain seeds, not valuable enough to pay postage, but which I would wish to be sent by the stage, or any similar quick conveyance. The letters to Colo. Lewis & Mr. Eppes (who take care of my affairs) are particularly interesting to me. The package for Colo. Richd. Cary our judge of Admiralty near Hampton, contains seeds & roots, not to be sent by Post. Whether they had better go by the stage, or by water, you will be the best judge. I beg your pardon for giving you this trouble. But my situation & your goodness will I hope excuse it. In my letter to Mr. Jay, I have mentioned the meeting of the Notables appointed for the 29th inst. It is now put off to the 7th or 8th of next month. This event, which will hardly excite any attention in America, is deemed here the most important one which has taken place in their civil line during the present century. Some promise their country great things from it, some nothing. Our friend de La Fayette was placed on the list originally. Afterwards his name disappeared; but finally was reinstated. This shews that his character here is not considered as an indifferent one; and

---

[1] Peace, and order, and economy were what Jefferson was interested in preserving — and prosperity was the stable reward hoped for from their conjunction. The generalized form of class opposition is perhaps the most fundamental argument in Jefferson's artillery. It is the continuous background of his various complaints about bureaucracy and privilege. Its importance cannot be minimized, since it is wholly in accord with the theory of republicanism of the populist form to which Jefferson adhered. Good republican society must avoid above all, as stated in this letter to his fellow Virginian and Society of the Cincinnati member, Edward Carrington, "the general prey of the rich on the poor." This, in Jefferson's opinion, is exactly what ruined the "governments of Europe," which had adopted the terrible practice of dividing their subjects into a sheep like majority, while the governors, the wealthy, and the priests were the wolves who fed upon them.' (Koch 1957, 174.)

that it excites agitation. His education in our school has drawn on him a very jealous eye from a court whose principles are the most absolute despotism. But I hope he has nearly passed his crisis. The King, who is a good man, is favorably disposed towards him: & he is supported by powerful family connections, & by the public good will. He is the youngest man of the Notables except one whose office placed him on the list.

The Count de Vergennes has within these ten days had a very severe attack of what is deemed an unfixed gout. He has been well enough however to do business to-day. But anxieties for him are not yet quieted. He is a great & good minister, and an accident to him might endanger the peace of Europe.

The tumults in America, I expected would have produced in Europe an unfavorable opinion of our political state. But it has not. On the contrary, the small effect of these tumults seems to have given more confidence in the firmness of our governments. The interposition of the people themselves on the side of government has had a great effect on the opinion here. I am persuaded myself that the good sense of the people will always be found to be the best army. They may be led astray for a moment, but will soon correct themselves. The people are the only censors of their governors: and even their errors will tend to keep these to the true principles of their institution. To punish these errors too severely would be to suppress the only safeguard of the public liberty. The way to prevent these irregular interpositions of the people is to give them full information of their affairs thro' the channel of the public papers, & to contrive that those papers should penetrate the whole mass of the people. The basis of our governments being the opinion of the people, the very first object should be to keep that right; and were it left to me to decide whether we should have a government without newspapers or newspapers without a government, I should not hesitate a moment to prefer the latter. But I should mean that every man should receive those papers & be capable of reading them. I am convinced that those societies (as the Indians) which live without government enjoy in their general mass an infinitely greater degree of happiness than those who live under the European governments. Among the former, public opinion is in the place of law, & restrains morals as powerfully as laws ever did anywhere. Among the latter, under pretense of governing they have divided their nations into two classes, wolves & sheep. I do not exaggerate. This is a true picture of Europe. Cherish therefore the spirit of our people, and keep alive their attention. Do not be too severe upon their errors, but reclaim them by enlightening them. If once they become inattentive to the public affairs, you & I, & Congress & Assemblies, judges & governors shall all become wolves. It seems to be the law of our general nature, in spite of individual exceptions; and experience declares that man is the only animal which devours his own kind, for I can apply no milder term to the governments of Europe, and to the general prey of the rich on the poor. The want of news has led me into disquisition instead of narration, forgetting you have every day enough of that. I shall be happy to hear from you sometimes, only observing that whatever passes thro' the post is read, & that when you write what should be read by myself only, you must be so good as to confide your letter to some passenger or officer of the packet. I will ask your permission to write to you sometimes, and to assure you of the esteem & respect with which I have honor to be Dear Sir your most obedient & most humble servt.

To James Madison[1]
Paris, Jan 30, 1787
Dear Sir,

My last to you was of the 16th of Dec, since which I have received yours of Nov 25, & Dec 4, which afforded me, as your letters always do, a treat on matters public, individual & economical. I am impatient to learn your sentiments on the late troubles in the Eastern states. So far as I have yet seen, they do not appear to threaten serious consequences. Those states have suffered by the stoppage of the channels of their commerce, which have not yet found other issues. This must render money scarce, and make the people uneasy. This uneasiness has produced acts absolutely unjustifiable; but I hope they will provoke no severities from their governments. A consciousness of those in power that their administration of the public affairs has been honest, may perhaps produce too great a degree of indignation: and those characters wherein fear predominates over hope may apprehend too much from these instances of irregularity. They may conclude too hastily that nature has formed man insusceptible of any other government but that of force, a conclusion not founded in truth, nor experience. Societies exist under three forms sufficiently distinguishable. 1. Without government, as among our Indians. 2. Under governments wherein the will of everyone has a just influence, as is the case in England in a slight degree, and in our states, in a great one. 3. Under governments of force: as is the case in all other monarchies and in most of the other republics. To have an idea of the curse of existence under these last, they must be seen. It is a government of wolves over sheep. It is a problem, not clear in my mind, that the first condition is not the best. But I believe it to be inconsistent with any great degree of population. The second state has a great deal of good in it. The mass of mankind under that enjoys a precious degree of liberty & happiness. It has it's evils too: the principal of which is the turbulence to which it is subject. But weigh this against the oppressions of monarchy, and it becomes nothing. Malo periculosam libertatem quam quietam servitutem. Even this evil is productive of good. It prevents the degeneracy of government, and nourishes a general attention to the public affairs. I hold it that

---

[1] This letter to Madison reflects Jefferson's remarkable rhetoric about the virtues of rebellion. "I hold it," he claimed, "that a little rebellion, now and then, is a good thing, and as necessary in the political world as storms in the physical." Written in early 1787 — and doubtless in reaction to political events in Paris and America (this time to Shays' rebellion) — Jefferson continued to believe that the people's censorship of government was the only way to correct tyranny and injustice. Even if the people were wrong in rising against some governmental act, the action would call attention to public affairs. "I hold that a little rebellion now and then is a good thing," he wrote to Madison, "and is necessary for the sound health of government." But it seems that Jefferson is advocating not liberty but license....thoughts grounded far less in the soil of Jacobin France than that of prerevolutionary Virginia. (Young 1996, 83; Hatzenbuehler 1988, 31)

a little rebellion now and then is a good thing, & as necessary in the political world as storms in the physical. Unsuccessful rebellions indeed generally establish the encroachments on the rights of the people which have produced them. An observation of this truth should render honest republican governors so mild in their punishment of rebellions, as not to discourage them too much. It is a medicine necessary for the sound health of government. If these transactions give me no uneasiness, I feel very differently at another piece of intelligence, to wit, the possibility that the navigation of the Mississippi may be abandoned to Spain. I never had any interest westward of the Alleghany; & I never will have any. But I have had great opportunities of knowing the character of the people who inhabit that country. And I will venture to say that the act which abandons the navigation of the Mississippi is an act of separation between the Eastern & Western country. It is a relinquishment of five parts out of eight of the territory of the United States, an abandonment of the fairest subject for the payment of our public debts, & the chaining those debts on our own necks in perpetuum. I have the utmost confidence in the honest intentions of those who concur in this measure; but I lament their want of acquaintance with the character & physical advantages of the people who, right or wrong, will suppose their interests sacrificed on this occasion to the contrary interests of that part of the confederacy in possession of present power. If they declare themselves a separate people, we are incapable of a single effort to retain them. Our citizens can never be induced, either as militia or as soldiers, to go there to cut the throats of their own brothers & sons, or rather to be themselves the subjects instead of the perpetrators of the parricide. Nor would that country requite the cost of being retained against the will of its inhabitants, could it be done. But it cannot be done. They are able already to rescue the navigation of the Mississippi out of the hands of Spain, & to add New Orleans to their own territory. They will be joined by the inhabitants of Louisiana. This will bring on a war between them & Spain; and that will produce the question with us whether it will not be worth our while to become parties with them in the war, in order to reunite them with us, & thus correct our error? & were I to permit my forebodings to go one step further, I should predict that the inhabitants of the U S would force their rulers to take the affirmative of that question. I wish I may be mistaken in all these opinions.

We have for some time expected that the Chevalier de la Luzerne would obtain a promotion in the diplomatic line, by being appointed to some of the courts where this country keeps an ambassador. But none of the vacancies taking place which had been counted on, I think the present disposition is to require his return to his station in America. He told me himself lately, that he should return in the spring. I have never pressed this matter on the court, tho' I knew it to be desirable and desired on our part; because if the compulsion on him to return had been the work of Congress, he would have returned in such ill temper with them, as to disappoint us in the good they expected from it. He would forever have laid at their door his failure of promotion. I did not press it for another reason, which is that I have great reason to believe that the character of the Count de Moustier, who would go were the Chevalier to be otherwise provided for, would give the most perfect satisfaction in America.

As you are now returned into Congress it will become of importance that you should form a just estimate of certain public characters: on which therefore I will give you such notes as my knowledge of them has furnished me with. You will compare them with the materials you are otherwise possessed of, and decide on a view of the whole. Mr. *Carmichael*, is, I think, very little *known* in *America*. I never *saw him*, & while I was *in Congress I* formed rather a *disadvantageous idea* of him.[1] His letters, received then, showed him *vain*, & more attentive to *ceremony* & *etiquette* than we suppose men *of sense* should be. *I* have now a constant correspondence with him, and find *him* a little *hypochondriac* and *discontented.* He possesses very *good understanding*, tho' not of the *first order. I have* had great opportunities of *searching into* his *character*, and have availed myself *of them.* Many persons of different nations, *coming* from *Madrid* to *Paris*, all speak of *him as* in *high esteem*, & *I think* it certain that he has more of the Count de Florida Blanca's friendship, than any *diplomatic* character at *that court.* As long as this *minister* is in *office, Carmichael* can do *more than* any other *person who* could be *sent there.* You will see *Franks,* and doubtless he will be *asking some appointment.* I wish there may be any one for *which* he is *fit.* He is *light, indiscreet, active, honest, affectionate.* Tho' *Bingham* is not in *diplomatic office*, yet as he wishes to be so, I will mention such circumstances of *him, as you might* otherwise be *deceived in. He will* make *you believe he* was on the most intimate footing with the first *characters in Europe*, & versed in the *secrets* of every *cabinet.* Not a word of this *is true. He* had a rage for being *presented* to *great men*, & had no *modesty* in the methods by which he could if *he attained acquaintance.* Afterwards it was with such *90* who were susceptible of impression from the *beauty of his wife.* I must *except* the Marquis de Bonclearren who had been an *old acquaintance.*

The Marquis de La Fayette is a most valuable *auxiliary to me.* His *zeal* is unbounded, & his *weight* with those in *power, great.* His *education* having been merely *military, commerce* was an unknown field to him. But his good sense enabling him to *comprehend* perfectly whatever is *explained to him, his agency* has been very *efficacious. He* has a great deal of *sound genius*, is well *remarked* by the *King*, & rising in *popularity. He* has nothing against *him, but* the *suspicion* of *republican principles.* I think he will one day *be of* the *ministry.* His foible is, a *canine appetite for popularity and fame;* but he will get *above this. The Count de Vergennes is ill.* The possibility of his *recovery*, renders it dangerous for *us to express a doubt of it: but* he is *in danger.* He is *a great minister in European affairs*, but has very *imperfect ideas* of *our institutions, and no confidence in* them. His *devotion* to the principles of *pure despotism*, renders him *unaffectionate to our governments.* But *his fear* of *England makes him value us* as a *make weight.* He is *cool, reserved in political conversations, but free and familiar* on other *subjects*, and a very *attentive, agreeable person* to *do business with.* It is *impossible* to have a clearer, better *organized head;* but *age* has *chilled his heart.* Nothing should be spared, on our part, to attach this country to us. It is the only one on which we can rely for support, under every event. Its inhabitants

---

[1] These and subsequent words in italics were originally written in cipher. (Boyd 1990)

love us more, I think, than they do any other nation on earth. This is very much the effect of the good dispositions with which the French officers returned. In a former letter, I mentioned to you the dislocation of my wrist. I can make not the least use of it, except for the single article of writing, though it is going on five months since the accident happened. I have great anxieties, lest I should never recover any considerable use of it. I shall, by the advice of my surgeons, set out in a fortnight for the waters of Aix, in Provence. I chose these out of several they proposed to me, because if they fail to be effectual, my journey will not be useless altogether. It will give me an opportunity of examining the canal of Languedoc, and of acquiring knowledge of that species of navigation, which may be useful hereafter; but more immediately, it will enable me to make the tour of the ports concerned in commerce with us, to examine, on the spot, the defects of the late regulations respecting our commerce, to learn the further improvements which may be made in it, and on my return, to get this business finished. I shall be absent between two and three months, unless anything happens to recall me here sooner, which may always be effected in ten days, in whatever part of my route I may be. In speaking *of characters*, I omitted *those of Reyneval and Hennin*, the *two eyes* of Count de Vergennes. The *former* is the most important *character, because possessing* the most of the *confidence* of the *Count. He* is rather *cunning* than *wise*, his views of things being neither *great* nor *liberal. He governs* himself by *principles* which he has *learned* by *rote*, and is *fit only* for the *details* of *execution. His heart* is susceptible of little *passions* but not of *good ones. He* is *brother-in-law* to M. *Gerard*, from whom he received *disadvantageous impressions* of *us, which* cannot be *effaced. He* has much *duplicity. Hennin* is a *philosopher, sincere, friendly, liberal, learned, beloved* by everybody; the *other* by *nobody*. I *think* it a great *misfortune* that the *United States* are in the *department* of the *former*. As particulars of this kind may be useful to you, in your present situation, I may hereafter continue the chapter. I know it will be safely lodged in your discretion.

Feb. 5. Since writing thus far, *Franks* is *returned* from *England. I learn* that *Mr. Adams* desires to be *recalled*, & that *Smith* should be *appointed chargé des affaires* there. It is not for me to decide whether any *diplomatic character* should be *kept* at a *court*, which *keeps* none with *us.* You can judge of *Smith's* abilities by *his letters.* They are not of the *first order*, but they are *good.* For his *honesty*, he is like our friend *Monroe;* turn his *soul* wrong side outwards, and there is not a speck on it. *He* has one *foible*, an *excessive inflammability* of *temper*, but he feels it when it comes on, and has *resolution enough* to *suppress* it, and to *remain silent* till it *passes* over.

I send you by Colo. Franks, your pocket telescope, walking stick & chemical box. The two former could not be combined together. The latter could not be had in the form you referred to. Having a great desire to have a portable copying machine, & being satisfied from some experiments that the principle of the large machine might be applied in a small one, I planned one when in England & had it made. It answers perfectly. I have since set a workman to making them here, & they are in such demand that he has his hands full. Being assured that you will be pleased to have one, when you shall have tried it's convenience, I send you one by Colo. Franks. The machine costs 96 livres, the appendages 24 livres, and I send you paper & ink for 12 livres; in all 132 livres. There is a printed paper of directions; but you must expect to make many essays before you succeed perfectly. A soft brush, like a shaving brush, is more convenient than the sponge. You can get as much ink & paper as you please from London. The paper costs a guinea a ream.

To Mrs. John (Abigail) Adams[1]
Paris, Feb. 22, 1787
Dear Madam,

I am to acknowledge the honor of your letter of Jan. 29. and of the papers you were so good as to send me. They were the latest I had seen or have yet seen. They left off too in a critical moment; just at the point where the Malcontents make their submission on condition of pardon, & before the answer of government was known. I hope they pardoned them. The spirit of resistance to government is so valuable on certain occasions, that I wish it to be always kept alive. It will often be exercised when wrong but better so than not to be exercised at all. I like a little rebellion now & then. It is like a storm in the atmosphere. It is wonderful that no letter or paper tells us who is president of Congress, tho' there are letters in Paris to the beginning of January. I suppose I shall hear when I come back from my journey, which will be eight months after he will have been chosen, and yet they complain of us for not giving them intelligence. Our Notables assembled to-day, and I hope before the departure of Mr. Cairnes I shall have heard something of their proceedings worth communicating to Mr. Adams. The most remarkable effect of this convention as yet is the number of puns & bon mots it has generated. I think were they all collected it would make a more voluminous work than the Encyclopedie. This occasion, more than anything I have seen, convinces me that this nation is incapable of any serious effort but under the word of command. The people at large view every object only as it may furnish puns and bon mots; and I pronounce that a good punster would disarm the whole nation were they ever so seriously disposed to revolt. Indeed, Madam, they are gone, when a measure so capable of doing good as the calling the Notables is treated with so much ridicule; we may conclude the nation desperate, & in charity pray that heaven may send them good kings.

The bridge at the place Louis XV is begun, the hotel dieu is to be abandoned & new ones to be built. The old houses on the bridges are in a course of demolition. This is all I know of Paris. We are about to lose the Count d'Arande, who has desired & obtained his recall. Fernand Nunner, before destined for London,

---

[1] Most observers, on both sides of the Atlantic, saw political turbulence in America as evidence of a failure of public virtue and republican government. But Jefferson turned incidents such as Shays Rebellion into reassuring signs of Americans' continued vigilance against possible encroachments on their liberty. He unabashedly reiterates his beliefs when, in this letter, he remarks to Abigail Adams, "The spirit of resistance to government is so valuable on certain occasions, that I wish it to be always kept alive. It will often be exercised when wrong but better so than not to be exercised at all. I like a little rebellion now & then. It is like a storm in the atmosphere." (Baseler 1998, 187)

is to come here. The Abbes' Arnoux & Chalut are well. The Duchess Danville somewhat recovered from the loss of her daughter. Mrs. Barrett very homesick and fancying herself otherwise sick. They will probably remove to Honfleur. This is all our news. I have only to add then that Mr. Cairnes has taken charge of 15 aunes of black lace for you at 9 livres the aune, purchased by Petit & therefore I hope better purchased than some things have been for you; and that I am, dear Madam, your affectionate & humble servant.

To Martha Jefferson[1]
Aix en Provence, March 28, 1787

I was happy, my dear Patsey, to receive, on my arrival here, your letter, informing me of your good health and occupation. I have not written to you sooner because I have been almost constantly on the road. My journey hitherto had been a very pleasing one. It was undertaken with the hope that the mineral waters of this place might restore strength to my wrist. Other considerations also concurred — instruction, amusement, and abstraction from business, of which I had too much at Paris. I am glad to learn that you are employed in things new and good, in your music and drawing. You know what have been my fears for some time past — that you did not employ yourself so closely as I could wish. You have promised me a more assiduous attention, and I have great confidence in what you promise. It is your future happiness which interests me, and nothing can contribute more to it (moral rectitude always excepted) than the contracting a habit of industry and activity. Of all the cankers of human happiness none corrodes with so silent, yet so baneful an influence, as indolence. Body and mind both unemployed, our being becomes a burthen, and every object about us loathsome, even the dearest. Idleness begets ennui, ennui the hypochondriac, and that a diseased body. No laborious person was ever yet hysterical. Exercise and application produce order in our affairs, health of body and cheerfulness of mind, and these make us precious to our friends. It is while we are young that the habit of industry is formed. If not then, it never is afterwards. The fortune of our lives, therefore, depends on employing well the short period of youth. If at any moment, my dear, you catch yourself in idleness, start from it as you would from the precipice of a gulf. You are not, however, to consider yourself as unemployed while taking exercise. That is necessary for your health, and health is the first of

---

[1] The connection among exercise, productive activity, and health was a theme that Jefferson often touched upon. Here, during a visit to Aix-en Provence, he wrote Martha, who had remained in Paris, urging her to keep to a busy and productive schedule: "Idleness begets ennui, ennui the hypochondria, and that a diseased body. No laborious person was ever yet hysterical. Exercise and application produce order in our affairs, health of body, cheerfulness of mind, and these make us precious to our friends." Similarly, in a letter to his nephew the same year, he maintained that "an attention to health ... should take the place of every other object." Jefferson, whose life experiences had graphically taught him the value of good physical health, was himself a constant whirlwind of physical and intellectual energy and, as his writings demonstrate, he seems to have also possessed some measure of psychological insight regarding mental health. (Abrams 2013, 190)

all objects. For this reason, if you leave your dancing-master for the summer, you must increase your other exercises.

I do not like your saying that you are unable to read the ancient print of your Livy but with the aid of your master. We are always equal to what we undertake with resolution. A little degree of this will enable you to decipher your Livy. If you always lean on your master, you will never be able to proceed without him. It is part of the American character to consider nothing as desperate, to surmount every difficulty by resolution and contrivance. In Europe there are shops for every want; its inhabitants, therefore, have no idea that their wants can be supplied otherwise. Remote from all other aid, we are obliged to invent and to execute; to find means within ourselves, and not to lean on others. Consider, therefore, the conquering your Livy as an exercise in the habit of surmounting difficulties; a habit which will be necessary to you in the country where you are to live, and without which you will be thought a very helpless animal, and less esteemed. Music, drawing, books, invention, and exercise, will be so many resources to you against ennui. But there are others which, to this object, add that of utility. These are the needle and domestic economy. The latter you cannot learn here, but the former you may. In the country life of America there are many moments when a woman can have recourse to nothing but her needle for employment. In a dull company, and in dull weather, for instance, it is ill-manners to read, ill-manners to leave them; no card-playing there among genteel people — that is abandoned to blackguards. The needle is then a valuable resource. Besides, without knowing how to use it herself, how can the mistress of a family direct the work of her servants?

You ask me to write you long letters. I will do it, my dear, on condition you will read them from time to time, and practice what they inculcate. Their precepts will be dictated by experience, by a perfect knowledge of the situation in which you will be placed, and by the fondest love for you. This it is which makes me wish to see you more qualified than common. My expectations from you are high, yet not higher than you may attain. Industry and resolution are all that are wanting. Nobody in this world can make me so happy, or so miserable, as you. Retirement from public life will ere long become necessary for me. To your sister and yourself I look to render the evening of my life serene and contented. Its morning has been clouded by loss after loss, till I have nothing left but you. I do not doubt either your affections or dispositions. But great exertions are necessary, and you have little time left to make them. Be industrious then, my child. Think nothing insurmountable by resolution and application, and you will be all that I wish you to be.

You ask if it is my desire that you should dine at the Abbess's table? It is. Propose it as such to Madame de Frauleinheim, with my respectful compliments, and thanks for her care of you. Continue to love me with all the warmth with which you are beloved by, my dear Patsey, yours affectionately.

To Martha Jefferson[1]
Toulon, April 7th, 1787
My Dear Patsey

I received yesterday, at Marseilles, your letter of March 25th, and I received it with pleasure, because it announced to me that you are well. Experience learns us to be always anxious about the health of those whom we love. I have not been able to write to you as often as I expected, because I am generally on the road, and when I stop anywhere I am occupied in seeing what is to be seen. It will be some time now, perhaps, three weeks, before I shall be able to write you again. But this need not slacken your writing to me, because you have leisure and your letters come regularly to me. I have received letters which inform me that our dear Polly will certainly come to us this summer. By the time I return it will be time to expect her. When she arrives she will become a precious charge on your hands. The difference of your age and your common loss of a mother, will put that office on you. Teach her above all things to be good, because without that we can neither be valued by others nor set any value on ourselves. Teach her to be always true; no vice is so mean as the want of truth, and at the same time so useless. Teach her never to be angry; anger only serves to torment ourselves, to divert others, and alienate their esteem. And teach her industry, and application to useful pursuits. I will venture to assure you that if you inculcate this in her mind, you will make her a happy being herself, a most inestimable friend to you, and precious to all the world. In teaching her these dispositions of mind, you will be more fixed in them yourself, and render yourself dear to all your acquaintances. Practice them, then, my dear, without ceasing. If ever you find yourself in difficulty, and doubt how to extricate yourself, do what is right, and you will find it the easiest way of getting out of the difficulty. Do it for the additional incitement of increasing the happiness of him who loves you infinitely, and who is, my dear Patsey, yours affectionately.

To The Secretary for Foreign Affairs (John Jay)[2]

---

[1] Patsy's progress to womanhood pleased her father both because he anticipated her future life in Virginia and because, before that, he would depend on her to care for "our dear Polly." Jefferson envisioned fifteen-year old Patsy as a maternal figure for her younger sister, who was not yet nine in the summer of 1787 when she was due to arrive in Paris. Jefferson's advice to Patsy on assuming responsibility for this "precious charge" amounted to a summary of his own prescriptions for domestic tranquility, which he valued above all else. "Teach her above all things to be good.... Teach her always to be true.... Teach her never to be angry.... And teach her industry and application to useful pursuits. I will venture to assure you that if you inculcate this in her mind you will make her a happy being in herself, a most inestimable friend to you, and precious to all the world." Eagerly awaiting the arrival of his "dear Polly," he reminded his elder daughter that she, too, should practice these virtues "for the additional incitement of increasing the happiness of him who loves you infinitely." (Kierner 2012, 61)

[2] Jefferson, in this note, explains to Jay that Italy — the seat of Rome, of classical culture, the darling of the poets and the artists — now beckoned. But not for any of the more artistic reasons. On the contrary, Jefferson had heard that in the Piedmont region they possessed a machine for cleaning rice which brought

Marseilles, May 4, 1787
Sir,

I had the honor of receiving at Aix your letter of Feb. 9, and immediately wrote to the Count de Montmorin, explaining the delay of the answer of Congress to the King's letter, and desired Mr. Short to deliver that answer with my letter to Monsieur de Montmorin, which he accordingly informs me he has done.

My absence prevented my noting to you in the first moment the revolution which has taken place at Paris in the department of Finance, by the substitution of Monsieur de Fourqueux in the place of Monsieur de Calonnes, so that you will have heard of it through other channels before this will have the honor of reaching you.

Having staid at Aix long enough to prove the inefficacy of the waters, I came on to this place for the purpose of informing myself here, as I mean to do at the other sea-port towns, of whatever may be interesting to our commerce. So far as carried on in our own bottoms, I find it almost nothing; & so it must probably remain till something can be done with the Algerines. Tho' severely afflicted with the plague, they have come out within these few days, & shewed themselves in force along the coast of Genoa, cannonading a little town & taking several vessels.

Among other objects of inquiry, this was the place to learn something more certain on the subject of rice, as it is a great emporium for that of the Levant & of Italy. I wished particularly to know whether it was the use of a different machine for cleaning which brought European rice to market less broken than ours, as had been represented to me by those who deal in that article in Paris. I found several persons who had passed thro' the rice country of Italy, but not one who could explain to me the nature of the machine. But I was given

---

European rice to the market less broken into fragments than the American product. No one who had seen the machine had been able to explain to Jefferson either its construction or how it worked. Since American rice, though above the European in quality and color, met with less favor in European markets because it came half- crushed by the existing American methods, Jefferson, the inventor, now determined to spend the three weeks he projected for the journey to examine this wonderful machine for himself and, if possible, to copy it for American use. This letter also reflects the young republic's — and Jefferson's — continuing, and palpable interest in South America. The early relationship between the North American colonists and Brazil was facilitated by the relationship between Britain and Portugal. The alliance between London and Lisbon was long-standing — a trend that was evident at the surrender at Yorktown, where the man who presented Cornwallis's sword was Charles O'Hara, the "bastard son of Lord Tyrawley, English Ambassador to Portugal" and "his mistress, Anna, a Portuguese lady." This was reflective of the fact that "many English, because of old social ties and economic trading positions, did business with and lived in both Brazil and Portugal." The London-Lisbon alliance, in turn, facilitated ties between North America and Brazil, and the relationship did not cease after the Revolution, as U.S. businessmen were prominent in the slave trade to Montevideo in the late 18th century. Here Jefferson instructs Jay about the prospects for the ousting of Portugal from Brazil; however, his opinion that "the slaves will take the side of their masters" seems like a bit of self-interested wishful thinking on his part. (Schachner, 1957, 332; Horne 2007, 18)

to believe that I might see it myself immediately on entering Piedmont. As this would require but about three weeks I determined to go & ascertain this point; as the chance only of placing our rice above all rivalship in quality as it is in color, by the introduction of a better machine, if a better existed, seemed to justify the application of that much time to it. I found the rice country to be in truth Lombardy, 100 miles further than had been represented, & that tho' called Piedmont rice, not a grain is made in the country of Piedmont. I passed thro the rice fields of the Venellese & Milanese, about 60 miles, & returned from thence last night, having found that the machine is absolutely the same as ours, and of course that we need not listen more to that suggestion. It is a difference in the species of grain, of which the government of Turin is so sensible, that, as I was informed, they prohibit the exportation of rough rice on pain of death. I have taken measures however for obtaining a quantity of it which I think will not fail & I bought on the spot a small parcel which I have with me. As further details on this subject to Congress would be misplaced, I propose on my return to Paris to communicate them, & send the rice to the society at Charlestown for promoting agriculture, supposing that they will be best able to try the experiment of cultivating the rice of this quality, and to communicate the species to the two states of S Carolina & Georgia if they find it answer. I thought the staple of these two states was entitled to this attention, and that it must be desirable to them to be able to furnish rice of the two qualities demanded in Europe, especially as the greater consumption is in the forms for which the Lombardy quality is preferred. The mass of our countrymen being interested in agriculture, I hope I do not err in supposing that in a time of profound peace as the present, to enable them to adapt their productions to the market, to point out markets for them, and endeavor to obtain favorable terms of reception, is within the line of my duty.

My journey into this part of the country has procured me information which I will take the liberty of communicating to Congress. In October last I received a letter dated Montpelier Octob. 2. 1786. announcing to me that the writer was a foreigner who had a matter of very great consequence to communicate to me, and desired I would indicate the channel thro which it might pass safely. I did so. I received soon after a letter in the following words, omitting only the formal parts. As by this time I had been advised to try the waters of Aix, I [wrote] to the gentleman my design, and that I would go off my road as far as Nismes, under the pretext of seeing the antiquities of that place, if he would meet me there. He met me, and the following is the sum of the information I received from him. 'Brazil contains as many inhabitants as Portugal. They are 1. Portuguese. 2. Native whites. 3. black and mulatto slaves. 4. Indians civilized and savage. 1. The Portuguese are few in number, mostly married there, have lost sight of their native country, as well as the prospect of returning to it, and are disposed to become independent. 2. The native whites form the body of their nation. 3. The slaves are as numerous as the free. 4. The civilized Indians have no energy, and the savage would not meddle. There are 20,000 regular troops. Originally these were Portuguese; but as they died off they were replaced by natives, so that these compose at present the mass of the troops and may be counted on by their native country. The officers are partly Portuguese, partly Brazilians: their bravery is not doubted, and they understand the parade but not the science of their profession. They have no bias for Portugal, but no energy neither for anything. The Priests are partly Portuguese, partly Brazilians, and will not interest themselves much. The Noblesse are scarcely known as such. They will in no manner be distinguished from the people. The men of letters are those most desirous of a revolution. The people are not much under the influence of their priests, most of them read and write, possess arms, and are in the habit of using them for hunting. The slaves will take the side of their masters. In short, as to the question of revolution, there is but one mind in that country. But there appears no person capable of conducting a revolution, or willing to venture himself at its head, without the aid of some powerful nation, as the people of their own might fail them. There is no printing press in Brazil. They consider the North American revolution as a precedent for theirs. They look to the United States as most likely to give them honest support, and from a variety of considerations have the strongest prejudices in our favor. This informant is a native and inhabitant of Rio Janeiro the present metropolis, which contains 50,000 inhabitants, knows well St. Salvador the former one, and the Mines d'or which are in the center of the country. These are all for a revolution, and, constituting the body of the nation, the other parts will follow them. The king's fifth of the mines yields annually 13. millions of crusadoes or half dollars. He has the sole right of searching for diamonds and other precious stones, which yields him about half as much. His income alone then from these two resources, is about 10. millions of dollars annually. But the remaining part of the produce of the mines, being 26. millions, might be counted on for effecting a revolution. Besides the arms in the hands of the people, there are public magazines. They have abundance of horses, but only a part of their country would admit the service of horses. They would want cannon, ammunition, ships, sailors, soldiers, and officers, for which they are disposed to look to the U.S., always understood that every service and furniture will be well paid. Corn costs about 20 livres the 100 ℔. They have flesh in the greatest abundance, insomuch that in some parts they kill beeves for the skin only. The whale fishery is carried on by Brazilians altogether, and not by Portuguese; but in very small vessels, so that the fishermen know nothing of managing a large ship. They would want of us at all times shipping, corn, and salt fish. The latter is a great article, and they are at present supplied with it from Portugal. Portugal being without either army or navy, could not attempt an invasion under a twelvemonth: Considering of what it would be composed it would not be much to be feared, and, if it failed, they would probably never attempt a second. Indeed, this source of their wealth being intercepted, they are scarcely capable of a first effort. The thinking part of the nation are so sensible of this, that they consider an early separation as inevitable. There is an implacable hatred between the Brazilians and Portuguese: to reconcile which a former minister adopted the policy of letting the Brazilians into a participation of public offices; but subsequent administrations have reverted to the antient policy of keeping the administration in the hands of native Portuguese. There is a mixture of natives of the old appointments still remaining in office. If Spain should invade them on their Southern extremities, these are so distant from the body of their settlements that they could not penetrate thence, and Spanish enterprise is not formidable. The Mines d'or are among mountains, inaccessible to any army. And Rio Janeiro is considered as the strongest port in the world after Gibraltar. In case of a successful revolution, a republican government in a single body, would probably be established.'

I took care to impress on him thro' the whole of our conversation that I had neither instructions nor authority to say a word to anybody on this subject, and that I could only give him my own ideas as a single individual: which were that we were not in a condition at present to meddle nationally in any war; that we wished particularly to cultivate the friendship of Portugal, with whom we have an advantageous commerce. That yet a successful revolution in Brazil could not be uninteresting to us. That prospects of lucre might possibly draw numbers of individuals to their aid, and purer motives our officers, among whom are many excellent. That our citizens, being free to leave their own country individually without the consent of their governments, are equally free to go to any other.

A little before I received the first letter of the Brazilian, a gentleman informed me there was a Mexican in Paris, who wished to have some conversation with me. He accordingly called on me. The substance of the information I drew from him was as follows. He is himself a native of Mexico, where his relations are principally. He left it at about 17. years of age, and seems now to be about 33. or 34. He classes and characterizes the inhabitants of that country as follows. 1. The natives of old Spain, possessed of most of the offices of government, and firmly attached to it. 2. The clergy equally attached to the government. 3. The natives of Mexico, generally disposed to revolt, but without instruction, without energy, and much under the dominion of their priests. 4. The slaves, mulatto and black, the former enterprising and intelligent, the latter brave, and of very important weight, into whatever scale they throw themselves; but he thinks they will side with their masters. 5. The conquered Indians, cowardly, not likely to take any side, nor important which. 5. The free Indians, brave and formidable, should they interfere, but not likely to do so as being at a great distance. I asked him the numbers of these several classes, but he could not give them. The first he thought very inconsiderable: that the 2d. formed the body of the freemen: the 3d. equal to the two first: the 4th. to all the preceding: and as to the 5th. he could form no idea of their proportion. Indeed it appeared to me that his conjectures as to the others were on loose grounds. He said he knew from good information there were 300,000 inhabitants in the city of Mexico. I was still more cautious with him than with the Brazilian, mentioning it as my private opinion (unauthorized to say a word on the subject otherwise) that a successful revolution was still at a distance with them; that I feared they must begin by enlightening and emancipating the minds of their people; that as to us, if Spain should give us advantageous terms of commerce, and remove other difficulties, it was not probable that we should relinquish certain and present advantages tho' smaller, to uncertain and future ones, however great. I was led into this caution by observing that this gentleman was intimate at the Spanish Ambassador's, and that he was then at Paris, employed by Spain to settle her boundaries with France on the Pyrenees. He had much the air of candor, but that can be borrowed: so that I was not able to decide about him in my own mind.

Led by a unity of subject, and a desire to give Congress as general a view of the dispositions of our Southern countrymen as my information enables me, I will add an article which, old and insulated, I did not think important enough to mention at the time I received it. You will remember, Sir, that during the late war, the British papers often gave details of a rebellion in Peru. The character of those papers discredited the information. But the truth was that the insurrections were so general, that the event was long on the poise. Had Commodore Johnson, then expected on that coast, touched and landed there 2000 men, the dominion of Spain in that country was at an end. They only wanted a point of union which this body would have constituted. Not having this, they acted without concert, and were at length subdued separately. This conflagration was quenched in blood, 200,000 souls on both sides having perished; but the remaining matter is very capable of combustion. I have this information from a person who was on the spot at the time, and whose good faith, understanding, and means of information leave no doubt of the facts. He observed however that the numbers above supposed to have perished were on such conjectures only as he could collect.

I trouble Congress with these details, because, however distant we may be both in condition and dispositions, from taking an active part in any commotions in that country, nature has placed it too near us to make it's movements altogether indifferent to our interests or to our curiosity.

I hear of another Arrêt of this court increasing the duties on foreign stock fish, and the premiums on their own, imported into their islands; but not having yet seen it I can say nothing certain on it. I am in hopes the effect of this policy will be defeated by the practice which I am told takes place on the banks of Newfoundland of putting our fish into the French fishing boats and the parties sharing the premium, instead of ours paying the duty.

I am in hopes Mr. Short will be able to send you the medals of General Gates by this packet. I await a general instruction as to these medals. The academies of Europe will be much pleased to receive each a set.

I propose to set out the day after tomorrow for Bourdeaux (by the canal of Languedoc), Nantes, Lorient and Paris.

I have the honor to be with sentiments of the most perfect esteem & respect, Sir, your most obedient & most humble servant,

To Martha Jefferson[1]

---

[1] At the very least the recurrent moral comparisons between English society and American indicated a widespread recognition that for the Revolution to be really significant it had to affect the ways and values of everyday life. Reflecting this ethic, here, Jefferson tells his daughter, "Determine never to be idle. No person will have occasion to complain of the want of time who never loses any. It is wonderful how much may be done if we are always doing." (Ketcham 1974, 165)

Marseilles, May 5th, 1787

My Dear Patsey,

I got back to Aix the day before yesterday, and found there your letter of the 9th of April, from which I presume you to be well, though you do not say so. In order to exercise your geography, I will give you a detail of my journey. You must therefore take your map and trace out the following places: Dijon, Lyons, Pont St. Esprit, Nismes, Arles, St. Remis, Aix, Marseilles, Toulon, Hières, Fréjus, Antibes, Nice, Col de Tende, Coni, Turin, Vercelli, Milan, Pavia, Tortona, Novi, Genoa, by sea to Albenga, by land to Monaco, Nice, Antibes, Fréjus, Brignolles, Aix, and Marseilles. The day after morrow, I set out hence for Aix, Avignon, Pont du Gard, Nismes, Montpellier, Narbonne, along the canal of Languedoc to Toulouse, Bordeaux, Rochefort, Rochelle, Nantes, L'Orient, Nantes, Tours, Orleans, and Paris — where I shall arrive about the middle of June, after having travelled something upwards of a thousand leagues.

From Genoa to Aix was very fatiguing; the first two days having been at sea, and mortally sick — two more clambering the cliffs of the Apennines, sometimes on foot, sometimes on a mule, according as the path was more or less difficult — and two others travelling through the night as well as day without sleep. I am not yet rested, and shall therefore shortly give you rest by closing my letter, after mentioning that I have received a letter from your sister, which though a year old gave me great pleasure. I inclose for your perusal, as I think it will be pleasure for you also. But take care of it, and return it to me when I shall get back to Paris, for, trifling as it seems, it is precious to me.

When I left Paris I wrote to London to desire that your harpsicord might be sent during the months of April and May, so that I am in hopes it will arrive a little before I shall, and give me an opportunity of judging whether you have got the better of that want of industry which I began to fear would be the rock on which you would split. Determine never to be idle. No person will have occasion to complain of the want of time who never loses any. It is wonderful how much may be done if we are always doing. And that you may always be doing good, my dear, is the ardent prayer of, yours affectionately.

To Martha Jefferson[1]

May 21st, 1787

I write you, my dear Patsey, from the canal of Languedoc, on which I am at present sailing, as I have been for a week past, cloudless skies above, limpid waters below, and on each hand a row of nightingales in full chorus. This delightful bird had given me a rich treat before, at the fountain of Vaucluse. After visiting the tomb of Laura at Avignon, I went to see this fountain—a noble one of itself, and rendered famous forever by the songs of Petrarch, who lived near

---

[1] Though Jefferson conveyed his ideas in many different ways over the course of his trip, similar patterns run through his various forms of travel writing. And while his letters to Martha may seem overly didactic, he held himself to a similar standard in that he, too, was using his travels as a way of learning. He never lost sight of what he saw as the main purpose of traveling: to learn new ideas that could help improve mankind. (Hayes 2008, 354)

it. I arrived there somewhat fatigued and sat down by the fountain to repose myself. It gushes, of the size of a river, from a secluded valley of the mountains, the ruins of Petrarch's chateau being perched on a rock two hundred feet perpendicular above. To add to the enchantment of the scene, every tree and bush was filled with nightingales in full song. I think you told me that you had not yet noticed this bird. As you have trees in the garden of the convent, there might be nightingales in them, and this is the season of their song. Endeavor, my dear, to make yourself acquainted with the music of this bird, that when you return to your own country, you may be able to estimate its merit in comparison with that of the mocking-bird. The latter has the advantage of singing through a great part of the year, whereas the nightingale sings about five or six weeks in the spring, and a still shorter term, and with a more feeble voice, in the fall.

I expect to be at Paris about the middle of the next month. By that time we may begin to expect our dear Polly. It will be a circumstance of inexpressible comfort to me to have you both with me once more. The object most interesting to me for the residue of my life, will be to see you both developing daily those principles of virtue and goodness, which will make you valuable to others and happy in yourselves, and acquiring those talents and that degree of science which will guard you at all times against ennui, the most dangerous poison of life. A mind always employed is always happy. This is the true secret, the grand recipe, for felicity. The idle are only the wretched. In a world which furnishes so many employments which are so useful, so many which are amusing, it is our own fault if we ever know what ennui is, or if we are ever driven to the miserable resources of gaming, which corrupts our dispositions, and teaching us a habit of hostility against all mankind. We are now entering the port of Toulouse, where I quit my bark, and of course must conclude my letter. Be good and be industrious, and you will be what I shall most love in the world. Adieu, my dear child. Yours affectionately.

To James Madison[1]
Paris, June 20, 1787
Dear Sir

---

[1] Written during the opening meetings of 1787 Constitutional Convention, Jefferson could not contemplate the idea of such a convention without great anxiety. His counsel was solicited by Madison during the progress of the convention, and he responded, stating his opinions of the necessary reformations with modesty and frankness. Here, Jefferson straightforwardly promotes the idea of a single executive. "The idea of separating the executive business of the confederacy from Congress, as the judiciary is already in some degree, is just & necessary. I had frequently pressed on the members individually, while in Congress, the doing this by a resolution of Congress for appointing an Executive committee to act during the sessions of Congress, as the Committee of the states was to act during their vacations. But the referring to this Committee all executive business as it should present itself, would require a more persevering self-denial than I supposed Congress to possess. It will be much better to make that separation by a federal act." (Rayner 1832, 262)

I wrote you last on the 30th of Jan. with a postscript of Feb. 5. Having set out the last day of that month to try the waters of Aix, and been journeying since till the 10th inst. I have been unable to continue my correspondence with you. In the meantime I have received your several favors of Feb. 15, Mar. 18 19, & Apr. the 23. The last arrived here about the 25th of May, while those of Mar. 18 & 19, tho' written five weeks earlier arrived three weeks later. I mention this to shew you how uncertain is the conveyance thro' England.

The idea of separating the executive business of the confederacy from Congress, as the judiciary is already in some degree, is just & necessary. I had frequently pressed on the members individually, while in Congress the doing this by a resolution of Congress for appointing an Executive committee to act during the sessions of Congress, as the Committee of the states was to act during their vacations. But the referring to this Committee all executive business as it should present itself, would require a more persevering self-denial than I suppose Congress to possess. It will be much better to make that separation by a federal act. The negative proposed to be given them on all the acts of the several legislatures is now for the first time suggested to my mind. Primâ facie I do not like it. It fails in an essential character that the hole & the patch should be commensurate. But this proposes to mend a small hole by covering the whole garment. Not more than one out of 100 state acts concern the confederacy. This proposition then in order to give them 1. degree of power which they ought to have, gives them 99. more which they ought not to have, upon a presumption that they will not exercise the 99. But upon every act there will be a preliminary question Does this act concern the confederacy? And was there ever a proposition so plain as to pass Congress without a debate? Their decisions are almost always wise; they are like pure metal. But you know of how much dross this is the result. Would not an appeal from the state judicatures to a federal court in all cases where the act of Confederation controlled the question, be as effectual a remedy, & exactly commensurate to the defect? A British creditor, e.g., sues for his debt in Virginia; the defendant pleads an act of the state excluding him from their courts; the plaintiff urges the Confederation & the treaty made under that, as controlling the state law; the judges are weak enough to decide according to the views of their legislature. An appeal to a federal court sets all to rights. It will be said that this court may encroach on the jurisdiction of the state courts. It may. But there will be a power, to wit, Congress, to watch & restrain them. But place the same authority in Congress itself, and there will be no power above them to perform the same office. They will restrain within due bounds a jurisdiction exercised by others much more rigorously than if exercised by themselves. I am uneasy at seeing that the sale of our Western lands is not yet commenced. That precious fund for the immediate extinction of our debt will I fear be suffered to slip thro' our fingers. Every delay exposes it to events which no human foresight can guard against. When we consider the temper of the people of that country, derived from the circumstances which surround them, we must suppose their *separation impossible*, at every moment.[1] If they can be *retained till* their governments *become* settled & wise, they will *remain* with us always, and be a precious part of our strength & of our virtue. *But* this affair of the *Mississippi*, by shewing that *Congress is capable* of hesitating on a question, which proposes a *clear sacrifice* of the *western* to the *maritime States*, will with difficulty be *obliterated*. The proposition of *my going to Madrid*, to *try* to *recover* there the ground which has been *lost* at *New York*, by the *concession* of the vote of *seven States*, I should think desperate. With respect to *myself*, weighing the pleasure of *the journey* & bare possibility of *success*, in one scale, and the strong *probability* of *failure* and the public *disappointment directed* on *me*, in the other, the latter preponderates. Add to this that *jealousy* might be *excited* in the *breast* of a *person*, who could find occasions of making *me uneasy*.

The late changes in the ministry here excite considerable hopes. I think we *gain in them all*. I am particularly happy at the *re-entry* of *Malesherbes* into the *Council*. His knowledge, his integrity render his value inappreciable, and the greater *to me*, because while he had no *views of office, we* had established together the most unreserved *intimacy*. So far too *I am pleased* with *Montmorin*. His honesty proceeds from *the heart* as well as *the head*, and therefore may be more surely *counted on*. *The King* loves *business, economy, order, & justice, and* wishes sincerely the good of *his people; but he* is *irascible, rude,* very *limited in his understanding, and religious*, bordering only on *bigotry*. He has no *mistress, loves his queen*, and is too much *governed by her. She is capricious* like *her brother, and governed* by *him*; devoted to *pleasure and expense; and not remarkable* for any other *vices or virtues. Unhappily the King* shews a propensity for the *pleasures* of the *table*, that for *drink* has *increased lately*, or at least it is *become more known*. For European news in general, I will refer you to my letter to Mr. Jay. Is it not possible that the occurrences in Holland may excite a desire in many of fleeing that country & transferring their effects out of it may make an opening for shifting into their hands the debts due to this country, to its officers and Farmers? It would be surely eligible. I believe Dumas, if put on the watch, might alone suffice; but surely, if Mr. Adams should go when the moment offers. *Dumas* has been in the habit of sending his *letters open* to *me*, to *be forwarded* to Mr. *Jay*. During my absence they passed through Mr. *Short's* hands who made *extracts* from them by which I see he has been recommending himself and *me* for the *money negotiations in Holland*. It might be thought perhaps that *I have* encouraged *him in* this. Be assured my dear Sir, that no such idea ever entered my head. On the contrary it is a business which would be the most *disagreeable to me* of all others, & for which *I am* the most *unfit person living. I do* not understand *bargaining*, nor possess the *dexterity* requisite to them. On the other hand Mr. *Adams*, whom I expressly and sincerely recommend, stands already on ground for that business, which *I* could not gain in years. Pray set *me* to rights in the minds of those who may have supposed *me privy* to this proposition. En passant, I will observe with respect to Mr. *Dumas*, that the death of the Count de Vergennes places *Congress* more at *their* ease, how to dispose of *him*. Our credit has been ill-treated here in public debate, and our *debt* deemed *apocryphal*. We should try to transfer this *debt*

---

[1] These and subsequent words in italics were originally written in cipher. (Boyd 1990)

elsewhere, & leave nothing capable of exciting ill thoughts between us. I shall mention in my letter to Mr. Jay a disagreeable affair in which *Mr. Barclay* has been thrown into, at *Bordeaux*. An honester man cannot be found, nor a *slower*, nor more *indecisive one. His affairs*, too, *are so embarrassed and desperate*, that the *public reputation* is every moment in danger of being *compromitted* with *him*. He is perfectly amiable & honest, with all his *embarrassments*.

By the next packet I shall be able to send you some books as also your watch & pedometer. The two last are not yet done. To search for books and forward them to Havre will require more time than I had between my return & the departure of this packet. You did perfectly right as to the payment by the Mr. Fitzhughs. Having been a witness heretofore to the divisions in Congress on the subject of their foreign ministers, it would be a weakness in me to suppose none with respect to myself, or to count with any confidence on the renewal of my commission, which expires on the 10th day of March next: and the more so as, instead of requiring the disapprobation of 7. states as formerly, that of one suffices for a recall when Congress consists of only 7. states, 2. when of 8. &c which I suppose to be habitually their numbers at present. Whenever I leave this place, it will be necessary to begin my arrangements 6. months before my departure; and these, once fairly begun and under way, and my mind set homewards, a change of purpose could hardly take place. If it should be the desire of Congress that I should continue still longer, I could wish to know it at farthest by the packet which will sail from New York in September. Because were I to put off longer the quitting my house, selling my furniture &c. I should not have time left to wind up my affairs; and having once quitted, and sold off my furniture, I could not think of establishing myself here again. I take the liberty of mentioning this matter to you not with a desire to change the purpose of Congress, but to know it in time. I have never fixed in my own mind the epoch of my return so far as shall depend on myself, but I never supposed it very distant. Probably I shall not risk a second vote on this subject. Such trifling things may draw on one the displeasure of one or two states & thus submit me to the disgrace of a recall.

I thank you for the Peccan nuts which accompanied your letter of March. Could you procure me a copy of the bill for proportioning crimes & punishments in the form in which it was ultimately rejected by the house of delegates? Young Mr. Bannister desired me to send him regularly the Mercure de France. I will ask leave to do this thro' you, & that you will adopt such method of forwarding them to him as will save him from being submitted to postage which they would not be worth. As a compensation for your trouble you will be free to keep them till you shall have read them.

To John Adams[1]

---

[1] A central complication in Franco-American relations in the years of the Confederation remained the American default on repayment of money France had loaned the United States during the Revolutionary War. France was not the only creditor to suffer. The Congress of the Confederation was powerless to pay installments on the principal or to keep up the interest payments on any foreign loans. Being the major creditor, however, France was the main sufferer.

Paris, July 1, 1787

Dear Sir,

I returned about three weeks ago from a very useless voyage, useless, I mean, as to the object which first suggested it, that of trying the effect of the mineral waters of Aix en Provence on my hand. I tried these because recommended among six or eight others as equally beneficial, & because they would place me at the beginning of a tour to the seaports of Marseilles, Bordeaux, Nantes & L'Orient which I had long meditated, in hopes that a knowledge of the places & persons concerned in our commerce & the information to be got from them might enable me sometimes to be useful. I had expected to satisfy myself at Marseilles of the causes of the difference of quality between the rice of Carolina & that of Piedmont which is brought in quantities to Marseilles. Not being able to do it I made an excursion of three weeks into the rice country beyond the Alps, going through it from Vercelli to Pavia, about 60 miles. I found the difference to be not in the management as had been supposed both here & in Carolina, but in the species of rice, & I hope to enable them in Carolina to begin the cultivation of the Piedmont rice & carry it on hand in hand with their own that they may supply both qualities, which is absolutely necessary at this market. I had before endeavored to lead the depôt of rice from Cowes to Honfleur, and hope to get it received there on such terms as may draw that branch of commerce from England to this country. It is an object of 250.000 guineas a year.

While passing thro' the towns of Turin, Milan & Genoa, I satisfied myself of the practicability of introducing our whale oil for their consumption & I suppose it would be equally so in the other great cities of that country. I was sorry that I was not authorized to set the matter on foot. The merchants with whom I chose to ask conferences, met me freely, and communicated fully, knowing I was in a public character. I could however only prepare a disposition to meet our oil merchants. On the article of tobacco I was more in possession of my ground, and put matters into a train for inducing their government to draw their tobaccos directly from the U. S. & not as heretofore from Gr. B. I am now occupied with the new ministry here to put the concluding hand to the new regulations for our commerce with this country, announced in the letter of M. de Calonnes which I sent you last fall. I am in hopes in addition to those, to obtain a suppression of the duties on Tar, pitch, & turpentine, and an extension of the privileges of American whale oil, to their fish oils in general. I find that the quantity of Codfish oil brought to L'Orient is considerable. This being got off hand (which will be in

---

Only by levying import duties or by requisitioning the states could Congress raise money. No longer faced with an immediate foreign danger, the states were deaf to congressional demands. Congress, however, could not ignore the vexing solicitations of French agents on the subject of debt payment, nor could Jefferson for that matter, at least in his position of American minister to France. As he advised Adams here, the question of debts "draws on us a great deal of censure, & occasioned a language in the Assemblée des Notables very likely to produce dissatisfaction between us." Yet the French government applied no pressure, even when faced with bankruptcy, to force payment; it was reconciled, by 1789, to never being paid. (Deconde 1958. 16)

a few days) the chicaneries & vexations of the farmers on the article of tobacco, and their elusions of the order of Bernis, call for the next attention. I have reason to hope good dispositions in the new ministry towards our commerce with this country. Besides endeavoring on all occasions to multiply the points of contact & connection with this country, which I consider as our surest mainstay under every event, I have had it much at heart to remove from between us every subject of misunderstanding or irritation. Our debts to the King, to the officers, & to the farmers are of this description. The having complied with no part of our engagements in these draws on us a great deal of censure, & occasioned a language in the Assemblée des Notables very likely to produce dissatisfaction between us.

Dumas being on the spot in Holland, I had asked of him some time ago, in confidence, his opinion on the practicability of transferring these debts from France to Holland, & communicated his answer to Congress, pressing them to get you to go over to Holland & try to effect their business. Your knowledge of the ground & former successes occasioned me to take this liberty without consulting you, because I was sure you would not weigh your personal trouble against public good. I have had no answer from Congress; but hearing of your journey to Holland have hoped that some money operation had led you there. If it related to the debts of this country I would ask a communication of what you think yourself at liberty to communicate, as it might change the form of my answers to the eternal applications I receive. The debt to the officers of France carries an interest of about 2000 guineas, so we may suppose its principle is between 30 & 40.000. This makes more noise against us than all our other debts put together.

To Monsieur de Calonnes[1]
July 5, 1787

---

[1] Charles Alexandre de Calonne was a French statesman who seems to have been a man of great business capacity, gay and careless in temperament, and thoroughly unscrupulous in political action. In the terrible crisis of affairs preceding the French Revolution, when minister after minister tried in vain to replenish the exhausted royal treasury and was dismissed for want of success, Calonne was summoned to take the general control of affairs. He assumed office on the 3rd of November 1783 and owed the position to Vergennes. In taking office he found "600 millions to pay and neither money nor credit." At first he attempted to develop the latter, and to carry on the government by means of loans in such a way as to maintain public confidence in its solvency. In October 1785 he recoined the gold coinage, and he developed the caisse d'escompte. But these measures failing, he proposed to the king the suppression of internal customs, duties and the taxation of the property of nobles and clergy. Therefore he had an assembly of "notables" called together in January 1787. Before it he exposed the deficit in the treasury, and proposed the establishment of a subvention territoriale, which should be levied on all property without distinction. This suppression of privileges was badly received by the privileged notables. Calonne, angered, printed his reports and so alienated the court. Louis XVI dismissed him on April 8, 1787, and exiled him to Lorraine. The joy was general in Paris, where Calonne, accused of wishing to augment the imposts, was known as "Monsieur Deficit." Jefferson was delighted to hear that the Notables had rejected Calonne's

Observations on the Letter of Monsieur De Calonnes to Monsieur Jefferson, Dated Fontainebleau, October 22, 1786.

A committee was appointed, in the course of the last year to take a view of the subjects of commerce which might be brought from the United States of America, in exchange for those of France, and to consider what advantages and facilities might be offered to encourage that commerce. The letter of Monsieur de Calonnes was founded on their report. It was conclusive as to the articles on which satisfactory information had been then obtained, and reserved for future consideration certain others needing further enquiry. It is proposed now to review those unfinished articles, that they also may be comprehended in the Arrêt, and the regulations on this branch of commerce be rendered complete.

1. The letter promises to diminish the Droits du roi et d' amirauté, paiable by an American vessel entering into a port of France, & to reduce what should remain into a single duty, which shall be regulated by the draught of the vessel, or her number of masts. It is doubted whether it will be expedient to regulate the duty in either of these ways. If by the draught of water, it will fall unequally on us as a Nation; because we build our vessels sharp-bottomed, for swift sailing, so that they draw more water than those of other nations, of the same burthen; if by the number of masts it will fall unequally on individuals, because we often see ships of 180 tons, & brigs of 360. This then would produce an inequality among individuals of 6. to 1. The present principle is the most just, to regulate by the burthen. It is certainly desirable that these duties should be reduced to a single one. Their names and numbers perplex & harass the merchant more than their amount, subject him to imposition, & to the suspicion of it where there is none. An intention of general reformation in this article has been accordingly announced with augmentation as to foreigners. We are in hopes that this augmentation is not to respect us; because it is proposed as a measure of reciprocity; whereas in some of our states no such duties exist, & in the others they are extremely light; because we have been made to hope a diminution instead of augmentation; and because this distinction cannot draw on France any just claims from other nations, the Jura gentis amicissimæ conferred by her late treaties having reference expressly to the nations of Europe only, & those conferred by the more ancient ones not being susceptible of any other interpretation, nor admitting a pretension of reference to a nation which did not then exist, and which has come into existence under circumstances distinguishing its commerce from that of all other nations. Merchandise received from them take employment from the poor of France; ours give it; theirs is brought in the last stage of manufacture, ours in the first; we bring our tobaccos to be manufactured into snuff, our flax & hemps into linen and cordage, our furs into hats, skins into saddlery, shoes & clothing; we take nothing till it has received the last hand.

2. Fish-oils. The Hanseatic treaty was the basis on which the diminution of duty on this article was asked & granted. It is expressly referred to as such in the letter of Monsieur de Calonnes. Instead however of the expression

---

plan and that after his failure he had been dismissed in disgrace. (Chisholm 1910, 60; Thompson 2013 , 109)

"huile et graisse de baleine & d'autres poissons" used in that treaty, the letter uses the terms "huiles de baleine, spermaceti, et tout ce qui est compris sous ces denominations." And the farmers have availed themselves of this variation to refuse the diminution of duty on the oils of the vache marine, chien de mer, esturgeon & other fish. It is proposed therefore to re-establish in the Arrêt the expressions of the Hanseatic treaty, & to add from the same treaty the articles "baleine coupee et fanon de baleine." The letter states these regulations as finally made by the king. The merchants on this supposition entered into speculations. But they found themselves called on for the old duties, not only on other fish oils, but on the whale oil. Monsieur de Calonnes always promised that the Arrêt should be retrospective to the date of the letter, so as to refund to them the duties they had thus been obliged to pay. To this attention is prayed in forming the Arrêt. His majesty having been pleased as an encouragement to the importation of our fish oils, to abolish the Droits de fabrication, it is presumed that the purpose announced of continuing those duties on foreign oils will not be extended to us.

3. Rice. The duty on this is only 7½ deniers the Quintal, or about one quarter per cent on its first cost. While this serves to inform the government of the quantities imported, it cannot discourage that importation. Nothing further therefore is necessary on this article.

4. Potashe. This article is of principal utility to France in her bleacheries of linen, glass works, & soap-works; & the potash of America, being made of green wood, is known to be the best in the world. All duty on it was therefore abolished by the king. But the city of Rouen levies on it a duty of 20 sols the Quintal, which is very sensible in its price, brings it dearer to the bleacheries near Paris, to those of Beauvais, Laval &c., & to the glass works, and encourages them to give a preference to the potash or soda of other nations. This is a counteraction of the views of the king expressed in the letter which it is hoped will be prevented.

5. Turpentine, tar, & pitch, were not decided on the former occasion. Turpentine (Terebenthine) pays 10. sols the Quintal and 10. sols the livre, making 15 sols the quintal; which is 10. per cent. on its prime cost. Tar, (goudron, braigras) pays 8 livres the length of 12 barrels, & 10. sols the livre, amounting to 20 sols the barrel, which is 12½ per cent. on its prime cost. Pitch (brai sec) pays 10. sols the Quintal & 10 sols the livre, making 15 sols the Quintal, which is 20 per cent. on its prime cost. Duties of from 10 to 20 per cent. on articles of heavy carriage, prevent their importation. They eat up all the profits of the merchants, & often subject him to loss. This has been much the case with respect to turpentine, tar, & pitch, which are a principal article of remittance for the state of North Carolina. It is hoped that it will coincide with the views of government in making the present regulations, to suppress the duties on these articles, which of all others can bear them least.

To Thomas Mann Randolph[1]

---

[1] With an eye to the future and education, Jefferson felt that there were very good reasons why the coming generation needed to know not only French but

Paris, July 6, 1787

Dear Sir,

Your favor of April 14, came here during my absence on a journey through the Southern parts of France and Northern of Italy, from which I am but lately returned. This cause alone has prevented your receiving a more early answer to it. I am glad to find that among the various branches of science presenting themselves to your mind you have fixed on that of Politics as your principal pursuit. Your country will derive from this a more immediate and sensible benefit. She has much for you to do. For tho' we may say with confidence that the worst of the American constitutions is better than the best which ever existed before in any other country, & that they are wonderfully perfect for a first essay, yet every human essay must have defects. It will remain therefore to those now coming on the stage of public affairs to perfect what has been so well begun by those going off it. Mathematics, Natural philosophy, Natural history, Anatomy, Chemistry, Botany, will become amusements for your hours of relaxation, and auxiliaries to your principal studies. Precious and delightful ones they will be. As soon as such a foundation is laid in them as you may build on as you please hereafter, I suppose you will proceed to your main objects, Politics, Law, Rhetoric, & History. As to these, the place where you study them is absolutely indifferent. I should except Rhetoric, a very essential member of them and which I suppose must be taught to advantage where you are. You would do well therefore to attend the public exercises in this branch also, and to do it with every particular diligence. This being done, the question arises, where you shall fix yourself for studying Politics, Law, & History? I should not hesitate to decide in favor of France, because you will at the same time be learning to speak the language of that country, become absolutely essential under our present circumstances. The best method of doing this would be to fix yourself in some family where there are women & children, in Passey, Auteuil or some other of the little towns in reach of Paris. The principal hours of the day you will attend to your studies, & in those of relaxation associate with the family. You will learn to speak better from women & children in three months, than from men in a year. Such a situation too will render more easy a due attention to economy of time & money. Having pursued your main studies here about two years, & acquired a facility in speaking French, take a tour of 4 or 5 months through this country & Italy, return then to Virginia & pass a year in Williamsburg under the care of Mr. Wythe, and you will be ready to enter on the public stage, with superior advantages. I have proposed to you to carry on the study of the law with that of Politics & History. Every political measure will forever have an intimate connection with the laws of the land; and he who knows nothing of these will always be perplexed & often

also Spanish. The commercial and diplomatic relationship between Spain and the United States, as Jefferson told young Randolph in this letter, "is already important and will become daily more so. Besides this the antient part of American history is written chiefly in Spanish." Jefferson took his own advice to heart. Having expanded his collection of Spanish Americana in Europe, his collection included a book by Francisco López de Gómara, the Spanish historian who served as secretary to Hernando Cortés. (Hayes 2008, 389)

foiled by adversaries having the advantage of that knowledge over him. Besides it is a source of infinite comfort to reflect that under every change of fortune we have a resource in ourselves from which we may be able to derive an honorable subsistence. I would therefore propose not only the study, but the practice of the law for some time, to possess yourself of the habit of public speaking. With respect to modern languages, French, as I have before observed, is indispensable. Next to this the Spanish is most important to an American. Our connection with Spain is already important & will become daily more so. Besides this the antient part of American history is written chiefly in Spanish. To a person who would make a point of reading & speaking French & Spanish, I should doubt the utility of learning Italian. These three languages, being all degeneracies from the Latin, resemble one another so much that I doubt the possibility of keeping in the head a distinct knowledge of them all. I suppose that he who learns them all will speak a compound of the three, & neither perfectly. The journey which I propose to you need not be expensive, and would be very useful. With your talents & industry, with science, and that steadfast honesty which eternally pursues right, regardless of consequences, you may promise yourself everything,—but health, without which there is no happiness. An attention to health then should take place of every other object. The time necessary to secure this by active exercises, should be devoted to it in preference to every other pursuit. I know the difficulty with which a studious man tears himself from his studies at any given moment of the day. But his happiness & that of his family depend on it. The most uninformed mind with a healthy body, is happier than the wisest valetudinarian. I need not tell you that if I can be useful to you in any part of this or any other plan you shall adopt, you will make me happy by commanding my services.

Will you be so good, Sir, as to return my most respectful thanks for the diploma with which I am honored by the society instituted with you for the encouragement of the study of Natural history? I am afraid it will never be in my power to contribute anything to the object of the institution. Circumstances have thrown me into a very different line of life; and not choice as I am happy to find in your case. In the year 1781, while confined to my room by a fall from my horse, I wrote some Notes in answer to the inquiries of M. de Marbois as to the natural & political state of Virginia. They were hasty & undigested; yet as some of these touch slightly on some objects of its natural history, I will take the liberty of asking the society to accept a copy of them. For the same reason, & because too they touch on the political condition of our country, I will beg leave to present you with a copy, and ask the favor of you to find a conveyance for them from London to Edinburgh. They are printed by Stockdale, bookseller Piccadilly, and will be ready in 3 or 4 weeks from this time. I will direct him to deliver two copies to your order. Repeating constantly the proffer of my services, I shall only add assurances of the esteem & attachment with which I am Dear

To Edward Rutledge[1]

---

[1] Rice was the great theme of Jefferson's agricultural letters. The vast national importance of the matter, together with the warm responses which he had

Paris, July 14, 1787

Dear Sir,

I received your favor of the 14th of October in the moment I was setting out on a tour of the seaport towns of this country, from which I have been not long returned. I received it too with that kind of heartfelt pleasure which always attends the recollection of antient affections. I was glad to find that the adoption of your rice to this market was considered worth attention as I had supposed it. I set out from hence impressed with the idea the rice-dealers here had given me that the difference between your rice & that of Piedmont proceeded from a difference in the machine for cleaning it. At Marseilles I hoped to know what the Piedmont machine was: but I could find nobody who knew anything of it. I determined therefore to sift the matter to the bottom by crossing the Alps into the rice country. I found the machine exactly such a one as you had described to me in Congress in the year 1775. There was but one conclusion then to be drawn, to wit, that the rice was of a different species, & I determined to take enough to put you in seed:

They informed me however that it's exportation in the husk was prohibited; so I could only bring off as much as my coat & surtout pockets would hold. I took measures with a muleteer to run a couple of sacks across the Apennines to Genoa, but have not great dependence on its success. The little therefore which I brought myself must be relied on for fear we should get no more, and because also it is genuine from Vercelli where the best is made of all the Sardinian Lombardy, the whole of which is considered as producing a better rice than the Milanese. This is assigned as the reason of the strict prohibition. Piedmont rice sold at Nice (the port of its exportation) when I was there at 17 livres French, the French hundredweight. It varies from time to time as the price of wheat does with us. The price of Carolina rice at Bordeaux, Nantes, Lorient & Havre varies from 16# to 24# the French quintal, which is equal to 109 lb. our weight. The best ports to send it to are Bordeaux & Havre (or Rouen which is the same thing as

---

received from Charleston to his letters upon rice, induced him to cross the Alps and traverse the rice-country on purpose to examine the hulling-mill employed there, to the vise of which he supposed the higher price of the Italian rice was due. "I found their machine," he wrote here to Edward Rutledge of South Carolina, "exactly such a one as you had described to me in Congress in the year 1783!" But he did not cross the Alps in vain. Seeing that the Italians cleaned their rice by the very mill used in South Carolina, he concluded that the Italian rice was of a better kind, and resolved to send some of the seed to Charleston. It was, however, part of the barbaric protective system to prevent the exportation of whatever could most signally bless other nations; and no one was allowed to send seed-rice out of the country. Jefferson, falling back on the higher law, took measures with a muleteer to transport a couple of sacks across the Apennines to Genoa; but, having little faith in the muleteer's abilities, he also filled the pockets of his own coat and overcoat with the best rice of the best rice-producing district in Italy, and sent it, in two parcels by different ships, to Charleston. The muleteer indeed failed to complete the task; but Jefferson's modest samples reached Charleston where it was distributed it among the rice-planters, a dozen or two of grains to each. These were carefully sown and watched, usually under the master's eye. The species succeeded well in the rice country, and enabled the South-Carolina planters to substantially increase the quality of their rice. (Parton 1874, 308)

Havre) but it is essential that it arrive here a month before the commencement of Lent, when the principal demand is made for it. Carolina rice after being sorted here into several qualities, sells from 6 sols to 10 sols the French pound, retail, according to the quality. Unsorted and wholesale about 30# the French quintal.

Piedmont rice is but of one quality, which sells retail at 10 sous the Fr. pound, & wholesale is about 3 or 4# dearer than yours. In order to induce your countrymen to ship their rice here directly, I have proposed to some merchants here to receive consignments allowing the consignor to draw on the moment of shipping for as much as he could sell for on the spot & the balance when it should be sold. But they say that is impossible. They are to consider & inform me what are the most favorable terms on which they can receive it. I am told that freight insurance & commission are about 4# the Fr. quintal, to a seaport town. I have written so long a letter on the subject of rice to Mr. Drayton for the society of agriculture, that I will trouble you with no farther particulars but refer you to that. Indeed I am sensible I have written too much on the subject. Being absolutely ignorant of it myself, it was impossible for me to know what particulars merited communication. I thought it best therefore to communicate everything. After writing that letter, I received one from Mr. Izard, by which I found that he had examined the rice-process in Lombardy. He was so much more capable than myself of giving the details that I had at one moment determined to suppress my letter. However observing that he considered the rice of Piedmont to be of the same species with yours, and suspecting myself certainly that it is not, I determined to hazard my letter and all those criticisms which fall justly on an ignorant person writing on a subject to those much more learned in it than himself. A part of my letter too related to the olive tree & caper, the first of which would surely succeed in your country & would be an infinite blessing after some 15 or 20 years; the caper would also probably succeed & would offer a very great and immediate profit. I thank you for your obliging mention of my worthless *Notes on Virginia.* Worthless & bad as they are they have been rendered more so, as I am told, by a translation into French. That I may have neither merit nor demerit not my own, I have consented to their publication in England. I advised the bookseller to send 200 copies to Philadelphia & 200 to Richmond, supposing that number might be sold in the United States: but I do not know whether he will do it. If you give me leave I will send you a copy of the original impression.

I congratulate you, my dear friend, on the law of your state for suspending the importation of slaves, and for the glory you have justly acquired by endeavoring to prevent it forever. This abomination must have an end, and there is a superior bench reserved in heaven for those who hasten it. The distractions of Holland thicken apace. They begin to cut one another's throats heartily. I apprehend the neighboring powers will interfere: but it is not yet clear whether in concert, or by taking opposite sides. It is a poor contest, whether they shall have one, or many masters. Your nephew is arrived here in good health. My first interview with him has impressed me much in his favor. Present me very respectfully to Mrs. Rutledge, as well as to your brother & his house. Accept yourself assurances of the sincere esteem & respect with which I am Dear Sir your most obedient & most humble servt.

To Mrs. John Bolling[1]
Paris, July 23d, 1787
Dear Sister,

I received with real pleasure your letter of May 3d, informing me of your health and of that of your family. Be assured it is, and ever has been, the most interesting thing to me. Letters of business claiming their rights before those of affection, we often write seldomest to whom we love most. The distance to which I am removed has given a new value to all I valued before in my own country, and the day of my return to it will be the happiest I expect to see in my life. When it will come is not yet decided, as far as depends on myself. My dear Polly is safely arrived here, and in good health. She had got so attached to Captain Ramsey that they were obliged to decoy her from him. She staid three weeks in London with Mrs. Adams, and had got up such an attachment to her, that she refused to come with the person I sent for her. After some days she was prevailed on to come. She did not know either her sister or myself, but soon renewed her acquaintance and attachment. She is now in the same convent with her sister, and will come to see me once or twice a week. It is a house of education altogether, the best in France, and at which the best masters attend. There are in it as many Protestants as Catholics, and not a word is ever spoken to them on the subject of religion. Patsey enjoys good health, and longs much to return to her friends. We shall doubtless find much change when we get back; many of our older friends withdrawn from the stage, and our younger ones grown out of our knowledge. I suppose you are now fixed for life at Chestnut Grove. I take a part of the misfortune to myself, as it will prevent my seeing you as often as would be practicable at Lickinghole. It is still a greater loss to my sister Carr. We must look to Jack for indemnification, as I think it was the plan that he should live at Lickinghole. I suppose he is now become the father of a family, and that we may all hail you as grandmother. As we approach that term it becomes less fearful. You mention Mr. Bolling's being unwell, so as not to write to me. He has just been sick enough all his life to prevent his writing to anybody. My prayer is, therefore, only that he may never be any worse; were he to be so, nobody would

---

[1] Mary Jefferson Bolling was Thomas Jefferson's older sister. She married John Bolling in January 1760 and they had ten children. The Bollings lived at Fairfields in Goochland County and Lickinghole Creek, just west of Goochland Courthouse; in 1785 they moved to Chestnut Grove, Bolling's family plantation in Chesterfield County, Virginia, while their oldest son Jack assumed ownership of Fairfields. Letters between Thomas Jefferson, Mary, their sister Martha, and Jefferson's daughter Maria Jefferson Eppes reveal affectionate family relationships. However, it is apparent that John Bolling suffered from alcoholism, and that this was the cause of major strain in the family. As Jefferson writes here, "You mention Mr. Bolling's being unwell, so as not to write to me. He has just been sick enough all his life to prevent his writing to anybody. My prayer is, therefore, only that he may never be any worse...." (Thomas Jefferson Foundation 2016)

feel it more sensibly than myself, as nobody has a more sincere esteem for him than myself. I find as I grow older, that I love those most whom I loved first. Present me to him in the most friendly terms; to Jack also, and my other nephews and nieces of your fireside, and be assured of the sincere love with which I am, dear sister, your affectionate brother.

To A. Donald[1]
Paris, July 28, 1787
Dear Sir,

I received with infinite satisfaction your letter of the 1st of March: it was the first information I had of your being in America. There is no person whom I shall see again with more cordial joy whenever it shall be my lot to return to my native country; nor any one whose prosperity in the meantime will be more interesting to me. I find as I grow older that I set a higher value on the intimacies of my youth, and am more afflicted by whatever loses one of them to me. Should it be in my power to render any service in your shipment of tobacco to Havre de Grace, I shall do it with great pleasure. The order of Berni has I believe been evaded by the farmers general as much as possible. At this moment I receive information from most of the seaports that they refuse taking any tobacco under pretext that they have purchased their whole quantity. From Havre I have heard nothing, and believe you will stand a better chance there than anywhere else. Being one of the ports of manufacture too it is entitled to a higher price. I have now desired that the farmers may make a distinct return of their purchases which are conformable to the order of Berni. If they have really bought their quantity on those terms, we must be satisfied: if they have not, I shall propose their being obliged to make it up instantly. There is a considerable accumulation of tobacco in the ports.

Among many good qualities which my countrymen possess some of a different character, unhappily mix themselves. The most remarkable are indolence, extravagance, & infidelity to their engagements. Cure the two first, and the last would disappear, because it is a consequence of them, and not proceeding from a want of morals. I know of no remedy against indolence & extravagance but a free course of justice. Everything else is merely palliative; but unhappily the evil has gained too generally the mass of the nation to leave the course of justice unobstructed. The maxim of buying nothing without the money in our pocket to pay for it, would make of our country one of the happiest upon earth. Experience during the war proved this; as I think every man will remember that under all the privations it obliged him to submit to during that period he slept sounder & awaked happier than he can do now. Desperate of finding relief from a free course of justice, I look forward to the abolition of all credit as the only other remedy which can take place. I have seen therefore with pleasure the exaggerations of our want of faith with which the London papers teem. It is indeed a strong medicine for sensible minds, but it is a medicine. It will prevent their crediting us abroad, in which case we cannot be credited at home. I have been much concerned at the

---

[1] Alexander Donald was a Richmond tobacco merchant and close friend of Jefferson (Risjord 1978, 299)

losses produced by the fire at Richmond. I hope you have escaped them. It will give me much pleasure to hear from you as often as you can spare a moment to write. Be assured that nobody entertains for you sentiments of more perfect and sincere esteem than Dear Sir your friend & servant.

To Nicholas Lewis[1]
Paris, July 29, 1787
Dear Sir,

In my letter of Dec. 19, 1786, I informed you that, as you had supposed in yours of March 14, that the balance of bonds & profits of the estate to that time would pay all the debts then known to you except my sister Nancy's, I was desirous of laying our shoulder seriously to the paiment of Farrell & Jones' & McCaul's debts; & that I should make propositions to them on that subject. I did so. These propositions were, to pay to Jones 400 £ sterl. a year & to McCaul 200£ sterl., or to the former if he preferred it two thirds of the profits of my estate & to the latter one third. 2. That the crop of 1787, should commence these paiments. 3. That no interest should be allowed on their debts from Apr. 19. 1775 to Apr. 19, 1783 (being 8 years.) 4. That their accounts should remain perfectly open to settlement & rectification, notwithstanding the paiments which should be made. McCaul has acceded very contentedly to these proposals; I added some other conditions to Jones, not worth mentioning as he does not accede as yet, I think however he will accede. I consider myself as so much bound in honor to the sacred execution of this agreement that when the profits fall short of enabling us to pay at any time, I would choose to have made up by a sale of something or another. I mentioned to you in my letter also that I could always get 30/ Virginia money for my tobacco delivered at Havre & proposed your having it sent there. Further reflection and information of the Virginia prices convince me it would be best to send them either to Havre or to Bordeaux, at either of which places I could have them attended to. I find that my old friend A. Donald is settled at Richmond, is concerned in the Tobacco trade, & particularly sends to Havre. I am confident he would take on himself the having my tobaccos shipped to me. The earlier they would come in the season, the better always. So far I had settled in my own mind the plan for extinguishing as fast as we could these two great debts, when I received from Mr. Eppes a letter of May 1. 1787, wherein he tells me he had been with you in Sep. 1786. that you had computed together, all the former debts (except my sister Nancy's) due from the estate, & all due to it; and

---

[1] Certainly not limited to Jefferson's financial position, debts destroyed not only lives and families but the personal independence that free Virginians cherished. In eighteenth-century Virginia, though, they were seen as a terrible burden. Further, the men and women that loathed debt found themselves falling deeper and deeper into it as they sought to explain what had happened. Here, reflecting on this dismal economic scenario, Jefferson tells Lewis, "The torment of mind I endure till the moment shall arrive when I shall not owe a shilling on earth is such really as to render life of little value. I cannot decide to sell my lands. I have sold too much of them already, and they are the only sure provision for my children, nor would I willingly sell the slaves as long as there remains any prospect of paying my debts with their labor." (Holton 1999, 44-45)

that there was still a balance of 1200£ against it, to pay which there would be nothing but the crop of 1786, two thirds of which would be consumed by negroes clothing & taxes. This account threatens a total derangement of my plan for payment of my great debts. I had observed that by a statement in your letter of March 14. of the probable proceeds of the crop of 1785, (about 50 hogsheads of tobacco) that the profits of the few house servants & tradesmen hired out were as much as those of the whole estate, & therefore suggested to you the hiring out the whole estate. The torment of mind I endure till the moment shall arrive when I shall not owe a shilling on earth is such really as to render life of little value. I cannot decide to sell my lands. I have sold too much of them already, and they are the only sure provision for my children, nor would I willingly sell the slaves as long as there remains any prospect of paying my debts with their labor. In this I am governed solely by views to their happiness which will render it worth their while to use extraordinary exertions for some time to enable me to put them ultimately on an easier footing, which I will do the moment they have paid the debts due from the estate, two thirds of which have been contracted by purchasing them. I am therefore strengthened in the idea of renting out my whole estate; not to any one person, but in different parts to different persons, as experience proves that it is only small concerns that are gainful, & it would be my interest that the tenants should make a reasonable gain. The lease I made to Garth & Moseley would be a good model. I do not recollect whether in that there was reserved a right of distraining on the lands for the whole rent. If not, such a clause would be essential, especially in the present relaxed state of the laws, I know there was in that no provision against paper money. This is still more essential, the best way of stating the rent would be in ounces of silver. The rent in that lease, tho' expressed in current money, was meant to be 11£. sterling a titheable. When we consider the rise in the price of tobacco, it should balance any difference for the worse which may have taken place in the lands in Albemarle, so as to entitle us there to equal terms. In Cumberland, Goochland, Bedford, where the lands are better, perhaps better terms might be expected. Calculating this on the number of working slaves, it holds up to us a clear revenue capable of working off the debts in a reasonable time. Think of it, my dear Sir, & if you do not find it disadvantageous be so good as to try to execute it, by leases of 3, 4 or 5 years; not more, because no dependence can be reposed in our laws continuing the same for any length of time. Indeed 3 years might be the most eligible term. The mill should be separate from the lease, finished, & rented by itself. All the lands reserved to my own use in Garth & Mosley's lease should still be reserved, and the privileges of that lease in general. House negroes still to be hired separately. The old and infirm, who could not be hired, or whom it would be a pity to hire, could perhaps be employed in raising cotton, or some other easy culture on lands to be reserved; George still to be reserved to take care of my orchards, grasses &c. The lands in Albemarle should be relieved by drawing off a good number of the laborers to Bedford, where a better hire might be expected & more lands be opened there. I feel all the weight of the objection, that we cannot guard the negroes perfectly against the usage, but in a question between hiring & selling them (one of which is necessary) the hiring will be temporary only, and will end in their happiness; whereas if we sell them, they will be subject to equal ill usage, without a prospect of change. It is for their good therefore ultimately, and it appears to promise a relief to me within such a term as I would be willing to wait for. I do not mention the rate of hire with a view to tie you up to that, but merely to show that hiring presents a hopeful prospect. I should rely entirely on your judgment for that, for the choice of kind & helpful tenants, & for every other circumstance.

The bacon hams you were so kind as to send to Mr. Buchanan for me, I never heard of. The difficulty of getting them here renders it not worth attempting again. I will put into this letter some more seeds of the Spanish St. Foin lest those formerly sent should have miscarried. The present situation of Europe threatens a war, which if it breaks out will probably be a very general one. France & England are so little in a condition for war that we may still expect they will do much to avoid it. Should it take place, I fear the scale against this country would be too heavy.

I must pray of you to make all the arrangements possible for enabling me to comply with the first years paiment of my debts, that is to say the paiment for this present year, which is to be made in the city of London the next spring. Apologies for all the trouble I give you would only show you how sensible I am of your goodness. I have proposed the extraordinary trouble of the leases with less reluctance, because it will be taken once for all, & will be a relief in the end. Be so good as to assure Mrs. Lewis of my attachment and my wishes for her health & happiness as well as that of your whole family.

To James Madison[1]
Paris, Aug. 2, 1787
Dear Sir,

My last was of June 20. Your's received since that date are May 15 and June 6. In mine I acknowledged the receipt of the Paccan nuts which came sealed up. I have reason to believe those in the box are arrived at L'Orient. By the Mary [ship name], Capt. Howland lately sailed from Havre to N York I shipped three boxes of books one marked J. M. for yourself, one marked B. F. for Doctr Franklin, &

---

[1] Here, despite prefacing the matter with, "I did not intend to have said anything to you on political subjects," Jefferson writes Madison that he had heard Adams had managed to raise some money in Holland. If this was so, then Congress must borrow sufficient to pay off *all* the French debt. Matters had taken such a turn that France was on the verge of bankruptcy. For the first time he noted the possibility of a convulsion. "Such a spirit has risen within a few weeks as could not have been believed," he declared. Revenues were deficient, Parliament had refused to register any new taxes, demanding instead the convocation of a States-General; the king had taken to drink, the queen is detested; "and an explosion of some sort is not impossible." To be sure, the payment of debts was more than a mere general problem to Jefferson; it was deeply personal as well. In spite of all his own promises, he had been unable to clear away even a part of his own accumulated and long-outstanding accounts of the British merchants. (Schachner 1957, 348)

one marked W. H. for William Hay in Richmond. I have taken the liberty of addressing them all to you as you will see by the enclosed bill of lading, in hopes you would be so good as to forward the other two. You will have opportunities of calling on the gentlemen for freight &c. In yours you will find the books noted in the account enclosed herewith. You have now Mably's works complete except that on Poland, which I have never been able to get, but shall not cease to search for. Some other volumes are wanting to complete your collection of Chronologies. The 4th vol of D'Albon was lost by the bookbinder, & I have not yet been able to get one to replace it. I shall continue to try. The Memoires sur les droits et impositions en Europe (cited by Smith) was a scarce & excessively dear book. They are now reprinting it. I think it will be in three or four parts of from 9 to 12$^\#$ a volume. When it is finished I shall take a copy for you. Amelot's travels into China, I can learn nothing of. I put among the books sent you two somewhat voluminous, & the object of which will need explanation; these are the Tableau de Paris & L'espion Anglois. The former is truly a picture of private manners in Paris, but presented on the dark side & a little darkened moreover. But there is so much truth in its ground work that it will be well worth your reading. You will then know Paris (& probably the other large cities of Europe) as well as if you had been here years. L'espion Anglois is no caricature. It will give you a just idea of the wheels by which the machine of government is worked here. There are in it also many interesting details of the last war, which in general may be relied on. It may be considered as the small history of great events. I am in hopes when you shall have read them you will not think I have misspent your money for them. My method for making out this assortment was to revise the list of my own purchases since the invoice of 1785, and to select such as I had found worth your having. Besides this I have casually met with & purchased some few curious & cheap things. I have made out the Dr. side of the account, taking for my ground work yours of March 18. 1786. correcting two errors of computation in that which were to your prejudice. The account of Mr. Fitzhughs stood thus: 1785. Sep. 1. cash 600$^\#$. Nov. 10. pd their bill of exchange in favor of Limozin 480$^\#$. making 1080$^\#$. The money they paid you was worth 1050$^\#$. according to our mode of settling at 18$^\#$ for 20/ Virginia money. The difference of 30$^\#$ will never be worth notice unless you were to meet with them by chance, & hardly then. I must trouble you on behalf of a Mr. Thos Burke at Loughburke near Loughrea in Ireland, whose brother James Burke is supposed to have died in 1785 on his passage from Jamaica, or St. Eustatius to New York. His property on board the vessel is understood to have come to the hands of alderman Groom at New York. The enclosed copy of a letter to him will more fully explain it. A particular friend of mine here applies to me for information, which I must ask the favor of you to procure and forward to me.

Writing news to others, much pressed in time & making this letter one of private business, I did not intend to have said anything to you on political subjects. But I must press one subject. Mr. Adams informs me he has borrowed money in Holland, which if confirmed by Congress will enable them to pay not only the interest due here to the foreign officers but the principal. Let me beseech you to reflect on the expediency of transferring this debt to Holland. All our other debts in Europe do not injure our reputation so much as this. These gentlemen have connections both in & out of office, & these again their connections, so that our default on this article is further known, more blamed, & excites worse dispositions against us than you can conceive. If you think as I do, pray try to procure an order for paying off their capital. Mr. Adams adds that if any certain tax is provided for the paiment of interest, Congress may borrow enough in Holland to pay off their whole debts in France, both public & private, to the Crown, to the farmers & to Beaumarchais. Surely it will be better to transfer these debts to Holland. So critical is the state of that country that I imagine the monied men of it would be glad to place their money in foreign countries, & that Mr. Adams could borrow there for us without a certain tax for the interest, & saving our faith too by previous explanations on that subject. This country is really supposed on the eve of a *bankruptcy*.[1] Such a spirit has risen within a few weeks as could not have been believed. They see the great deficit in their revenues, & the hopes of economy lessen daily. The parliament refuse to register any act for a new tax, & require an assembly of the states. The object of this assembly is evidently to give law to the King, to fix a constitution, to limit expenses. These views are said to gain upon the nation. The *King's passion* for *drink* is *diverting him* of all *respect*, the *Queen* is *detested* and an *explosion* of some sort is not impossible. The *ministry* is alarmed, & the surest reliance at this moment for the *public peace* is on their *two hundred thousand men*. I cannot write these things in a public dispatch because they would *get* into a *newspaper* and *be back here*.

A final decision of some sort should be made on Beaumarchais' affairs.

I am with sentiments of the most perfect esteem Dear Sir your friend and servt.

P. S. The watch and pedometer are not done. In the box of books are some for the colleges of Philadelphia & Williamsburg & two vols of the *Encyclopedie* for Congress, presented by the author of that part.

To Edward Carrington[2]

---

[1] These and subsequent words in italics were originally written in cipher. (Boyd 1990)

[2] As suggested in this letter to Carrington, Jefferson still believed that Congress was not as helpless to enforce its decisions on the States under the old Articles of Confederation as was pretended, particularly in the collection of money levies. Even though no such power was expressly mentioned in the Articles, "...they have it by the law of nature," he argues to Carrington. "When two parties make a compact, there results to each a power of compelling the other to execute it. Compulsion was never so easy as in our case, where a single frigate would soon levy on the commerce of any state the deficiency of its contributions." Jefferson looks to have reverted to this idea of compulsion on several occasions; and it furnishes a clue to some of the seeming inconsistencies in Jefferson's philosophy of government. How, for example, reconcile this assertion of the power of the central government to employ force, if necessary, to compel State obedience to its decrees with the later doctrine of the Kentucky Resolution that the States were sovereign entities who could declare an act of Congress null and void? The answer lies in Jefferson's reiterated distinction between foreign and domestic

Paris, Aug 4, 1787
Dear Sir,

   Since mine of the 16th of January I have been honored by your favors of Ap 24 & June 9. I am happy to find that the states have come so generally into the scheme of the Federal convention, from which I am sure we shall see wise propositions. I confess I do not go as far in the reforms thought necessary as some of my correspondents in America; but if the convention should adopt such propositions I shall suppose them necessary. My general plan would be to make the states one as to everything connected with foreign nations, & several as to everything purely domestic. But with all the imperfections of our present government, it is without comparison the best existing or that ever did exist. It's greatest defect is the imperfect manner in which matters of commerce have been provided for. It has been so often said, as to be generally believed, that Congress have no power by the confederation to enforce anything, for e. g., contributions of money. It was not necessary to give them that power expressly; they have it by the law of nature. When two parties make a compact, there results to each a power of compelling the other to execute it. Compulsion was never so easy as in our case, where a single frigate would soon levy on the commerce of any state the deficiency of its contributions; nor more safe than in the hands of Congress which has always shown that it would wait, as it ought to do, to the last extremities before it would execute any of its powers which are disagreeable. I think it very material to separate in the hands of Congress the Executive & Legislative powers, as the Judiciary already are in some degree. This I hope will be done. The want of it has been the source of more evil than we have experienced from any other cause. Nothing is so embarrassing nor so mischievous in a great assembly as the details of execution. The smallest trifle of that kind occupies as long as the most important act of legislation, & takes place of everything else. Let any man recollect, or look over, the files of Congress, he will observe the most important propositions hanging over from week to week & month to month, till the occasions have past them, & the thing never done. I have ever viewed the executive details as the greatest cause of evil to us, because they in fact place us as if we had no federal head, by diverting the attention of that head from great to small objects; and should this division of power not be recommended by the Convention, it is my opinion Congress should make it itself by establishing an Executive committee.

To Benjamin Hawkins[1]

---

affairs, in foreign matters — for which the contributions were intended — Congress was supreme and representative of a unity. In domestic matters, on the other hand — even under the Constitution — the States were supreme and Congress representative of a federated group of sovereign powers. (Schachner 1957, 342)

[1] Benjamin Hawkins, a North Carolinian, studied French at the College of New Jersey (now Princeton University) and was appointed official interpreter for General George Washington during the Revolutionary War. After the war, he served in the North Carolina House of Commons and the Continental

Paris, Aug. 4, 1787
Dear Sir,

I have to acknowledge the receipt of your favors of Mar. 8 & June 9. and to give you many thanks for the trouble you have taken with the Dionasa Muscipula [a carnivorous plant]. I have not yet heard anything of them, which makes me fear they have perished by the way. I believe the most effectual means of conveying them hither will be by the seed. I must add my thanks too for the vocabularies. This is an object I mean to pursue, as I am persuaded that the only method of investigating the filiation of the Indian nations is by that of their languages.

I look up with you to the Federal convention for an amendment of our federal affairs. Yet I do not view them in so disadvantageous a light at present as some do. And above all things I am astonished at some people's considering a kingly government as a refuge. Advise such to read the fable of the frogs who solicited Jupiter for a king. If that does not put them to rights, send them to Europe to see something of the trappings of monarchy, and I will undertake that every man shall go back thoroughly cured. If all the evils which can arise among us from the republican form of our government from this day to the day of judgment could be put into a scale against what this country suffers from its monarchical form in a week, or England in a month, the latter would preponderate. Consider the contents of the red book in England, or the Almanac royale of France, and say what a people gain by monarchy. No race of kings has ever presented above one man of common sense in twenty generations. The best they can do is to leave things to their ministers, & what are their ministers but a committee, badly chosen? If the king ever meddles it is to do harm. It is still undecided whether we shall have war or not. If war, I fear it will not be a successful one for our friends against England & Prussia. Such a war by sea, & such a one by land, are too much for this country at this time. Add to this that the condition of her finances threatens bankruptcy, & that the hope of mending them lessens daily. Good will result from other late operations of the government, but as to money matters they have lost more confidence than they have gained. Were it possible for us to borrow money in Holland to pay them the principal of our debt at this time, it would be felt by them with gratitude as if we had given them so much. I think it probable they would do something clever for us in our commerce; & would be very sure to help us again whenever our affairs would require it. Mr. Adams thinks the money could be borrowed in Holland if there was a tax laid to pay the interest. But I think it possible that the present storm in Holland may make the monied men wish to transfer their money anywhere else. I wish Mr. Adams put

---

Congress before representing North Carolina in the U.S. Senate from 1789 to 1795. Responding to reports that had filtered back to France that there were those in America who thought a kingly government was the only one that could avoid anarchy and chaos. Jefferson responded vehemently. Here he suggests that Hawkins advise the advocates of a monarchy to read the fable of the frogs and King Stork. "If that does not put them to rights," he added, "send them to Europe to see something of the trappings of monarchy, and I will undertake that every man shall go back thoroughly cured." (Foster 2013; Schachner 1957, 342)

on this business before he leaves Europe. Adieu, my dear Sir, & be assured of the esteem of your friend & servt.

To Peter Carr[1]
Paris, Aug. 10, 1787
Dear Peter,

I have received your two letters of Decemb. 30 and April 18, and am very happy to find by them, as well as by letters from Mr. Wythe, that you have been so fortunate as to attract his notice & good will; I am sure you will find this to have been one of the most fortunate events of your life, as I have ever been sensible it was of mine. I inclose you a sketch of the sciences to which I would wish you to apply in such order as Mr. Wythe shall advise; I mention also the books in them worth your reading, which submit to his correction. Many of these are among your father's books, which you should have brought to you. As I do not recollect those of them not in his library, you must write to me for them, making out a catalogue of such as you think you shall have occasion for in 18 months from the date of your letter, & consulting Mr. Wythe on the subject. To this sketch I will add a few particular observations.

1. Italian. I fear the learning this language will confound your French and Spanish. Being all of them degenerated dialects of the Latin, they are apt to mix in conversation. I have never seen a person speaking the three languages who did not mix them. It is a delightful language, but late events having rendered the Spanish more useful, lay it aside to prosecute that.

2. Spanish. Bestow great attention on this, & endeavor to acquire an accurate knowledge of it. Our future connections with Spain & Spanish America will render that language a valuable acquisition. The antient history of a great part of America, too, is written in that language. I send you a dictionary.

3. Moral philosophy. I think it lost time to attend lectures in this branch. He who made us would have been a pitiful bungler if he had made the rules of our moral conduct a matter of science. For one man of science, there are thousands who are not. What would have become of them? Man was destined for society. His morality therefore was to be formed to this object. He was endowed with a sense of right & wrong merely relative to this. This sense is as much a part of his nature as the sense of hearing, seeing, feeling; it is the true foundation of morality, & not the kalon [moral beauty] truth, &c. as fanciful writers have imagined. The moral sense, or conscience, is as much a part of man as his leg or

---

[1] Peter Carr was born in Goochland County, Virginia, most likely at the Spring Forest plantation of his parents, Dabney Carr, a lawyer, and Martha Jefferson Carr, Jefferson's sister. Dabney Carr and Jefferson had formed so close a friendship that after Carr's death, Jefferson took full responsibility for the education of Peter Carr. During his time in France, Jefferson entrusted his informal guardianship to James Madison. Here, Jefferson seeks to advise Carr on matters of education, while also expounding on the innate goodness of man with some measure of persistence. To Jefferson, the moral sense was an integral part of the social sense, and here, to Carr, he writes that "the moral sense of conscience is as much a part of a man as his leg or arm." Further, that "Man was destined for society. His morality, therefore, was to be formed to this object." (Looney 2013; Berman 1927, 33)

arm. It is given to all human beings in a stronger or weaker degree, as force of members is given them in a greater or less degree. It may be strengthened by exercise, as may any particular limb of the body. This sense is submitted indeed in some degree to the guidance of reason; but it is a small stock which is required for this: even a less one than what we call common sense. State a moral case to a ploughman & a professor. The former will decide it as well, & often better than the latter, because he has not been led astray by artificial rules. In this branch therefore read good books because they will encourage as well as direct your feelings. The writings of Sterne particularly form the best course of morality that ever was written. Besides these read the books mentioned in the enclosed paper; and above all things lose no occasion of exercising your dispositions to be grateful, to be generous, to be charitable, to be humane, to be true, just, firm, orderly, courageous &c. Consider every act of this kind as an exercise which will strengthen your moral faculties, & increase your worth.

4. Religion. Your reason is now mature enough to examine this object. In the first place divest yourself of all bias in favor of novelty & singularity of opinion. Indulge them in any other subject rather than that of religion. It is too important, & the consequences of error may be too serious. On the other hand shake off all the fears & servile prejudices under which weak minds are servilely crouched. Fix reason firmly in her seat, and call to her tribunal every fact, every opinion. Question with boldness even the existence of a god; because, if there be one, he must more approve of the homage of reason, than that of blindfolded fear. You will naturally examine first the religion of your own country. Read the bible then, as you would read Livy or Tacitus. The facts which are within the ordinary course of nature you will believe on the authority of the writer, as you do those of the same kind in Livy & Tacitus. The testimony of the writer weighs in their favor in one scale, and their not being against the laws of nature does not weigh against them. But those facts in the bible which contradict the laws of nature, must be examined with more care, and under a variety of faces. Here you must recur to the pretensions of the writer to inspiration from god. Examine upon what evidence his pretensions are founded, and whether that evidence is so strong as that its falsehood would be more improbable than a change in the laws of nature in the case he relates. For example in the book of Joshua we are told the sun stood still several hours. Were we to read that fact in Livy or Tacitus we should class it with their showers of blood, speaking of statues, beasts, &c. But it is said that the writer of that book was inspired. Examine therefore candidly what evidence there is of his having been inspired. The pretension is entitled to your inquiry, because millions believe it. On the other hand you are astronomer enough to know how contrary it is to the law of nature that a body revolving on its axis as the earth does, should have stopped, should not by that sudden stoppage have prostrated animals, trees, buildings, and should after a certain time have resumed its revolution, & that without a second general prostration. Is this arrest of the earth's motion, or the evidence which affirms it, most within the law of probabilities? You will next read the new testament. It is the history of a personage called Jesus. Keep in your eye the opposite pretensions 1. of those

who say he was begotten by god, born of a virgin, suspended & reversed the laws of nature at will, & ascended bodily into heaven: and 2. of those who say he was a man of illegitimate birth, of a benevolent heart, enthusiastic mind, who set out without pretensions to divinity, ended in believing them, & was punished capitally for sedition by being gibbeted according to the Roman law which punished the first commission of that offence by whipping, & the second by exile or death in furcâ. See this law in the Digest Lib. 48. tit. 19. §. 28. 3. & Lipsius Lib. 2. de cruce. cap. 2. These questions are examined in the books I have mentioned under the head of religion, & several others. They will assist you in your inquiries, but keep your reason firmly on the watch in reading them all. Do not be frightened from this inquiry by any fear of its consequences. If it ends in a belief that there is no god, you will find incitements to virtue in the comfort & pleasantness you feel in its exercise, and the love of others which it will procure you. If you find reason to believe there is a god, a consciousness that you are acting under his eye, & that he approves you, will be a vast additional incitement; if that there be a future state, the hope of a happy existence in that increases the appetite to deserve it; if that Jesus was also a god, you will be comforted by a belief of his aid and love. In fine, I repeat that you must lay aside all prejudice on both sides, & neither believe nor reject anything because any other persons, or description of persons have rejected or believed it. Your own reason is the only oracle given you by heaven, and you are answerable not for the rightness but uprightness of the decision. I forgot to observe when speaking of the new testament that you should read all the histories of Christ, as well of those whom a council of ecclesiastics have decided for us to be Pseudo-evangelists, as those they named Evangelists. Because these Pseudo-evangelists pretended to inspiration as much as the others, and you are to judge their pretensions by your own reason, & not by the reason of those ecclesiastics. Most of these are lost. There are some however still extant, collected by Fabricius which I will endeavor to get & send you.

5. Travelling. This makes men wiser, but less happy. When men of sober age travel, they gather knowledge which they may apply usefully for their country, but they are subject ever after to recollections mixed with regret, their affections are weakened by being extended over more objects, & they learn new habits which cannot be gratified when they return home. Young men who travel are exposed to all these inconveniences in a higher degree, to others still more serious, and do not acquire that wisdom for which a previous foundation is requisite by repeated & just observations at home. The glare of pomp & pleasure is analogous to the motion of their blood, it absorbs all their affection & attention, they are torn from it as from the only good in this world, and return to their home as to a place of exile & condemnation. Their eyes are forever turned back to the object they have lost, & its recollection poisons the residue of their lives. Their first & most delicate passions are hackneyed on unworthy objects here, & they carry home only the dregs, insufficient to make themselves or anybody else happy. Add to this that a habit of idleness, an inability to apply themselves to business is acquired & renders them useless to themselves & their country.

These observations are founded in experience. There is no place where your pursuit of knowledge will be so little obstructed by foreign objects as in your own country, nor any wherein the virtues of the heart will be less exposed to be weakened. Be good, be learned, & be industrious, & you will not want the aid of travelling to render you precious to your country, dear to your friends, happy within yourself. I repeat my advice to take a great deal of exercise, & on foot. Health is the first requisite after morality. Write to me often & be assured of the interest I take in your success, as well as of the warmth of those sentiments of attachment with which I am, dear Peter, your affectionate friend.

P. S. Let me know your age in your next letter. Your cousins here are well & desire to be remembered to you.

To Dr. George Gilmer[1]
Paris, August 12, 1787
Dear Doctor,

Your letter of Jan 9, 1787, came safely to hand in the month of June last. Unluckily you forgot to sign it, and your handwriting is so Protean that one cannot be sure it is yours. To increase the causes of incertitude it was dated Penpark, a name which I only know as the seat of John Harmer. The handwriting too being somewhat in his style made me ascribe it hastily to him, indorse it with his name, and let it lie in my bundle to be answered at leisure. That moment of leisure arriving, I set down to answer it to John Harmer, & now for the first time discover marks of its being yours, & particularly those expressions of friendship to myself and family which you have ever been so good as to entertain, and which are to me among the most precious possessions. I wish my sense of this, & my desires of seeing you rich & happy may not prevent my seeing any difficulty in the case you state of George Harmer's wills; which as you state them are thus:

1. A will dated Dec 26, 1779, written in his own hand & devising to his brother the estates he had received from him.

2. Another will dated June 25, 1782, written also in his own hand, devising his estate to trustees to be conveyed to such of his relations. I. H. I. L. or H. L. as should become capable of acquiring property, or, on failure of that, to be sold & the money remitted them.

---

[1] Dr. George Gilmer was one of Jefferson's oldest friends and a former classmate at the College of William and Mary. Here, Jefferson provides a bit of legal counsel drawn from the death of George Harmer and Gilmer's mention in the estate papers. Years earlier, in 1766, it was Gilmer who encouraged Jefferson to be inoculated for smallpox. At the time, Jefferson was a tall, fit, lanky young man in fine health, but he undertook the then-controversial treatment to prevent contracting an acute future case of the devastating disease. The procedure was effected in Philadelphia, as inoculation was illegal in Virginia at the time, where many feared the procedure would spread infection. Jefferson's warm feelings toward the Gilmers are straightforward: "I shall be very happy to eat at Pen-park some of the good mutton & beef of Marrowbone, Horse-pasture & Poisonfield, with yourself & Mrs. Gilmer & my good old neighbors. I am as happy nowhere else & in no other society, & all my wishes end, where I hope my days will end, at Monticello." (Abrams 2013, 169)

3. A third will dated Sep 12, 1786, devising all his estate at Marrowbone, & his tracts at Horsepasture & Poisonfield to you, which will is admitted to record & of course has been duly executed.

You say the learned are divided on these wills. Yet I see no cause of division, as it requires little learning to decide that "the first deed, & last will must always prevail." I am afraid therefore the difficulty may arise on the want of words of inheritance in the devise to you: for you state it as a devise to "George Gilmer" (without adding "& to his heirs") of "all the estate called Marrowbone" "the tract called Horsepasture" and "the tract called Poisonfield." If the question is on this point, and you have copied the words of the will exactly, I suppose you take an estate in fee simple in Marrowbone, & for life only in Horsepasture & Poisonfield, the want of words of inheritance in the two last cases being supplied as to the first by the word "estate" which has been repeatedly decided to be descriptive of the quantum of interest devised, as well as of its locality. I am in hopes however you have not copied the words exactly, that there are words of inheritance to all the devises, as the testator certainly knew their necessity, & that the conflict only will be between the different wills, in which case I see nothing which can be opposed to the last. I shall be very happy to eat at Pen-park some of the good mutton & beef of Marrowbone, Horse-pasture & Poisonfield, with yourself & Mrs. Gilmer & my good old neighbors. I am as happy nowhere else & in no other society, & all my wishes end, where I hope my days will end, at Monticello. Too many scenes of happiness mingle themselves with all the recollections of my native woods & fields, to suffer them to be supplanted in my affection by any other. I consider myself here as a traveler only, & not a resident. My commission expires next spring, & if not renewed, I shall of course return then. If renewed, I shall remain here some time longer. How much I cannot say; yet my wishes shorten the period. Among the strongest inducements will be that of your society & Mrs. Gilmer's, which I am glad to find brought more within reach by your return to Pen-park. My daughters are importunate to return also. Patsy enjoys good health, & is growing to my stature. Polly arrived here about a month ago, after a favorable voyage, & in perfect health. My own health has been as good as ever, after the first year's probation. The accident of a dislocated wrist, badly set, has I fear deprived me forever of almost every use of my right hand. Nor is the extent of the evil as yet known, the hand withering, the fingers remaining swelled & crooked, & losing rather than gaining in point of suppleness. It is now eleven months since the accident. I am able to write, tho for a long time I was not so. This inability was succeeded by a journey into the Southern parts of France and Northern of Italy, which added to the length of the chasm in my correspondence with my friends. If you knew how agreeable to me are the details of the small news of my neighborhood, your charity would induce you to write frequently. Your letters lodged in the post office at Richmond (to be forwarded to N York) come with certainty. We are doubtful yet whether there will be war or not. Present me with warm affection to Mrs. Gilmer & be assured yourself of the unvarying sentiments of esteem & attachment with which I am Dear Doctor your sincere friend & servant

To Joseph Jones[1]
Paris, Aug. 14, 1787
Dear Sir,

I have never yet thanked you, but with the heart, for the act of assembly confirming the agreement with Maryland, the pamphlet & papers I received from you a twelve month ago. Very soon after their receipt I got my right wrist dislocated which prevented me long from writing & as soon as that was able to bear it I took a long journey from which I am but lately returned. I am anxious to hear what our federal convention recommends & what the states will do in consequence of their recommendation. I wish to see our states made one as to all foreign, & several as to all domestic matters, a peaceable mode of compulsion over the states given to Congress, & the powers of this body divided, as in the states, into three departments legislative, executive, & judiciary. It is my opinion the want of the latter organization has already done more harm than all the other federal defects put together, & that every evil almost may be traced to that source, but with all the defects of our constitutions, whether general or particular, the comparison of our governments with those of Europe, are like a comparison of heaven & hell. England, like the earth, may be allowed to take the intermediate station. And yet I hear there are people among you who think the experience of our governments has already proved that republican governments will not answer. Send those gentry here to count the blessings of monarchy. A king's sister for instance stopped on the road, & on a hostile journey, is sufficient cause for him to march immediately 20,000 men to revenge this insult, when he had shown himself little moved by the matter of right then in question.

I apprehend this hasty movement of the King of Prussia may perhaps decide the crisis of Europe to war, when it was before doubtful. The English squadron has sailed Westwardly: the French will doubtless do the same, & they are moving an army into the neighborhood of Holland. Still however the negotiations are not broken off, and the desperate state of finances both in England & France give a hope they will yet arrange matters in this country. A great & sudden discontent has arisen, since the separation of the Assemblee des Notables. It is not easy to fix the causes, since it is certain that great improvements of their laws & constitution have actually taken place & others are promised, great reforms in expense have been effected & are effecting. But the investigation of the horrid depredation in the late administration of their finances, some new and

---

[1] Jefferson's perception of what concepts should be preserved from Europe and what should be dropped was immediate and sure, for his idea of patriotism was based upon a keen awareness of the fundamental differences between the Old and New Worlds. Again and again he expressed this awareness, deriving from the comparison a reassuring picture of the way of life he so passionately preferred. And, perhaps nowhere are these glaring differences so succinctly contrasted than in this letter to the Virginia Anti-Federalist Joseph Jones: "With all the defects of our constitutions, whether general or particular, the comparison of our governments with those of Europe are like a comparison of heaven and hell. England, like the earth, may be allowed to take an intermediate station." (Berman 1947, 55-56)

inconsiderable expenses of the court, and the new taxes have probably excited this discontent. The opposition of the parliament to the new taxes is carried to its last point, and their exile is a measure which may very possibly take place. The principal security against it is the mild & patriotic character of the new ministry.

From all these broils we are happily free, and that God may keep us long so, and yourself in health & happiness is the prayer of, dear Sir, your most obedient, & most humble servant.

P. S. Aug. 15. The Parliament is exiled to Troyes this morning.

To The Editor of The Journal De Paris[1]
Paris, Aug. 29, 1787
Sir,

I am a citizen of the United States of America, and have passed in those states almost the whole of my life. When young, I was passionately fond of reading books of history & travels. Since the commencement of the late revolution which separated us from Great Britain, our country too has been thought worthy to employ the pens of historians & travelers. I cannot paint to you, Sir, the agonies which these have cost me, in obliging me to renounce these favorite branches of reading and in discovering to me at length that my whole life has been employed in nourishing my mind with fables & falsehoods. For thus I reason. If the histories of d'Auberteuil & of Longchamps, and the travels of the Abbé Robin can be published in the face of the world, can be read & believed by those who are cotemporary with the events they pretend to relate, how may we expect that future ages shall be better informed? Will those rise from their graves to bear witness to the truth, who would not, while living, lift their voices against falsehood? If cotemporary histories are thus false, what will future compilations be? And what are all those of preceding times? In your Journal of this day you announce & criticize a book under the title of "les ligues Acheenne, Suisse, & Hollandoise, et revolution des etats unis de l'Amerique par M. de Mayer." I was no part of the Achaean Swiss or Dutch confederacies, & have therefore nothing to say against the facts related of them. And you cite only one fact from his account of the American revolution. It is in these words. "Monsieur Mayer assure qu'une seule voix, un seul homme, prononça l'independance des

---

[1] All of the evidence indicates that Jefferson wrote this letter in a burst of indignation over the mistaken account of the adoption of the Declaration of Independence that he had read in the *Journal de Paris*. Then, with customary prudence, permitted himself a cooling-off period; and finally, on reflection, decided not to dispatch the document. This evidence may be summarized as follows: (1) Being generally averse to newspaper controversy, Jefferson usually sent his remarks intended for publication to some third person who could be depended upon to make a good translation, and there is no evidence that he did so in this instance; (2) The letter was never published in the *Journal de Paris*; and, probably most importantly, (3) Jefferson was known in Paris as the author of the Declaration of Independence. Still, the letter possesses considerable value as it details, from Jefferson's unique personal perspective, the scenarios leading up to the document's adoption. (Boyd 1990)

Etats unis. Ce fut, dit il, John Dickinson, un des Deputés de la Pensilvanie au Congrés. La veille, il avoit vôté pour la soumission, l'egalité des suffrages avoit suspendu la resolution; s'il eut persisté, le Congrés ne deliberoit point, il fut foible; il ceda aux instances de ceux qui avoient plus d'energie, plus d'eloquence, et plus de lumieres; il donna sa voix: l'Amerique lui doit une reconnaissance eternelle; c'est Dickinson qui l'a affranchie." The modesty and candour of Mr. Dickinson himself, Sir, would disavow every word of this paragraph, except these — "il avoit voté pour la soumission." These are true, every other tittle false. I was on the spot, & can relate to you this transaction with precision. On the 7th of June, 1776, the delegates from Virginia moved, in obedience to instructions from their constituents, that Congress should declare the 13 united colonies to be independant of Great Britain, that a Confederation should be formed to bind them together, and measures be taken for procuring the assistance of foreign powers. The house ordered a punctual attendance of all their members the next day at ten o'clock, & then resolved themselves into a Committee of the whole and entered on the discussion. It appeared in the course of the debates that 7. states. viz., N Hampshire, Massachusetts, Rhode Island, Connecticut, Virginia, North Carolina & Georgia, were decided for a separation; but that 6. others still hesitated, to wit. New York, New Jersey, Pennsylvania, Delaware, Maryland, & South Carolina. Congress, desirous of unanimity, & seeing that the public mind was advancing rapidly to it, referred the further discussion to the 1st of July, appointing in the meantime a Committee to prepare a declaration of independence, a second to form Articles for the confederation of the states, and a third to propose measures for obtaining foreign aid. On the 28th of June, the Declaration of Independence was reported to the house, and was laid on the table for the consideration of the members. On the 1st day of July they resolved themselves into a committee of the whole, and resumed the consideration of the motion of June 7. It was debated through the day, and at length was decided in the affirmative by the vote of 9. states. viz New Hampshire, Massachusetts, Connecticut, Rhode island, New Jersey, Maryland, Virginia, N. Carolina and Georgia. Pennsylvania and S. Carolina voted against it. Delaware, having but two members present, was divided. The delegates from New York declared they were for it, & their constituents also; but that the instructions against it which had been given them a twelvemonth before, were still unrepealed; that their convention was to meet in a few days, and they asked leave to suspend their vote till they could obtain a repeal of their instructions. Observe that all this was in a committee of the whole Congress, and that according to the mode of their proceedings, the Resolution of that Committee to declare themselves independent was to be put to the same persons reassuming their form as a Congress. It was now evening, the members exhausted by a debate of 9 hours, during which all the powers of the soul had been distended with the magnitude of the object, and the delegates of S. Carolina desired that the final decision might be put off to the next morning that they might still weigh in their own minds their ultimate vote. It was put off, and in the morning of the 2d of July they joined the other nine states in voting for it. The members of the Pennsylvania delegation too, who had been absent the day before, came in & turned the vote of their state in favor of independence, and a 3d member of the state of Delaware, who, hearing of the division in the sentiments of his two colleagues, had travelled post to arrive in time, now came in and decided the vote of that state also for the resolution. Thus twelve states voted for it at the time of its passage, and the delegates of New York, the 13th state, received instructions within a few days to add theirs to the general vote; so that, instead of the "egalité des suffrages" spoken of by M. Mayer, there was not a dissenting voice. Congress proceeded immediately to consider the Declaration of Independence which had been reported by their committee on the 28th of June. The several paragraphs of that were debated for three days, viz. the 2d, 3d, & 4th of July. In the evening of the 4th they were finally closed, and the instrument approved by a unanimous vote and signed by every member, except Mr. Dickinson. Look into the Journal of Congress of that day, Sir, and you will see the instrument, and the name of the signers, and that Mr. Dickinson's name is not among them. Then read again those words of your paper. "Il (M. Mayer) assure qu'une seule voix, un seul homme, prononça l'independance des etats unis, ce fut John Dickinson. — l'Amerique lui doit une reconnoissance eternelle; c'est Dickinson qui l'a affranchie." With my regrets, & my Adieus to History, to Travels, to Mayer, & to you, Sir, permit me to mingle assurances of the great respect with which I have the honor to be, Sir, your most obedient & most humble servant.

To George Wythe[1]
Paris, Sep. 16, 1787
Dear Sir,

I am now to acknowledge the receipt of your favors of Dec. 13 & 22 1786 & of Jan. 1787. These should not have been so long unanswered, but that they arrived during my absence on a journey of between 3 & 4 months through the Southern parts of France & northern of Italy. In the latter country my time allowed me to go no further than Turin, Milan, and Genoa: consequently I scarcely got into classical ground. I took with me some of the writings in which endeavors have been made to investigate the passage of Hannibal over the Alps, and was just able to satisfy myself, from a view of the country, that the descriptions given of his march are not sufficiently particular to enable us at this day even to guess at his track across the Alps. In architecture, painting, sculpture, I found much amusement: but more than all in their agriculture, many objects of which might

---

[1] The absence of personal letters from Jefferson's time in Italy means that "Notes of a Tour" constitutes the main source of information for his Italian experience. But, the matter-of-fact nature of "Notes," however, detracts from a trip that, by all other indications, involved exciting adventure, culinary delight, aesthetic pleasure, and new information. One exception is this letter in which he describes his trip to his old mentor, George Wythe, and provides a measure of scholarly insight into the history of the area: "I took with me some of the writings in which endeavors have been made to investigate the passage of Hannibal over the Alps, and was just able to satisfy myself, from a view of the country, that the descriptions given of his march are not sufficiently particular to enable us at this day even to guess at his tract across the Alps." (Hayes 2008, 346)

be adopted with us to great advantage. I am persuaded there are many parts of our lower country where the olive tree might be raised, which is assuredly the richest gift of heaven. I can scarcely except bread. I see this tree supporting thousands in among the Alps where there is not soil enough to make bread for a single family. The caper too might be cultivated with us. The fig we do raise. I do not speak of the vine, because it is the parent of misery. Those who cultivate it are always poor, and he who would employ himself with us in the culture of corn, cotton, &c. can procure in exchange much more wine, & better than he could raise by its direct culture. I sent you formerly copies of the documents on the Tagliaferro family which I had received from Mr. Febroni. I now send the originals. I have procured for you a copy of Polybius, the best edition; but the best edition of Vitruvius, which is with the commentaries of Ticinus, is not to be got here. I have sent to Holland for it. In the meantime the Polybius comes in a box containing books for Peter Carr & for some of my friends in Williamsburg & its vicinities. I have taken the liberty of addressing this box to you. It goes to New York in the packet boat which carries this letter, & will be forwarded to you by water, by Mr. Madison. Its freight to New York is paid here. The transportation from thence to Williamsburgh will be demanded of you, and shall stand as the equivalent to the cost of Polybius & Vitruvius if you please. The difference either way will not be worth the trouble of erecting & transmitting accounts. I send you herewith a state of the contents of the box, and for whom each article is. Among these are some as you will perceive, of which I ask your acceptance. It is a great comfort to me that while here I am able to furnish some amusement to my friends by sending them such productions of genius, antient & modern, as might otherwise escape them; and I hope they will permit me to avail myself of the occasion, while it lasts. This world is going all to war. I hope our's will remain clear of it. It is already declared between the Turks & Russians, and, considering the present situation of Holland, it cannot fail to spread itself all over Europe. Perhaps it may not be till the next spring that the other powers will be engaged in it: nor is it as yet clear how they will arrange themselves. I think it not impossible that France & the two empires may join against all the rest. The Patriotic party in Holland will be saved by this, and the Turks sacrificed.

The only thing which can prevent the union of France & the two empires, is the difficulty of agreeing about the partition of the spoils. Constantinople is the key of Asia. Who shall have it is the question? I cannot help looking forward to the reestablishment of the Greeks as a people, and the language of Homer becoming again a living language, as among possible events. You have now with you Mr. Paradise, who can tell you how easily the modern may be improved into the antient Greek. You ask me in your letter what ameliorations I think necessary in our federal constitution. It is now too late to answer the question, and it would always have been presumption in me to have done it. Your own ideas & those of the great characters who were to be concerned with you in these discussions will give the law, as they ought to do, to us all. My own general idea was that the states should severally preserve their sovereignty in whatever concerns themselves alone, & that whatever may concern another state, or any foreign nation, should be made a part of the federal sovereignty. That the exercise of the federal sovereignty should be divided among three several bodies, legislative, executive, & judiciary, as the state sovereignties are: and that some peaceable means should be contrived for the federal head to enforce compliance on the part of the states.

I have reflected on your idea of wooden or ivory diagrams for the geometrical demonstrations. I should think wood as good as ivory; & that in this case it might add to the improvement of the young gentlemen; that they should make the figures themselves. Being furnished by a workman with a piece of veneer, no other tool than a penknife & a wooden rule would be necessary. Perhaps pasteboards, or common cards might be still more convenient. The difficulty is, how to reconcile figures which must have a very sensible breadth, to our ideas of a mathematical line, which, having neither breadth nor thickness, will revolt more at these than at simple lines drawn on paper or slate. If after reflecting on this proposition you would prefer having them made here, lay your commands on me and they shall be executed.

I return you a thousand thousand thanks for your goodness to my nephew. After my debt to you for whatever I am myself, it is increasing it too much to interest yourself for his future fortune. But I know that, to you, a consciousness of doing good is a luxury ineffable. You have enjoyed it already beyond all human measure, and that you may long live to enjoy it and to bless your country & friends is the sincere prayer of him who is with every possible sentiment of esteem & respect, dear Sir, your most obedient & most humble servant.

To Charles Thomson[1]
Paris, Sep. 20, 1787
Dear Sir,

Your favor of April 28 did not come to my hands till the 1st inst. Unfortunately the boxes of plants, which were a day too late to come by the April packet, missed the packet of June 10 also, & only came by that of July 25. They are not yet arrived at Paris, but I expect them daily. I am sensible of your kind attention to them, and that as you were leaving New York you took the course which bade fair to be the best. That they were forgotten in the hands in which you placed them, was probably owing to too much business & more important. I have desired Mr. Madison to refund to you the money you were so kind as to advance for me. The delay of your letter will apologize for this delay of the repayment. I thank you also for the extract of the letter you were so kind as to communicate to me on the antiquities found in the Western country. I wish that the persons who go thither would make very exact descriptions of what they see of that kind, without forming any theories. The moment a person forms

---

[1] As previously indicated, Charles Thomson was an Irish émigré and political leader during the American Revolution. He served as secretary of the Continental Congress (1774–89) and is credited as being the moving spirit in the committee that obtained the design for the Great Seal of the United States. (Wood 2009, 555)

a theory his imagination sees in every object only the traits which favor that theory. But it is too early to form theories on those antiquities. We must wait with patience till more facts are collected. I wish your philosophical society would collect exact descriptions of the several monuments as yet known, and insert them naked in their transactions, and continue their attention to those hereafter to be discovered. Patience & observation may enable us in time to solve the problem whether those who formed the scattering monuments in our Western country, were colonies sent off from Mexico, or the founders of Mexico itself? Whether both were the descendants or the progenitors of the Asiatic red men. The Mexican tradition mentioned by Dr. Robertson, is an evidence, but a feeble one, in favor of the one opinion. The number of languages radically different, is a strong evidence in favor of the contrary one. There is an American of the name of Ledyard, he who was with Captain Cook on his last voyage & wrote an account of that voyage, who is gone to St. Petersburg, from thence he was to go to Kamschatka, to cross over thence to the northwest coast of America, & to penetrate through the main continent to our side of it. He is a person of ingenuity & information. Unfortunately he has too much imagination. However, if he escapes safely, he will give us new, curious, & useful information. I had a letter from him dated last March, when he was about to leave St. Petersburgh on his way to Kamschatka.

With respect to the information of the strata of rocks, I had observed them between the Blue Ridge & North Mountain in Virginia to be parallel with the pole of the earth. I observed the same thing in most instances in the Alps between Cette & Turin: but in returning along the precipices of the Pyrinees where they hang over the Mediterranean, their direction was totally different and various; and you mention that in our Western country they are horizontal. This variety proves they have not been formed by subsidence as some writers of theories of the earth have pretended, for then they should always have been in circular strata, & concentric. It proves too that they have not been formed by the rotation of the earth on its axis, as might have been suspected had all these strata been parallel with that axis. They may indeed have been thrown up by explosions, as Whitehurst supposes, or have been the effect of convulsions. But there can be no proof of the explosion, nor is it probable that convulsions have deformed every spot of the earth. It is now generally agreed that rock grows, and it seems that it grows in layers in every direction, as the branches of trees grow in all directions. Why seek further the solution of this phenomenon? Everything in nature decays. If it were not reproduced then by growth, there would be a chasm. I remember you asked me in a former letter whether the steam mill in London was turned by the steam immediately or by the intermediate agency of water raised by the steam. When I was in London Boulton made a secret of his mill. Therefore I was permitted to see it only superficially. I saw no water wheels, & therefore supposed none. I answered you accordingly that there were none. But when I was at Nismes, I went to see the steam mill there, & they showed it to me in all its parts. I saw that their steam raised water, & that this water turned a wheel. I expressed my doubts of the necessity of the inter-agency of water, &

that the London mill was without it. But they supposed me mistaken; perhaps I was so; I have had no opportunity since of clearing up the doubt.

To William Carmichael[1]
Paris, Sep. 25, 1787
Dear Sir,

The copy of your letter of July 9. and that of Aug. 22. came to hand together. The original of the former I never received. My last to you was dated June 14. I heard indirectly that Mr. *Grand* had refused to pay *a bill* of *yours*.[2] But he never said a word to me on the subject, nor mentioned any *letter of yours* in consequence of it. I have stated the matter to the *board of Treasury*. I also wrote to Mr. Adams a state of the same fact. There are at Amsterdam 100.000 *florins at his disposal*. Colo. Smith will endeavor to get *for you an order* to draw on that *fund*. The subject of *Smith's mission to Portugal* appeared to me so *causeless as given out* that I imagined it was only the *ostensible* one, the *real cause remaining a secret between him and Congress*, yet I never heard *any other hinted*. With respect to the reimbursement to the Count d'Expilly for the maintenance of our prisoners at Algiers, I wrote to Mr. Jay what you had formerly communicated to me, but am not authorized to give any answer. I think it important to destroy at Algiers every idea that Congress will redeem our captives there, perhaps at any price, much less at that paid by Spain. It seems to be the general opinion that the redeeming them would occasion the capture of greater numbers by increasing the incitements to cruise against us. We must never make it their interest to go out of the straights in quest of us, and we must avoid entering into the straights at least till we are rich enough to arm in that sea. The Spanish consul therefore cannot too soon withdraw himself from all responsibility for our prisoners. As to the affair of the frigate of South Carolina, I communicated to you everything I knew on the subject, by inclosing you all the papers which had come to my hands. I have received letters & gazettes from America to the 25. of July. The federal convention was likely to sit to the month of October. A thin Congress was sitting at the same time. They had passed an Ordinance dividing the country North of Ohio into three states, & providing

---

[1] This letter represents the first use of a coded message in the correspondence between Jefferson and Ambassador to Spain, Carmichael. Ironically, the most significant passage in it — the assertion that the Mississippi Question was the "only bone of contention which can arise between Spain and US for ages" and that it would therefore be wise "to take arrangements according to what must happen" — was one that Jefferson must have intended Carmichael to pass on to Spain's Chief Minister, José Moñino, 1st Count of Floridablanca. But, to make doubly sure, he left this passage uncoded. Further, this letter can only assume its proper perspective in the light of Carmichael's insistence through more than two years that he could not safely or fully discuss international affairs or the domestic policies and court intrigues of Madrid without being possessed of a cipher. Carmichael first broached the subject in June, 1785, and it is perhaps significant that he then suggested to Jefferson that Congress would do well to send a common cipher to each of their ministers and chargé d'affaires. (Boyd 1990)
[2] These and subsequent words in italics were originally written in cipher. (Ibid.)

both a present and a future form of government for them. The sale of their lands commence this month. An idea had got abroad in the Western country that Congress was ceding to Spain the navigation of the Mississippi for a certain time. They had taken flame at it, & were assembling conventions on the subject, wherein the boldest & most dangerous propositions were to be made. They are said to be now 60.000 strong, and are more formidable from their spirit than numbers. This is the only bone of contention which can arise between Spain & us for ages. It is a pity it could not be settled amicably. When we consider that the Mississippi is the only issue to the ocean for five eights of the territory of the U. S. & how fast that territory peoples, the ultimate event cannot be mistaken. It would be wise then to take arrangements according to what must happen.

There had been a hope that the affairs of Holland might be accommodated without a war. But this hope has failed. The Prussian troops have entered the territories of the republic. The stadtholder is now at the Hague, and there seems to be no force capable of opposing him. England too has notified this court by her envoy, two days ago, that she is arming. In the meantime *little provision* has been *made here* against such an *event*. M. de *Segur declares* that six weeks ago he *proposed in council* to *march 24,000 men* into *Holland.* The archbishop is *charged* principally with having *prevented this.* He seems to have been *duped by his* strong desire for peace, and by calculating that the K. of Prussia would have acted on principles of common sense. To complicate the game still more, you know of the war which has arisen between Russia & the Turks. You know also that it was excited there, as well as at Berlin by the English. Former alliances thus broke, Prussia having thrown herself into the scale opposed to France, Turkey having abandoned her councils and followed the instigations of her enemies, what remains for this country to do? *I know* that *Russia proposed a confederation* with *this court,* that *this court* without committing *itself wished* 1481. 941. I know the *final determination* of the *emperor was that he* came into *the proposition,* has formed a line from the Russian to the Turkish confines by 4. camps of 30,000 men in one, & 50,000 in each of the others. Yet it does *not seem that France has closed* the *proposal* in favor of which every principle of common sense enlists itself. *The queen, Breteuil and Montmorin* have been for some time *decidedly* for this *triple alliance* which especially if *aided by Spain* would *give law to the world.* The *premier is* still accused *with hesitation.* They begin to say that tho' *he is* a patriotic *Minister and an able one for peace he* has not *energy enough for war. If* this *takes place* the consequences to Prussia and the *Stadtholder* may be easily foreseen. *Whether it does or not* the Turks must *quit Europe.* Neutrality should be our plan: because no nation should without urgent necessity begin a second war while the debts of the former remain unpaid. The accumulation of debts is a most fearful evil. But ever since the accession of the present King of England, that court has unerringly done what common sense would have dictated not to do. Now common sense dictates that they should avoid forcing us to take part against them, because this brings on them a heavy land war. Therefore they will not avoid it: they will stop our ships, visit and harass them, seize them on the most frivolous pretexts and oblige us to take from them Canada & Nova Scotia, which it is not our interest to possess. Mr. Eden sets out in a few days for Madrid. You will have to oppose in him the most bitter enemy against our country which exists. His late and sudden elevation makes the remembrance of the contempt we shewed to his mission in America rankle the more in his breast. Whether his principle will restrain him to fair modes of opposition, I am not well enough acquainted with him to say. I know nothing of him but his parliamentary history, and that is not in his favor. As he wishes us every possible ill, all the lies of the London papers are true history in his creed, and will be propagated as such, to prejudice against us the mind of the Court where you are. You will find it necessary to keep him well in your eye, and to trace all his foot-steps.

You know doubtless that M. de Brienne has been appointed Minister of War, & the Count de la Luzerne Minister of Marine. He is brother of the Chevalier, & at present in St. Domingo of which he is commandant. The Count de Moustier goes Minister to America, the Chevalier de la Luzerne preferring the promise of the first vacant embassy. Lambert is Comptrolleur general. De la Borde & Cabarus have successively refused the office of Directeur du tresor royale.

Having now got the maps for the *Notes on Virginia*, I will send by the Count d'Aranda two copies, one for yourself, & one for Monsr de Campomenes. By the same conveyance I will forward the Ratification of the treaty with Morocco, & ask the favor of you to contrive it to that court. Mr. Barclay is gone to America.

To John Adams[1]
Paris, Sep. 28, 1787
Dear Sir,

I received your favor by Mr. Cutting, and thank you sincerely for the copy of your book. The departure of a packet boat, which always gives me full employment for some time before has only permitted me to look into it a little. I judge of it from the first volume which I thought formed to do a great deal of good. The first principle of a good government is certainly a distribution of its powers into executive, judiciary & legislative and a subdivision of the latter into two or three branches. It is a good step gained, when it is proved that the English constitution, acknowledged to be better than all which have preceded it, is only better in proportion as it has approached nearer to this distribution of powers. From this the last step is easy, to shew by a comparison of our constitutions with that of England, how much more perfect they are. The article of Confederations is surely worthy of your pen. It would form a most interesting addition to shew what have been the nature of the Confederations which have existed hitherto, what were their excellences & what their defects. A comparison of ours with

---

[1] While Jefferson's hatred of the English and admiration of the French are well known, in this letter to Adams his opinions are particularly venomous: "We I hope shall be left free to avail ourselves of the advantages of neutrality: and yet much I fear the English, or rather their stupid king, will force us out of it. For thus I reason. By forcing us into the war against them they will be engaged in an expensive land war as well as a sea war. Common sense dictates therefore that they should let us remain neuter: *ergo* they will not let us remain neuter. I never yet found any other general rule for foretelling what they will do, but that of examining what they ought not to do." (Walsh 1834, 199)

them would be to the advantage of ours, and would increase the veneration of our countrymen for it. It is a misfortune that they do not sufficiently know the value of their constitutions & how much happier they are rendered by them than any other people on earth by the governments under which they live.

You know all that has happened in the United Netherlands. You know also that our friends Van Staphorsts will be among the most likely to become objects of severity, if any severities should be exercised. Is the money in their hands entirely safe? If it is not, I am sure you have already thought of it. Are we to suppose the game already up, and that the Stadtholder is to be reestablished, perhaps erected into a monarch, without this country lifting a finger in opposition to it? If so, it is a lesson the more for us. In fact what a crowd of lessons do the present miseries of Holland teach us? Never to have an hereditary officer of any sort: never to let a citizen ally himself with kings: never to call in foreign nations to settle domestic differences, never to suppose that any nation will expose itself to war for us, &c. Still I am not without hopes that a good rod is in soak for Prussia, and that England will feel the end of it. It is known to some that Russia made propositions to the emperor & France for acting in concert, that the emperor consents and has disposed four camps of 180,000 men from the limits of Turkey to those of Prussia. This court hesitates, or rather it's premier hesitates; for the queen, Montmorin & Breteuil are for the measure. Should it take place, all may yet come to rights, except for the Turks, who must retire from Europe, and this they must do were France Quixotic enough to undertake to support them. We I hope shall be left free to avail ourselves of the advantages of neutrality: and yet much I fear the English, or rather their stupid king, will force us out of it. For thus I reason. By forcing us into the war against them they will be engaged in an expensive land war as well as a sea war. Common sense dictates therefore that they should let us remain neuter: ergo they will not let us remain neuter. I never yet found any other general rule for foretelling what they will do, but that of examining what they ought not to do.

You will have heard doubtless that M. Lambert is Comptroller general, that the office of Directeur general du tresor royal, has been successively refused by Monsr. de la Borde & Monsr. Cabarrus; that the Conte de Brienne, brother of the Archbishop, is Minister of War, and the Count de la Luzerne Minister of Marine. They have sent for him from his government in the West Indies. The Chevalier de la Luzerne has a promise of the vacant Embassy. It will be that of London if Adhemar can be otherwise disposed of. The Chevalier might have had that of Holland if he would. The Count de Moustier will sail about the middle of next month. Count d'Aranda leaves us in a few days. His successor is hourly expected.

I have the honor to be with my best respects to Mrs. Adams, & sentiments of perfect esteem & regard to yourself dear Sir your most obedient & most humble servant.

P.S. Since writing the above, I learn through a *very good* [*channel*] *that this court is decided* and is *arranging* with the *two empires*. Perhaps as a proof of this we may soon *see them recall their officers in the Dutch service.*[1]

---

[1] The words in italics were originally written in cipher. (Boyd 1990)

To Comte De Buffon[1]
Paris, Octob. 1, 1787
Sir,

I had the honor of informing you some time ago that I had written to some of my friends in America, desiring they would send me such of the spoils of the Moose, Caribou, Elk & deer as might throw light on that class of animals; but more particularly to send me the complete skeleton, skin, & horns of the Moose, in such condition as that the skin might be sewed up & stuffed on its arrival here. I am happy to be able to present to you at this moment the bones & skin of a Moose, the horns of the Caribou, the elk, the deer, the spiked horned buck, and the Roebuck of America. They all come from New Hampshire & Massachusetts. I give you their popular names, as it rests with yourself to decide their real names. The skin of the Moose was dressed with the hair on, but a great deal of it has come off, and the rest is ready to drop off. The horns of the elk are remarkably small. I have certainly seen of them which would have weighed five or six times as much. This is the animal which we call elk in the Southern parts of America, and of which I have given some description in the *Notes on Virginia*, of which I had the honor of presenting you a copy. I really doubt whether the flat-horned elk exists in America; and I think this may be properly classed with the elk, the principal difference being in the horns. I have seen the Daim, the Cerf, the Chevreuil of Europe. But the animal we call Elk, and which may be distinguished as the Round Horned elk, is very different from them. I have never seen the Brand-hirtz or Cerf d'Ardennes, nor the European elk. Could I get a sight of them I think I should be able to say to which of them the American elk resembles most, as I am tolerably well acquainted with that animal. I must observe also that the horns of the Deer, which accompany these spoils, are not of the fifth or sixth part of the weight of some that I have seen. This individual has been of age, according to our method of judging. I have taken measures particularly to be furnished with large horns of our elk & our deer, & therefore beg of you not to consider those now sent as furnishing a specimen of their ordinary size. I really suspect you will find that the Moose, the Round horned elk, & the American deer are species not existing in Europe. The Moose is perhaps of a new class. I wish these spoils, Sir, may have the merit of adding anything new to the treasures of nature which have so fortunately come under your observation, & of which she seems

---

[1] This letter is indicative of Jefferson's profound displeasure with the work of one of the most distinguished naturalists of his day: French scientist Georges-Louis Leclerc, the Comte de Buffon. Buffon expressed the view that the climates of the colonies in America were degenerative, "that nature is less active, less energetic on one side of the globe than she is on the other" (Jefferson's translation), and asserted that climate in turn led to smaller and less diverse plant and animal life in the New World as compared to the Old. By way of counter-evidence, a proud Jefferson sent Buffon the skeleton of a moose along with the written descriptions — in this letter — of the massive antlers such animals often possessed, expressing the hope that it "may have the merit of adding anything new to the treasures of nature which have so fortunately come under your observation." (Solomon, Daniel and mien and Druckenbrod 200, 430)

to have given you the key: they will in that case be some gratification to you, which it will always be pleasing to me to have procured, having the honor to be with sentiments of the most perfect esteem & respect, Sir, your most obedient, & most humble servant.

To The Governor of South Carolina (John Rutledge)[1]
Paris, Oct. 4, 1787
Sir,

  I am informed that the persons having claims against the state of South Carolina on account of the frigate of the same name, have appointed Mr. Cutting their attorney for settling those claims with the state. It becomes my duty therefore to inform you that a claim of the state against the court of Spain for services performed by that frigate was transmitted to me the last spring by Mr. Jay, together with the papers on which it was founded, & that I was instructed to forward the same to Mr. Carmichael at Madrid to be solicited by him, and at the same time to confer with the Prince of Luxemburg on the subject & engage the assistance of the French ambassador at Madrid in the solicitation. All this was done, and I have lately received a letter from Mr. Carmichael inclosing the copy of one from the Count de Florida Blanca by which it appears that the court of Spain has referred the adjustment of your claim to Mr. Gardoqui & your delegates at New York, where perhaps the whole business may be most conveniently settled. In my conference with the Prince of Luxemburg I undertook to quiet his mind by assurances which I knew I might make with truth, that the state of South Carolina would settle his claim finally with justice & honor, & would take measures for paying it as soon as their situation would permit. A recent instance of arrangements taken in a like case by the state of Maryland has had a good effect in counteracting those calumnies against us which our enemies on the other side the channel disseminate industriously through all Europe.

---

[1] This letter relates to what became known as the "Luxembourg Claims." While the state's obligations to the veterans who served on the frigate *South Carolina* were the most enduring of the claims generated by the frigate, the most famous debt was that owed to the prince of Luxembourg, the principal actor in the second class of obligations — those stemming from the contract of May 1780, in which Luxembourg had leased, and assigned control over, the warship to Commodore Alexander Gillon of South Carolina. In the lease document the Commodore had committed a percentage of prize money to the prince. Indeed the prince's banker, Ferdinand Grand of Paris, had been appointed to distribute all prize money; as noted, however, with the exception of the ill-fated *Alexander*, captured off the coast of Ireland and recaptured by the British on her way to France, Gillon had been unable to send any prizes or money to Grand. Moreover, as also noted, the Commodore had promised the prince compensation if the frigate was utilized for any other purpose than capturing enemy ships on the high seas, and that the *South Carolina* would be returned to a French port after three years. If she were lost or simply not returned, the contract stipulated that Gillon pay the prince three hundred thousand livres. (Lewis 1999, 112)

To James Madison[1]
Paris, Oct. 8, 1787
Dear Sir,

The bearer hereof the Count de Moustier, successor to Monsr de la Luzerne, would from his office need no letter of introduction to you or to anybody. Yet I take the liberty of recommending him to you to shorten those formal approaches which the same office would otherwise expose him to in making your acquaintance. He is a great enemy to formality, etiquette, ostentation & luxury. He goes with the best dispositions to cultivate society without poisoning it by ill example. He is sensible, disposed to view things favorably, & being well acquainted with the constitution of England, it's manners & language, is the better prepared for his station with us. But I should have performed only the lesser, & least pleasing half of my task, were I not to add my recommendations of Madame de Brehan. She is goodness itself. You must be well acquainted with her. You will find her well-disposed to meet your acquaintance & well worthy of it. The way to please her is to receive her as an acquaintance of a thousand years' standing. She speaks little English. You must teach her more, and learn French from her. She hopes by accompanying Monsieur de Moustier to improve her health which is very feeble, & still more to improve her son in his education & to remove him to a distance from the seductions of this country. You will wonder to be told that there are no schools in this country to be compared to ours, in the sciences. The husband of Madame de Brehan is an officer, & obliged by the times to remain with the army. Monsieur de Moustier brings your watch. I have worn it two months and really find her a most incomparable one. She will not want the little redressing which new watches generally do after going about a year. She cost 600 livres. To open her in all her parts, press the little pin on the edge, with the point of your nail, that opens the crystal, then open the dial plate in the usual way, then press the stem, at the end within the loop, & it opens the back for winding up or regulating. De Moustier is remarkably communicative. With adroitness he may be pumped of anything. His openness is from character, not from affectation. An intimacy with him may, on this account be politically valuable.[2]

---

[1] Here Jefferson initiates what will soon become an object lesson in the disparity between the French and American sexual and social codes, which could only have served to reinforce his realization that to escort Maria Cosway about Paris was one thing, and to travel about with her in America without her husband quite another. The new French minister to the United States, the Comte de Moustier, had embarked for the New World with the beautiful Madame de Brehan, who was his sister-in-law and also his mistress. Here, Jefferson writes a warm letter of introduction on her behalf to Madison, describing her as "goodness itself," as "modest and amiable," adding that her husband, as an officer, was "obliged by the times to remain with the army." He was shortly chilled and saddened to learn that Americans treated the couple frostily. Madison later stiffly wrote him that the Comte de Moustier "suffers also from his illicit connection with Madame de Brehan which is universally known and offensive to American manners.... On their journeys it is said they often neglect the most obvious precautions for veiling their intimacy." (Brodie 1974, 221)

[2] The words in italics were originally written in cipher. (Boyd 1990)

To John Jay[1]
Paris, Nov 3, 1787
Sir,

I shall take the liberty of confiding sometimes to a private letter such details of the small history of the court or cabinet as may be worthy of being known, and yet not proper to be publicly communicated. I doubt whether the administration is yet in a permanent form. The Count de Montmorin & Baron de Breteuil are I believe firm enough in their places. It was doubted whether they would wait for the count de la Lucerne, if the war had taken place; but at present I suppose they will. I wish it also; because M. de Hector, his only competitor, has on some occasions shewn little value for the connection with us. Lambert, the Comptroller general is thought to be very insecure. I should be sorry also to lose him. I have worked several days with him, the M. de la Fayette, and Monsr. du Pont (father of the young gentleman gone to America with the Count de Moustier) to reduce into one arret whatever concerned our commerce. I have found him a man of great judgment & application, possessing good general principles on subjects of commerce, & friendly dispositions towards us. He passed the arret in a very favorable form, but it has been opposed in the council, & will I fear suffer some alteration in the article of whale oil. That of tobacco, which was put into a separate instrument, experiences difficulties also, which do not come from him. Mr. du Pont has rendered us essential service on these occasions. I wish his son could be so well noticed as to make a favorable report to his father; he would I think be gratified by it, & his good dispositions be strengthened, & rendered further useful to us. Whether I shall be able to send you these regulations by the present packet, will depend on their getting thro' the council in time. The Archbishop continues well with his patroness. Her object is, a close connection with her brother. I suppose he convinces her that peace will furnish the best occasions of cementing that connection. It may not be uninstructive to give you the origin & nature of his influence with the queen.

When the D. de Choiseul proposed the marriage of the dauphin with this lady, he thought it proper to send a person to Vienna to perfect her in the language. He asked his friend the Archbishop of Toulouse to recommend to him a proper person. He recommended a certain Abbé. The Abbé, from his first arrival at Vienna, either tutored by his patron, or prompted by gratitude, impressed on the queen's mind the exalted talents and merit of the Archbishop, and continually

---

[1] Jefferson's opening sentence requires careful consideration: "I shall take the liberty of confiding sometimes to a private letter such details of the small history of the court or cabinet as may be worthy of being known, and yet not proper to be publicly communicated." Further, his pointed reference to European habits of bribing clerks; his remarks about use of the post office by intelligence agencies; and his expression of confidence in Jay's treatment of letters from foreign ministers — these are all indicative of the unexpressed fear that the real danger lay in a possibly inappropriate bit of information being shared by Jay with Congress. This potential resulted in Jefferson becoming extremely sensitive to the danger of publication and the consequent handicap placed upon him as an effective minister. (Ibid.)

represented him as the only man fit to be placed at the helm of affairs. On his return to Paris, being retained near the person of the queen, he kept him constantly in her view. The Archbishop was named of the assembly des notables, had occasion enough there to prove his talents, & count de Vergennes his great enemy, dying opportunely, the Queen got him into place. He uses the abbé even yet, for instilling all his notions into her mind. That he has imposing talents, and patriotic dispositions I think is certain. Good judges think him a theorist only, little acquainted with the details of business & spoiling all his plans by a bungled execution. He may perhaps undergo a severe trial. His best actions are exciting against him a host of enemies, particularly the reduction of the pensions & reforms in other branches of economy. Some think the ministers are willing he should stay in till he has effected this odious, yet necessary work, & that they will then make him the scape-goat of the transaction. The declarations too which I send you in my public letter, if they should become public, will probably raise an universal cry. It will all fall on him, because Montmorin & Breteuil say without reserve, that the sacrifice of the Dutch has been against their advice. He will perhaps not permit these declarations to appear in this country. They are absolutely unknown, they were communicated to me by the D. of Dorset, and I believe no other copy has been given here. They will be published, doubtless, in England, as a proof of their triumph, & may thence make their way into this country. If the premier can stem a few months, he may remain long in office & will never make war if he can help it. If he should be removed, the peace will probably be short. He is solely chargeable with the loss of Holland. True they could not have raised money by taxes to supply the necessities of war; but could they do it were their finances ever so well arranged? No nation makes war now-a-days but by the aid of loans: and it is probable that in a war for the liberties of Holland, all the treasures of that country would have been at their service. They have now lost the cow which furnishes the milk of war. She will be on the side of their enemies, whenever a rupture shall take place: & no arrangement of their finances can countervail this circumstance.

I have no doubt, you permit access to the letters of your foreign ministers by persons only of the most perfect trust. It is in the European system to bribe the clerks high in order to obtain copies of interesting papers.

I am sure you are equally attentive to the conveyance of your letters to us, as you know that all are opened that pass thro' any post office of Europe. Your letters which come by the packet, if put into the mail at New York, or into the post office at Havre, wear proofs that they have been opened. The passenger to whom they are confided, should be cautioned always to keep them in his own hands till he can deliver them personally in Paris.

To William Stephens Smith[1]

---

[1] During Jefferson's absence from the United States, his friend and closest political ally, James Madison, spearheaded a movement to replace the wartime Articles of Confederation with a constitution that would rein in the powers of the virtually sovereign thirteen states. Sharing Madison's vision of America's destiny

Paris, Nov 13, 1787
Dear Sir,

I am now to acknowledge the receipt of your favors of October the 4th, 8th, & 26th. In the last you apologies for your letters of introduction to Americans coming here. It is so far from needing apology on your part, that it calls for thanks on mine. I endeavor to shew civilities to all the Americans who come here, & will give me opportunities of doing it: and it is a matter of comfort to know from a good quarter what they are, & how far I may go in my attentions to them. Can you send me Woodmason's bills for the two copying presses for the M. de la Fayette, & the M. de Chastellux? The latter makes one article in a considerable account, of old standing, and which I cannot present for want of this article.

I do not know whether it is to yourself or Mr. Adams I am to give my thanks for the copy of the new constitution. I beg leave through you to place them where due. It will be yet three weeks before I shall receive them from America. There are very good articles in it: & very bad. I do not know which preponderate. What we have lately read in the history of Holland, in the chapter on the Stadtholder, would have sufficed to set me against a chief magistrate eligible for a long duration, if I had ever been disposed towards one: & what we have always read of the elections of Polish kings should have forever excluded the idea of one continuable for life. Wonderful is the effect of impudent & persevering lying. The British ministry have so long hired their gazetteers to repeat and model into every form lies about our being in anarchy, that the world has at length believed them, the English nation has believed them, the ministers themselves have come to believe them, & what is more wonderful, we have believed them ourselves. Yet where does this anarchy exist? Where did it ever exist, except in the single instance of Massachusetts? And can history produce an instance of rebellion so honorably conducted? I say nothing of its motives. They were founded in ignorance, not wickedness. God forbid we should ever be 20 years without such a rebellion. The people cannot be all, & always, well informed. The part which is wrong will be discontented in proportion to the importance of the facts they misconceive. If they remain quiet under such misconceptions it is a lethargy, the forerunner of death to the public liberty. We have had 13. states independent 11. years. There has been one rebellion. That comes to one rebellion in a century & a half for each state. What country before ever existed a century & half without a rebellion? & what country can preserve its liberties if their rulers are not warned from time to time that their people preserve the spirit of resistance? Let them take arms. The remedy is to set them right as to facts, pardon & pacify them.

---

as a continental nation, Jefferson disagreed with those who feared the political awakening of ordinary men which the states' autonomy had fostered. When he heard that an armed band of indebted farmers in western Massachusetts had closed the county courts, Jefferson, in this letter to John Adams' son-in-law, penned some of his most memorable lines: "The tree of liberty must be refreshed from time to time with the blood of patriots and tyrants. It is its natural manure." Shays' Rebellion, which fearful conservatives and creditors viewed as part of a larger plot being hatched by democrats and debtors, was seen by Jefferson as a useful purgative of the body politic. (Appleby 1999, xviii)

What signify a few lives lost in a century or two? The tree of liberty must be refreshed from time to time with the blood of patriots & tyrants. It is it's natural manure. Our Convention has been too much impressed by the insurrection of Massachusetts: and in the spur of the moment they are setting up a kite to keep the hen-yard in order. I hope in God this article will be rectified before the new constitution is accepted.

You ask me if anything transpires here on the subject of S. America. Not a word. I know that there are combustible materials there, and that they wait the torch only. But this country probably will join the extinguishers.

The want of facts worth communicating to you has occasioned me to give a little loose to dissertation. We must be contented to amuse, when we cannot inform.

To William Carmichael[1]
Paris, Dec. 15, 1787
Dear Sir,

I am later in acknowledging the receipt of your favors of Oct. 15, Nov. 5 & 15, because we have been long expecting a packet which I hoped would bring communications worth detailing to you, and she arrived only a few days ago, after a very long passage indeed. I am very sorry you have not been able to make out the cipher of my letter of Sept. 25, because it contained things which I wished you to know at that time. They have lost now a part of their merit; but still I wish you could decipher them, there remains a part which it might still be agreeable to you to understand. I have examined the cipher, from which it was written. It is precisely a copy of those given to Messieurs Barclay & Lamb. In order that you may examine whether yours corresponds I will now translate into cipher the three first lines of my letter of June 14. 1420. 1250. 1194. 1307. 1531. 458. 48. 1200. 134. 1140. 1469. 519. 563. 1129. 1057. 1201. 1199. 1531. 1571. 1040. 870. 423. 1001. 855. 521. 1173. 917. 1559. 505. 1196. 51. 1152. 698. 141. 1569. 996. 861. 804. 1337. 1199.

This will serve to show whether your cipher corresponds with mine, as well as my manner of using it. But I shall not use it in future till I know from you the result of your re-examination of it. I have the honor now to return you the letter you had been so good as to enclose to me. About the same time of Liston's conversation with you, similar ones were held with me by Mr. Eden. He

---

[1] In a conflict between France and England Jefferson could never be neutral in the sense of being indifferent. With Jefferson it was a question of honestly trying to maintain an actual neutrality in spite of those predilections that were often expressed by each, within the inner circle of his friends. Too, Jefferson was convinced that the fate of the American experiment was bound up with the success of the French Revolution. But while he was firmly convinced that the United States should take no part in any European War, in this letter to William Carmichael, the American Ambassador to Spain, he notes that, "...without hesitation that our treaty obliged us to receive the armed vessels of France with their prizes into our ports, & to refuse admission to the prizes made on her by her enemies: that there was a clause by which we guaranteed to France her American possessions, and which might perhaps force us into the war if these were attacked." (Thomas 1931, 15)

particularly questioned me on the effect of our treaty with France in the case of a war, and what might be our dispositions. I told him without hesitation that our treaty obliged us to receive the armed vessels of France with their prizes into our ports, & to refuse admission to the prizes made on her by her enemies: that there was a clause by which we guaranteed to France her American possessions, and which might perhaps force us into the war if these were attacked. "And it is certain, said he, that they would have been attacked." I added that our dispositions would have been to be neutral, & that I thought it the interest of both those powers that we should be so, because it would relieve both from all anxiety as to the feeding their West Indian islands, and England would moreover avoid a heavy land war on our continent which would cripple all her proceedings elsewhere. He expected these sentiments from me personally, and he knew them to be analogous to those of our country. We had often before had occasions of knowing each other: his peculiar bitterness towards us had sufficiently appeared, & I had never concealed from him that I considered the British as our natural enemies, and as the only nation on earth who wished us ill from the bottom of their souls. And I am satisfied that were our continent to be swallowed up by the ocean, Great Britain would be in a bonfire from one end to the other. Mr. Adams, as you know, has asked his recall. This has been granted, & Colonel Smith is to return too; Congress having determined to put an end to their commission at that court. I suspect, and hope they will make no new appointment.

Our new constitution is powerfully attacked in the American newspapers. The objections are, that its effect would be to form the 13 states into one; that proposing to melt all down into one general government they have fenced the people by no declaration of right, they have not renounced the power of keeping a standing army, they have not secured the liberty of the press, they have reserved a power of abolishing trials by jury in civil cases, they have proposed that the laws of the federal legislature shall be paramount the laws & constitutions of the states, they have abandoned rotation in office; & particularly their president may be re-elected from 4. years to 4 years for life, so as to render him a king for life, like a King of Poland, & have not given him either the check or aid of a council. To these they add calculations of expense &c. &c. to frighten people. You will perceive that these objections are serious, and some of them not without foundation. The constitution however has been received with a very general enthusiasm, and as far as can be judged from external demonstrations the bulk of the people are eager to adopt it. In the eastern states the printers will print nothing against it unless the writer subscribes his name. Massachusetts & Connecticut have called conventions in January to consider of it. In New York there is a division. The Governor (Clinton) is known to be hostile to it. Jersey it is thought will certainly accept it. Pennsylvania is divided, & all the bitterness of her factions has been kindled anew on it. But the party in favor of it is strongest both in & out of the legislature. This is the party antiently of Morris, Wilson &c. Delaware will do what Pennsylvania shall do. Maryland is thought favorable to it: yet it is supposed Chase & Paca will oppose it. As to Virginia two of her delegates in the first place refused to sign it. These were Randolph, the governor,

& George Mason. Besides these, Henry, Harrison, Nelson, & the Lees are against it. Gen'l. Washington will be for it, but it is not in his character to exert himself much in the case. Madison will be its main pillar; but tho an immensely popular one, it is questionable whether he can bear the weight of such a host. So that the presumption is that Virginia will reject it. We know nothing of the disposition of the states South of this. Should it fall thro', as is possible notwithstanding the enthusiasm with which it was received in the first moment, it is probable that Congress will propose that the objections which the people shall make to it being once known, another Convention shall be assembled to adopt the improvements generally acceptable, & omit those found disagreeable. In this way union may be produced under a happy constitution, and one which shall not be too energetic, as are the constitutions of Europe. I give you these details, because possibly you may not have received them all. The sale of our Western lands is immensely successful. 5. millions of acres had been sold at private sale for a dollar an acre in certificates, and at the public sales some of them had sold as high as 24/10 dollars the acre. The sale had not been begun two months. By these means, taxes, &c. our domestic debt, originally 28. millions of dollars was reduced by the 1st day of last October to 12. millions & they were then in treaty for 2. millions of acres more at a dollar private sale. Our domestic debt will thus be soon paid off, and that done, the sales will go on for money, at a cheaper rate no doubt, for the payment of our foreign debt. The petite guerre always waged by the Indian seems not to abate the ardor of purchase or emigration. Kentucky is now counted at 60.000. Franklin is also growing fast.

I inclose you a letter from Mr. Littlepage on the subject of money he owes you. The best thing you can do, I think, will be to desire your banker at Madrid to give orders to his correspondent here to receive the money and remit it to you. I shall cheerfully lend my instrumentality as far as it can be useful to you. If any sum of money is delivered me for you before you write on the subject I shall place it in Mr. Grand's hands subject to your order, & give you notice of it. No money-news yet from our board of treasury.

You ask me if there is any French translation of my notes? There is one by the Abbé Morellet: but the whole order is changed and other differences made, which, with numerous typographical errors, render it a different book, in some respects perhaps a better one, but not mine. I am flattered by the Count de Campomane's acceptance of the original. I wish I had thought to have sent one to Don Ulloa (for I suppose him to be living, tho' I have not heard of him lately,) a person so well acquainted with the Southern part of our world, & who has given such excellent information on it, would perhaps be willing to know something of the Northern part.

I have been told that the cutting thro' the isthmus of Panama, which the world has so often wished & supposed practicable, has at times been thought of by the government of Spain, & that they once proceeded so far as to have a survey & examination made of the ground; but that the result was either impracticability or too great difficulty. Probably the Count de Campomanes or Don Ulloa can give you information on this head. I should be exceedingly pleased to get as minute details as possible on it, and even copies of the survey, report, &c., if they could be obtained at a moderate expense. I take the liberty of asking your assistance in this.

To James Madison[1]
Paris, Dec. 20, 1787
Dear Sir,

My last to you was of Oct. 8 by the Count de Moustier. Yours of July 18. Sep. 6. &Oct. 24. have been successively received, yesterday, the day before & three or four days before that. I have only had time to read the letters, the printed papers communicated with them, however interesting, being obliged to lie over till I finish my dispatches for the packet, which dispatches must go from hence the day after tomorrow. I have much to thank you for. First and most for the ciphered paragraph respecting myself. These little informations are very material towards forming my own decisions. I would be glad even to know when any individual member thinks I have gone wrong in any instance. If I know myself it would not excite ill blood in me, while it would assist to guide my conduct, perhaps to justify it, and to keep me to my duty, alert. I must thank you too for the information in Tho⁵. Burke's case, tho' you will have found by a subsequent letter that I have asked of you a further investigation of that matter. It is to gratify the lady who is at the head of the Convent wherein my daughters are, & who, by her attachment & attention to them, lays me under great obligations. I

---

[1] With respect to insight, this is arguably one of Jefferson's most important letter. After the Constitutional Convention was over, and after carefully studying the Constitution, here Jefferson writes Madison a candid letter explaining his approval of certain sections, while taking exception to others and to the omissions. Jefferson was pleased with the separation of powers, the promised vigor of the government, and the grant of power to levy and collect taxes. The compromise on representation "captivated" him, and several other important features, such as the veto power of the executive, received his approval. The bulk of his letter was reserved for what he found distasteful. "I will now add what I do not like," Jefferson wrote; "first the omission of a bill of rights providing clearly & without the aid of sophisms" for the whole catalog of civil rights commonly accepted as fundamental in America. To these guarantees for personal freedom, Jefferson added a restriction against government-granted monopolies. The argument that James Wilson was employing in Pennsylvania, that these rights were beyond the scope of a general government and dearly unnecessary, was to Jefferson "a *gratis dictum*" that might please a Philadelphia audience but which left him uneasy. Whereas the second section of the Articles of Confederation had assured to each state the retention of its sovereignty and jurisdiction in all cases where specific powers had not been delegated to the central government, no such assurance was found in the proposed Constitution. The lack of uniformity in the states on the matter of jury trials in civil cases should have stimulated the Convention to conclude that errant states must have their mistakes pointed out, "to have established a general right instead of a general wrong." Then as an afterthought, Jefferson scribbled between the lines of his letter a closing remark. "Let me add that a bill of rights" is what the people are entitled to against every government on earth, general or particular, & what no just government should refuse, or rest on inference." (Rutland 1955, 129)

shall hope therefore still to receive from you the result of the further enquiries my second letter had asked.

The parcel of rice which you informed me had miscarried accompanied my letter to the Delegates of S. Carolina. Mr. Bourgoin was to be the bearer of both & both were delivered together into the hands of his relation here who introduced him to me, and who at a subsequent moment undertook to convey them to Mr. Bourgoin. This person was an engraver particularly recommended to D^r. Franklin & Mr. Hopkinson. Perhaps he may have mislaid the little parcel of rice among his baggage.

I am much pleased that the sale of Western lands is so successful. I hope they will absorb all the Certificates of our Domestic debt speedily, in the first place, and that then offered for cash they will do the same by our foreign one.

The season admitting only of operations in the Cabinet, and these being in a great measure secret, I have little to fill a letter. I will therefore make up the deficiency by adding a few words on the Constitution proposed by our Convention. I like much the general idea of framing a government which should go on of itself peaceably, without needing continual recurrence to the state legislatures. I like the organization of the government into Legislative, Judiciary & Executive. I like the power given the Legislature to levy taxes, and for that reason solely approve of the greater house being chosen by the people directly. For tho' I think a house chosen by them will be very illy qualified to legislate for the Union, for foreign nations &c. yet this evil does not weigh against the good of preserving inviolate the fundamental principle that the people are not to be taxed but by representatives chosen immediately by themselves. I am captivated by the compromise of the opposite claims of the great & little states, of the latter to equal, and the former to proportional influence. I am much pleased too with the substitution of the method of voting by persons, instead of that of voting by states: and I like the negative given to the Executive with a third of either house, though I should have liked it better had the Judiciary been associated for that purpose, or invested with a similar and separate power. There are other good things of less moment. I will now add what I do not like. First the omission of a bill of rights providing clearly & without the aid of sophisms for freedom of religion, freedom of the press, protection against standing armies, restriction against monopolies, the eternal & unremitting force of the habeas corpus laws, and trials by jury in all matters of fact triable by the laws of the land & not by the law of nations. To say, as Mr. Wilson does that a bill of rights was not necessary because all is reserved in the case of the general government which is not given, while in the particular ones all is given which is not reserved, might do for the audience to whom it was addressed, but is surely a gratis dictum, opposed by strong inferences from the body of the instrument, as well as from the omission of the clause of our present confederation which had declared that in express terms. It was a hard conclusion to say because there has been no uniformity among the states as to the cases triable by jury, because some have been so incautious as to abandon this mode of trial, therefore the more prudent states shall be reduced to the same level of calamity. It would have been much more just & wise to have concluded the other way that as most of the states had judiciously preserved this palladium, those who had wandered should be brought back to it, and to have established general right instead of general wrong. Let me add that a bill of rights is what the people are entitled to against every government on earth, general or particular, & what no just government should refuse, or rest on inferences. The second feature I dislike, and greatly dislike, is the abandonment in every instance of the necessity of rotation in office, and most particularly in the case of the President. Experience concurs with reason in concluding that the first magistrate will always be re-elected if the Constitution permits it. He is then an officer for life. This once observed, it becomes of so much consequence to certain nations to have a friend or a foe at the head of our affairs that they will interfere with money & with arms. A Galloman or an Angloman will be supported by the nation he befriends. If once elected, and at a second or third election out voted by one or two votes, he will pretend false votes, foul play, hold possession of the reins of government, be supported by the States voting for him, especially if they are the central ones lying in a compact body themselves & separating their opponents: and they will be aided by one nation of Europe, while the majority are aided by another. The election of a President of America some years hence will be much more interesting to certain nations of Europe than ever the election of a king of Poland was. Reflect on all the instances in history antient & modern, of elective monarchies, and say if they do not give foundation for my fears. The Roman emperors, the popes, while they were of any importance, the German emperors till they became hereditary in practice, the kings of Poland, the Deys of the Ottoman dependences. It may be said that if elections are to be attended with these disorders, the seldomer they are renewed the better. But experience shews that the only way to prevent disorder is to render them uninteresting by frequent changes. An incapacity to be elected a second time would have been the only effectual preventative. The power of removing him every fourth year by the vote of the people is a power which will not be exercised. The king of Poland is removeable every day by the Diet, yet he is never removed.

Smaller objections are the Appeal in fact as well as law, and the binding all persons Legislative Executive & Judiciary by oath to maintain that constitution. I do not pretend to decide what would be the best method of procuring the establishment of the manifold good things in this constitution, and of getting rid of the bad. Whether by adopting it in hopes of future amendment, or, after it has been duly weighed & canvassed by the people, after seeing the parts they generally dislike, & those they generally approve, to say to them 'We see now what you wish. Send together your deputies again, let them frame a constitution for you omitting what you have condemned, & establishing the powers you approve. Even these will be a great addition to the energy of your government.'

At all events I hope you will not be discouraged from other trials, if the present one should fail of its full effect.

I have thus told you freely what I like & dislike: merely as a matter of curiosity, for I know your own judgment has been formed on all these points after having heard everything which could be urged on them. I own I am not a friend to a very energetic government. It is always oppressive. The late rebellion in Massachusetts has given more alarm than I think it should have done. Calculate that one rebellion in 13 states in the course of 11 years, is but one for each state in a century & a half. No country should be so long without one. Nor will any degree of power in the hands of government prevent insurrections. France, with all its despotism, and two or three hundred thousand men always in arms has had three insurrections in the three years I have been here in every one of which greater numbers were engaged than in Massachusetts & a great deal more blood was spilt. In Turkey, which Montesquieu supposes more despotic, insurrections are the events of every day. In England, where the hand of power is lighter than here, but heavier than with us they happen every half dozen years. Compare again the ferocious depredations of their insurgents with the order, the moderation & the almost self-extinguishment of ours. After all, it is my principle that the will of the majority should always prevail. If they approve the proposed Convention in all its parts, I shall concur in it cheerfully, in hopes that they will amend it whenever they shall find it work wrong. I think our governments will remain virtuous for many centuries; as long as they are chiefly agricultural; and this will be as long as there shall be vacant lands in any part of America. When they get piled upon one another in large cities, as in Europe, they will become corrupt as in Europe. Above all things I hope the education of the common people will be attended to; convinced that on their good sense we may rely with the most security for the preservation of a due degree of liberty. I have tired you by this time with my disquisitions & will therefore only add assurances of the sincerity of those sentiments of esteem & attachment with which I am Dear Sir your affectionate friend & servant

P. S. The instability of our laws is really an immense evil. I think it would be well to provide in our constitutions that there shall always be a twelvemonth between the engrossing a bill & passing it: that it should then be offered to its passage without changing a word: and that if circumstances should be thought to require a speedier passage, it should take two thirds of both houses instead of a bare majority.

To Edward Carrington[1]

---

[1] Any mention of a war in Europe into which France might be drawn, invariably evoked from Jefferson an announcement that the true interests of the United States lay in a neutral position. Yet the opportunity to derive pecuniary advantages through the expansion of American commerce during a great war appealed to him as it did to most other Americans. Alternatively, he foresaw danger to the United States, too, if France were weakened, and he even contemplated, as had been suggested, the notion of America becoming something akin to pirates operating under French colors. But Jefferson, in the end, remained convinced that ultimate neutrality was the best course of action. And his opinions on European connections had settled into the conviction that the American system should either exclude treaties entirely or make them exceptions, promoting commerce but not entangling it with the politics of the old world. His decision is succinctly reinforced in this letter to Carrington, "I know too that it is a maxim with us, and I think it a wise one, not to entangle ourselves with the affairs of Europe." (Woolery 1927, 103)

Paris, Dec. 21, 1787

Dear Sir,

I have just received your two favors of October 23 and that of Nov. 10. I am much obliged to you for your hints in the Danish business. They are the only information I have on that subject except the resolution of Congress, & warn me of a rock on which I should most certainly have split. The vote plainly points out an Agent, only leaving it to my discretion to substitute another. My judgment concurs with that of Congress as to his fitness. But I shall enquire for the surest banker at Copenhagen to receive the money, not because I should have had any doubts, but because I am informed others would have had them. Against the failure of a banker, were such an accident or any similar one to happen, I cannot be held accountable in a case where I act without particular interest. My principal idea in proposing the transfer of the French debt was to obtain in the new loans a much longer day for the reimbursement of the principal, hoping that the resources of the U. S. could have been equal to the article of interest alone. But I shall endeavor to quiet, as well as I can, those interested. A part of them will probably sell at any rate: and one great claimant may be expected to make a bitter attack on our honor. I am very much pleased to hear that our Western lands sell so successfully. I turn to this precious resource as that which will in every event liberate us from our Domestic debt, and perhaps too from our foreign one: and this much sooner than I had expected. I do not think anything could have been done with them in Europe. Individual speculators & sharpers had duped so many with their unlocated land warrants that every offer would have been suspected. As to the new Constitution I find myself nearly a Neutral. There is a great mass of good in it, in a very desirable form: but there is also to me a bitter pill or two. I have written somewhat lengthily to Mr. Madison on this subject and will take the liberty to refer you to that part of my letter to him. I will add one question to what I have said there. Would it not have been better to assign to Congress exclusively the article of imposts for federal purposes, & to have left direct taxation exclusively to the states? I should suppose the former fund sufficient for all probable events, aided by the land office.

The form which the affairs of Europe may assume is not yet decipherable by those out of the Cabinet. The Emperor gives himself at present the air of a Mediator. This is necessary to justify a breach with the Porte. He has his eye at the same time on Germany, and particularly on Bavaria, the elector of which has for a long time been hanging over the grave. Probably France would now consent to the exchange of the Austrian Netherlands to be created into a kingdom for the Duke de Deuxponts against the electorate of Bavaria. This will require a war. The Empress longs for Turkey; & viewing France as her principal obstacle would gladly negotiate her acquiescence. To spur on this she is coquetting it with England. The king of Prussia too is playing a double game between France & England. But I suppose the former incapable of forgiving him or of ever reposing confidence in him. Perhaps the spring may unfold to us the final arrangement which will take place among the powers of this continent.

I often doubt whether I should trouble Congress or my friends with these details of European politics. I know they do not excite that interest in America of which it is impossible for one to divest himself here. I know too that it is a maxim with us, and I think it a wise one, not to entangle ourselves with the affairs of Europe. Still, I think, we should know them. The Turks have practiced the same maxim of not meddling in the complicated wrangles of this continent. But they have unwisely chosen to be ignorant of them also, and it is this total ignorance of Europe, it's combinations & it's movements which exposes them to that annihilation possibly about taking place. While there are powers in Europe which fear our views, or have views on us, we should keep an eye on them, their connections & oppositions, that in a moment of need we may avail ourselves of their weakness with respect to others as well as ourselves, and calculate their designs & movements on all the circumstances under which they exist. Tho' I am persuaded therefore that these details are read by many with great indifference, yet I think it my duty to enter into them, and to run the risk of giving too much, rather than too little information. I have the honor to be with perfect esteem & respect, Dear Sir, your most obedient & most humble servant.

P. S. The resolution of Congress relative to the prize money received here speaks of that money as paid to me. I hope this matter is properly understood. The treasury board desired me to receive it, and apply it to such & such federal purposes; & that they would pay the dividends of the claimants in America. This would save the expense of remittance. I declined however receiving the money, & ordered it into the hands of their banker, who paid it away for the purposes to which they had destined it. I should be sorry, an idea should get abroad that I had received the money of these poor fellows & applied it to other purposes. I shall in like manner order the Danish & Barbary money into the hands of bankers, carefully avoiding ever to touch a sou of it, or having any other account to make out than what the banker will furnish.

To Colonel Forrest[1]
Paris, Dec. 31. 1787
Dear Sir,

Just before I received your favor asking my opinion of our new proposed constitution, I had written my sentiments on the subject fully to my friend Mr. Madison, they concurred so exactly with yours that the communication of them could answer no end but that of showing my readiness to obey you. I therefore extracted that part from my letter to him, & have reserved it for a good private conveyance which has never offered till now by Mr. Parker. Tho I pretend to make no mystery of my opinion, yet my distance from the scene gives me too much diffidence in my views of it to detail them lengthily & publicly. This diffidence is increased by my high opinion of the abilities & honesty of the framers of the

---

[1] A successful tobacco exporter and delegate in the Continental Congress, Federalist Uriah Forrest, of Georgetown, Maryland, had served with distinction in the Revolution, was wounded in the Battle of Germantown and lost a leg at the Battle of Brandywine. (Ecker 1933, 16)

Constitution, yet we cannot help thinking for ourselves. I suppose I see much precious improvement in it, but some seeds of danger which might have been kept out of sight of the framers by a consciousness of their own honesty & a presumption that all succeeding rulers would be as honest as themselves. Make what use you please of the contents of the paper, but without quoting its author, who has no pretentions to see what is hidden from others.

1788

To William Stephens Smith[1]
Paris, Feb. 2, 1788
Dear Sir,

 With respect to Mr. Adams's picture I must again press it to be done by Brown, because Trumbul does not paint of the size of the life & could not be asked to hazard himself on it. I have sent to Florence for those of Columbus (if it exists) of Americus Vesputius, Magellan &c., and I must not be disappointed of Mr. Adams's when done. Mr. Trumbul will receive & forward it to me. Be so good also as to let me know who undertook the Map of S. America, & even to get from him some acknowledgment in writing, of what he is to do. I am glad to learn by letters which come down to the 20th of December that the new Constitution will undoubtedly be received by a sufficiency of the States to set it a going. Were I in America, I would advocate it warmly till nine should have adopted & then as warmly take the other side to convince the remaining four that they ought not to come into it till the declaration of rights is annexed to it. By this means we should secure all the good of it, & procure so respectable an opposition as would induce the accepting states to offer a bill of rights. This would be the happiest turn the thing could take. I fear much the effects of the perpetual re-eligibility of the President. But it is not thought of in America, & have therefore no prospect of a change of that article. But I own it astonishes me to find such a change wrought in the opinions of our countrymen since I left them, as that three fourths of them should be contented to live under a system which leaves to their governors the power of taking from them the trial by jury in civil cases, freedom of religion, freedom of the press, freedom of commerce, the habeas corpus laws, & of yoking

---

[1] Further reflection on the need for a Bill or Rights continued to solidify Jefferson's now firm position. In this note to Colonel William Smith, in the American legation at London, Jefferson revealed his own ideas on how a Bill of Rights might be added to the Constitution. If I were in America now, Jefferson wrote, "I would advocate it [Constitution] warmly till nine [states] should have adopted, & then as warmly take the other side to convince the remaining four that they ought not to come into it till the declaration of rights is annexed to it. By this means we should secure all the good of it, & procure so respectable an opposition as would induce the accepting states to offer a bill of rights. This would be the happiest turn the thing could take." Indeed, after Jefferson shaped this idea of ratification he made no secret of it and would continue to advance his ideas whenever possible so that his vision would eventually be known from New York south to the Carolinas. (Rutland 1955, 129-130)

them with a standing army. This is a degeneracy in the principles of liberty to which I had given four centuries instead of four years. But I hope it will all come about. We are now vibrating between too much and too little government, & the pendulum will rest finally in the middle. Adieu, yours affectionately.

To William Rutledge[1]
Paris, Feb. 2, 1788
Dear Sir,

I should sooner have answered your favor of Jan. 2. but that we have expected for some time to see you here. I beg you not to think of the trifle I furnished you with, nor to propose to return it till you shall have that sum more than you know what to do with. And on every other occasion of difficulty I hope you will make use of me freely. I presume you will now remain at London to see the trial of Hastings. Without suffering yourself to be imposed on by the pomp in which it will be enveloped, I would recommend to you to consider & decide for yourself these questions: If his offence is to be decided by the law of the land, why is he not tried in that court in which his fellow citizens are tried, i. e., the king's bench? If he is cited before another court that he may be judged, not according to the law of the land, but by the discretion of his judges, is he not disfranchised of his most precious right, the benefit of the laws of his country in common with his other fellow citizens? I think you will find on investigating this subject that every solid argument is against the extraordinary court, & that everyone in its favor is specious only. It is a transfer from a judicature of learning & integrity to one, the greatness of which is both illiterate & unprincipled. Yet such is the force of prejudice with some, & of the want of reflection in others, that many of our constitutions have copied this absurdity without suspecting it to be one. I am glad to hear that our new constitution is pretty sure of being accepted by states enough to secure the good it contains, & to meet such opposition in some

---

[1] Jefferson, the political thinker, was a doctrinaire of the most radical type. Jefferson, the practical statesman, confronting actual conditions, seeking a feasible issue, knew how to adapt and trim, if not suppress his theories quite easily. He viewed all the efforts of the progressive party with optimistic sympathy. Yet he rarely lost his judgment, could criticize unfavorably as well as favorably. He plainly had a sober estimate of the capacities of Frenchmen for larger political life, and believed that they should enjoy the extensive political rights that were their due only after some training in practical politics. And even the attempts of the government to be liberal he regarded with something like open scorn. Here, speaking of the French edict emancipating the Protestants — the 1787 Edict of Toleration — which was hailed as a triumph of enlightened legislation, he tells Rutledge, "The long expected edict of the Protestants at length appears here. It is an acknowledgment (hitherto withheld by the laws) that Protestants can beget children, and that they can die and be offensive unless buried. It does not give them permission to think, to speak, or to worship. It enumerates the limitations to which they shall remain subject, and the burthens to which they shall continue to be unjustly exposed. What are we to think of the condition of the human mind in a country where such a wretched thing as this has thrown the state into convulsions, and how must we bless our own situation in a country, the most illiterate peasant of which is a Solon compared with the authors of this law." (Hazen 1897, 25)

others as to give us hopes it will be accommodated to them by the amendment of its most glaring faults, particularly the want of a declaration of rights.

The long expected edict for the protestants at length appears here. It's analysis is this. It is an acknowledgment (hitherto withheld by the laws) that protestants can beget children and that they can die & be offensive unless buried. It does not give them permission to think, to speak, or to worship. It enumerates the humiliations to which they shall remain subject, & the burthens to which they shall continue to be unjustly exposed. What are we to think of the condition of the human mind in a country where such a wretched thing as this has thrown the state into convulsions, and how must we bless our own situation in a country the most illiterate peasant of which is a Solon compared with the authors of this law. There is modesty often which does itself injury. Our countrymen possess this. They do not know their own superiority. You see it; you are young, you have time & talents to correct them. Study the subject while in Europe in all the instances which will present themselves to you, and profit your countrymen of them by making them to know & value themselves.

To James Madison[1]
Paris, Feb. 6. 1788
Dear Sir,

I am glad to hear that the New Constitution is received with favor. I sincerely wish that the 9 first conventions may receive & the 4 last reject it. The former will receive it finally, while the latter will oblige them to offer a declaration of rights in order to complete the union. We shall thus have all its good, and cure its principal defect. You will of course be so good as to continue to mark to me it's progress. I will thank you also for as exact a data as you can procure me of the impression made on the sum of our domestic debt by the sale of lands, & by federal & state exertions in any other manner. I have not yet heard whether the law passed in Virginia for *prohibiting the importn. of brandies. If it did, the late Arret*

---

[1] Madison had spent the last two years thoroughly immersed in the political campaign to draft the Constitution and oversee its ratification. Jefferson, on the other hand, was an ocean away in Paris, and although Madison had kept him informed of the state-by-state developments in the ratification process, Jefferson was blissfully oblivious to the supercharged political atmosphere that Madison was trying to manage. This helps to explain the rather strange proposal that Jefferson offers here, when ratification remained problematic: "I sincerely wish that the first nine conventions, may receive [the Constitution], and the last four reject it. The former will secure it finally, while the latter will oblige them to offer a declaration of rights in order to complete the union. We shall thus have all its good, without its principal defect." One can only imagine the sense of horror that seized Madison when he read these words, for they came perilously close to the second convention option that he regarded as the political equivalent of a poison pill designed to kill the Constitution under the pretext of amending it. Jefferson obviously thought that the absence of a bill of rights was a fatal flaw in the document and, though he probably did not realize it, was willing to put ratification at risk in order to include what he called a "declaration of rights." (Ellis 2015, 202)

---

for encouraging our commerce will be repealed. The Minister will be glad of such a pretext for pacifying the opposition.[1]

To Jean Pierre Brissot De Warville[2]
Paris, Feb. 11, 1788
Sir,

I am very sensible of the honor you propose to me of becoming a member of the society for the abolition of the slave trade. You know that nobody wishes more ardently to see an abolition not only of the trade but of the condition of slavery: and certainly nobody will be more willing to encounter every sacrifice for that object. But the influence & information of the friends to this proposition in France will be far above the need of my association. I am here as a public servant; and those whom I serve having never yet been able to give their voice against this practice, it is decent for me to avoid too public a demonstration of my wishes to see it abolished. Without serving the cause here, it might render me less able to serve it beyond the water. I trust you will be sensible of the prudence of those motives therefore which govern my conduct on this occasion, & be assured of my wishes for the success of your undertaking, and the sentiments of esteem & respect with which I have the honor to be Sir your most obedt. humble servt:

To George Washington[3]

---

[1] The words in italics were originally written in cipher. (Boyd 1990)

[2] Jefferson's appreciation of the differences in the political environments of France and America had been fortified by his 1787 tour of southern France. The people, he noted in his travels, had little in common with American yeomen, for the ignorance and passivity of the peasants which facilitated their exploitation by their government and their landlords were almost incomprehensible to him. Here was no material for self-government. Granted that his disgust was primarily for the government of the *Ancien Régime*, it must necessarily have extended to people who would permit themselves to be so misgoverned. Not only are the French not the free-minded people we in America think they are, he informed George Wythe, but it would take them a thousand years to achieve America's political accomplishments. Even the intelligentsia did not escape this judgment, despite Jefferson's reliance upon their connections at Versailles. The idealization of America in the writings of Brissot and Crèvecoeur disturbed as well as flattered him; but he knew well that reality would never satisfy those Frenchmen nurtured on a Utopian myth. Here, in this note, he seeks to subtly temper some of the enthusiasm he had generated in France by declining Brissot's invitation to join his abolitionist society and by privately urging other friends making the journey to America not to expect too much from the New World. He had learned from his French experience that although admiration in France for America might be sincere, it would be shallow if not based upon a true understanding. Indeed France and her Revolution may have lessened Jefferson's objectivity in interpreting the course of America's development during his absence from home, but his experience as an American prevented his confusing the American Revolution with the French Revolution. (Kaplan 1957, 29)

[3] Jefferson was particularly concerned over the threat of monarchy and strongly opposed to unlimited reelection of a President, a point that the new Constitution did not cover. As he candidly puts in this letter to Washington, "This, I fear, will make that an office for life, first, then hereditary. I was much an enemy of monarchies before I came to Europe, and am ten thousand times more so since I

Paris, May 2, 1788
Sir,

I am honored with your Excellency's letter by the last packet & thank you for the information it contains on the communication between the Cayahoga & Big beaver. I have ever considered the opening a canal between those two water courses as the most important work in that line which the state of Virginia could undertake. It will infallibly turn thro' the Potomac all the commerce of Lake Erie & the country West of that, except what may pass down the Mississippi, and it is important that it be soon done, lest that commerce should in the meantime get established in another channel. Having in the spring of last year taken a journey through the Southern parts of France, & particularly examined the canal of Languedoc through its whole course, I take the liberty of sending you the notes I made on the spot, as you may find in them something perhaps which may be turned to account some time or other in the prosecution of the Potomac canal. Being merely a copy from my travelling notes they are undigested & imperfect, but may still perhaps give hints capable of improvement in your mind.

I had intended to have written a word to your Excellency on the subject of the new constitution, but I have already spun out my letter to an immoderate length. I will just observe therefore that according to my ideas there is a great deal of good in it. There are two things however which I dislike strongly. 1. The want of a declaration of rights. I am in hopes the opposition of Virginia will remedy this, & produce such a declaration. 2. The perpetual re-eligibility of the President. This I fear will make an office for life first, & then hereditary. I was much an enemy to monarchy before I came to Europe. I am ten thousand times more so since I have seen what they are. There is scarcely an evil known in these countries which may not be traced to their king as its source, nor a good which is not derived from the small fibers of republicanism existing among them. I can further say with safety there is not a crowned head in Europe whose talents or merits would entitle him to be elected a vestryman by the people of any parish in America. However I shall hope that before there is danger of this change taking place in the office of President, the good sense & free spirit of our countrymen will make the changes necessary to prevent it. Under this hope I look forward to the general adoption of the new constitution with anxiety, as necessary for us under our present circumstances.

---

have seen what they are. There is scarcely an evil known in these countries which may not be traced to their king as its source, nor a good which is not derived from the small fibers of republicanism existing among them. I can further say, with safety, there is not a crowned head in Europe whose talents or merits would entitle him to be elected vestryman by the people of any parish in America." Of course, in reality, Washington had no desire to be King; what he wanted was to retire to a quiet life at Mount Vernon, from which he could conduct his highly profitable business as a real estate operator. He was already one of the richest men in the country, and the emoluments and duties of a monarch did not attract him. (Coyle 1960, 3)

To Mrs. William Bingham[1]
Paris, May 11, 1788
Dear Madam,

A gentleman going to Philadelphia furnishes me the occasion of sending you some numbers of the Cabinet des Modes & some new theatrical pieces. These last have had great success on the stage, where they have excited perpetual applause. We have now need of something to make us laugh, for the topics of the times are sad and eventful. The gay and thoughtless Paris is now become a furnace of Politics. All the world is now politically mad. Men, women, children talk nothing else, & you know that naturally they talk much, loud & warm. Society is spoilt by it, at least for those who, like myself, are but lookers on.

You too have had your political fever. But our good ladies, I trust, have been too wise to wrinkle their foreheads with politics. They are contented to soothe & calm the minds of their husbands returning ruffled from political debate. They have the good sense to value domestic happiness above all other, and the art to cultivate it beyond all others. There is no part of the earth where so much of this is enjoyed as in America. You agree with me in this; but you think that the pleasures of Paris more than supply its wants; in other words that a Parisian is happier than an American. You will change your opinion, my dear Madam, and come over to mine in the end. Recollect the women of this capital, some on foot, some on horses, & some in carriages hunting pleasure in the streets, in routs & assemblies, and forgetting that they have left it behind them in their nurseries; compare them with our own countrywomen occupied in the tender and tranquil amusements of domestic life, and confess that it is a comparison of Americans and Angels.

You will have known from the public papers that Monsieur de Buffon, the father, is dead & you have known long ago that the son and his wife are separated. They are pursuing pleasure in opposite directions. Madame de Rochambeau is well: so is Madame de la Fayette. I recollect no other Nouvelles de societé interesting to you. And as for political news of battles & sieges, Turks & Russians, I will not detail them to you, because you would be less handsome after reading them. I have only to add then, what I take a pleasure in repeating, tho' it will be the thousandth time that I have the honor to be with sentiments

---

[1] In the general sense, as clearly reflected in this letter to the fashionable Anne Willing Bingham, of Philadelphia, Jefferson scorned women's interest in politics. Commenting on the tumult leading up to the French Revolution, he remarked, "Gay and thoughtless Paris is now become a furnace of Politics. All the world is run politically mad. Men, women, children talk of nothing else." Obviously disapproving, he hoped that was not the case in America: "Our good ladies, I trust, have been too wise to wrinkle their foreheads with politics. They are contented to soothe and calm the minds of their husbands returning ruffled from political debate. They have the good sense to value domestic happiness above all other, and the art to cultivate it beyond all others." He continues, "And as for political news of battles and sieges, Turks and Russians, I will not detail them to you, because you would be less handsome after reading them." (Zagarri, 2007, 159)

of very sincere respect & attachment, dear Madam, your most obedient & most humble servant.

To The Comte De Moustier[1]
Paris, May 17, 1788
Dear Sir,

I have at length an opportunity of acknowledging the receipt of your favors of Feb. & Mar 14., and of congratulating you on your resurrection from the dead among whom you had been confidently entombed by the news dealers of Paris. I am sorry that your first impressions have been disturbed by matters of etiquette, where surely they should least have been expected to occur. These disputes are the most insusceptible of determination, because they have no foundation in reason. Arbitrary & senseless in their nature, they are arbitrarily decided by every nation for itself. These decisions are meant to prevent disputes, but they produce ten where they prevent one. It would have been better therefore in a new country to have excluded etiquette altogether; or, if it must be admitted in some form or other, to have made it depend on some circumstance founded in nature, such as the age or stature of the parties. However you have got over all this, and I am in hopes have been able to make up a society suited to your own dispositions. Your situation will doubtless be improved by the adoption of the new constitution, which I hope will have taken place before you receive this. I see in this instrument a great deal of good. The consolidation of our government, a just representation, an administration of some permanence and other features of great value will be gained by it. There are indeed some faults which revolted me a good deal in the first moment; but we must be contented to travel on towards perfection, step by step. We must be contented with the ground which this constitution will gain for us, and hope that a favorable moment will come for correcting what is amiss in it. I view in the same light the innovations making here. The new organization of the judiciary department is undoubtedly for the better. The reformation of the criminal code is an immense step taken towards good. The composition of the plenary court is indeed vicious in the extreme, but the basis of that court may be retained and its composition changed. Make of it a representative of the people, by composing it of members sent from the provincial assemblies, and it becomes a valuable member of the constitution. But it is said the court will not consent to do this. The court however has consented to call the States general, who will consider the plenary court but as a canvas for them to work

---

[1] Here, Jefferson confirmed to Elénor-François-Élie, Marquis de Moustier, French Ambassador the Unites States at Philadelphia, the rumor that the desperate king was planning to call the Estates-General, on the heels of a series of disturbances in Paris and the provinces. "The public mind is manifestly advancing on the abusive prerogatives of their governors, and bearing them down. No force in the government can withstand this in the long run. Courtiers had rather give up power than pleasures: they will barter therefore the usurped prerogatives of the king for the money of the people." As if to accentuate his prediction, he adds, "This is the agent by which modern nations will recover their rights." (Howard 1997, 297)

on. The public mind is manifestly advancing on the abusive prerogatives of their governors, and bearing them down. No force in the government can withstand this in the long run. Courtiers had rather give up power than pleasures: they will barter therefore the usurped prerogatives of the king for the money of the people. This is the agent by which modern nations will recover their rights. I sincerely wish that in this country they may be contented with a peaceable & passive opposition. At this moment we are not sure of this, tho' as yet it is difficult to say what form the opposition will take. It is a comfortable circumstance that their neighboring enemy is under the administration of a minister disposed to keep the peace.

To James Madison[1]
Paris, May 25, 1788
Dear Sir,

The enclosed letter for Mr. Jay being of a private nature, I have thought it better to put it under your cover lest it might be opened by some of his clerks in the case of his absence. But I inclose a press copy of it for yourself as you will perceive the subject of it referred to you as well as to him. I ask your aid in it so far as you think right, and to have done what you think right. If you will now be so good as to cast your eye over the copy enclosed, what follows the present sentence will be some details, supplementary to that only, necessary for your information, but not proper for me to state to Mr. Jay.

Mr. Jay[2] tho appointed a minister resident at the court of *Madrid* he never was *received* in that character. He was continually passing from *Paris* to *Madrid* and *Madrid* to *Paris*, so that he had no occasion to establish a household at either. Accordingly, he stayed principally in furnished lodgings. Of all our ministers he had the least occasion for an outfit, and I suppose spent almost nothing on that article. He was of a disposition too to restrain himself within any limits of expense whatever, and it suited his recluse turn which is to avoid society. Should he judge of what others should do, by what he did, it would be an improper criterion. He was in Europe as a *voyageur* only, and it was while the salary was 500 guineas more than at present.

J. Adams. He came over when, instead of outfit & salary, all expenses were paid. Of rigorous honesty, and careless of appearances he lived for a considerable time as an economical private individual. After he was fixed at *the Hague* and the salary at a sum certain, he continued his economical stile till out of the difference between his expenses and his salary, he could purchase furniture for his house. This was the easier as the salary was at 2500 guineas then. He was obliged too to be passing between *Paris* and *the Hague*, so as to avoid any regular current of expense. When he established himself, his pecuniary affairs were under the

---

[1] Here, Jefferson suggested that the Confederation Congress settle his accounts as Minister to France before the new government under the Constitution began; however, the accounts were not settled until 1792. (Jefferson Madison and Smith 1995, 539)
[2] All italics were originally written in cipher. (Boyd 1990)

---

direction of *Mistress Adams*, one of the most estimable characters on earth, and the most attentive & honorable economists. Neither had a wish to lay up a copper, but both wished to make both ends meet. I suspected however, from an expression dropped in conversation, that they were not able to do this, and that a deficit in their accounts appeared in their winding up. If this conjecture be true, it is a proof that the salary, so far from admitting savings, is unequal to a very plain stile of life, for such was theirs. I presume Congress will be asked to allow it, and it is evident to me, from what I saw while in *London*, that it ought to be done, as they did not expend a shilling which should have been avoided. Would it be more eligible to set the example of making good a deficit, or to give him an Outfit, which will cover it? The impossibility of living on the sum allowed, respectably, was the true cause of his insisting on his recall.

Doct. Franklin. He came over while all expenses were paid. He rented a house with standing furniture, such as tables, chairs, presses &c. and bought all other necessaries. The latter were charged in his account, the former was included in the article of house rent and paid during the whole time of his stay here; and as the established rate of hire for furniture is from 30 to 40 per cent. per annum, the standing furniture must have been paid for three times over during the 8. years he stayed here. His salary too was 2500 guineas. When Congress reduced it to less than 2000. he refused to accede to it, asked his recall, and insisted that whenever they chose to alter the conditions on which he came out, if he did not approve of it, they ought to replace him in America on the old conditions. He lived plain, but as decently as his salary would allow. He saved nothing, but avoided debt. He knew he could not do this on the reduced salary & therefore asked his recall with decision.

To *him* I succeeded. He had established a certain stile of living. The same was expected from *me* and there were 500 guineas a year less to do it on. It has been aimed at however as far as was practicable. This rendered it constantly necessary to step neither to the right nor to the left to incur any expense which could possibly be avoided & it called for an almost womanly attention to the details of the household, equally perplexing, disgusting, & inconsistent with business. You will be sensible that in this situation no savings could be made for reimbursing the half year's salary ordered to be advanced under the former commission & more than as much again which was unavoidably so applied, without order, for the purchase of the Outfit. The reason of the thing, the usage of all nations, the usage of our own by paying all expenses of preceding ministers, which gave them the outfit as far as their circumstances appeared to them to render it necessary, have made me take for granted all along that it would not be refused to me; nor should I have mentioned it now but that the administration is passing into other hands, and more complicated forms. It would be disagreeable to me to be presented to them in the first instance as a suitor. Men come into business at first with visionary principles. It is practice alone which can correct & conform them to the actual current of affairs. In the meantime those to whom their errors were first applied have been their victims. The government may take up the project of appointing foreign ministers without outfits and they may ruin two or three individuals before they find that that article is just as indispensable as the salary. They must then fall into the current of general usage, which has become general only because experience has established it's necessity.

Upon the whole, be so good as to reflect on it, and to do, not what your friendship to me, but your opinion of what is right will dictate. Accept, in all cases, assurances of the sincere esteem & respect with which I am Dear Sir your friend & servant.

To John Brown[1]
Paris, May 26, 1788
Dear Sir,

It was with great pleasure I saw your name on the roll of Delegates, but I did not know you had actually come on to New York, till Mr. Paradise informed me of it. Your removal from Carolina to Kentucky was not an indifferent event to me. I wish to see that country in the hands of people well disposed, who know the value of the connection between that & the Maritime states, and who wish to cultivate it. I consider their happiness as bound up together, and that every measure should be taken which may draw the bands of union tighter. It will be an efficacious one to receive them into Congress, as I perceive they are about to desire. If to this be added an honest & disinterested conduct in Congress as to everything relating to them we may hope for a perfect harmony. The navigation of the Mississippi was perhaps the strongest trial to which the justice of the federal government could be put. If ever they thought wrong about it, I trust they have got to rights. I should think it proper for the Western country to defer pushing their right to that navigation to extremity as long as they can do without it tolerably; but that the moment it becomes absolutely necessary for them, it will become the duty of the maritime states to push it to every extremity to which they would their own right of navigating the Chesapeake, the Delaware, the Hudson or any other water. A time of peace will not be the surest for obtaining this object. Those therefore who have influence in the new country would act wisely to endeavor to keep things quiet till the western parts of Europe shall be engaged in war. Notwithstanding the aversion of the courts of London & Versailles to war, it is not certain that some incident may not engage them in it. England, France, Spain, Russia, Sweden & Denmark will all have fleets at sea, or ready to put to sea immediately. Who can answer for the prudence of all their

---

[1] John Brown, who was tutored in the law by Jefferson, was the youngest member of the Confederation Congress. Here, Jefferson opines on the importance of international commerce, telling Brown: "I cannot think that but that it would be desirable to all commercial nations to have that nation & all its dependencies driven from the sea-coast into the interior parts of Asia & Africa. What a field would thus be restored to commerce!" Jefferson's reflection on commerce was not merely a celebration of the economic possibilities. He lamented, "The finest parts of the old world are now dead in a great degree, to commerce, to arts, to science & to society. Greece, Syria, Egypt & the whole northern coast of Africa constituted the whole world to the Romans, and to us they are scarcely accessible at all." Privately, Jefferson was delighted at the thought that Greece might be liberated from its Ottoman overlords. (Gallimore 2003, 16)

officers? War is their interest. Even their courts are pacific from impotence only, not from disposition. I wish to heaven that our new government may see the importance of putting themselves immediately into a respectable position. To make provision for the speedy paiment of their foreign debts will be the first operation necessary. This will give them credit. A concomitant one should be magazines & manufactures of arms. This country is at present in a crisis of very uncertain issue. I am in hopes it will be a favorable one to the rights & happiness of the people; and that this will take place quietly. Small changes in the late regulations will render them wholly good. The campaign opens between the Turks & the two empires with an aspect rather favorable to the former. The Russians seem not yet thawed from the winter's torpitude. They have no army yet in motion, and the Emperor has been worsted in two-thirds of the small actions which they have had as yet. He is said to be rather retiring. I do not think however that the success of the Turks in the partisan affairs which have taken place, can authorize us to presume that they will be superior also in great decisions. Their want of discipline and skill in military maneuvers is of little consequence in small engagements & of great in larger ones. Their grand army was at Adrianople by the last accounts, and to get from thence to Belgrade will require a month. It will be that time at least then before we can have any very interesting news from them. In the meantime the plague rages at Constantinople to a terrible degree. I cannot think but that it would be desirable to all commercial nations to have that nation & all its dependencies driven from the sea-coast into the interior parts of Asia & Africa. What a field would thus be restored to commerce! The finest parts of the old world are now dead in a great degree, to commerce, to arts, to science, & to society. Greece, Syria, Egypt & the northern coast of Africa constituted the whole world almost for the Romans, and to us they are scarcely known, scarcely accessible at all. The present summer will enable us to judge what turn this contest will take.

I am greatly anxious to hear that nine states accept our new constitution. We must be contented to accept of it's good, and to cure what is evil in it hereafter. It seems necessary for our happiness at home; I am sure it is so for our respectability abroad. I shall at all times be glad to hear from you, from New York, from Kentucky or whatever region of the earth you inhabit being with sentiments of very sincere esteem & attachment Dear Sir Your friend &

To Edward Carrington[1]

[1] The Constitution first encountered powerful opposition in Massachusetts. For a while it seemed doubtful that enough votes in favor could be mustered. Samuel Adams, whose democratic convictions had highlighted the prerevolutionary years, noted signs of reaction against "the Natural Rights of Man" developing even before the conclusion of that struggle. John Hancock, initially inclined to be negative, finally supplied the formula that won Adams' acquiescence: "I give my assent to the Constitution, in full confidence that the amendments proposed will soon become a part of the system." "Recommendatory," not "conditional amendments" was the price exacted. This outcome created "a blemish," Madison admitted, but one "least offensive" in form. The size of the minority, 187 to 168, was "disagreeably large"; but the temper of it supplied "some atonement."

Paris, May 27, 1788
Dear Sir,

I have received with great pleasure your friendly letter of Apr. 24. It has come to hand after I had written my letters for the present conveyance, and just in time to add this to them. I learn with great pleasure the progress of the new Constitution. Indeed I have presumed it would gain on the public mind, as I confess it has on my own. At first, tho' I saw that the great mass & ground work was good, I disliked many appendages. Reflection and discussion have cleared off most of these. You have satisfied me as to the query I had put to you about the right of direct taxation. My first wish was that 9 States would adopt it in order to ensure what was good in it, & that the others might, by holding off, produce the necessary amendments. But the plan of Massachusetts is far preferable, and will I hope be followed by those who are yet to decide. There are two amendments only which I am anxious for. 1. A bill of rights, which it is so much the interest of all to have, that I conceive it must be yielded. The 1st amendment proposed by Massachusetts will in some degree answer this end, but not so well. It will do too much in some instances & too little in others. It will cripple the federal government in some cases where it ought to be free, and not restrain it in some others where restraint would be right.

The 2d amendment which appears to me essential is the restoring the principle of necessary rotation, particularly to the Senate & Presidency: but most of all to the last. Re-eligibility makes him an officer for life, and the disasters inseparable from an elective monarchy, render it preferable, if we cannot tread back that step, that we should go forward & take refuge in a hereditary one. Of the correction of this Article however I entertain no present hope, because I find it has scarcely excited an objection in America. And if it does not take place ere long, it assuredly never will. The natural progress of things is for liberty to yield, & government to gain ground. As yet our spirits are free. Our jealousy is only put to sleep by the unlimited confidence we all repose in the person to whom we all look as our president. After him inferior characters may perhaps succeed and awaken us to the danger which his merit has led us into. For the present however, the general adoption is to be prayed for; and I wait with great anxiety for the news from Maryland & S. Carolina which have decided before this, and

---

Meanwhile, Maryland (April 28, 1788) and South Carolina (May 23, 1788) ratified with comfortable margins. New Hampshire (June 21, 1788) voted to add the "*seventh* pillar" to the Federal Temple by vote of 57 to 47. The Bay State's procedure had worked so well that Madison now advocated its use wherever the vote promised to be close. "A conditional ratification or a second convention," he wrote Governor Edmund Randolph, "appears to me utterly irreconcilable... with the dictates of prudence and safety." Recommendatory alterations alone provided ground for coalition among real federalists. The Massachusetts formula caught on. "My idea is," Virginia delegate Francis Corbin observed, "that we should go hand in hand with Massachusetts; adopt it first, and then propose amendments...." Here in this letter to Carrington, a Virginia delegate to the Continental Congress from 1786 to 1788, Jefferson, who had earlier urged that ratification be delayed until a bill of rights could be added, now surrendered. "[T]he plan of Massachusetts is far preferable," he agreed, "and will I hope be followed by those who are yet to decide." (Mason 1962, 52-53)

with that Virginia, now in session, may give the 9th vote of approbation. There could then be no doubt of N. Carolina, N. York, & New Hampshire, but what do you propose to do with Rhode island? As long as there is hope, we should give her time. I cannot conceive but that she will come to rights in the long run. Force, in whatever form, would be a dangerous precedent.

There are rumors that the Austrian army is obliged to retire a little; that the Spanish squadron is gone to South America; that the English have excited a rebellion there, and some others equally unauthorized. I do not mention them in my letter to Mr. Jay, because they are unauthenticated. The bankruptcies in London have recommenced with new force. There is no saying where this fire will end. Perhaps in the general conflagration of all their paper. If not now, it must ere long. With only 20 millions of coin, & three or four hundred million of circulating paper, public & private, nothing is necessary but a general panic, produced either by failure, invasion or any other cause, and the whole residuary fabric vanishes into air & shews that paper is poverty, that it is only the ghost of money, & not money itself. 100 years ago they had 20. odd millions of coin. Since that they have brought in from Holland by borrowing 40. millions more. Yet they have but 20 millions left, and they talk of being rich and of having the balance of trade in their favor. Paul Jones is invited into the Empress's service with the rank of rear-admiral, & to have a separate command. I wish it corresponded with the views of Congress to give him that rank from the taking of the Serapis [a British warship]. I look to this officer as our great future dependence on the sea, where alone we should think of ever having a force. He is young enough to see the day when we shall be more populous than the whole British dominions and able to fight them ship to ship. We should procure him then every possible opportunity of acquiring experience.

To William Carmichael[1]
Paris, June 3, 1788

---

[1] During this period, the proposed amendments to the Constitution found the various party leaders viewing the maneuver with mixed feelings. Madison thought that the introduction of amendments was a blemish on the ratification, while Washington believed that the presence of amendments and the small majority lightened the impact of ratification on the Antifederalists. From Jefferson's perspective, although, as indicated in his May 27 letter to Carrington that the Massachusetts plan held promise, he still felt that the Massachusetts proposal which limited the powers of Congress was only a half-way solution to this problem. In particular, he feared it would cripple the federal government in some cases where it ought to be free, and not restrain it in some others where restraint should be exercised. Still, upon reflection, Jefferson seems to have resolved, at least in part, his earlier misgivings and here he confidently tells Carmichael, "But I am now convinced that the plan of Massachusetts is the best. That is, to accept, and to amend afterwards. If the states which were to decide after her should all do the same, it is impossible but they must obtain the essential amendments. It will be more difficult if we lose this instrument, to recover what is good in it, than to correct what is bad after we shall have adopted it. However, not all America was in accord with Jefferson's conciliatory mood, even after his revised views became known. (Rutland 1955, 148-149)

Dear Sir,

Your favors of Apr. 14. and 29. and May 8. have lately come to hand. That of Jan. 29. by M. de Molinedo had been left here during my absence on a journey to Amsterdam. That gentleman was gone, as I presume from my being unable to learn anything of him. I had been led to Amsterdam in order to meet with Mr. Adams and to endeavor in conjunction with him to take arrangements for answering the most pressing of our European calls for money till the end of the year 1790, by which time our new government will have been probably established, put under way, and enabled to draw money from its own resources. We succeeded in obtaining enough to last to the end of the present year, and in arranging a plan for two years more if it shall be approved by Congress. In the estimate I gave in to our bankers was comprehended a sum to be drawn either monthly or quarterly, by yourself, Mr. Dumas, and myself: so that for the present year you need be under no further anxieties, nor, as I hope, for two more to come. You mention that you had been authorized to draw on a house in Amsterdam for 3000 Dollars. Whenever the term shall be expired to which that portion of salary was appropriated, if you will make your draught on Messrs. Willem & Jan Willink, Nicholas & Jacob Van Staphorst at Amsterdam, and send the first draught through me, I will write to them such an explanatory letter as may leave you under no future doubts, unless the dispositions already made at Amsterdam should be controlled by the Treasury board, which I have no reason to apprehend.

The ciphered words in your letter of Apr. 14. prove to me that Mr. Barclay left you a wrong cipher. In those of May 8. taken from the cipher I sent you, are several things which I cannot make out. From an expression in your letter I suppose some of these to have been intended, others I ascribe to the equivocal hand writing in the cipher, which I believe was by one of Mr. Barclay's clerks. I cannot always distinguish the letter e. from o. n. from u. t. from f. and sometimes from s. I observe you use repeatedly 1360. instead of 1363. which I presume to be an error of the copyist to be corrected in your cipher. I cite the following passage, drawing lines under the numbers I do not understand. '1001. 739. 1264. 1010. 1401. 1508. <u>1237</u>. <u>1509</u>. <u>950</u>. <u>1509</u>. <u>694</u>. <u>861</u>. 221. 742. 658. 233. 1017. 1077. 1097.' and I do it that we may come to a perfect understanding of our cipher. The separating the numbers by a dot, as above, would add a facility to the deciphering of yours.

Mr. *Littlepage*[1] is returned to Poland. He expressed concern that you had not drawn on him, and appeared to me not to have a distinct idea of the sum, so that I think you will have to specify it to him. I will forward your letter to him whenever you shall be good enough to send it to me.

With respect to the *isthmus of Panama* I am assured by *Burgoine* (who would not choose to be named however) that *a survey* was made, that a *canal* appeared very practicable, and that the idea was suppressed for *political reasons* altogether. He has seen and minutely examined the *report*. This *report* is to me a vast desideratum for *reasons political and philosophical*. I cannot help suspecting the Spanish squadron to be gone to S. America, and that some disturbances have been excited there by the British. The court of Madrid may suppose we would

---

[1] All italics were originally written in cipher. (Boyd 1990)

not see this with an unwilling eye. This may be true as to the uninformed part of our people: but those who look into futurity farther than the present moment or age, and who combine well what is, with what is to be, must see that our interests, well understood, and our wishes are that Spain shall (not forever, but) very long retain her possessions in that quarter: and that her views and ours must, in a good degree, and for a long time, concur. It is said in our gazettes that the Spaniards have sunk one of our boats on the Mississippi, and that our people retaliated on one of theirs. But my letters not mentioning this fact have made me hope it is not true, in which hope your letter confirms me. There are now 100,000 inhabitants at Kentucky. They have accepted the offer of independence on the terms proposed by Virginia, and they have decided that their independent government shall begin on the 1st. day of the next year. In the meantime they claim admittance into Congress. Georgia has ceded her Western territory to the U.S. to take place with the commencement of the new federal government. I do not know the boundaries. There has been some dispute of etiquette with [the] *new French minister which has disgusted him.* The following is a state of the progress and prospect of the new plan of government.

The Conventions of 6. states have accepted it, to wit,

1. Massachusetts by	187	Ayes against	168 Noes.
2. Connecticut		148.	40.
3. Pennsylvania		46.	23.
4. Delaware		22	0
5. New Jersey		39	0
6. Georgia		33	0
		475	231

The other Conventions were to meet as follows.

7. Maryland.	April 21.
8. S. Carolina	May. 12.
9. Virginia	May. 26.
10. New York	June. 17.
11. New Hampshire	June. 18
12. North Carolina	July.

13. Rhode island referred the question to their people.

About one third of these gave their votes, and of these there were about nine tenths against accepting the Constitution. In Maryland there was respectable opposition: yet it is thought they will accept. In S. Carolina there is scarcely any opposition. In Virginia the opposition is very formidable. Yet on the whole it is thought to have lessened and that that state will accede. New York is perhaps more doubtful: but if the 9. preceding states should have adopted it, this will surely induce her to do it. The New Hampshire convention met. Many of the delegates came instructed and determined to vote against it. The discussions brought them over to the side of the Constitution. But they could not vote against their instructions. They therefore asked an adjournment that they might go back to their constituents and ask a repeal of their instructions. Little doubt is entertained that they will accede. The conduct of Massachusetts has been noble. She accepted the constitution, but voted that it should stand as a perpetual instruction to their delegates to endeavor to obtain such and such reformations; and the minority, tho very strong both in numbers and abilities, declared viritim et seriatim that, acknowleging the principle that the Majority must give the law, they would now support the new constitution with their tongues and with their blood if necessary. I was much pleased with many and essential parts of this instrument from the beginning. But I thought I saw in it many faults, great and small. What I have read and reflected has brought me over from several of my objections of the first moment, and to acquiesce under some others. Two only remain, of essential consideration, to wit, the want of a bill of rights, and the expunging the principle of necessary rotation in the offices of President and Senate. At first I wished that when 9. states should have accepted the constitution, so as to ensure us what is good in it, the other 4. might hold off till the want of the bill of rights at least might be supplied. But I am now convinced that the plan of Massachusetts is the best. That is, to accept, and to amend afterwards. If the states which were to decide after her should all do the same, it is impossible but they must obtain the essential amendments. It will be more difficult if we lose this instrument, to recover what is good in it, than to correct what is bad after we shall have adopted it. It has therefore my hearty prayers, and I wait with anxiety for news of the votes of Maryland, S. Carolina, and Virginia. There is no doubt that Genl. Washington will accept the presidentship, tho' he is silent on the subject. He would not be chosen to the Virginia convention.

A riot has taken place in New York which I will state to you from an eye-witness. It has long been a practice with the Surgeons of that city to steal from the grave bodies recently buried. A citizen had lost his wife. He went, the 1st. or 2d. evening after her burial, to pay a visit to her grave. He found that it had been disturbed and suspected from what quarter. He found means to be admitted to the anatomical lecture of that day, and on his entering the room, saw the body of his wife, naked and under dissection. He raised the people immediately. The body in the meantime was secreted. They entered into and searched the houses of the Physicians whom they most suspected. But found nothing. One of them however, more guilty or more timid than the rest, took asylum in the Prison. The mob considered this as an acknowledgement of guilt. They attacked the prison. The governor ordered militia to protect the culprit and suppress the mob. The militia, thinking the mob had just provocation, refused to turn out. Hereupon the people of more reflection, thinking it more dangerous that even a guilty person should be punished without the forms of law, than that he should escape, armed themselves and went to protect the physician. They were received by the mob with a volley of stones, which wounded several of them. They hereupon fired on the mob and killed four. By this time they received a reinforcement of other citizens of the militia horse, the appearance of which in the critical moment dispersed the mob. So ended this chapter of history, which I have detailed to you because it may be represented as a political riot, when politics had nothing to do with it. Mr. Jay and Baron Steuben were both grievously wounded in the head by stones. The former still kept his bed, and the latter his room when the packet sailed which was the 24th. of April.

You have no doubt seen the reformations proposed in this country. They are all good as to the matter, the manner alone being exceptionable. They say if the king can of his own authority abolish bad and erect good institutions co-eval with his own, he may do the reverse. When I said the changes were all good, I should have excepted the Cour plenière. The composition of that is undoubtedly vicious. If the minister will so far yield to the public wish as to take the members of that court from the Provincial assemblies by free election, so that it shall become a representative of the nation, and will call the States general to ratify and establish it beyond the reach of the royal authority, this country will have made a vast stride towards political reformation. More than half the grand bailliages have accepted their offices. The Chatelet is disposed to accept, but their advocates still hold off. If these jurisdictions can be set a going, government will be relieved from the most embarrassing difficulty, and will, in my opinion, be able to go through with their measure.

Do you see Don Miguel de Lardizabal ever? If you do be so good as to present my compliments to him, and to remind him of my catalogue of books, in which he was so kind as to promise me his aid.

Mr. Young, the bearer of this is on the set-out, and in a very distant quarter from me. This obliges me to omit all other European details, and to assure you here of the sentiments of esteem & respect with which I have the honor to be Dear Sir Your most obedient & most humble servt,

To Mr. Thomas Digges[1]
Paris, June 19, 1788
Sir,

I have duly received your favor of May 12, as well as that of the person who desires information on the state of cotton manufactures in America, and for his interest & safety I beg leave to address to you the answers to his queries without naming him.

In general it is impossible that manufactures should succeed in America from the high price of labor. This is occasioned by the great demand of labor

---

[1] Thomas Attwood Digges, scion of a prominent Catholic family of Maryland whose seat lay across the Potomac from Mount Vernon, was trusted least by those who knew him best. The known testimony of contemporaries was almost unanimously negative, with Benjamin Franklin's famous appraisal being so damning and so current at the time that Horace Walpole recorded it in his journals. On learning that Digges had embezzled charitable funds placed in his hands for the relief of suffering American prisoners, Franklin declared in outrage: "We have no name in our Language for such atrocious Wickedness. If such a fellow is not damn'd it is not worthwhile to keep a Devil." Hutson suggests that Digges, "...also may have been a British spy." Further, noting that, "William Bell Clark [in his 1953 *Pennsylvania Magazine of History and Biography* essay, "In Defense of Thomas Digges"] does not refute the charge that Digges was a spy. That confirmation of Digges's spying is absent from papers of some members of the British ministry proves nothing. Only the discovery of the British Secret Service papers after 1778 will exonerate or convict Digges." (Hutson 1978, xii; Boyd 1990)

for agriculture. A manufacturer going from Europe will turn to labor of other kind if he find more to be got by it, & he finds some employment so profitable that he can soon lay up money enough to buy fifty acres of land, to the culture of which he is irresistibly tempted by the independence in which that places him, & the desire of having a wife & family around him. If any manufactures can succeed there, it will be that of cotton. I must observe for his information that this plant grows nowhere in the United States Northward of the Potomac, and not in quantity till you get Southward as far as York & James rivers. I know nothing of the manufacture which is said to be set up at Richmond. It must have taken place since 1783, when I left Virginia. In that state (for it is the only one I am enabled to speak of with certainty) there is no manufacture of wire or of cotton cards: or if any, it is not worth notice. No manufacture of stocking-weaving, consequently none for making the machine: none of cotton cloths of any kind whatever for sale; tho in almost every family some is manufactured for the use of the family, which is always good in quality, & often tolerably fine. In the same way they make excellent knit stockings of cotton, weaving it in like manner carried on principally in the family way: among the poor, the wife weaves generally, & the rich either have a weaver among their servants or employ their poor neighbors. Cotton cost in Virginia from 12d. to 18d. sterling the pound before the war, probably it is a little raised since. Richmond is as good a place for a manufactory as any in that State, & perhaps the best as to its resources for this business. Cotton clothing is very much the taste of the country. A manufacturer on his landing should apply to the well informed farmers and gentlemen of the country. Their information will be more disinterested than that of merchants, and they can better put him into the way of disposing of his workmen in the cheapest manner till he has time to look about him & decide how & where he will establish himself. Such is the hospitality in that country, & their disposition to assist strangers, that he may boldly go to any good house he sees, and make the inquiry he needs. He will be sure to be kindly received, honestly informed, and accommodated in a hospitable way, without any other introduction than an information who he is & what are his views. It is not the policy of the government in that country to give any aid to works of any kind. They let things take their natural course without help or impediment, which is generally the best policy. More particularly as to myself I must add that I have not the authority nor the means of assisting any persons in their passage to that country.

To Nicholas Lewis[1]

---

[1] In this letter of Nicholas Lewis, to whom Jefferson had entrusted his farms while serving in Paris, clearly reflects Jefferson's penchant for meticulous record-keeping. In fact, in this letter he boasts to Lewis, he had kept his memorandum books "with such scrupulous fidelity that I shall not be afraid to justify them on the bed of death, and so exact that in the course of 15 years which they comprehend, I never discovered that I had made but one omission of a payment." Of course, the irony of Jefferson's financial memoranda is that though he maintained a meticulous record of his expenditures, he never balanced his accounts. He was chronically in debt yet seldom faced that fact, the suggestion

Paris, July 11, 1788
Dear Sir,

Your favor of Aug. 20. 1787 came to hand some time ago; that of Apr. 15. 1788 I received last night. I had just written to Mr. Eppes on the subject of my affairs, and intended writing to you today. The opportune arrival of the last letter enables me to answer both at the same time. I am much pleased that you approve of my plan of hiring my estate. Besides that the profit will be greater, it will enable me to see a fixed term to my embarrassments. For the same reason I would prefer money to tobacco rents, because my engagements for annual paiments must be in money. Yet if you think the greater assurance of punctual paiments in tobacco overbalances the advantage of a fixed sum in money, I leave it to your discretion. One piece of information however I must give you, which is that there is no prospect that the European market for tobacco will improve. Our principal dependence is on this country, and the footing on which I have got that article placed here, is the best we can ever expect. In the leases therefore, tobacco of my own estate, or of the best warehouses cannot be counted on at more than from 20/ to 22/6 currency the utmost. But I am in hopes my dear Sir, that more can be obtained per hand than 12£ currency, which you mention. I found my hopes on these considerations. I rented to Garth & Mosley as well as I recollect for £11. sterling a hand, tobacco then from 18/ to 20/ the hundred and the legal exchange 25. per cent. Tobacco is now ten per cent. higher & legal exchange raised 5 per cent. This entitles us at present to ask £15. currency a hand. I never knew exactly what Garth & Mosley made. They only told me in general that they had made about a good overseer's or steward's lay each: suppose this 75£ each & calculate it on the number of workers they had, and it will prove how much more worth is a working hand with the lands and stock thrown in, than without them. Add to this that there is the addition of Hickman & Smith's lands in Albemarle (about 1000 acres) and that the lands in Bedford are much better for tobacco than those of Albemarle were when Garth & Mosley rented them. I only mention these considerations to enable you to demonstrate to those who enter into conference on the subject that a higher sum than £12. currency may be reasonably asked; but not to tie you down, for certainty I had rather rent for £12. currency than not to rent at all. I think I suggested in my former letters the necessity of stipulating a right to distrain when the rent is not paid. It might be a still greater security to stipulate also that their tobaccos shall be delivered at certain warehouses in your name, so that you may receive the money from the purchaser when the tenant has failed to pay.

I come over to your advice, Sir, to sell my lands in Cumberland & Goochland, and have accordingly desired Mr. Eppes to join you in doing it. As to the prices, I leave it to your discretions. I never had a direct offer for those lands, because I never meant to sell them. But from overtures made before a shilling of paper money had issued, I suppose I could get 1500£ for Cumberland and the same for Elkhill. This was before I purchased Smith's. I have promised to Jones three fifths

being that the records gave an artificial sense of order to Jefferson's oftentimes chaotic financial situation. (Hayes 2008, 100)

of what these lands shall sell for, and even that the bonds shall be given in his name, if he will acquit me so far, and on condition he will make a final settlement with me on the terms I have promised. I shall immediately write to Mr. McCaul that he shall have the other two fifths, as well as two fifths annually of the rents & profits of my estate, the other three fifths of these being proposed to Jones. The check on the tenants against abusing my slaves was, by the former lease, that I might discontinue it on a reference to arbitrators. Would it not be well to retain an optional right to sue them for ill-usage of the slaves or to discontinue it by arbitration, whichever you should choose at the time?

I will now proceed to take notice of some of the debts mentioned in your letters. As to Mr. Braxton's I still think his memory has led him into error on the subject, and that my memorandum books of that date would correct it. You mention "a considerable debt due to Dr. Walker not enumerated in my list." I settled with Doct^r. Walker just before I left Virginia, and gave my acknowledgment of the balance I owed him which was £40-11-9¾. This is stated in the list of my debts which I left you, & which I presume escaped your notice, as I know of no other debt of money to Doct^r. Walker, unless he should have taken an assignment from somebody. Be this as it will, I know his justice and honor so well that whatever he has demanded is right, & I would wish it to be paid of the first money possible, if it be no more than the balance I have named with its interest, rather than he should be incommoded. If you have not the money, be so good as to obtain it by drawing a bill on me at 60 days sight, which shall be honored. My friend, Mr. Donald, can dispose of this draft for you. 'Coutt's demand' 'Donald, Scott & Co.' I doubt both. I do not even remember the name of such a house as the latter. My papers, will perhaps throw light on these. They were alphabetically arranged, so as that any paper may be found in a moment. But most of all my memorandum books will shew. 'Doctor Read's account' is noted in my list £48-13-3 under the name of Col°. Bannister, because you will find among my papers Reid's account & his order to pay the money to Bannister. Since I left Virginia Col°. Bannister is fallen in my debt. If therefore he has not relinquished to Reid his claim on me, you can get his receipt for the money, for which I will credit him in the account of what I have paid for him.

'Boden of Norfolk £14.' If this is for Phripp & Bowden for leather (I believe) it may be right, by possibility, but I doubt it.

Hierom Gaines for timber, work &^c. £19. Frank Gaines owed me a certain number of days work. I agreed to take in exchange for it work from his father, whom I wished to employ in searching timber, searching the lines of my order of council &^c. I think there is no other claim of Hierom's against me, & of course that his services were to pay a debt. Before I left Monticello I made a point of settling every account I could get at, in order to state it in my list of debts. Where I could not settle the balance accurately, still I entered the name in the list I left you, as a note that there was something due. It is not probable that I could have over looked Hierom Gaines' account & especially for such a sum. I have great confidence in Hierom's integrity, and therefore hope that by the aid of these circumstances you will be able to settle this matter rightly.

'W^m. Chisholm. £26.' This is in my opinion impossible. He left my estate in Goochland when the British came there. He was in such distress afterwards that if I had owed him money, it was impossible I should not have raised it for him by some means or other, and much more so that I should have omitted it in my list, & lost every trace of it in my memory.

Johnson a carpenter thirty odd pounds for work many years ago.' I have forgot that ever such a person worked for me: but, if he did, that he has been paid is certain. I made a point of paying my workmen in preference to all other claimants. I never parted with one without settling with him, and giving him either his money or my note. Every person that ever worked for me can attest this, and that I always paid their notes pretty soon. I am sure there did not exist one of these notes unpaid when I left Virginia, except to Watson & Orr who were still at work for me. The debts in Bedford to Robinson, Bennett & Calloway I suppose have been contracted since I came away. In general I will beg of you to refer to my memorandum books. They are small books which I used to carry in my pocket. They are 6. or 8. in number. There is an alphabetical index of names to everyone, so that all the entries respecting any one person may be found in a moment in them. They are made with such scrupulous fidelity that I shall not be afraid to justify them on the bed of death, and so exact that in the course of 15 years which they comprehend, I never discovered that I had made but one omission of a payment. I do not mean to say that the accounts before questioned are not just decisively. I have not confidence enough in my memory to say that. But they should be examined under several points of view. They may be paper money accounts. They may have been transferred from some other person who has been paid. They may be due from some other person & the demand made on the without foundation. They may have been paid by me either directly or circuitously. The silence of my memorandum books as to a money paiment or receipt by me may be relied on as negative proof, and their entries of a paiment or receipt as a positive proof of that paiment or entry. Wherever credits have been transferred circuitously from one to another, and accounts discharged in that way, I did not always enter them, nor even generally, but as you know a great deal of business was done in this way, it should always be well enquired into as to any accounts presented since I came away, & not enumerated in my list. My omission there is a presumption that the account has been settled some way: tho' I do not pretend it to be infallible. I only made out as exact a list as I could.

I am so desirable of proceeding to the hiring of my estate, that I would not detain my sawyers to finish my bill of scantling. Only be so good as to put what stuff is ready into perfect security. The bricks also which are ready made I would wish to have well taken care of, that I may not have occasion to make any on my return.

I shall continue to reflect on the debts before observed on and which are mentioned to me for the first time in your letter received last night. Probably my recollection will enable me to be more particular on their subject in my next letter. So that the settlement of them had better be a little delayed, if my memorandum books do not satisfy you.

I shall give orders at Havre relative to the bacon whenever it arrives. But in future it will not be worthwhile to send me any, because its importation is prohibited, and I have never yet been able to obtain any article of this kind from the Custom house. I thank Mrs. Lewis kindly for the ears of corn & the seeds accompanying them which are safely come to hand. The hominy corn is a precious present. The corn of this country and of Italy, as far as I have seen it, cannot be eaten, either in the form of corn or of bread, by any person who has eaten that of America. I have planted some grains which may perhaps come to maturity as we have still 3 months & a half to frost.

One word more on my leases. I think the term should not exceed three years. The negroes too old to be hired, could they not make a good profit by cultivating cotton? Much enquiry is made of me here about the cultivation of cotton, & I would thank you to give me your opinion how much a hand would make cultivating that as his principal crop instead of tobacco. Great George, Ursula, Betty, Hennings not to be hired at all, nor Martin nor Bob otherwise than as they are now. I am sensible, my dear Sir, how much trouble & perplexity I am giving you with my affairs. The plan of leasing will in a great measure relieve you. I know Mrs. Lewis's goodness too & her attentions to them.

To Dr. William Gordon[1]
Paris, July 16, 1788
Sir,

In your favor of the 8th instant you mention that you had written to me in February last. This letter never came to hand. That of Apr. 24. came here during my absence on a journey thro' Holland & Germany, and having been obliged to devote the first moments after my return to some very pressing matters, this must be my apology for not having been able to write to you till now. As soon as I knew that it would be agreeable to you to have such a disposal of your work for

---

[1] This letter to William Gordon, an Englishman who had fought on the American side in the Revolution and returned to Great Britain in 1786, offers a somewhat insightful glimpse into Jefferson's feeling on slavery. The context is associated with the depredations of Lord Cornwallis and his troops when they overran his estate in 1781. Here, Jefferson tells Gordon, "he carried off also about thirty slaves; had this been to give them their freedom, he would have done right, but it was to consign them to inevitable death from the smallpox and putrid fever then raging in his camp." But this account differs markedly from the cold facts recorded in his "Farm Book" when these events took place. In that document, which was not intended for the public eye, he listed the names of the slaves that he had lost and described what had befallen them. Next to eight entries in a group he wrote: "fled to the enemy and died". Another two slaves were said to have "joined the enemy and died"; while four more, "joined the enemy, returned and died". Beside three names he wrote laconically: "joined enemy"; and it is presumed that they managed to survive the war. One slave, Barnaby, was described as having "joined the enemy, but came back again and lived." Nowhere in this account is the term "carried off" seen, and Jefferson's later use of the phrase glosses over the fact that more than one seventh of his blacks chose to desert him. So, it seems that Jefferson's statement that Cornwallis would have done right if he had taken the Negroes to free them is at variance with his own behavior both before and after 1781. (O'Brien 1996, 267)

translation as I had made for Dr. Ramsay, I applied to the same bookseller with propositions on your behalf. He told me that he had lost so much by that work that he could hardly think of undertaking another, and at any rate not without first seeing & examining it. As he was the only bookseller I could induce to give anything on the former occasion, I went to no other with my proposals, meaning to ask you to send me immediately as much of the work as is printed. This you can do by the Diligence which comes three times a week from London to Paris. Furnished with this, I will renew my propositions and do the best for you I can, tho' I fear that the ill success of the translation of Dr. Ramsay's work, and of another work on the subject of America, will permit less to be done for you than I had hoped. I think Dr. Ramsay failed from the inelegance of the translation, & the translator's having departed entirely from the Doctor's instructions. I will be obliged to you to set me down as a subscriber for half a dozen copies, and to ask Mr. Trumbull (No. 2, North street, Rathbone place) to pay you the whole subscription price for me, which he will do on showing him this letter. These copies can be sent by the Diligence. I have not yet received the pictures Mr. Trumbull was to send me, nor consequently that of M. de La Fayette. I will take care of it when it arrives. His title is simply le Marquis de la Fayette. You ask, in your letter of Apr 24, details of my sufferings by Colo Tarleton. I did not suffer by him. On the contrary, he behaved very genteelly with me. On his approach to Charlottesville, which is within 3 miles of my house at Monticello he dispatched a troop of horse under Capt McLeod with the double object of taking me prisoner with the two Speakers of the Senate & delegates who then lodged with me and of remaining there in vedette, my house commanding a view of 10 or 12 counties round about. He gave strict orders to Capt McLeod to suffer nothing to be injured. The troops failed in one of their objects, as we had notice so that the two speakers had gone off about two hours before their arrival at Monticello, & myself with my family about five minutes. But Capt McLeod preserved everything with sacred care during about 18 hours that he remained there. Colo Tarleton was just so long at Charlottesville being hurried from thence by the news of the rising of the militia, and by a sudden fall of rain which threatened to swell the river and intercept his return. In general he did little injury to the inhabitants on that short & hasty excursion, which was about 60 miles from their main army then in Spotsylvania, & ours in Orange. It was early in June, 1781. Lord Cornwallis then proceeded to the point of fork, and encamped his army from thence all along the main James river to a seat of mine called Elk-hill, opposite to Elk island, & a little below the mouth of the Byrd creek. (You will see all these places exactly laid down in the map annexed to my *Notes on Virginia* printed by Stockdale.) He remained in this position ten days, his own headquarters being in my house at that place. I had had time to remove most of the effects out of the house. He destroyed all my growing crops of corn & tobacco, he burned all my barns containing the same articles of the last year, having first taken what he wanted, he used, as was to be expected, all my stocks of cattle, sheep & hogs for the sustenance of his army, and carried off all the horses capable of service: of those too young for service he cut the throats, and he burned all the fences on the plantation, so as to leave it an absolute waste. He carried off also about 30. slaves. Had this been to give them freedom he would have done right, but it was to consign them to inevitable death from the small pox & putrid fever then raging in his camp. This I knew afterwards to have been the fate of 27. of them. I never had news of the remaining three, but presume they shared the same fate. When I say that Lord Cornwallis did all this, I do not mean that he carried about the torch in his own hands, but that it was all done under his eye, the situation of the house in which he was, commanding a view of every part of the plantation, so that he must have seen every fire. I relate these things on my own knowledge in a great degree, as I was on the ground soon after he left it. He treated the rest of the neighborhood somewhat in the same stile but not with that spirit of total extermination with which he seemed to rage over my possessions. Wherever he went, the dwelling houses were plundered of everything that could be carried off. Lord Cornwallis's character in England would forbid the belief that he shared in the plunder but that his table was served with the plate thus pillaged from private houses can be proved by many hundred eye witnesses. From an estimate I made at that time, on the best information I could collect, I supposed the state of Virginia lost under Lord Cornwallis's hands that year about 30,000 slaves, and that of these about 27,000 died of the small pox and camp fever and the rest were partly sent to the West Indies & exchanged for rum, sugar, coffee & fruit, & partly sent to New York, from whence they went at the peace either to Nova Scotia or England. From this last place I believe they have been lately sent to Africa. History will never relate the horrors committed by the British army in the Southern states of America. They raged in Virginia 6 months only, from the middle of April to the middle of October, 1781. when they were all taken prisoners, & I give you a faithful specimen of their transactions for 10. days of that time & on one spot only. Ex pede Herculem [from the sample we are able to estimate the whole] I suppose their whole devastations during those 6 months amounted to about three millions sterling. The copiousness of this subject has only left me space to assure you of the sentiments of esteem & respect with which I am, Sir, your most obedt. humble servt.

To Edward Rutledge[1]

---

[1] Jefferson's attitude toward the Constitution is distinguishable from that of friends and enemies alike. As we have seen, particular provisions of the document impressed him less than did the Constitution as a convincing demonstration that reason is the most efficacious solvent of varying interests and divergent points of view, there was nonetheless a measure of satisfaction reflected in this note to Edward Rutledge: "We can surely boast of having set the world a beautiful example of a government reformed by reason alone without bloodshed." But, interestingly, despite the political intrigues — both in France and America — unfolding during this period, Jefferson also made time to continue his more scholarly pursuits. About this same time, Jefferson had developed an interest in the theory of Dr. Andrew Turnbull, a Scottish physician of Charleston, South Carolina, that the Creek Indians were descended from Carthaginians whose ships strayed from Hannibal's fleet and wound up in America. Here, he tells, Rutledge, "I see nothing impossible in his conjecture. I am glad he means to appeal to the similarity of language..." But he does not mention the speculation that there were

Paris, July 18, 1788
My Dear Sir,

You promise, in your letter of Octob 23. 1787. to give me in your next, at large, the conjectures of your Philosopher on the descent of the Creek Indians from the Carthaginians, supposed to have been separated from Hanno's fleet during his periplus. I shall be very glad to receive them, & see nothing impossible in his conjecture. I am glad he means to appeal to the similarity of language, which I consider as the strongest kind of proof it is possible to adduce. I have somewhere read that the language of the ancient Carthaginians is still spoken by their descendants inhabiting the mountainous interior parts of Barbary to which they were obliged to retire by the conquering Arabs. If so, a vocabulary of their tongue can still be got, and if your friend will get one of the Creek languages, the comparison will decide. He probably may have made progress in this business: but if he wishes any enquiries to be made on this side the Atlantic, I offer him my services cheerfully, my wish being, like his, to ascertain the history of the American aborigines.

I congratulate you on the accession of your state to the new federal constitution. This is the last I have yet heard of, but I expect daily that my own has followed the good example, & suppose it to be already established. Our government wanted bracing. Still we must take care not to run from one extreme to another; not to brace too high. I own I join those in opinion who think a bill of rights necessary. I apprehend too that the total abandonment of the principle of rotation in the offices of President & Senator will end in abuse. But my confidence is that there will for a long time be virtue & good sense enough in our countrymen to correct abuses. We can surely boast of having set the world a beautiful example of a government reformed by reason alone without bloodshed. But the world is too far oppressed to profit of the example. On this side of the Atlantic the blood of the people is become an inheritance, and those who fatten on it, will not relinquish it easily. The struggle in this country is as yet of doubtful issue. It is in fact between the monarchy and the parliaments. The nation is no otherwise concerned but as both parties may be induced to let go some of its abuses to court the public favor. The danger is that the people, deceived by a false cry of liberty may be led to take side with one party, & thus give the other a pretext for crushing them still more. If they can avoid the appeal to arms, the nation will be sure to gain much by this controversy. But if that appeal is made it will depend entirely on the dispositions of the army whether it issue in liberty or despotism. Those dispositions are not as yet known. In the meantime there is great probability that the war kindled in the east will spread from nation to nation & in the long run become general.

---

mounds of Carthaginian origin and would probably have rejected the idea, as he did other theories of trans-Atlantic origins for the mound-builders. (Mason 1962, 22; Wallace 2001, 137)

To James Madison[1]
Paris, July 31, 1788
Dear Sir,

My last letters to you were of the 3d. & 25th of May. Yours from Orange, of Apr 22, came to hand on the 10th inst.

My letter to Mr. Jay containing all the public news that is well authenticated, I will not repeat it here, but add some details in the smaller way which you may be glad to know. *The disgrace of the Marquis de la Fayette,*[2] which at any other period of their history would have had the worst consequences for *him*, will on the contrary mark him favorably to the nation at present. During the present administration he can expect nothing, but perhaps it may serve him with their successors, whenever a change shall take place. No change of *the Principal* probably take place before the meeting of the States general *though a change is to be wished, for his operations do not answer the expectations formed of him. These had been calculated on his brilliancy in society. He is very feebly aided, too. Montmorin is weak, though a most worthy character. He is indolent and inattentive, too, in the extreme. Luzerne is considerably inferior in abilities to his brother, whom you know. He is a good man, too, but so much out of his element, that he has the air of one huskanoyed. The Garde des sceaux is considered as the Principal's bull dog, braving danger like that animal. His talents do not pass mediocrity. The Archbishop's brother, and the new minister Villedeuil, and Lambert, have no will of their own. They cannot raise money for the peace establishment the next year, without the States General; much less if there be war; and their administration will probably end with the States General.*

Littlepage, who was here as a *secret agent for the King of Poland*, rather *overreached* himself. He wanted more money. The King furnished it more than once. Still he wanted more and thought to obtain a high bid by saying he was called for *in America*, and asking leave to go there. Contrary to his expectation, he received leave; but he went to Warsaw instead of *America*, and from thence to join the *Russian army*. I do not know these facts certainly, but re-collect them, by putting several things together. *The King* then sent an *ancient secretary* here, in whom he had much confidence, to look out for a *correspondent, a mere letter writer* for him. A happy hazard threw *Mazzei* his way. He recommended him, and he is appointed. He has no *diplomatic character* whatever, but is to receive *eight thousand livres a year*,

---

[1] Of course, Jefferson was not present when the Constitution and First Amendment were adopted by Congress. But these documents merely made explicit the jurisdictional policies that were already implicit in the constitutional order. The federal Bill of Rights, which includes the First Amendment, served a dual purpose: to assure the citizenry that the federal government would not encroach upon the civil and religious liberties of individuals and to guarantee the states that the federal government would not usurp the states' jurisdiction over civil and religious liberties. Jefferson still held deep concerns about the Constitution and topping his list was the lack of express and broad protection for religious liberty. In this letter, he tells Madison, "I hope therefore a bill of rights will be formed to guard the people against the federal government, as they are already guarded against their state governments in most instances." (Dreisbach 202, 188; Ragosta, 2012, 83-84)

[2] All italics were originally written in cipher. (Boyd 1990)

as an intelligencer. I hope this *employment* may have some permanence. The danger is, that he will overact his part.

The Marquis de la Luzerne had been for many years *married* to his *brother's wife's sister, secretly. She* was ugly and deformed, but sensible, amiable, and rather rich. When he was *named ambassador to London,* with ten thousand *guineas a year,* the *marriage* was avowed, and he relinquished his *cross of Malta,* from which he derived a handsome revenue for life, and which was very open to advancement. She stayed here and not long after died. His real *affection for her,* which was great and *unfeigned,* and perhaps the loss of his *order* for so short-lived a satisfaction, has thrown him almost *into a state of despondency.* He is *now here.*

I send you a book of Dupont's on the subject of the commercial treaty with England. Tho it's general matter may not be interesting, yet you will pick up in various parts of it such excellent principles and observations as will richly repay the trouble of reading it. I send you also two little pamphlets of the Marquis de Condorcet, wherein is the most judicious statement I have seen of the great questions which agitate this nation at present. The new regulations present a preponderance of good over their evil, but they suppose that the King can model the constitution at will, or in other words that his government is a pure despotism. The question then arising is whether a pure despotism in a single head, or one which is divided among a king, nobles, priesthood, & numerous magistracy is the least bad. I should be puzzled to decide: but I hope they will have neither, and that they are advancing to a limited, moderate government, in which the people will have a good share.

I sincerely rejoice at the acceptance of our new constitution by nine states. It is a good canvass, on which some strokes only want retouching. What these are, I think are sufficiently manifested by the general voice from North to South, which calls for a bill of rights. It seems pretty generally understood that this should go to Juries, Habeas corpus, Standing armies, Printing, Religion & Monopolies. I conceive there may be difficulty in finding general modifications of these, suited to the habits of all the states. But if such cannot be found then it is better to establish trials by Jury, the right of Habeas corpus, freedom of press & freedom of religion, in all cases, and to abolish standing armies in time of peace, and Monopolies in all cases, than not do it in any. The few cases wherein these things may do evil, cannot be weighed against the multitude wherein the want of them will do evil. In disputes between a foreigner & a native, a trial by jury may be improper. But if this exception cannot be agreed to, the remedy will be to model the jury by giving the mediatas linguæ in civil as well as criminal cases. Why suspend the Hab. Corp. in insurrections & rebellions? The parties who may be arrested may be charged instantly with a well-defined crime, of course the judge will remand them. If public safety requires that the government should have a man imprisoned on less probable testimony in those than in other emergencies; let him be taken & tried, retaken & retried, while the necessity continues, only giving him redress against the government for damages. Examine the history of England. See how few of the cases of the suspension of the Habeas corpus law have been worthy of that suspension. They have been either real treasons wherein the parties might as well have been charged at once, or sham plots where it was shameful they should ever have been suspected. Yet for the few cases wherein the suspension of the hab. corp. has done real good, that operation is now become habitual, & the minds of the nation almost prepared to live under its constant suspension. A declaration that the federal government will never restrain the presses from printing anything they please, will not take away the liability of the printers for false facts printed. The declaration that religious faith shall be unpunished, does not give impunity to criminal acts dictated by religious error. The saying there shall be no monopolies lessens the incitements to ingenuity, which spurred on by the hope of a monopoly for a limited time, as of 14 years; but the benefit even of limited monopolies is too doubtful to be opposed to that of their general suppression. If no check can be found to keep the number of standing troops within safe bounds, while they are tolerated as far as necessary, abandon them altogether, discipline well the militia, & guard the magazines with them. More than magazine guards will be useless if few, & dangerous if many. No European nation can ever send against us such a regular army as we need fear, & it is hard if our militia are not equal to those of Canada or Florida. My idea then is, that tho' proper exceptions to these general rules are desirable, & probably practicable, yet if the exceptions cannot be agreed on, the establishment of the rules in all cases will do ill in very few. I hope therefore a bill of rights will be formed to guard the people against the federal government, as they are already guarded against their state governments in most instances.

The abandoning the principle of necessary rotation in the Senate, has I see been disapproved by many; in the case of the President, by none. I readily therefore suppose my opinion wrong, when opposed by the majority as in the former instance, & the totality as in the latter. In this however I should have done it with more complete satisfaction, had we all judged from the same position.

Solicitations, which cannot be directly refused, oblige me to trouble you often with letters recommending & introducing to you persons who go from hence to America. I will beg the favor of you to distinguish the letters wherein I appeal to recommendations from other persons, from those which I write on my own knowledge. In the former, it is never my intention to compromise myself, nor you. In both instances I must beg you to ascribe the trouble I give you to circumstances which do not leave me at liberty to decline it.

To William Short[1]
Paris, Sept 20, 1788
Dear Sir,

---

[1] Jefferson was a lifelong mentor to William Short, who served as Jefferson's private secretary when Jefferson was a peace commissioner and then the United States Minister to France in Paris, from 1784 to 1789. When Jefferson left Paris — on the assumption of an early return to his post — the business of the legation was put in the Short's capable hands, though Congress had not seen fit to give him an official title. Short would serve as America's chargé d'affaires in France during the French Revolution from 1789–1792, as America's Minister to the Netherlands, and as a treaty commissioner to Spain. (Peterson 1975, 385)

The evening of your departure came a letter by the way of London & N. York, addressed to you, and probably from Virginia. I think you wished your American letters to remain here; I shall therefore keep it. The passport now enclosed came the day after your departure: so also did a mass of American letters for me, as low down as August 10. I shall give you their substance.

The convention of Virginia annexed to their ratification of the new Constitution a copy of the state Declaration of rights, not by way of Condition, but to announce their attachment to them. They added also propositions for specific alterations of the constitution. Among these was one for rendering the President incapable of serving more than 8 years in any term of 16. New York has followed the example of Virginia, expressing the substance of her bill of rights, (i.e. Virginia's) & proposing amendments; these last differ much from those of Virginia, but they concur as to the President, only proposing that he shall be incapable of being elected more than twice. But I own I should like better than either of these, what Luther Martin tells us was repeatedly voted & adhered to by the federal convention, & only altered about 12. days before their rising when some members had gone off, to wit, that he should be elected for 7 years & incapable for ever after. But New York has taken another step which gives uneasiness, she has written a circular letter to all the legislatures, asking their concurrence in an immediate Convention for making amendments. No news yet from N. Carolina. Electors are to be chosen the 1st Wednesday in January, the President to be elected the 1st Wednesday in February, the new legislature to meet the 3d week in March, the place is not yet decided on. Philadelphia was first proposed & had 6½ votes, the half vote was Delaware, one of whose members wanted to take a vote on Wilmington, then Baltimore was proposed & carried, and afterwards rescinded, so that the matter stood open as ever on the 10th of August; but it was allowed the dispute lay only between N. York & Philadelphia, & rather thought in favor of the last. The R. island delegates had retired from Congress. Dr. Franklin was dangerously ill of the gout & stone on the 21st of July. My letters of Aug. 10 not mentioning him, I hope he was recovered. Warville, &c. were arrived. Congress had referred the decision as to the independence of Kentucky to the new government. Brown ascribes this to the jealousy of the Northern states, who want Vermont to be received at the same time in order to preserve a balance of interests in Congress. He was just setting out for Kentucky disgusted, yet disposed to persuade to an acquiescence, tho' doubting they would immediately separate from the Union. The principal obstacle to this, he thought, would be the Indian war.

The following is a quotation from a letter from Virginia dated July 12. "P[endleto]n, tho' much impaired in health, & in every respect in the decline of life, shewed as much zeal to carry the new const, as if he had been a young man; perhaps more than he discovered in the commencement of the late revolution in his opposition to Great Britain. W[yth]e acted as chairman to the comee. of the whole & of course took but little part in the debate; but was for the adoption, relying on subsequent amendments. B[lai]r said nothing, but was for it. The G[overno]r exhibited a curious spectacle to view. Having refused to sign the paper, everybody supposed him against it, but he afterwards had written a letter; & having taken a part which might be called rather vehement, than active, he was constantly laboring to shew that his present conduct was consistent with that letter, & that letter with his refusal to sign. M[a]d[iso]n took the principal share in the debate for it, in which, together with the aid I have already mentioned, he was somewhat assisted by I-nn[e]s, Lee, M[arshal]l, C[orbi]n & G. N[ichola]s. M[a]s[o]n, H[enr]y & Gr[ayso]n were the principal supporters of the opposition. The discussion, as might be expected where the parties were so nearly on a balance, was conducted generally with great order, propriety & respect of either party to the other."

The assembly of Virginia, hurried to their harvests, would not enter into a discussion of the District bill, but suspended it to the next session. E. Winston is appointed a judge, vice Gab. Jones resigned. R. Goode & Andrew Moore, counsellors, vice B. Starke dead, & Jos Egglestone resigned.

It is said Wilson, of Philadelphia, is talked of, to succeed Mr. A[dams] in London. Qu?

The dispute about Virgil's tomb & the laurel seems to be at length settled by the testimony of two travelers, given separately & without a communication with each other. These both say, that attempting to pluck off a branch of the Laurel, it followed their hand, being in fact nothing more than a plant or bough recently cut & stuck in the ground for the occasion. The Cicerone acknowledged the roguery, & said they practiced it with almost every traveler, to get money. You will of course tug well at the laurel which shall be shewn you, to see if this be the true solution.

The President Dupaty is dead. Monsr de Barentin, premier president de la cour des aides, is appointed Garde des sceaux. The stocks are rather lower than when you left this. Present me in the most friendly terms to Messrs. Shippen & Rutledge. I rely on your communicating to them the news, & therefore on their pardoning me for not repeating it in separate letters to them. You can satisfy them how necessary this economy of my time & labor is. This goes to Geneva, poste restante. I shall not write again till you tell me where to write to.

To James Madison[1]
Paris, Nov. 18, 1788

---

[1] Considering his relationship with Madison, Jefferson's antifederalist arguments had doubtless been constructive in helping to stimulate discussion leading to *The Federalist*, a series of eighty-five essays urging the citizens of New York to ratify the new United States Constitution. Written by Alexander Hamilton, James Madison, and John Jay, the essays originally appeared anonymously in New York newspapers in 1787 and 1788 under the pen name "Publius," and are considered one of the most important sources for interpreting and understanding the original intent of the Constitution. In this note, Jefferson, well realizing that the essays have become a political classic — despite that they were initially prepared more as a propaganda tract rather than as a treatise on political theory — tells Madison that he read them "with care, pleasure and improvement"; further that it was "the best commentary on the principles of government ever written." (McCormick 1959, 145-146)

Dear Sir,

My last to you was of the 31st July: since which I have received yours of July 24, Aug. 10 & 23. The first part of this long silence in me was occasioned by a knowledge that you were absent from N. York; the latter part by a want of opportunity, which has been longer than usual. Mr. Shippen being just arrived here, and to set out to-morrow for London, I avail myself of that channel of conveyance. Mr. Carrington was so kind as to send me the 2d vol. of the *American Philosophical Transactions*, the *Federalist*, and some other interesting pamphlets; and I am to thank you for another copy of the *Federalist* and the report of the instrns. to the ministers for negotiating peace. The latter unluckily omitted exactly the passage I wanted, which was what related to the navigation of the Mississippi. With respect to the *Federalist*, the three authors had been named to me. I read it with care, pleasure & improvement, and was satisfied there was nothing in it by one of those hands, & not a great deal by a second. It does the highest honor to the third, as being, in my opinion, the best commentary on the principles of government which ever was written. In some parts it is discoverable that the author means only to say what may be best said in defense of opinions in which he did not concur. But in general it establishes firmly the plan of government. I confess it has rectified me in several points. As to the bill of rights however I still think it should be added and I am to see that three states have at length considered the perpetual re-eligibility of the president as an article which should be amended. I should deprecate with you indeed the meeting of a new convention. I hope they will adopt the mode of amendment by Congress & the Assemblies, in which case I should not fear any dangerous innovation in the plan. But the minorities are too respectable not to be entitled to some sacrifice of opinion in the majority especially when a great proportion of them would be contented with a bill of rights. Here things internally are going on well. The Notables, now in session, have indeed passed one vote which augurs ill to the rights of the people, but if they do not obtain now so much as they have a right to, they will in the long run. The misfortune is that they are not yet ripe for receiving the blessings to which they are entitled. I doubt, for instance, whether the body of the nation, if they could be consulted, would accept of a Habeas corpus law, if offered them by the King. If the Etats generaux, when they assemble, do not aim at too much, they may begin a good constitution. There are three articles which they may easily obtain, 1, their own meeting periodically. 2, the exclusive right of taxation. 3, the right of registering laws & proposing amendments to them as exercised now by the parliaments. This last would be readily approved by the courts on account of their hostility against the parliaments, & would lead immediately to the origination of laws. The 2d has been already solemnly avowed by the King; and it is well understood there would be no opposition to the first. If they push at much more, all may fail. I shall not enter further into public details, because my letter to Mr. Jay will give them. That contains a request of permission to return to America the next spring, for the summer only. The reasons therein urged, drawn from my private affairs, are very cogent. But there is another more cogent on my mind, tho' of a nature not to be explained in a public letter. It is the necessity of attending my daughters myself to their own country, and depositing them safely in the hands of those with whom I can safely leave them. I have deferred this request as long as circumstances would permit, and am in hopes it will meet with no difficulty. I have had too many proofs of your friendship not to rely on your patronage of it, as, in all probability, nothing can suffer by a short absence. But the immediate permission is what I am anxious about; as by going in April & returning in October I shall be sure of pleasant & short passages out & in. I must entreat your attention, my friend, to this matter, and that the answers may be sent me thro' several channels.

Mr. Limozin at Havre, sent you by mistake a package belonging to somebody else. I do not know what it contained, but he has written to you on the subject, & prayed me to do the same. He is likely to suffer if it be not returned.

Supposing that the funding their foreign debt will be among the first operations of the new government, I send you two estimates, the one by myself, the other by a gentleman infinitely better acquainted with the subject, shewing what fund will suffice to discharge the principal and interest as it shall become due, aided by occasional loans, which the same fund will repay. I inclose them to you, because collating them together, and with your own ideas, you will be able to devise something better than either. But something must be done. This government will expect, I fancy, a very satisfactory provision for the paiment of their debt, from the first session of the new Congress. Perhaps in this matter, as well as the arrangement of your foreign affairs, I may be able when on the spot with you, to give some information & suggest some hints, which may render my visit to my native country not altogether useless. I consider as no small advantage the resuming the tone of mind of my constituents, which is lost by long absence, and can only be recovered by mixing with them: and shall particularly hope for much profit & pleasure, by contriving to pass as much time as possible with you. Should you have a trip to Virginia in contemplation for that year, I hope you will time it so as that we may be there together. I will camp you at Monticello where, if illy entertained otherwise, you shall not want for books. In firm hope of a happy meeting with you in the spring or early in summer I conclude with assurances of the sincere esteem & attachment with which I am, Dear Sir, your affectionate friend & servant.

To George Washington[1]
Paris, Dec. 4, 1788

---

[1] Despite the fact that his initial opinions of the Constitution were, as we have seen, arguably unfavorable, after he had learned that the new Government was to be a fact, in this letter, Jefferson writes Washington: "I have seen with infinite pleasure our new constitution accepted." Careful study had taught him, he said, "that circumstances may arise, and probably will arise, wherein all the resources of taxation will be necessary for the safety of the state." He saw probability of war which "requires every resource of taxation & credit." Adding that "the power of making war often prevents it." Jefferson thus walks a rather fine political line: he could be quoted on both sides and claimed by neither or by both. (Beveridge 1916. 47)

Sir,

Your favor of Aug. 31. came to hand yesterday; and a confidential conveyance offering, by the way of London, I avail myself of it to acknowledge the receipt. I have seen, with infinite pleasure, our new constitution accepted by 11. states, not rejected by the 12th. and that the 13th. happens to be a state of the least importance. It is true that the minorities in most of the accepting states have been very respectable, so much so as to render it prudent, were it not otherwise reasonable, to make some sacrifices to them. I am in hopes that the annexation of a bill of rights to the constitution will alone draw over so great a proportion of the minorities, as to leave little danger in the opposition of the residue; and that this annexation may be made by Congress and the assemblies, without calling a convention which might endanger the most valuable parts of the system. Calculation has convinced me that circumstances may arise, and probably will arise, wherein all the resources of taxation will be necessary for the safety of the state. For tho I am decidedly of opinion we should take no part in European quarrels, but cultivate peace and commerce with all, yet who can avoid seeing the source of war in the tyranny of those nations who deprive us of the natural right of trading with our neighbors? The produce of the U.S. will soon exceed the European demand. What is to be done with the surplus, when there shall be one? It will be employed, without question, to open by force a market for itself with those placed on the same continent with us, and who wish nothing better. Other causes too are obvious which may involve us in war; and war requires every resource of taxation and credit. The power of making war often prevents it, and in our case would give efficacy to our desire of peace. If the new government wears the front which I hope it will I see no impossibility in the availing ourselves of the wars of others to open the other parts of America to our commerce, as the price of our neutrality.

The campaign between the Turks and two empires has been clearly in favor of the former. The emperor is secretly trying to bring about a peace. The alliance between England, Prussia and Holland, (and some suspect Sweden also) renders their mediation decisive wherever it is proposed. They seemed to interpose it so magisterially between Denmark and Sweden, that the former submitted to its dictates, and there was all reason to believe that the war in the North-Western parts of Europe would be quieted. All of a sudden a new flame bursts out in Poland. The king and his party are devoted to Russia. The opposition rely on the protection of Prussia. They have lately become the majority in the confederated diet, and have passed a vote for subjecting their army to a commission independent of the king, and propose a perpetual diet, in which case he will be a perpetual cipher. Russia declares against such a change in their constitution, and Prussia has put an army into readiness for marching at a moment's warning on the frontiers of Poland. These events are too recent to see as yet what turn they will take, or what effect they will have on the peace of Europe. So is that also of the lunacy of the king of England, which is a decided fact, notwithstanding all the stuff the English papers publish about his fevers, his deliriums &c. The truth is that the lunacy declared itself almost at once, and with as few concomitant complaints as usually attend the first development of that disorder. I suppose a regency will be established, and if it consist of a plurality of members it will probably be peaceable. In this event it will much favor the present wishes of this country, which are so decidedly for peace, that they refused to enter into the mediation between Sweden and Russia, lest it should commit them. As soon as the convocation of the States general was announced, a tranquility took place thro' the whole kingdom. Happily no open rupture had taken place in any part of it. The parliaments were re-instated in their functions at the same time. This was all they desired, and they had called for the States general only through fear that the crown could not otherwise be forced to re-instate them. Their end obtained, they began to foresee danger to themselves in the States general. They began to lay the foundations for cavilling at the legality of that body, if it's measures should be hostile to them. The court, to clear itself of the dispute, convened the Notables who had acted with general approbation on the former occasion, and referred to them the forms of calling and organizing the States-general. These Notables consist principally of nobility and clergy, the few of the tiers etat among them being either parliament-men, or other privileged persons. The court wished that in the future States general the members of the Tiers-etat should equal those of both the other orders, and that they should form but one house, all together, and vote by persons, not by orders. But the Notables, in the true spirit of priests and nobles, combining together against the people, have voted by 5 bureaux out of 6. that the people or tiers etat shall have no greater number of deputies than each of the other orders separately, and that they shall vote by orders: so that two orders concurring in a vote, the third will be overruled; for it is not here as in England where each of the three branches has a negative on the other two. If this project of theirs succeeds, a combination between the two houses of clergy and nobles, will render the representation of the Tiers etat merely nugatory. The bureaux are to assemble together to consolidate their separate votes; but I see no reasonable hope of their changing this. Perhaps the king, knowing that he may count on the support of the nation and attach it more closely to him, may take on himself to disregard the opinion of the Notables in this instance, and may call an equal representation of the people, in which precedents will support him. In every event, I think the present disquiet will end well. The nation has been awaked by our revolution, they feel their strength, they are enlightened, their lights are spreading, and they will not retrograde. The first states general may establish 3. important points without opposition from the court. 1. their own periodical convocation. 2. their exclusive right of taxation (which has been confessed by the king.) 3. The right of registering laws and of previously proposing amendments to them, as the parliaments have by usurpation been in the habit of doing. The court will consent to this from its hatred to the parliaments, and from the desire of having to do with one rather than many legislatures. If the states are prudent they will not aim at more than this at first, lest they should shock the dispositions of the court, and even alarm the public mind, which must be left to open itself by degrees to successive improvements. These will follow from the nature of things. How far they can proceed, in the end, towards a thorough reformation of abuse, cannot be foreseen. In my opinion a kind of influence, which none of their plans of reform take into account, will elude them all; I mean the influence of women in the government. The manners of the nation allow them to visit, alone, all persons in office, to solicit the affairs of the husband, family, or friends, and their solicitations bid defiance to laws and regulations. This obstacle may seem less to those who, like our countrymen, are in the precious habit of considering Right, as a barrier against all solicitation. Nor can such an one, without the evidence of his own eyes, believe in the desperate state to which things are reduced in this country from the omnipotence of an influence which, fortunately for the happiness of the sex itself, does not endeavor to extend itself in our country beyond the domestic line.

Your communications to the Count de Moustier, whatever they may have been, cannot have done injury to my endeavors here to open the W. Indies to us. On this head the ministers are invincibly mute, tho' I have often tried to draw them into the subject. I have therefore found it necessary to let it lie till war or other circumstances may force it on. Whenever they are in war with England, they must open the islands to us, and perhaps during that war they may see some price which might make them agree to keep them always open. In the meantime I have laid my shoulder to the opening the markets of this country to our produce, and rendering it's transportation a nursery for our seamen. A maritime force is the only one by which we can act on Europe. Our navigation law (if it be wise to have any) should be the reverse of that of England. Instead of confining importations to home-bottoms or those of the producing nation, I think we should confine exportations to home bottoms or to those of nations having treaties with us. Our exportations are heavy, and would nourish a great force of our own, or be a tempting price to the nation to whom we should offer a participation of it in exchange for free access to all their possessions. This is an object to which our government alone is adequate in the gross. But I have ventured to pursue it here, so far as the consumption of our productions by this country extends. Thus in our arrangements relative to tobacco, none can be received here but in French or American bottoms. This is employment for near 2000 seamen, and puts nearly that number of British out of employ. By the arret of Dec. 1787. it was provided that our whale oils should not be received here but in French or American bottoms, and by later regulations all oils but those of France and America are excluded. This will put 100 English whale vessels immediately out of employ, and 150. ere long: and call so many of French and American into service. We have had 6000 seamen formerly in this business, the whole of whom we have been likely to lose. The consumption of rice is growing fast in this country, and that of Carolina gaining ground on every other kind. I am of opinion the whole of the Carolina rice can be consumed here. It's transportation employs 2500. sailors, almost all of them English at present, the rice being deposited at Cowes and brought from thence here. It would be dangerous to confine this transportation to French and American bottoms the ensuing year, because they will be much engrossed by the transportation of wheat and flour hither, and the crop of rice might lie on hand for want of vessels: but I see no objections to the extension of our principle to this article also, beginning with the year 1790. However before there is a necessity of deciding on this I hope to be able to consult our new government in person, as I have asked of Congress a leave of Absence for 6. months, that is to say from April to November next. It is necessary for me to pay a short visit to my native country, first to reconduct my family thither, and place them in the hands of their friends, and secondly to place my private affairs under certain arrangements. When I left my own house I expected to be absent but 5. months, and I have been led by events to an absence of 5. years. I shall hope therefore for the pleasure of personal conferences with your Excellency on the subjects of this letter and others interesting to our country, of getting my own ideas set to rights by a communication of yours, and of taking again the tone of sentiment of my own country which we lose in some degree after a certain absence. You know doubtless of the death of the Marquis de Chastellux. The Marquis de la Fayette is out of favor with the court, but high in favor with the nation. I once feared for his personal liberty. But I hope him on safe ground at present.

On the subject of the whale fishery I inclose you some observations I drew up for the ministry here, in order to obtain a correction of their Arret of Sep. last, whereby they had involved our oils with the English in a general exclusion from their ports. They will accordingly correct this, so that our oils will participate with theirs in the monopoly of their markets. There are several things incidentally introduced which do not seem pertinent to the general question. They were rendered necessary by particular circumstances the explanation of which would add to a letter already too long. I will trespass no further then, than to assure you of the sentiments of sincere attachment and respect with which I have the honor to be your Excellency's most obedt. humble servant,

P. S. The observations enclosed, tho' printed, have been put into confidential hands only.

1789

To John Jay[1]

---

[1] In this letter to Jay, Jefferson offers a few sketches of personages of the time. These were in the tradition of the "characters" of the eighteenth century and his sharpness of observation combines with a felicitous power of description to create lasting images. An example that accurately reflects the particular flavor of their style relates to his observations on George IV, at that time Prince of Wales: "He has not a single element of Mathematics, of Natural or Moral Philosophy, or of any other science on earth, nor has the society he has kept been such as to supply the void of education. It has been that of the lowest, the most illiterate and profligate persons of the kingdom, without choice of rank or mind, and with whom the subjects of conversation are only horses, drinking-matches, bawdy houses, and in terms the most vulgar... He has not a single idea of justice, morality, religion, or of the rights of men, or any anxiety for the opinion of the world. He carries that indifference for fame so far, that he would probably not be hurt were he to lose his throne provided he could be assured of having always meat, drink, horses, and women." (Berman, 1947, 245)

Paris, January 11, 1789

Dear Sir,

As the character of the Prince of Wales is becoming interesting, I have endeavored to learn what it truly is. This is less difficult in his case than it is in other persons of rank, because he has taken no pains to hide himself from the world. The information I most rely on is from a person here, with whom I am intimate, who divides his time between Paris and London — an Englishman by birth, of truth, sagacity, and science. He is of a circle, when in London, which has had good opportunities of knowing the Prince, but he has also, himself, had special occasions of verifying their information by his own personal observations. He happened, when last in London, to be invited to a dinner of three persons. The Prince came by chance, and made the fourth. He ate half a leg of mutton; and did not taste of small dishes, because small; drank Champagne and Burgundy as small beer during dinner, and Bourdeaux after dinner, as the rest of the company. Upon the whole, he ate as much as the other three, and drank about two bottles of wine without seeming to feel it.

My informant sat next him, and being until then unknown to the Prince personally (though not by character) and lately from France, the Prince confined his conversation to him almost entirely.[1] Observing to the Prince that he spoke French, without the slightest foreign accent, the Prince told him that, when very young, his father had put only French servants about him, and it was to that circumstance he owed his pronunciation. He led him from this to give an account of his education, the total of which was the learning a little Latin. He has not a single element of mathematics, of natural or moral philosophy, or any other science on earth, nor has the society he has kept been such as to supply the void of education. It has been that of the lowest, the most illiterate and profligate persons of the kingdom, without choice of rank or mind, and with whom the subjects of conversation are only horses, drinking-matches, bawdy-houses, and in terms the most vulgar. The young nobility who begin by associating with him soon leave him disgusted by the insupportable profligacy of his society; and Mr. Fox, who has been supposed his favorite, and not over-nice in the choice of company, would never keep his company habitually. In fact, he never associated with a man of sense. He has not a single idea of justice, morality, religion, or of the rights of men, or any anxiety for the opinion of the world. He carries that indifference for fame so far, that he probably would not be hurt if he were to lose his throne, provided he could be assured of having always meat, horses and women. In the article of women, nevertheless, he has become more correct since his connection with Mrs. Fitzherbert, who is an honest and worthy woman; he is even less crapulous than he was.

---

[1] Jefferson's informant about the Prince of Wales was very likely Dr. Richard Gem — an atheist Welsh physician who supported the French Revolution — who was almost a daily visitor at Hôtel de Langeac during the fall and winter of 1788–1789, and who not only was a man of truth, sagacity, and science, but had been born in England, made frequent visits to London, and belonged to a circle there that had good opportunities of knowing the prince. (Boyd 1990)

He had a fine person, but it is becoming coarse. He possesses good native common sense, is affable, polite, and very good-humored — saying to my informant, on another occasion, "Your friend such a one dined with me yesterday, and I made him damned drunk"; he replied, "I am sorry for it. I had heard that your royal highness had left off drinking." The Prince laughed, tapped him on the shoulder very good-naturedly, without saying a word, or ever after showing any displeasure.

The Duke of York, who was for some time cried up as the prodigy of the family, is as profligate and of less understanding. To these particular traits, from a man of sense and truth, it would be superfluous to add the general terms of praise or blame in which he is spoken of by other persons, in whose impartiality and penetration I have less confidence. A sample is better than a description. For the peace of Europe, it is best that the King should give such gleanings of recovery as would prevent the Regent or his ministry from thinking themselves firm, and yet that he should not recover.

To James Madison
Paris, Jan. 12. 1789
Dear Sir,

My last to you was of the 18th of Nov. since which I have received yours of Sep. 21 and Oct. 8. with the pamphlet on the Mohican language, for which receive my thanks. I endeavor to collect all the vocabularies I can of the American Indians, as of those of Asia, persuaded that if they ever had a common parentage it will appear in their languages. I was pleased to see the vote of Congress, of Sep. 16, on the subject of the Mississippi, as I had before seen with great uneasiness the pursuits of other principles which I could never reconcile to my own ideas of probity or wisdom, and from which, and my knowledge of the character of our Western settlers, I saw that the loss of that country was a necessary consequence.[1] I wish this return to true policy may be in time to prevent evil. There has been little foundation for the reports and fears relative to the M. de la Fayette. He has from the beginning taken openly part with those who demand a constitution: and there was a moment that we apprehended the Bastille: but they venture on nothing more than to take from him a temporary service on which he had been ordered: and this more to save appearances for their own authority than anything else; for at the very time they pretended that they had put him into disgrace, they were constantly conferring & communicating with him. Since this he has stood on safe ground, and is viewed as among the foremost of the patriots. Everybody here is trying their hand at forming declarations of rights.

---

[1] In September 1788, a congressional resolution was introduced "designed to remove the apprehension and uneasiness produced by a report that Congress are disposed to treat with Spain for the surrender of their claim to the navigation of the river Mississippi." The resolutions stated that since the rumor was not founded in fact the delegates were at liberty to contradict it, that free navigation of the Mississippi was an essential right of the United States, and that negotiations on this subject should "be referred to the new government." (Abernethy 1959. 359-360)

As something of that kind is going on with you also, I send you two specimens from hence. The one is by our friend of whom I have just spoken. You will see that it contains the essential principle of ours accommodated as much as could be to the actual state of things here. The other is from a very sensible man, a pure theorist, of the sect called the economists, of which Turgot was considered as the head. The former is adapted to the existing abuses; the latter goes to those possible as well as to those existing. With respect to Doct^r. Spence, supposed to have been taken by the Algerians, I think the report extremely [im]probable. O'Bryan, one of our captives there, has constantly written to me, and given me information on every subject he thought interesting. He could not have failed to know if such a capture had been made, tho' before his time, nor to inform me of it. I am under perpetual anxiety for our captives there. The money indeed is not yet ready at Amsterdam; but when it shall be, there are no orders from the board of Treasury to the bankers to furnish what may be necessary for the redemption of the captives: and it is so long since Congress approved the loan, that the orders of the Treasury for the application of the money would have come if they had intended to send any. I wrote to them early on the subject & pointedly. I mentioned it to Mr. Jay also merely that he might suggest it to them. The paiments to the foreign officers will await the same formality. I thank you for your attention to the case of Mrs. Burke.

We have no news of Dr. Franklin since July last when he was very ill. Tho' the silence of our letters on that subject is a proof that he is well, yet there is an anxiety here among his friends. We have lately had three books published which are of great merit in different lines. The one is in 7. vols, 8.vo, by an Abbé Barthelemy, wherein he has collected every subject of Grecian literature, after a labor of 30. years. It is called Les voyages d'Anacharsis. I have taken a copy for you, because the whole impression was likely to be run off at once. The second is a work on government by the Marquis de Condorcet, 2. v. 8vo. I shall secure you a copy. The 3.d are the works of the K. of Prussia, in 16. vols, 8vo. These were a little garbled at Berlin, before printed. The government lays its hands on all which come here, and change some leaves. There is a genuine edition published at Basle, where even the garblings of Berlin are reestablished. I doubt the possibility of getting a copy, so vigilant is the government as to this work. I shall obtain you one if it be possible. As I write all the public news to Mr. Jay, I will not repeat it to you. I have just received the [botanical manuscript] *Flora Caroliniana* of [Thomas] Walter; a very learned and good work.[1]

---

[1] Again, Jefferson casts an eye toward science. Among the South Carolina planters there were three who showed a marked interest in science for its own sake during the Jeffersonian period: Thomas Walter and John Drayton in the early years of independence and Stephen Elliott somewhat later. Arriving in South Carolina from England shortly before the Revolution, Walter began work on a Flora of the region. He established a botanical garden on his plantation on the Santee River and planted more than 600 species of plants collected within a radius of fifty miles. He was greatly aided in this enterprise by a visiting Scottish nurseryman, John Fraser, who ranged the countryside as far as the foothills of the Appalachians. Fraser added several hundred plants to Walter's garden before returning to England in 1788, carrying Walter's herbarium and the manuscript

To Dr. Edward Bancroft[1]
Paris, Jan. 26, 1789
Dear Sir,

I have deferred answering your letter on the subject of slaves because you permitted me to do it till a moment of leisure, and that moment rarely comes, and because too I could not answer you with such a degree of certainty as to merit any notice. I do not recollect the conversation at Vincennes to which you allude but can repeat still on the same ground, on which I must have done then, that as far as I can judge from the experiments which have been made to give liberty to, or rather, to abandon persons whose habits have been formed in slavery is like abandoning children. Many Quakers in Virginia seated their slaves on their lands as tenants. They were distant from me, and therefore I cannot be particular in the details, because I never had very particular information. I cannot say whether they were to pay a rent in money, or a share of the produce: but I remember that the landlord was obliged to plan their crops for them, to direct all their operations during every season & according to the weather. But what is more afflicting, he was obliged to watch them daily & almost constantly to make them work, & even to whip them. A man's moral sense must be unusually strong, if slavery does not make him a thief. He who is permitted by law to have no property of his own, can with difficulty conceive that property is founded in anything but force. These slaves chose to steal from their neighbors rather

---

of his *Flora Caroliniana* with him. Published in London in 1788, Walter's *Flora* was the first such regional work by an American. (Greene 1984, 109)

[1] The discussion of slavery continued during this period, bringing about a reformulation of the relationship between master and slave, as the harsh patriarchal ethos of the colonial era gave way to the ideal of paternalism. And scholars continue to debate precisely when paternalism appeared in the southern states, as well as what factors allowed for its maturation. Some point to the end of North America's involvement in the Atlantic slave trade in 1808 and the emergence of a wholly Creole slave population with no memory of freedom in Africa and few hopes of liberation in the United States, a phenomenon already present in Virginia with its large native-born slave class. Others attribute the evolution of ruthless patriarchalism into paternalism to the moderating influence of evangelical Christianity, while yet other historians regard it as only a pose adopted by planters to disguise the cruelty of their regime. If Chesapeake slavery became somewhat less harsh in the decades after the war, it was because planters wished to make it more permanent and create a stable slave society. In the process, masters increasingly adopted the excuse that maintaining unfree labor was their responsibility to those who lived on their lands and under their care. As was so often the case, in this letter to Bancroft, Jefferson succinctly sums up his position, "To give liberty to, or rather, to abandon persons whose habits have been formed in slavery is like abandoning children." With respect to his own farms, one plan Jefferson had been considering for two decades involved turning his slaves into *metayers*, or sharecroppers. He would inaugurate his own scheme for filling Virginia with small farms by settling his slaves on 50-acre parcels of his land, intermingled with free white farmers. The enslaved children, he tells Bancroft, would learn "habits of property and foresight" from their neighbors, and "I have no doubt but that they will be good citizens" (Egerton 2009, 144-145; Stanton 2012, 257)

than work; they became public nuisances and in most instances were reduced to slavery again. But I will beg of you to make no use of this imperfect information (unless in common conversation). I shall go to America in the Spring & return in the fall. During my stay in Virginia I shall be in the neighborhood where many of these trials were made. I will inform myself very particularly of them, & communicate the information to you. Besides these there is an instance since I came away of a young man (Mr. Mayo) who died and gave freedom to all his slaves, about 200. This is about 4 years ago. I shall know how they have turned out. Notwithstanding the discouraging result of these experiments, I am decided on my final return to America to try this one. I shall endeavor to import as many Germans as I have grown slaves. I will settle them and my slaves, on farms of 50 acres each, intermingled, and place all on the footing of the Metayers (Medietani) of Europe. Their children shall be brought up, as others are, in habits of property and foresight, & I have no doubt but that they will be good citizens. Some of their fathers will be so: others I suppose will need government. With these, all that can be done is to oblige them to labor as the laboring poor of Europe do, and to apply to their comfortable subsistence the produce of their labor, retaining such a moderate portion of it as may be a just equivalent for the use of the lands they labor and the stocks & other necessary advances.

A word now on Mr. Paradise's affairs: you were informed at the time, of the arrangement they had established in their affairs, to wit. reserving 400 £ a year for their subsistence, abandoning the rest of their income about 400 £ more, all their credits (one of which is 800 £ from an individual and another is 1000 £ from the state) and the cutting of a valuable wood, to their creditors. Their whole debts amounting but to 2300 £, the term of paiment cannot be long, if this arrangement can be preserved. I had hope that the journey to Italy would have fixed Mrs. Paradise with her daughter and left him free to travel or tarry where he liked best. But this journey has been a burthen instead of a relief to their affairs. In fact it is evident to me that the society of England is necessary for the happiness of Mrs. Paradise, and is perhaps the most agreeable to Mr. Paradise also. It is become an object therefore to obtain the concurrence of their creditors in the arrangements taken. The inducement to be proposed to them is Mrs. Paradise's joining in a deed in which these dispositions shall be stipulated (which by the laws of Virginia will bind her property there) so that the creditors will be secured of their debts in the event of Mr. Paradise's death. The inducement to Mr. & Mrs. Paradise is that their persons & property shall be free from molestation & their substance not consumed at law. We suppose that the creditors will name one trustee & Mr. Paradise another (yourself) fully & solely authorized to receive all remittances from America, to pay to them first their subsistence money & the rest to the creditors till they are fully paid. Mrs. Paradise will set out in a few days for London to set her hand to this accommodation. In the meantime they hope you will prepare the ground by negotiating the settlement with the creditors. As far as I have any influence with Mr. or Mrs. Paradise I have used it & shall use it for the joint interests of their creditors & themselves. For I view it as clearly their interest to reduce themselves to as moderate an expense as possible till their debts are paid. If this can be effected before my departure in April I will not only aid it here, but have anything done which may be necessary in Virginia when I go there, such as the recording the deed &c. This journey of Mrs. Paradise will also be an experiment whether their distresses will not be lighter when separate than while together.

I shall always be glad to hear from you. Since Mr. Adams's departure I have need of information from that country, and should rely much on yours. It will always therefore be acceptable.

To William Short
Paris, Feb. 9, 1789
Dear Sir,

I wrote you last on the 22d of Jan on which day I received yours of Dec 31, and since that the other of Jan 14. We have now received news from America down to the middle of December They had then had no cold weather. All things relative to our new constitution were going on well. Federal Senators are; N Hampshire Presid^t. Langdon and Bartlett. Massach. Strong & Dalton. Connect. Dr. Johnson & Ellsworth. New Jersey Patterson & Ellmer. Pennsylvania Rob Morris & McClay. Delaware Reed & Bassett. Virga. R. H. Lee & Grayson. Meryl. Charles Carrol of Carrolton & John Henry. All of these are federalists except those of Virga: so that a majority of federalists are secured in the Senate and expected in the H of representatives. Gen'l. Washington will be president and probably Mr. Adams vice president. So that the constitution will be put under way by those who will give it a fair trial. It does not seem probable that the attempt of N York to have another convention to make amendments will succeed, tho' Virginia concurs in it. It is tolerably certain that Congress will propose amendments to the assemblies, as even the friends of the constitution are willing to make amendments, some from a conviction they are necessary, others from a spirit of conciliation. The addition of a bill of rights will probably be the most essential change. A vast majority of Antifederalists have got into the assembly of Virginia, so that Mr. Henry is omnipotent there. Mr. Madison was left out as a Senator by 8. or 9. votes and Henry has so modelled the districts for representatives as to tack Orange to counties where he himself has great influence that Madison may not be elected in the lower federal house, which was the place Madison had wished to serve in, & not the Senate. Henry pronounced a Philippic against Madison in open assembly, Madison being then at Philadelphia. Mifflin is Presidt. of Pennsylvania and Peters speaker. Colo Howard is Govr of Maryland. Beverly Randolph Govr of Virginia (this last is said by a passenger only & he seems not very sure). Colo Humphreys is attacked in the papers for his French airs, for bad poetry, bad prose, vanity, &c. It is said his dress in so gay a style gives general disgust against him. I have received a letter from him. He seems fixed with Gen'l Washington. Mayo's bridge over Richmond was completed, & carried away in a few weeks. While up, it was so profitable that he had great offers for it. A turnpike is established at Alexandria & succeeds. Rhode island has again refused to call a Convention. Spain has granted to Colo Morgan of

New Jersey a vast tract of land on the Western side of the Mississippi with the monopoly of the navigation of that river. He is inviting settlers & they swarm to him.[1] Even the settlement of Kentucky is likely to be much weakened by emigrations to Morgan's grant. Warville is returned charmed with our country. He is going to carry his wife & children to settle there. Governor Morris is just arrived here, deputed, as is supposed, to settle R. Morris's affairs which continue still deranged. Dr. Franklin was well when he left America, which was about the middle of December.

To William Carmichael[2]
Paris, Mar. 4. 1789
Dear Sir,
 My last to you was of the 25th of December. Tho' the establishment of packet boats with you, and suppression of them with us, puts it in your power perhaps to give me better details of American affairs than I can you, I shall nevertheless continue to communicate to you what I know, persuaded it is better you should hear a thing twice than not hear it at all.

---

[1] Colonel George Morgan, of New Jersey, a revolutionary soldier, had of late been trying to induce Congress to help him found a colony near Kaskaskia, in what is now Illinois. This pending, Spain's Minister to the United States, Don Diego María de Gardoqui y Arriquibar Gardoqui sought him with an offer of conceding twelve or fifteen million acres of land at New Madrid, a settlement on the Mississippi River between what is now St. Louis, Missouri and Natchez, Mississippi. On October 3, 1788, the terms were settled. It was expected that his followers would be Protestants, and guarantees against religious interference were made. Free trade down the river satisfied the commercial requirements. The position of New Madrid, nearly opposite the mouth of the Ohio, gave earnest of a large town. Morgan issued a circular setting forth the advantages of the plan. It promised land at an eighth of a dollar an acre, with aid in building dwellings. It set forth the richness of the country, the abundance of buffalo and other game, which, if furnished by contractors, would cost a penny the pound. Free transportation down the Ohio of all household effects would be given. Schoolmasters would accompany the emigrants. Here, Jefferson notes his concern, "Even the settlement of Kentucky is likely to be much weakened by emigrations to Morgan's grant." (Winsor 1897, 366)
[2] Although Jefferson's optimism about the movement of revolutionary events in France was tempered by the unusual severity of the winter of 1788-1789, when temperatures in Paris dropped to nine below zero, increasing the problems of the government, in this letter to Carmichael he nonetheless states, "The revolution in this country seems to be going on well. In Burgundy & Franche compté indeed there is great stubbornness in the privileged orders, and in Bretagne they have proceeded to blows, which however are stopped for the present." But, too, he ponders the potential conflict, "The circumstance from which I fear the worst is that the States general are too numerous. I see great difficulty in preventing 1200 people from becoming a mob." As for the future of the revolution, he seems resigned to something less than ideal, when he opines, "I suppose the states general, with the consent of the King, will establish some of the leading features of a good constitution. They have indeed a miserable old canvas to work on, covered with daubings which it will be difficult to efface. But some they will efface, & some soften, so as to make a tolerable thing of it, perhaps a good one." (Cunningham, 1987, 123)

I mentioned to you in my last that the Convention of Virginia had proposed to Congress the method of amending by Congress & the assemblies. Since that the assembly of that state, a much more anti-federal body, has proposed the other method of amendment by a federal convention. But this will not take. The elections for the new Congress are almost universally federal, which proves the people in general to be so. The following is a list of the federal Senate so far as Notice of the elections have reached me. 1. N. Hampshire Presid^t. Langdon & Judge Bartlett. 2. Massachusetts, Strong & Dalton. 3. Connecticut D^r. Johnson & Elsworth. 4. N. Jersey. Patterson & Elmer. 5. Pennsylvania. R. H. Morris & McClurg. 6. Delaware. Reed & Basset. 7. Virginia. R. H. Lee & Grayson. 8. Maryland Chas. Carroll of Carrolton, & John Henry. It is thought Mr. Izard will be one from S. Carolina. Gen'l. Schuyler is expected for N. York, but as late as the 10th. of January that assembly had not yet been able to agree on Senators. I hear nothing from Georgia. N. Carolina has fixed a day for another convention, but a very distant one. It is the anti-federalism of Virginia which levens the mass. Rhode island has again refused to call a convention. Gen'l. Washington, tho' with vast reluctance, will undertake the presidency if called to it, & there was no doubt he would be so called. The only candidates for the vice presidency, with their own consent, are Mr. Hancock and Mr. J. Adams. The latter, it was thought, would be chosen. The friends of the new constitution agree pretty generally to add a declaration of rights to it, and the opposition becomes daily weaker, so that the government, confided generally to friendly hands, and gaining on the esteem of the nation, begins this very day, under the most auspicious appearances.

The revolution in this country seems to be going on well. In Burgundy & Franche compté indeed there is great stubbornness in the privileged orders, and in Bretagne they have proceeded to blows, which however are stopped for the present. In the west of the Kingdom it seems as if the rights of the tiers etat would be acknowledged and by a majority of the nobles. The circumstance from which I fear the worst is that the States general are too numerous. I see great difficulty in preventing 1200 people from becoming a mob. Should confusion be prevented from this circumstance, I suppose the states general, with the consent of the King, will establish some of the leading features of a good constitution. They have indeed a miserable old canvas to work on, covered with daubings which it will be difficult to efface. But some they will efface, & some soften, so as to make a tolerable thing of it, perhaps a good one. The war in the North is likely to spread: & the King of England seems recovering his senses. But time will be requisite to shew whether it be a lucid interval only, whether it be permanent, or whether it be anything more than a recovery from insanity to imbecility which is the most ordinary case. In either event, time is necessary to give such confidence in his state of mind, as that his Ministers may venture to take a part in the war; and that time will suffice to enable this nation to arrange its internal affairs so solidly as to put them more in condition, than ever they were at any period of their history, to act the part they may choose in foreign affairs. How happy is it for us that we are beyond the reach of those storms which are eternally desolating Europe. We have indeed a neighbor with whom misunderstandings are possible: but they must be the effect of interests ill calculated. Nothing is more demonstrable than is the unity of their & our interest for ages to come.

I have had a letter from Admiral Paul Jones dated St. Petersburgh Jan. 31. He was well and just arrived there on the call of the Empress. He has commanded on the Black Sea during the last campaign, but does not know where he is to act the ensuing one.

My last accounts from Lediard (another bold countryman of ours) were from Grand Cairo. He was just then plunging into the unknown regions of Africa, probably never to emerge again. If he returns, he has promised me to go to America and penetrate from Kentucky to the Western side of the Continent. I do not know whether you are informed that in the years 1787–1788. he went from here bound for Kamschatka, to cross over thence to the Western coast of our continent & pass through to the Eastern one. He was arrested par ordre superieure within two or three days journey of Kamschatka, conveyed back to the confines of Poland, & there turned adrift. He arrived here last June, & immediately set out for Africa. I received some time ago a very interesting history del luxo de España, and the charming poems of M. Yriarte, tho' they have not been mentioned in any of your letters I presume it is you I am to thank for them, which I do very cordially. I know nothing, since my last, more precise on the time of my departure, but I think it would be better you should address no letters to me at this place which may arrive between the middle of April & November. Mr. Short will transact the business of the legation during my absence, as I expect.

To Francis Hopkinson[1]
Paris, Mar. 13, 1789

[1] Francis Hopkinson, of Philadelphia, with whose mother Jefferson had placed Patsy during his Congressional duties at Annapolis, was almost as universal a man as Jefferson himself. Active in politics — he had been a member of Congress and had signed the Declaration of Independence on behalf of Pennsylvania — as well as a poet, judge, composer, musician, satirist and writer of essays and political tracts; an inventor and scientist; there was little in which his mind did not partake. Among his numerous inventions was a proposed improvement of the harpsichord: the substitution of tongues of leather and cork for the usual quill picks. As background to this letter, James Madison, his faithful friend, had been defeated in the Virginia Assembly for the United States Senate by a mere two or three votes. Madison's defeat could not but be a severe blow to Jefferson. One of his staunchest co-workers and supporters was no longer in government; and it meant that parties were crystallizing back home on the basis of adherence or nonadherence to the Constitution. It was shortly after the receipt of this unwelcome news that Jefferson penned his memorable protest to Hopkinson: "I am not a Federalist, because I never submitted the whole system of my opinions to the creed of any party of men whatever in religion, in philosophy, in politics, or in anything else where I was capable of thinking for myself. Such an addiction is the last degradation of a free and moral agent. If I could not go to heaven but with a party, I would not go there at all." But he was even further removed from the anti-Federalists. He was of neither party, "nor yet a trimmer between parties." Nevertheless, though he never had an opinion in politics or religion which he was afraid to avow, he owned frankly that "my great wish is to go on in a strict but silent performance of my duty; to avoid attracting notice & to keep my name out of newspapers, because I find the pain of a little censure, even when it is

Dear Sir,

Since my last, which was of Dec. 21. yours of Dec. 9. and 21. are received. Accept my thanks for the papers and pamphlets which accompanied them, and mine and my daughter's for the book of songs. I will not tell you how much they have pleased us nor how well the last of them merits praise for its pathos, but relate a fact only, which is that while my elder daughter was playing it on the harpsichord, I happened to look towards the fire and saw the younger one all in tears. I asked her if she was sick? She said "no; but the tune was so mournful."

The Editor of the Encyclopedie has published something as to an advanced price on his future volumes, which I understand alarms the subscribers. It was in a paper which I do not take and therefore I have not yet seen it, nor can say what it is.

I hope that by this time you have ceased to make wry faces about your vinegar, and that you have received it safe and good. You say that I have been dished up to you as an antifederalist, and ask me if it be just. My opinion was never worthy enough of notice to merit citing; but since you ask it I will tell it you. I am not a Federalist, because I never submitted the whole system of my opinions to the creed of any party of men whatever in religion, in philosophy, in politics, or in anything else where I was capable of thinking for myself. Such an addiction is the last degradation of a free and moral agent. If I could not go to heaven but with a party, I would not go there at all. Therefore I protest to you I am not of the party of federalists. But I am much farther from that of the Antifederalists. I approved, from the first moment, of the great mass of what is in the new constitution, the consolidation of the government, the organization into Executive legislative & judiciary, the subdivision of the legislative, the happy compromise of interests between the great & little states by the different manner of voting in the different houses, the voting by persons instead of states, the qualified negative on laws given to the Executive which however I should have liked better if associated with the judiciary also as in New York, and the power of taxation. I thought at first that the latter might have been limited. A little reflection soon convinced me it ought not to be. What I disapproved from the first moment also was the want of a bill of rights to guard liberty against the legislative as well as executive branches of the government, that is to say to secure freedom in religion, freedom of the press, freedom from monopolies, freedom from unlawful imprisonment, freedom from a permanent military, and a trial by jury in all cases determinable by the laws of the land. I disapproved also the perpetual reeligibility of the President. To these points of disapprobation I adhere. My first wish was that the 9. first conventions might accept the constitution, as the means of securing to us the great mass of good it contained, and that the 4. last might reject it, as the means of obtaining amendments. But I was corrected in this wish the moment I saw the much better plan of Massachusetts and which had never occurred to me. With respect to the declaration of rights I suppose the majority of the United States are of my opinion: for I apprehend all the antifederalists, and a very

unfounded, is more acute than the pleasure of much praise." (Schachner 1957, 284, 367-368)

respectable proportion of the federalists think that such a declaration should now be annexed. The enlightened part of Europe have given us the greatest credit for inventing this instrument of security for the rights of the people, and have been not a little surprised to see us so soon give it up. With respect to the re-eligibility of the president, I find myself differing from the majority of my countrymen, for I think there are but three states out of the 11. which have desired an alteration of this. And indeed, since the thing is established, I would wish it not to be altered during the life of our great leader, whose executive talents are superior to those I believe of any man in the world, and who alone by the authority of his name and the confidence reposed in his perfect integrity, is fully qualified to put the new government so under way as to secure it against the efforts of opposition. But having derived from our error all the good there was in it I hope we shall correct it the moment we can no longer have the same name at the helm. These, my dear friend, are my sentiments, by which you will see I was right in saying I am neither federalist nor antifederalist; that I am of neither party, nor yet a trimmer between parties. These my opinions I wrote within a few hours after I had read the constitution, to one or two friends in America. I had not then read one single word printed on the subject. I never had an opinion in politics or religion which I was afraid to own. A costive reserve on these subjects might have procured me more esteem from some people, but less from myself. My great wish is to go on in a strict but silent performance of my duty; to avoid attracting notice & to keep my name out of newspapers, because I find the pain of a little censure, even when it is unfounded, is more acute than the pleasure of much praise. The attaching circumstance of my present office is that I can do its duties unseen by those for whom they are done. You did not think, by so short a phrase in your letter, to have drawn on yourself such an egotistical dissertation.

To Madame De Brehan[1]

---

[1] Madame la Marquise de Brehan was the sister-in-law of the Comte de Moustier, the French minister to the United States. At this point in his posting to France, Jefferson had made up his mind: he would go back to Virginia—not permanently, just for a few months, time enough to bring his daughters home and straighten out his personal and financial affairs. When he had left Monticello in October 1783 to serve as delegate to the Continental Congress, he had planned to be away for only five months. It had now been five years since he had seen home. The third week of November 1788 he wrote Congress to ask for a leave of absence. He argued persuasively that he could make the trip without detriment to his responsibilities as American minister to France. His ministerial duties, he assured Congress, had reached a pause. His most pressing commitments had been fulfilled or would be in a matter of weeks. Most important, he had reached a new consular convention, which he was arranging to have printed. In addition, he had finished composing *Observations on the Whale-Fishery*, which would also be published soon. The harsh winter weather only reinforced his decision to return home. For most Parisians, the winter of 1788–89 was the coldest in memory; as he writes in this letter, "We have had such a winter Madam, as makes me shiver yet whenever I think of it. All communications almost were cut off. Dinners and suppers were suppressed, and the money laid out in feeding and warming the poor, whose labors were suspended by the rigor of the season. Loaded carriages past [i.e., crossed] the Seine on the ice, and it was covered with thousands of

Paris, March 14th, 1789

Dear Madam,

I had the honor of writing to you on the 15th of February, soon after which I had that of receiving your favor of December the 29th. I have a thousand questions to ask you about your journey to the Indian treaty, how you like their persons, their manners, their customs, cuisine, etc. But this I must defer until I can do it personally in New York where I hope to see you for a moment in the summer, and to take your commands for France. I have little to communicate to you from this place. It is deserted; everybody being gone into the country to choose or to be chosen deputies to the States General. I hope to see that great meeting before my departure. It is to be on the 27th of next month. A great political revolution will take place in your country, and that without bloodshed. A king, with two hundred thousand men at his orders, is disarmed by force of public opinion and want of money. Among the economies becoming necessary, perhaps one may be the Opera. They say it has cost the public treasury a hundred thousand crown in the last year. A new theatre is established since your departure — that of the Opera Buffons, where Italian operas are given, and good music. Paris is every day enlarging and beautifying. I do not count among its beauties, however, the wall with which they have enclosed us. They have made some amends for this by making fine Boulevards within and without the walls. These are in considerable forwardness, and will afford beautiful rides around the city of between fifteen and twenty miles in circuit. We have had such a winter, Madame, as makes me shiver yet whenever I think of it. All communications, almost, were cut off. Dinners and suppers were suppressed, and the money laid out in feeding and warming the poor, whose labors were suspended by the rigors of the season. Loaded carriages passed the Seine on the ice, and it was covered with thousands of people from morning to night, skating and sliding. Such sights were never seen before, and they continued two months. We have nothing new and excellent in your charming art of painting. In fact, I do not feel an interest in any pencil but that of David. But I must not hazard details on a subject wherein I am so ignorant and you are such a connoisseur. Adieu, my dear Madam; permit me always the honor of esteeming and being esteemed by you, and of tendering you the homage of that respectful attachment, with which I am and ever shall be, dear Madam, your most obedient, humble servant.

To James Madison[1]

---

people from morning to night, skating and sliding. Such sights were never seen before, and they continued two months." (Hayes 2008, 369)

[1] Madison continued to realize that violations of the Constitution would occur and, with respect to the public demands for a bill of rights, wondered if trying to protect liberties with written guarantees was not an exercise in futility. His chief concern was that "parchment barriers" would not be respected by "overbearing majorities, and complained that "experience proves the inefficacy of a bill of rights on those occasions when its control is most needed" and said that he was "inclined to think that *absolute* restrictions in cases that are doubtful, or where emergencies may overrule them, ought to be avoided" because "after repeated violations in extraordinary cases, they will lose even their ordinary

Paris, Mar 15, 1789
Dear Sir,

I wrote you last on the 12th of Jan. since which I have received yours of Octob 17, Dec 8 & 12. That of Oct. 17. came to hand only Feb 23. How it happened to be four months on the way, I cannot tell, as I never knew by what hand it came. Looking over my letter of Jan 12th, I remark an error of the word "probable" instead of "improbable," which doubtless however you had been able to correct. Your thoughts on the subject of the Declaration of rights in the letter of Oct 17. I have weighed with great satisfaction. Some of them had not occurred to me before, but were acknowledged just in the moment they were presented to my mind. In the arguments in favor of a declaration of rights, you omit one which has great weight with me, the legal check which it puts into the hands of the judiciary. This is a body, which if rendered independent & kept strictly to their own department merits great confidence for their learning & integrity. In fact what degree of confidence would be too much for a body composed of such men as Wythe, Blair & Pendleton? On characters like these the "civium ardor prava jubentium"[1] would make no impression. I am happy to find that on the whole you are a friend to this amendment. The Declaration of rights is like all other human blessings alloyed with some inconveniences, and not accomplishing fully it's object. But the good in this instance vastly overweighs the evil. I cannot refrain from making short answers to the objections which your letter states to have been raised. 1. That the rights in question are reserved by the manner in which the federal powers are granted. Answer. A constitutive act may certainly be so formed as to need no declaration of rights. The act itself has the force of a declaration as far as it goes; and if it goes to all material points nothing more is wanting. In the draught of a constitution which I had once a thought of proposing in Virginia, & printed afterwards, I endeavored to reach all the great objects of public liberty, and did not mean to add a declaration of rights. Probably the object was imperfectly executed; but the deficiencies would have been supplied by others, in the course of discussion. But in a constitutive act which leaves some precious articles unnoticed, and raises implications against others, a declaration of rights becomes necessary by way of supplement. This is the case of our new federal constitution. This instrument forms us into one state as to certain objects, and gives us a legislative & executive body for these

---

efficacy." In fact, Madison encountered significant political pressure to agree to a bill of rights, but it seems to have been Jefferson's enthusiasm for the idea that finally convinced him of its value. Here, in this note, Jefferson asked his old ally to remember "the legal check which it puts into the hands of the judiciary" — a check that, if independent of politics, would be able to protect freedoms. Jefferson also argued that it was better to have a bill of rights than not to have one. "A brace the more will often keep up the building which would have fallen with that brace the less," he told Madison. Jefferson's position remained that it was better to establish freedom of the press and other several other rights "in all cases" rather than not to do it in any. (Smith 1999, 34)

[1] The English translation reads: "The man tenacious of his purpose in a righteous cause is not shaken from his firm resolve by the frenzy of his fellow-citizens bidding what is wrong." (Boyd 1990)

---

objects. It should therefore guard us against their abuses of power within the field submitted to them. 2. A positive declaration of some essential rights could not be obtained in the requisite latitude. Answer. Half a loaf is better than no bread. If we cannot secure all our rights, let us secure what we can. 3. The limited powers of the federal government & jealousy of the subordinate governments afford a security which exists in no other instance. Answer. The first member of this seems resolvable into the 1st. objection before stated. The jealousy of the subordinate governments is a precious reliance. But observe that those governments are only agents. They must have principles furnished them whereon to found their opposition. The declaration of rights will be the text whereby they will try all the acts of the federal government. In this view it is necessary to the federal government also; as by the same text they may try the opposition of the subordinate governments. 4. Experience proves the inefficacy of a bill of rights. True. But tho it is not absolutely efficacious under all circumstances, it is of great potency always, and rarely inefficacious. A brace the more will often keep up the building which would have fallen with that brace the less. There is a remarkable difference between the characters of the Inconveniences which attend a Declaration of rights, & those which attend the want of it. The inconveniences of the Declaration are that it may cramp government in its useful exertions. But the evil of this is short-lived, trivial & reparable. The inconveniences of the want of a Declaration are permanent, afflicting & irreparable. They are in constant progression from bad to worse. The executive in our governments is not the sole, it is scarcely the principal object of my jealousy. The tyranny of the legislatures is the most formidable dread at present, and will be for long years. That of the executive will come in its turn, but it will be at a remote period. I know there are some among us who would now establish a monarchy. But they are inconsiderable in number and weight of character. The rising race are all republicans. We were educated in royalism; no wonder if some of us retain that idolatry still. Our young people are educated in republicanism, an apostasy from that to royalism is unprecedented & impossible. I am much pleased with the prospect that a declaration of rights will be added; and hope it will be done in that way which will not endanger the whole frame of the government, or any essential part of it.

I have hitherto avoided public news in my letters to you, because your situation insured you a communication of my letters to Mr. Jay. This circumstance being changed, I shall in future indulge myself in these details to you. There had been some slight hopes that an accommodation might be affected between the Turks & two empires but these hopes do not strengthen, and the season is approaching which will put an end to them for another campaign at least. The accident to the King of England has had great influence on the affairs of Europe. His mediation joined with that of Prussia, would certainly have kept Denmark quiet, and so have left the two empires in the hands of the Turks & Swedes. But the inactivity to which England is reduced, leaves Denmark more free, and she will probably go on in opposition to Sweden. The K. of Prussia too had advanced so far that he can scarcely retire. This is rendered the more difficult by the troubles he has excited in Poland. He cannot well abandon the party he had brought forward there so that it is very possible he may be engaged in the ensuing campaign. France will be quiet this year, because this year at least is necessary for settling her future constitution. The States will meet the 27th of April: and the public mind will I think by that time be ripe for a just decision of the Question whether they shall vote by orders or persons. I think there is a majority of the nobles already for the latter. If so, their affairs cannot but go on well. Besides settling for themselves a tolerably free constitution, perhaps as free a one as the nation is yet prepared to bear, they will fund their public debts. This will give them such a credit as will enable them to borrow any money they may want, & of course to take the field again when they think proper. And I believe they mean to take the field as soon as they can. The pride of every individual in the nation suffers under the ignominies they have lately been exposed to and I think the states general will give money for a war to wipe off the reproach. There have arisen new bickerings between this court & the Hague, and the papers which have passed shew the most bitter acrimony rankling at the heart of this ministry. They have recalled their ambassador from the Hague without appointing a successor. They have given a note to the Diet of Poland which shews a disapprobation of their measures. The insanity of the King of England has been fortunate for them as it gives them time to put their house in order. The English papers tell you the King is well: and even the English ministry say so. They will naturally set the best foot foremost: and they guard his person so well that it is difficult for the public to contradict them. The King is probably better, but not well by a great deal. 1. He has been bled, and judicious physicians say that in his exhausted state nothing could have induced a recurrence to bleeding but symptoms of relapse. 2. The Prince of Wales tells the Irish deputation he will give them a definitive answer in some days; but if the king had been well he could have given it at once. 3. They talk of passing a standing law for providing a regency in similar cases. They apprehend then they are not yet clear of the danger of wanting a regency. 4. They have carried the king to church; but it was his private chapel. If he be well why do not they shew him publicly to the nation, & raise them from that consternation into which they have been thrown by the prospect of being delivered over to the profligate hands of the prince of Wales. In short, judging from little facts which are known in spite of their teeth the King is better, but not well. Possibly he is getting well, but still, time will be wanting to satisfy even the ministry that it is not merely a lucid interval. Consequently they cannot interrupt France this year in the settlement of her affairs, & after this year it will be too late.

As you will be in a situation to know when the leave of absence will be granted me, which I have asked, will you be so good as to communicate it by a line to Mr. Lewis & Mr. Eppes? I hope to see you in the summer, and that if you are not otherwise engaged, you will encamp with me at Monticello for a while.

To David Humphreys[1]

---

[1] Born in Connecticut in 1752, David Humphreys served in the continental army aide-de-camp to Generals Putnam, Greene, and Washington. After the

Paris, Mar. 18, 1789
Dear Sir,
 Your favor of Nov. 29, 1788, came to hand the last month. How it happened that mine of Aug. 1787, was fourteen months on its way is inconceivable. I do not recollect by what conveyance I sent it. I had concluded however either that it had miscarried or that you had become indolent as most of our countrymen are in matters of correspondence.

 The change in this country since you left it is such as you can form no idea of. The frivolities of conversation have given way entirely to politics. Men, women & children talk nothing else: and all you know talk a great deal. The press groans with daily productions, which in point of boldness make an Englishman stare, who hitherto has thought himself the boldest of men. A complete revolution in this government has, within the space of two years (for it began with the Notables of 1787) been effected merely by the force of public opinion, aided indeed by the want of money which the dissipations of the court had brought on. And this revolution has not cost a single life, unless we charge to it a little riot lately in Bretagne which began about the price of bread, became afterwards political and ended in the loss of 4. or 5. lives. The assembly of the states general begins the 27th of April. The representation of the people will be perfect. But they will be alloyed by an equal number of nobility & clergy. The first great question they will have to decide will be whether they shall vote by orders or persons, & I have hopes that the majority of the nobles are already disposed to join the tiers etat in deciding that the vote shall be by persons. This is the opinion à la mode at present, and mode has acted a wonderful part in the present instance. All the handsome young women, for example, are for the tiers etat, and this is an army more powerful in France than the 200,000 men of the king. Add to this that the court itself is for the tiers etat, as the only agent which can relieve their wants; not by giving money themselves (they are squeezed to the last drop) but by pressing it from the non-contributing orders. The king stands engaged to pretend no more to the power of laying, continuing or appropriating taxes, to call the States general periodically, to submit lettres de cachet to legal restrictions, to consent to freedom of the press, and that all this shall be fixed by a fundamental constitution which shall bind his successors. He has not offered a participation in the legislature, but it will surely be insisted on. The public mind is so ripened on all these subjects, that there seems to be now but one opinion. The clergy indeed think separately, & the old men among the Nobles. But their voice is suppressed by the general one of the nation. The writings published on this occasion are some of them very valuable: because, unfettered by the prejudices under which the English labor, they give a full scope to reason,

---

war he was with Jefferson, for a time, at Paris on the commission for treaties with foreign powers, and also served as diplomat at Lisbon and Madrid where he was considered a favorite in numerous foreign circles of society. After he returned to America, he was invited to visit at Mount Vernon, and Washington offered him aid in pursuing a literary plan to write a history of the Revolution But Humphreys declined the offer, although he did go on to publish numerous nonfiction pieces and poetry until his death in 1818. (Marble 1907, 174-175)

and strike out truths as yet unperceived & unacknowledged on the other side the channel. An Englishman, dosing under a kind of half reformation, is not excited to think by such gross absurdities as stare a Frenchman in the face wherever he looks whether it be towards the throne or the altar. In fine I believe this nation will in the course of the present year have as full a portion of liberty dealt out to them as the nation can bear at present, considering how uninformed the mass of their people is. This circumstance will prevent their immediate establishment of the trial by jury. The palsied state of the executive in England is a fortunate circumstance for France, as it will give them time to arrange their affairs internally. The consolidation & funding their debts will give them a credit which will enable them to do what they please. For the present year the war will be confined to the two empires & Denmark, against Turkey & Sweden. It is not yet evident whether Prussia will be engaged. If the disturbances of Poland break out into overt acts, it will be a power divided in itself, & so of no weight. Perhaps by the next year England & France may be ready to take the field. It will depend on the former principally, for the latter, tho she may be then able, must wish still a little time to see her new arrangements well under way. The English papers & English ministry say the king is well. He is better, but not well: no malady requires a longer time to ensure against its return, than insanity. Time alone can distinguish accidental insanity from habitual lunacy.

The operations which have taken place in America lately, fill me with pleasure. In the first place they realize the confidence I had that whenever our affairs go obviously wrong the good sense of the people will interpose and set them to rights. The example of changing a constitution by assembling the wise men of the State, instead of assembling armies, will be worth as much to the world as the former examples we had given them. The constitution too which was the result of our deliberations, is unquestionably the wisest ever yet presented to men, and some of the accommodations of interest which it has adopted are greatly pleasing to me who have before had occasions of seeing how difficult those interests were to accommodate. A general concurrence of opinion seems to authorize us to say it has some defects. I am one of those who think it a defect that the important rights not placed in security by the frame of the constitution itself were not explicitly secured by a supplementary declaration. There are rights which it is useless to surrender to the government, and which governments have yet always been fond to invade. These are the rights of thinking, and publishing our thoughts by speaking or writing; the right of free commerce; the right of personal freedom. There are instruments for administering the government, so peculiarly trust-worthy, that we should never leave the legislature at liberty to change them. The new constitution has secured these in the executive & legislative departments; but not in the judiciary. It should have established trials by the people themselves, that is to say by jury. There are instruments so dangerous to the rights of the nation, and which place them so totally at the mercy of their governors, that those governors, whether legislative or executive, should be restrained from keeping such instruments on foot, but in well-defined cases. Such an instrument is a standing army. We are now allowed to say such a declaration of rights, as a supplement to the constitution where that is silent, is wanting to secure us in these points. The general voice has legitimated this objection. It has not however authorized me to consider as a real defect what I thought and still think one, the perpetual re-eligibility of the president. But three states out of 11. having declared against this, we must suppose we are wrong according to the fundamental law of every society, the lex majoris partis, to which we are bound to submit. And should the majority change their opinion, & become sensible that this trait in their constitution is wrong, I would wish it to remain uncorrected, as long as we can avail ourselves of the services of our great leader, whose talents and whose weight of character I consider as peculiarly necessary to get the government so under way as that it may afterwards be carried on by subordinate characters.

I must give you sincere thanks for the details of small news contained in your letter. You know how precious that kind of information is to a person absent from his country, and how difficult it is to be procured. I hope to receive soon permission to visit America this summer, and to possess myself anew, by conversation with my countrymen, of their spirits & their ideas. I know only the Americans of the year 1784. They tell me this is to be much a stranger to those of 1789. This renewal of acquaintance is no indifferent matter to one acting at such a distance as that instructions cannot be received hot and hot. One of my pleasures too will be that of talking over the old & new with you.

To The Marquis De La Fayette[1]
Paris, May 6, 1789
My Dear Friend,

As it becomes more & more possible that the noblesse will go wrong, I become uneasy for you. Your principles are decidedly with the tiers etat, and your instructions against them. A complaisance to the latter on some occasions and an adherence to the former on others, may give an appearance of trimming between the two parties which may lose you both. You will in the end go over wholly to the tiers etat, because it will be impossible for you to live in a constant sacrifice of your own sentiments to the prejudices of the Noblesse. But you would be received by the tiers etat at any future day, coldly and without confidence. It appears to me the moment to take at once that honest and manly stand with them which your own principles dictate. This will win their hearts forever, be approved by the world which marks and honors you as the man of the people, and will be an eternal consolation to yourself. The Noblesse, & especially

---

[1] Lafayette occupied a peculiar position. His feelings were aligned with the *Tiers Etat* (Third Estate), but he had received his election from the nobility of Auvergne, and he had been ordered by them to support their position. Jefferson correctly anticipated the uncompromising temper of the different orders, and this correspondence shows that he anticipated a schism most likely to result in civil war. He therefore advises Lafayette not take sides against the "nation, but to propose a compromise of two houses (equivalent to Lords and Commons), and having failed in that, to disobey his instructions, and act with the *Tiers Etat.* (Randall 1858, 519-520)

the Noblesse of Auvergne will always prefer men who will do their dirty work for them. You are not made for that. They will therefore soon drop you, and the people in that case will perhaps not take you up. Suppose a scission should take place. The priests and nobles will secede, the nation will remain in place and, with the King, will do its own business. If violence should be attempted, where will you be? You cannot then take side with the people in opposition to your own vote, that very vote which will have helped to produce the scission. Still less can you array yourself against the people. That is impossible. Your instructions are indeed a difficulty. But to state this at its worst, it is only a single difficulty, which a single effort surmounts. Your instructions can never embarrass you a second time, whereas an acquiescence under them will reproduce greater difficulties every day & without end. Besides, a thousand circumstances offer as many justifications of your departure from your instructions. Will it be impossible to persuade all parties that (as for good legislation two Houses are necessary) the placing the privileged classes together in one house and the unprivileged in another, would be better for both than a scission? I own I think it would. People can never agree without some sacrifices: and it appears but a moderate sacrifice in each party to meet on this middle ground. The attempt to bring this about might satisfy your instructions, and a failure in it would justify your siding with the people, even to those who think instructions are laws of conduct.

Forgive me, my dear friend, if my anxiety for you makes me talk of things I know nothing about. You must not consider this as advice. I know you and myself too well to presume to offer advice. Receive it merely as the expression of my uneasiness and the effusion of that sincere friendship with which I am, my dear Sir, your's affectionately.

To George Washington[1]
Paris, May 10, 1789
Sir,

I am now to acknowledge the honor of your two letters of Nov. 27 and Feb. 13, both of which have come to hand since my last to you of Dec. 4 & 5. The details you are so good as to give me on the subject of the navigation of the waters of the Potomac and Ohio are very pleasing to me, as I consider the union of these two rivers as among the strongest links of connection between the eastern & western sides of our confederacy. It will moreover add to the commerce of Virginia in particular all the upper parts of the Ohio & it's waters.

---

[1] Here, Jefferson congratulates Washington on his election; but, in a surprisingly candid statement, also cautions that Washington that he may well be risking his fame and good reputation by becoming president: "Nobody who has tried both public & private life can doubt but that you were much happier on the banks of the Potomac than you will be at New York. But there was nobody so well qualified as yourself to put our new machine into a regular course of action, nobody the authority of whose name could have so effectually crushed opposition at home, and produced respect abroad. I am sensible of the immensity of the sacrifice on your part. Your measure of fame was full to the brim: and therefore you have nothing to gain. But there are cases wherein it is a duty to risk all against nothing, and I believe this was exactly the case." (Frisch and Stevens 1971, 27)

Another vast object and of much less difficulty is to add also all the country on the lakes & their waters. This would enlarge our field immensely and would certainly be effected by an union of the upper waters of the Ohio & lake Erie. The Big beaver & Cayahoga offer the most direct line and according to information I received from Gen'l Hand, and which I had the honor of writing you in the year 1783, the streams in that neighborhood head in lagoons, and the country is flat. With respect to the doubts which you say are entertained by some whether the upper waters of Potomac can be rendered capable of navigation on account of the falls & rugged banks, they are answered by observing that it is reduced to a maxim that whenever there is water enough to float a batteau, there may be navigation for a batteau. Canals & locks may be necessary, & they are expensive; but I hardly know what expense would be too great for the object in question. Probably negotiations with the Indians, perhaps even settlement must precede the execution of the Cayahoga canal. The states of Maryland and Virginia should make a common object of it. The navigation again between Elizabeth river & the Sound is of vast importance and in my opinion it is much better that these should be done at public than private expense.

Tho' we have not heard of the actual opening of the New Congress, & consequently have not official information of your election as President of the U.S. yet as there never could be a doubt entertained of it, permit me to express here my felicitations, not to yourself, but to my country. Nobody who has tried both public & private life can doubt but that you were much happier on the banks of the Potomac than you will be at New York. But there was nobody so well qualified as yourself to put our new machine into a regular course of action, nobody the authority of whose name could have so effectually crushed opposition at home, and produced respect abroad. I am sensible of the immensity of the sacrifice on your part. Your measure of fame was full to the brim: and therefore you have nothing to gain. But there are cases wherein it is a duty to risk all against nothing, and I believe this was exactly the case. We may presume too, according to every rule of probability, that after doing a great deal of good you will be found to have lost nothing but private repose. In a letter to Mr. Jay of the 19 of November I asked a leave of absence to carry my children back to their own country, and to settle various matters of a private nature which were left unsettled because I had no idea of being absent so long. I expected that letter would have been received in time to be decided on by the government then existing. I know now that it would arrive when there was no Congress, and consequently that it must have awaited your arrival at New York. I hope you found the request not an unreasonable one. I am excessively anxious to receive the permission without delay, that I may be able to get back before the winter sets in. Nothing can be so dreadful to me as to be shivering at sea for two or three months in a winter passage. Besides there has never been a moment at which the presence of a minister here could be so well dispensed with, a certainty of no war this summer, and that the government will be so totally absorbed in domestic arrangements as to attend to nothing exterior. Mr. Jay will of course communicate to you some ciphered letters lately written, and one of this date. My public letter to him contains all the interesting public details. I inclose with the present some extracts of a letter from Mr. Payne which he desired me to communicate; your knowledge of the writer will justify my giving you the trouble of these communications which their interesting nature and his respectability will jointly recommend to notice.

I am in great pain for the M. de la Fayette. His principles you know are clearly with the people, but having been elected for the Noblesse of Auvergne they have laid him under express instructions to vote for the decision by orders & not persons. This would ruin him with the tiers etat, and it is not possible he could continue long to give satisfaction to the noblesse. I have not hesitated to press on him to burn his instructions & follow his conscience as the only sure clue which will eternally guide a man clear of all doubts & inconsistencies. If he cannot effect a conciliatory plan, he will surely take his stand manfully at once with the tiers etat [third estate]. He will in that case be what he pleases with them, and I am in hopes that base is now too solid to render it dangerous to be mounted on it.

In hopes of being able in the course of the summer to pay my respects to you personally in New York I have the honor to be with sentiments of the most perfect respect & attachment, Sir, Your most obedient & most humble servant.

To Comte De Moustier[1]
Paris, May 20, 1789
Dear Sir,

I had the honor of writing to you on the 13th of March by the way of London, another conveyance the same way now occurring, I avail myself of it to send you a list of the deputies to the States general, which I presume will be interesting to you. You will already have received the speeches of the King, Garde des sceaux, & Mr. Necker, as I know that M. de Montmorin wrote to you the evening of the day on which they appeared, & sent his letter by the Bordeaux packet. You are

---

[1] This letter rather signifies the end of what, in some circles, is believed to be one of more curious episodes of Jefferson's time in France. Drawn from was the appearance of an improper relationship between Count and Mme de Bréhan [see Jefferson's October 8, 1787, letter to James Madison and, in particular, the accompanying footnote] Moustier's conduct in the United States had remained to be politically and morally offensive to most American officialdom, and had finally resulting in a request for his recall. It was the first such request by the American government touching a foreign minister. Jay, then American Secretary for Foreign Affairs, handled the matter through Jefferson in France. Jefferson considered the question to be a delicate one, for in the event either of failure or of mismanagement friendship with France would be jeopardized. With the help of the Marquis de Lafayette, Jefferson brought the problem before the French Minister of Foreign Affairs, the Count de Montmorin, who desired close relations with the United States. Although Montmorin was willing to call Moustier back to France, he contended that there was no grievance of sufficient gravity against him to justify a recall. He had, moreover, no vacant post to which he could send Moustier if he were recalled. Finally, Montmorin hit upon the device of calling Moustier back to France on leave of absence, ostensibly in response to Moustier's own earlier-expressed desires. Without the difficulties of an actual recall, the Count de Moustier left the United States in October, 1789, never to return. (Deconde 1958, 167-168)

doubtless informed that a difference among the orders as to the manner of voting suspends all their proceedings. They continue inactive, and many despair of their ever getting under way. The truth is that this revolution has gone on so happily till now, and met with so few obstacles, that your countrymen are frightened at seeing that the machine is stopped and that no way yet presents itself of getting over the difficulty.

I see nothing to fear as yet, the nation is in a movement which cannot be stopped, their representatives, if they cannot get on one way, will try another.

The mind of man is full of expedients, and this is the case where all will be tried. I think that in the end the nobles will be obliged to yield to the vote by persons, because the Tiers are more unanimous, more inflexible, and more formidable. They have for them also a part of the Noblesse, the majority of the clergy (to wit, le bas-clergé) the nation, and the body of the army. The officers of the army, the bishops, and about four fifths of the nobles which form the opposition, cannot make head against such a mass.

The Cardinal de Lomenie is reposing under the shadow of his new hat at Pisa, where he is greatly courted, his colleague M. de Lamoignon late garde de sceaux, shot himself four days ago, as the world says, but as his friends say was killed by the accidental discharge of his own fusil. The Grand Seignior is dead. The Emperor will certainly soon follow him and the war will probably go on this year in the state in which it was at the close of the last campaign, that is to say, without any accession of other powers. The present state of the K. of England promises a long and wholesome inactivity in that kingdom, and may perhaps bridle the King of Prussia from making any effort to change the succession of the empire, which he would be disposed to attempt.

I should have observed to you that your parliaments have been for some time past as quiet as if they were already entombed. It is a great presumption in me to write to you, because you will get so much better information from your friends: but it is to shew you how acceptable your communications are to me, and how willing I am to do something for them. Present me with great affection to Madame de Brehan. I am in hourly expectation of receiving my leave of absence, and shall leave Paris the instant I receive it, and flatter myself soon to assure you both in person of those sentiments of esteem & respect with which I have the honor to be, Dear Sir, your most obedt. humble servt.

To The Marquis De La Fayette[1]

---

[1] On June 2nd, Jefferson was in the company of William Short (Jefferson's private secretary), Lafayette and Rabaut de St. Etienne, a Protestant who later acted a leading role in the Revolution. They discussed what could be done to break the political impasse drawn from the continuing revolution dialogue. St. Etienne left early, but the other three remained to continue the discussion. Someone — very likely Jefferson — proposed that the King, in a *séance royale*, should offer a Charter of Rights for France, which would be signed by him and by every member of the three Orders. Lafayette was impressed with the idea and Jefferson, after he went home, considered it afresh. With the weight of the royal influence thus placed behind it, with a series of reforms thus imperishably embodied in a written document to which all the parties could agree, the Revolution might well be

Paris, June 3, 1789

Dear Sir,

Revolving further in my mind the idea started yesterday evening of the King's coming forward in a seance royale and offering a charter containing all the good in which all parties agree I like it more and more. I have ventured to sketch such a charter merely to convey my idea, which I now inclose to you, as I do also to M. de St. Etienne. I write him a letter of apology for my meddling in a business where I know so little & you & he so much. I have thought it better to possess him immediately of the paper, because he may at the conference of to-day sound the minds of the conferees. Adieu. Your's affectionately.

To M. De St. Etienne[1]

Paris, June 3, 1789

Sir,

After you quitted us yesterday evening, we continued our conversation (Monsr. de la Fayette, Mr. Short & myself) on the subject of the difficulties which environ you. The desirable object being to secure the good which the King has offered & to avoid the ill which seems to threaten, an idea was suggested, which

---

resolved with resounding success. Excited by these thoughts — and perhaps by the consideration that thereby he might be the architect of this second revolution in which he found himself, as of the first — Jefferson sat down at his writing desk and drew up "A Charter of Rights, solemnly established by the King and Nation."

1. The States-General shall be elected triennially and meet annually without limitation.
2. The States-General alone shall levy money on the nation, and shall appropriate it.
3. Laws shall be made by the States-General only, with the consent of the King.
4. No person shall be restrained of his liberty except by due process of law, and the right of habeas corpus shall be instituted.
5. The military shall be subordinate to the civil authority.
6. The press shall be free and unrestricted.
7. All pecuniary privileges and exemptions shall be abolished.
8. Debts already contracted by the King shall be made the debts of the nation.
9. Eighty million livres now granted to the King shall be raised by a loan.
10. The States-General shall adjourn until November 1st.

The Charter which, in substance, Jefferson thus formulated was indeed only modestly liberal and reformist, and might well have received the plaudits of all Orders, with certain exceptions. The Nobles and Clergy did not wish their traditional privileges and exemptions taken away; the King was not prepared to have his money-raising power thus ruthlessly removed; and the Third Estate would have felt that the reforms did not strike at any economic roots. It certainly was not as radical as Jefferson's own draft constitution for Virginia, nor did it go as far even as the Federal Constitution of the United States.

The next morning, with this cover letter, Jefferson made copies of his proposals and sent one to Lafayette and the other to St. Etienne. Nothing came of it, but Lafayette was incorporating some of the provisions, together with others taken from the American Bill of Rights, with an obeisance to the Declaration of Independence, in a Declaration of the Rights of Man of his own, which he was to offer the Convention in the following month. (Schachner 1957, 373-374)

[1] Ibid.

appearing to make an impression on Mons[r]. de la Fayette, I was encouraged to pursue it on my return to Paris, to put it into form, & now to send it to you & him. It is this that the King, in a seance royale should come forward with a Charter of Rights in his hand, to be signed by himself & by every member of the three orders. This charter to contain the five great points which the Resultat of December offered on the part of the King, the abolition of pecuniary privileges offered by the privileged orders, & the adoption of the National debt and a grant of the sum of money asked from the nation. This last will be a cheap price for the preceding articles, and let the same act declare your immediate separation till the next anniversary meeting. You will carry back to your constituents more good than ever was effected before without violence, and you will stop exactly at the point where violence would otherwise begin. Time will be gained, the public mind will continue to ripen & to be informed, a basis of support may be prepared with the people themselves, and expedients occur for gaining still something further at your next meeting, & for stopping again at the point of force. I have ventured to send to yourself & Monsieur de la Fayette a sketch of my ideas of what this act might contain without endangering any dispute. But it is offered merely as a canvas for you to work on, if it be fit to work on at all. I know too little of the subject, & you know too much of it to justify me in offering anything but a hint. I have done it too in a hurry: insomuch that since committing it to writing it occurs to me that the 5th. article may give alarm, that it is in a good degree included in the 4th., and is therefore useless. But after all what excuse can I make, Sir, for this presumption. I have none but an unmeasurable love for your nation and a painful anxiety lest Despotism, after an unaccepted offer to bind its own hands, should seize you again with tenfold fury. Permit me to add to these very sincere assurances of the sentiments of esteem & respect with which I have the honor to be, Sir, Your most obed[t]. & most humble serv[t].

To L'abbé Arnoux[1]
Paris, July 19, 1789
Dear Sir.

Books on the subject of Juries – Complete juryman, or a Compendium of the Laws Relating to Jurors, Guide to English Juries, Hawles' Englishman's Right, Jurors Judges Both of Law and Fact by Jones, Security of Englishmen's Lives, or the Duty of Grand Juries, Walwin's Juries Justified.

The above is a catalogue of all the books I recollect on the subject of juries. With respect to the value of this institution I must make a general observation. We think in America that it is necessary to introduce the people into every department of government as far as they are capable of exercising it; and that this is the only way to ensure a long continued & honest administration of its powers.

---

[1] The Abbé Arnoux was a close friend of Benjamin Franklin who had provided letters of introduction when Jefferson travelled to the south of France. With respect to the letter itself, it should be noted that the structure and power of the judiciary became a major issue in the struggle between Jeffersonians and Federalists in Pennsylvania, partly because the principles of arbitration had become central to the legal process. (Adams 1997, 103; Steinberg 1989, 94)

1. They are not qualified to exercise themselves the Executive department; but they are qualified to name the person who shall exercise it. With us therefore they choose this officer every 4. years. 2. They are not qualified to Legislate. With us therefore they only choose the legislators. 3. They are not qualified to judge questions of law; but they are very capable of judging questions of fact. In the form of juries therefore they determine all matters of fact, leaving to the permanent judges to decide the law resulting from those facts. But we all know, that permanent judges acquire an Esprit de corps, that being known they are liable to be tempted by bribery, that they are misled by favor, by relationship, by a spirit of party, by a devotion to the Executive or Legislative; that it is better to leave a cause to the decision of cross & pile, than to that of a judge biased to one side; and that the opinion of 12. honest jurymen gives still a better hope of right, than cross & pile does. It is left therefore to the juries, if they think the permanent judges are under any bias whatever in any cause, to take on themselves to judge the laws as well as the fact. They never exercise this power but when they suspect partiality in the judges, and by the exercise of this power they have been the firmest bulwarks of English liberty. Were I called upon to decide whether the people had best be omitted in the Legislative or Judiciary department, I would say it is better to leave them out of the Legislature. The execution of the laws is more important than the making them. However it is best to have the people in all the three departments where that is possible. I write in great haste my dear Sir, & have therefore only time to add wishes for the happiness of your country, to which a new order of things is opening & assurances of the sincere esteem with which I have the honor to be, Dear Sir, your most obedient & humble servt.

To John Jay[1]
Paris, July 29, 1789
Dear Sir,

I am become very uneasy lest you should have adopted some channel for the conveyance of your letters to me which is unfaithful. I have none from you of later date than Nov. 25. 1788. and of consequence no acknowledgement of the receipt of any of mine since that of Aug. 11. 1788. Since that period I have written to you of the following dates. 1788. Aug. 20. Sep. 3. 5. 24. Nov. 14. 19. 29. 1789. Jan. 11. 14. 21. Feb. 4. Mar. 1. 12. 14. 15. May. 9. 11. 12. Jun. 17. 24. 29. I know through another person that you have received mine of Nov. 29. and that you have written an answer; but I have never received the answer, and it is this which suggests to me the fear of some general source of miscarriage.

The capture of three French merchant ships by the Algerines under different pretexts, has produced great sensation in the seaports of this country, and some in its government. They have ordered some frigates to be armed at Toulon to

---

[1] On July 14, 1789, Jefferson, was a witness to the events of a day in Paris that is commonly associated with the beginning of the French Revolution. Jefferson recorded the events of the day in this lengthy and detailed letter to John Jay, then Secretary of Foreign Affairs.

punish them. There is a possibility that this circumstance, if not too soon set to rights by the Algerines, may furnish occasion to the States general, when they shall have leisure to attend to matters of this kind, to disavow any future tributary treaty with them. These pirates respect still less their treaty with Spain, and treat the Spaniards with an insolence greater than was usual before the treaty.

The scarcity of bread begins to lessen in the Southern parts of France where the harvest is commenced. Here it is still threatening because we have yet two or three weeks to the beginning of harvest, and I think there has not been three days provision beforehand in Paris for two or three weeks past. Monsieur de Mirabeau, who is very hostile to Mr. Necker, wished to find a ground for censuring him in a proposition to have a great quantity of flour furnished from the United states, which he supposed me to have made to Mr. Necker, and to have been refused by him; and he asked time of the States general to furnish proofs. The Marquis de la Fayette immediately gave me notice of this matter, and I wrote him a letter to disavow having ever made any such proposition to Mr. Necker, which I desired him to communicate to the states. I waited immediately on Mr. Necker and Monsieur de Montmorin, satisfied them that what had been suggested was absolutely without foundation from me, and indeed they had not needed this testimony. I gave them copies of my letter to the Marquis de la Fayette, which was afterwards printed. The Marquis on the receipt of my letter, shewed it to Mirabeau, who turned then to a paper from which he had drawn his information, and found he had totally mistaken it. He promised immediately that he would himself declare his error to the States general, and read to them my letter, which he did. I state this matter to you, tho' of little consequence in itself, because it might go to you misstated in the English papers.

Our supplies to the Atlantic ports of France during the months of March, April, and May, were only 12,220 quintals 33 lb of flour, and 44,115 quintals 40 ℔ of wheat, in 21. vessels.

My letter of the 29th. of June brought down the proceedings of the States and Government to the reunion of the orders, which took place on the 27th. Within the Assembly matters went on well. But it was soon observed that troops, and particularly the foreign troops, were on their march towards Paris from various quarters and that this was against the opinion of Mr. Necker. The king was probably advised to this under pretext of preserving peace in Paris and Versailles, and saw nothing else in the measure. But his advisers are supposed to have had in view, when he should be secured and inspirited by the presence of the troops, to take advantage of some favorable moment and surprise him into an act of authority for establishing the Declaration of the 23d of June, and perhaps dispersing the States general. The Marshal de Broglio was appointed to command all the troops within the Isle of France, a high flying Aristocrat, cool and capable of everything. Some of the French guards were soon arrested under other pretexts, but in reality on account of their dispositions in favor of the national cause. The people of Paris forced the prison, released them, and sent a deputation to the States general to solicit a pardon. The States by a most moderate and prudent Arreté recommended these prisoners to the king, and peace to the people of Paris. Addresses came in to them from several of the great cities expressing sincere allegiance to the king, but a determined resolution to support the States general. On the 8th. of July they vote an address to the king to remove the troops. This piece of masculine eloquence, written by Monsieur de Mirabeau, is worth attention, on account of the bold matter it expresses or covers, thro the whole. The king refuses to remove the troops and says they may remove themselves if they please to Noyons or Soissons. They proceed to fix the order in which they will take up the several branches of their future constitution, from which it appears they mean to build it from the bottom, confining themselves to nothing in their antient form, but a king. A Declaration of rights, which forms the first chapter of their work was then proposed by the Marquis de la Fayette. This was on the 11th.

In the meantime troops to the number of about 125. or 30,000 had arrived and were posted in and between Paris and Versailles. The bridges and passes were guarded. At 3. o'clock in the afternoon the Count de la Luzerne was sent to notify Mr. Necker of his dismission, and to enjoin him to retire instantly without saying a word of it to anybody. He went home, dined, proposed to his wife a visit to a friend, but went in fact to his country house at St. Ouen, and at midnight set out from thence for Brussels. This was not known till the next day, when the whole ministry was changed except Villedeuil of the Domestic department and Barentin Garde des sceaux. These changes were as follows. The Baron de Breteuil President of the council of finance, and de la Galaisiere Comptroller General in the room of Mr. Necker; the Mareshal de Broglio minister of war, and Foulon under him, in the room of Puy-segur; Monsieur de la Vauguyon minister of foreign affairs instead of Monsieur de Montmorin; de la Porte, minister of marine, in place of the Count de la Luzerne; St. Priest was also removed from the council. It is to be observed that Luzerne and Puy-segur had been strongly of the aristocratical party in council; but they were not considered as equal to bear their shares in the work now to be done. For this change, however sudden it may have been in the mind of the king, was, in that of his advisers, only the second chapter of a great plan, of which the bringing together the foreign troops had been the first. He was now completely in the hands of men, the principal among whom had been noted thro' their lives for the Turkish despotism of their characters, and who were associated about the king as proper instruments for what was to be executed.

The news of this change began to be known in Paris about 1. or 2. o'clock. In the afternoon a body of about 100. German cavalry were advanced and drawn up in the Place Louis XV. and about 300 Swiss posted at a little distance in their rear. This drew people to that spot, who naturally formed themselves in front of the troops, at first merely to look at them. But as their numbers increased their indignation arose: they retired a few steps, posted themselves on and behind large piles of loose stone collected in that Place for a bridge adjacent to it, and attacked the horse with stones. The horse charged, but the advantageous position of the people, and the showers of stones obliged them to retire, and even to quit the field altogether, leaving one of their number on the ground. The Swiss in their rear were observed never to stir. This was the signal for universal insurrection, and this body of cavalry, to avoid being massacred, retired towards Versailles. The people now armed themselves with such weapons as they could find in Armourer's shops and private houses, and with bludgeons, and were roaming all night through all parts of the city without any decided and practicable object.

The next day the States press on the king to send away the troops, to permit the Bourgeoisie of Paris to arm for the preservation of order in the city, and offer to send a deputation from their body to tranquillize them. He refuses all their propositions. A Committee of magistrates and electors of the city are appointed, by their bodies, to take upon them its government. The mob, now openly joined by the French guards, force the prisons of St. Lazare, release all the prisoners, and take a great store of corn, which they carry to the corn market. Here they get some arms, and the French guards begin to form and train them. The City committee determine to raise 48,000 Bourgeois, or rather to restrain their numbers to 48,000.

On the 14th. they send one of their members (Monsieur de Corny, whom we knew in America) to the Hotel des Invalides to ask arms for their Garde Bourgeoise. He was followed by, or he found there, a great mob. The Governor of the Invalids came out and represented the impossibility of his delivering arms without the orders of those from whom he received them. De Corney advised the people then to retire, retired himself, and the people took possession of the arms. It was remarkable that not only the Invalids themselves made no opposition, but that a body of 5000 foreign troops, encamped within 400. yards, never stirred. Monsieur de Corny and five others were then sent to ask arms of Monsieur de Launai, Governor of the Bastille. They found a great collection of people already before the place, and they immediately planted a flag of truce, which was answered by a like flag hoisted on the parapet. The deputation prevailed on the people to fall back a little, advanced themselves to make their demand of the Governor, and in that instant a discharge from the Bastille killed 4. people of those nearest to the deputies. The deputies retired, the people rushed against the place, and almost in an instant were in possession of a fortification, defended by 100 men, of infinite strength, which in other times had stood several regular sieges and had never been taken. How they got in, has as yet been impossible to discover. Those, who pretend to have been of the party tell so many different stories as to destroy the credit of them all. They took all the arms, discharged the prisoners and such of the garrison as were not killed in the first moment of fury, carried the Governor and Lieutenant governor to the Greve (the place of public execution) cut off their heads, and set them through the city in triumph to the Palais royal. About the same instant, a treacherous correspondence having been discovered in Monsieur de Flesselles prevot des marchands, they seize him in the hotel de vile, where he was in the exercise of his office, and cut off his head. These events carried imperfectly to Versailles were the subject of two successive deputations from the States to the King, to both of which he gave dry and hard answers, for it has transpired that it had been proposed and agitated in Council to seize on the principal members of the States general, to march the whole army down upon Paris and to suppress it's tumults by the sword. But at night the Duke de Liancourt forced his way into the king's bedchamber, and obliged him to hear a full and animated detail of the disasters of the day in Paris. He went to bed deeply impressed.

The decapitation of de Launai worked powerfully thro' the night on the whole Aristocratical party, insomuch that in the morning those of the greatest influence on the Count d'Artois represented to him the absolute necessity that the king should give up everything to the states. This according well enough with the dispositions of the king, he went about 11. o'clock, accompanied only by his brothers, to the States general, and there read to them a speech, in which he asked their interposition to re-establish order. Tho this be couched in terms of some caution, yet the manner in which it was delivered made it evident that it was meant as a surrender at discretion. He returned to the chateau afoot, accompanied by the States. They sent off a deputation, the Marquis de la Fayette at their head, to quiet Paris. He had the same morning been named Commandant en chef of the milice Bourgeoise, and Monsieur Bailly, former President of the States general, was called for as Prevost des marchands.

The demolition of the Bastille was now ordered, and begun. A body of the Swiss guards, of the regiment of Ventimille, and the city horse guards join the people. The alarm at Versailles increases instead of abating. They believed that the Aristocrats of Paris were under pillage and carnage, that 150,000 men were in arms coming to Versailles to massacre the Royal family, the court, the ministers and all connected with them, their practices and principles. The Aristocrats of the Nobles and Clergy in the States general vied with each other in declaring how sincerely they were converted to the justice of voting by persons, and how determined to go with the nation all its lengths. The foreign troops were ordered off instantly. Every minister resigned. The king confirmed Bailly as Prevost des marchands, wrote to Mr. Necker to recall him, sent his letter open to the States general to be forwarded by them, and invited them to go with him to Paris the next day to satisfy the city of his dispositions: and that night and the next morning the Count d'Artois and a Monsieur de Montesson (a deputy) connected with him, Madame de Polignac, Madame de Guiche and the Count de Vaudreuil favorites of the queen, the Abbé de Vermont her confessor, the Prince of Condé and Duke de Bourbon, all fled, we know not whither.

The king came to Paris, leaving the queen in consternation for his return. Omitting the less important figures of the procession, I will only observe that the king's carriage was in the center, on each side of it the States general, in two ranks, afoot, at their head the Marquis de la Fayette as commander in chief, on horseback, and Bourgeois guards before and behind. About 60,000 citizens of all forms and colours, armed with the muskets of the Bastille and Invalids as far as they would go, the rest with pistols, swords, pikes, pruning hooks, scythes &c. lined all the streets thro' which the procession passed, and, with the crowds of people in the streets, doors and windows, saluted them everywhere with cries of "vive la nation." But not a single "vive le roy" was heard. The king landed at the

Hotel de ville. There Monsieur Bailly presented and put into his hat the popular cockade, and addressed him. The king being unprepared and unable to answer, Bailly went to him, gathered from him some scraps of sentences, and made out an answer, which he delivered to the Audience as from the king. On their return the popular cries were 'vive le roy et la nation.' He was conducted by a garde Bourgeoise to his palace at Versailles, and thus concluded such an Amende honorable as no sovereign ever made, and no people ever received. Letters written with his own hand to the Marquis de la Fayette remove the scruples of his position. Tranquillity is now restored to the Capital: the shops are again opened; the people resuming their labours, and, if the want of bread does not disturb our peace, we may hope a continuance of it.

The demolition of the Bastille is going on, and the milice Bourgeoise organising and training. The antient police of the city is abolished by the authority of the people, the introduction of king's troops will probably be proscribed, and a watch or city guards substituted, which shall depend on the city alone. But we cannot suppose this paroxysm confined to Paris alone. The whole country must pass successively thro' it, and happy if they get thro' it as soon and as well as Paris has done. I went yesterday to Versailles to satisfy myself what had passed there; for nothing can be believed but what one sees, or has from an eye witness. They believe there still that 3000 people have fallen victims to the tumults of Paris. Mr. Short and myself have been every day among them in order to be sure of what was passing. We cannot find with certainty that anybody has been killed but the three before mentioned, and those who fell in the assault or defense of the Bastille. How many of the garrison were killed no body pretends to have ever heard. Of the assailants accounts vary from 6. to 600. The most general belief is that there fell about 30. There have been many reports of instantaneous executions by the mob, on such of their body as they caught in acts of theft or robbery. Some of these may perhaps be true. There was a severity of honesty observed of which no example has been known. Bags of money offered on various occasions, thro fear or guilt, have been uniformly refused by the mobs. The churches are now occupied in singing "De profundis" and "Requiems for the repose of the souls of the brave and valiant citizens who have sealed with their blood the liberty of the nation."

Monsieur de Montmorin is this day replaced in the department of foreign affairs, and Monsieur de St. Priest is named to the Home department. The gazettes of France and Leyden accompany this. I send also a paper (called the Point du jour) which will give you some idea of the proceedings of the National assembly. It is but an indifferent thing; however it is the best.

I have the honor to be with great esteem and respect, Sir, your most obedient and most humble servt.,

P.S. July 21. Mr. Necker had left Brussels for Francfort before the Courier got there. We expect however to hear of him in a day or two. Monsieur le Comte de la Luzerne has resumed the department of the marine this day. Either this is an office of friendship effected by Monsr. de Montmorin (for tho they had taken different sides, their friendship continued) or he comes in as a stop-gap till somebody else can be found. Tho' very unequal to his office, all agree that he is an honest man. The Count d'Artois was at Valenciennes. The Prince of Condé and Duke de Bourbon had passed that place.

To James Madison[1]
Paris, July 29, 1789
Dear Sir,
   I wrote you on the 22d. since that I have received yours of the 23d of May. The *President's title as proposed by the senate was the most superlatively ridiculous thing I ever heard of.*[2] It is a proof the more of the justice of the *character given by Doctor Franklin of my friend. Always an honest one* [?] *often a great one but sometimes absolutely mad. I wish he* could have been here during the late scenes, if he could then have had one fiber of *aristocracy* left in his frame he would have been a proper subject for *bedlam.* The tranquility of this place has not been disturbed since the death of Foulon & Bertier. Supplies of bread are precarious but there has not as yet been such a want as to produce disorder, and we may expect the new wheat harvest to begin now in ten or twelve days. You will wonder to find the harvest here so late. But from my observations (I guess, because I have not calculated their result carefully) the sun does not shine here more than 5. hours of the 24. through the whole year. I inclose you some papers worth notice, which indeed have principally induced me to address you so soon after my last.

To James Swan[3]

---

[1]   Circumstances attending the actual setting up of the new Federal structures, in 1789, tended to increase Jefferson's fear of monarchical possibilities lurking in the new Constitution. For example, on May 23, Madison had written to Jefferson on the addresses of the Senate and the House of Representatives to Washington on the occasion of his inauguration: "My last enclosed copies of the President's inauguration Speech and the answer of the House of the Representatives. I now add the answer of the Senate. It will not have escaped you that the former was addressed with a truly republican simplicity to G. W. Presidt. of the U.S. The latter follows the example, with the omission of the personal name, but without any other than the constitutional tide. The proceeding on this point was in the House of Representatives spontaneous. The imitation by the Senate was extorted. The question became a serious one between the two houses. J. Adams espoused the cause of titles with great earnestness. His friend R. H. Lee altho elected as a republican enemy to an aristocratic constitution was a most zealous second. The projected title was His Highness the President of the U.S. and Protector of their Liberties. Had the project succeeded it would have subjected the President to a severe dilemma and given a deep wound to our infant government." In this note, Jefferson responds, "The president's title as proposed by the senate was the most superlatively ridiculous thing I ever heard of. It is a proof the more of the justice of the character given by Doctor Franklin of my friend [John Adams], "Always an honest man, often a great one, but sometimes absolutely mad." (O'Brien 1996, 75-76)
[2]   These and subsequent words in italics were originally written in cipher. (Boyd 1990)
[3]   The activities of James Swan, Boston merchant and financier, present an interesting example of efforts to increase Franco-American commerce at this time. In 1789-90 the French consul at Boston, Philippe André Joseph de Létombe,

Paris, Aug. 4, 1789
Sir,

Whenever foreigners, possessed of American funds, have come to consult me as to their solidity, I have made it a point to give them the best information in my power. But I have wished to avoid being consulted by those who desire to buy; because it is far from being among my duties to assist in converting the domestic debts of our country into foreign debts, and because too I have not been willing, by giving an opinion which might induce an individual to embark his fortune in a speculation, to take upon myself any responsibility or reproaches for the event of that speculation. The incident which I presume is the subject of your letter was the following. About a week ago one of my servants came and told me there was a person who wished to speak to me. I asked if he was an American or a foreigner? He said a foreigner. I had a good deal of company at the moment, and told him I could not receive him unless his business was extremely pressing. He went to ask his business, and returned with a letter too long to be read in that situation. But at one glance of the eye I saw that it related to the purchase of American funds. I told him to tell the person I did not meddle in that subject, but that unless he was well acquainted with it, he might lose. You know better than I do, Sir, that under the denomination of American funds are comprehended at least 20. kinds of paper of the United States & of the several states, and three times as many kinds of paper effects. Those of the confederacy I know to be as solid as the earth itself & would as soon lend money on them myself as on mortgages of land. Some of those of the several states are good: but I do not suppose all of them to be so. None but a broker living on the spot can distinguish the good from the bad. I therefore told the servant to say to him that 's'il ne s'y connaissait pas il pourrait bien y perdre.' How the servant or he could transform this into an answer 'that the American funds were of no great stability' is not for me to explain. The line or two of the letter which I read mentioned no names, nor specified any particular kind of funds. This, Sir, is the true answer, and the explanation of the motives which led to it: both of them very far from imputing a want of solidity to the funds of the United States. No body living I believe has been more uniformly confident in them than myself.

To James Madison[1]

---

had translated into French and published in Paris a refurbished memorial on Franco-American commerce which Swan had prepared, apparently in 1784, at the suggestion of Lafayette. The English title was *Causes Which Have Hindered the Growth of Trade between France and the United States, with the Means of Stimulating It.* (Deconde 1958, 144)

[1] As suggested in this letter, Jefferson felt reasonably optimistic about the eventual outcome of the French Revolution, in spite of the ominous excesses which had accompanied the July 14 storming of the Bastille, and in spite of the fact that what he called "The lees...of the patriotic party, [those] of wicked principles & desperate fortunes..." were swinging over to the Duc d' Orléans, a prince of the royal blood who saw a chance of fishing in troubled waters. Jefferson appraised the Duke as "a man of moderate understanding, of no principle, absorbed in low vice, and incapable of abstracting himself from the filth of that to direct anything

Paris, Aug. 28, 1789

Dear Sir,

My last to you was of July 29. Since that I have received yours of May 27. June 13. & 30. The tranquility of the city has not been disturbed since my last. Dissensions between the French & Swiss guards occasioned some private combats in which five or six were killed. These dissensions are made up. The want of bread for some days past has greatly endangered the peace of the city. Some get a little bread, some none at all. The poor are the best served because they besiege perpetually the doors of the bakers. Notwithstanding this distress, and the palpable impotence of the city administration to furnish bread to the city, it was not till yesterday that general leave was given to the bakers to go into the country & buy flour for themselves as they can. This will soon relieve us, because the wheat harvest is well advanced. Never was there a country where the practice of governing too much had taken deeper root & done more mischief. Their declaration of rights is finished. If printed in time I will inclose a copy with this. It is doubtful whether they will now take up the finance or the constitution first. The distress for money endangers everything. No taxes are paid, and no money can be borrowed. Mr. Necker was yesterday to give in a memoir to the Assembly on this subject. I think they will give him leave to put into execution any plan he pleases, so as to debarrass themselves of this & take up that of the constitution. No plan is yet reported; but the leading members (with some small differences of opinion) have in contemplation the following. The Executive power in a hereditary king, with a negative on laws and power to dissolve the legislature. To be considerably restrained in the making of treaties, and limited in his expenses. The legislative in a house of representatives. They propose a senate also, chosen on the plan of our federal senate by the provincial assemblies, but to be for life, of a certain age (they talk of 40. years) and certain wealth (4 or 500 guineas a year) but to have no other power as to laws but to remonstrate against them to the representatives, who will then determine their fate by a simple majority. This you will readily perceive is a mere council of revision like that of New York, which, in order to be something, must form an alliance with the king, to avail themselves of his veto. The alliance will be useful to both & to the nation. The representatives to be chosen every two or three

---

else." He was also aware that Orléans was the dupe of Mirabeau, brilliant, unprincipled and unscrupulous, who was hiding behind the royal duke's name in order to gain power for himself. But Jefferson was certain that the two conspirators would have only temporary success, if at all; that "the King, the mass of the substantial people of the whole country, the army, and the influential part of the clergy, form a firm phalanx which must prevail." If Jefferson miscalculated, it was because he had left out of consideration the swarming mobs of Paris and of the other cities of France — the congested proletariat of the towns which he was always to view with a certain horror and shrinking of the flesh. But, by this time, Jefferson was already on the verge of quitting France forever, so that he could follow only from a distance the long and bloody course of the Revolution which he now thought was proceeding in such orderly and satisfactory fashion, and which was to produce convulsions in both the Old and New Worlds for a generations to come. (Schachner 1957, 380)

years. The judiciary system is less prepared than any other part of their plan. However they will abolish the parliaments, and establish an order of judges & justices, general & provincial, a good deal like ours, with trial by jury in criminal cases certainly, perhaps also in civil. The provinces will have assemblies for their provincial government, & the cities a municipal body for municipal government, all founded on the basis of popular election. These subordinate governments, tho completely dependent on the general one, will be entrusted with almost the whole of the details which our state governments exercise. They will have their own judiciary, final in all but great cases, the Executive business will principally pass through their hands, and a certain local legislation will be allowed them. In short ours has been professedly their model, in which such changes are made as a difference of circumstance rendered necessary and some others neither necessary nor advantageous, but into which men will ever run when versed in theory and new in the practice of government, when acquainted with man only as they see him in their books & not in the world. This plan will undoubtedly undergo changes in the assembly, and the longer it is delayed the greater will be the changes: for that assembly, or rather the patriotic part of it, hooped together heretofore by a common enemy, are less compact since their victory. That enemy (the civil & ecclesiastical aristocracy) begins to raise its head. The lees too of the patriotic party, of wicked principles & desperate fortunes, hoping to pillage something in the wreck of their country, are attaching themselves to the faction of the Duke of Orleans, that faction is caballing with the populace, & intriguing at London, the Hague & Berlin and have evidently in view the transfer of the crown to the D. of Orleans. He is a man of moderate understanding, of no principle, absorbed in low vice, and incapable of abstracting himself from the filth of that to direct anything else. His name & his money therefore are mere tools in the hands of those who are duping him. Mirabeau is their chief.[1] They may produce a temporary confusion, and even a temporary civil war, supported as they will be by the money of England: but they cannot have success ultimately. The king, the mass of the substantial people of the whole country, the army, and the influential part of the clergy, form a firm phalanx which must prevail. Should those delays which necessarily attend the deliberations of a body of 1200 men give time to this plot to ripen & burst so as to break up the assembly before anything definitive is done, a constitution, the principles of which are pretty well settled in the minds of the assembly, will be proposed by the national militia urged by the individual members of the assembly, signed by the king, and supported by the nation, to prevail till circumstances shall permit it's revision and more regular sanction. This I suppose the pis-alle [last resort] of their affairs, while their probable event is a peaceable settlement of them. They fear a war from England Holland & Prussia. I think England will give money, but not make war. Holland would soon be afire internally were she to be embroiled in external difficulties. Prussia must know this & act accordingly.

---

[1] These and subsequent words in italics were originally written in cipher. (Boyd 1990)

It is impossible to desire better dispositions towards us, than prevail in this assembly. Our proceedings have been viewed as a model for them on every occasion; and tho in the heat of debate men are generally disposed to contradict every authority urged by their opponents, ours has been treated like that of the bible, open to explanation but not to question. I am sorry that in the moment of such a disposition anything should come from us to check it. The placing them on a mere footing with the English will have this effect. When of two nations, the one has engaged herself in a ruinous war for us, has spent her blood & money to save us, has opened her bosom to us in peace, and receive us almost on the footing of her own citizens, while the other has moved heaven, earth & hell to exterminate us in war, has insulted us in all her councils in peace, shut her doors to us in every part where her interests would admit it, libeled us in foreign nations, endeavored to poison them against the reception of our most precious commodities, to place these two nations on a footing, is to give a great deal more to one than to the other if the maxim be true that to make unequal quantities equal you must add more to the one than the other. To say in excuse that gratitude is never to enter into the motives of national conduct, is to revive a principle which has been buried for centuries with its kindred principles of the lawfulness of assassination, poison, perjury &c. All of these were legitimate principles in the dark ages which intervened between antient & modern civilization, but exploded & held in just horror in the 18th. century. I know but one code of morality for man whether acting singly or collectively. He who says I will be a rogue when I act in company with a hundred others but an honest man when I act alone, will be believed in the former assertion, but not in the latter. I would say with the poet 'hic niger est, hunc tu Romane caveto.' If the morality of one man produces a just line of conduct in him, acting individually, why should not the morality of 100 men produce a just line of conduct in them acting together? But I indulge myself in these reflections because my own feelings run me into them: with you they were always acknowledged. Let us hope that our new government will take some other occasion to shew that they mean to proscribe no virtue from the canons of their conduct with other nations. In every other instance the new government has ushered itself to the world as honest, masculine and dignified. It has shewn genuine dignity in my opinion in exploding adulatory titles; they are the offerings of abject baseness, and nourish that degrading vice in the people. I must now say a word on the declaration of rights you have been so good as to send me. I like it as far as it goes; but I should have been for going further. For instance the following alterations & additions would have pleased me. Art. 4. 'The people shall not be deprived or abridged of their right to speak to write or otherwise to publish anything but false facts affecting injuriously the life, liberty, property, or reputation of others or affecting the peace of the confederacy with foreign nations. Art. 7. All facts put in issue before any judicature shall be tried by jury except 1. in cases of admiralty jurisdiction wherein a foreigner shall be interested, 2. in cases cognizable before a court martial concerning only the regular officers & soldiers of the U. S. or members of the militia in actual service in time of war or insurrection, & 3. in impeachments allowed by the constitution. Art. 8. No person shall be held in confinement more than _____ days after they shall have demanded & been refused a writ of Hab. corp. by the judge appointed by law nor more than _____ days after such writ shall have been served on the person holding him in confinement & no order given on due examination for his remandment or discharge, nor more than _____ hours in any place at a greater distance than _____ miles from the usual residence of some judge authorized to issue the writ of Hab. corp. nor shall that writ be suspended for any term exceeding one year nor in any place more than _____ miles distant from the station or encampment of enemies or of insurgents. Art. 9. Monopolies may be allowed to persons for their own productions in literature & their own inventions in the arts, for a term not exceeding _____ years but for no longer term & no other purpose. Art. 10. All troops of the U. S. shall stand ipso facto disbanded at the expiration of the term for which their pay & subsistence shall have been last voted by Congress, and all officers & soldiers not natives of the U. S. shall be incapable of serving in their armies by land except during a foreign war.' These restrictions I think are so guarded as to hinder evil only. However if we do not have them now, I have so much confidence in my countrymen as to be satisfied that we shall have them as soon as the degeneracy of our government shall render them necessary. I have no certain news of P. Jones. I understand only in a general way that some persecution on the part of his officers occasioned his being called to Petersburgh, & that tho protected against them by the empress, he is not yet restored to his station. Silas Deane is coming over to finish his days in America, not having one sou to subsist on elsewhere. He is a wretched monument of the consequences of a departure from right. I will before my departure write Colo. Lee fully the measures I pursued to procure success in his business, & which as yet offer little hope, & shall leave it in the hands of Mr. Short to be pursued if any prospect opens on him. I propose to sail from Havre as soon after the 1st. of October as I can get a vessel: & shall consequently leave this place a week earlier than that. As my daughters will be with me, & their baggage somewhat more than that of mere voyageurs, I shall endeavor if possible to obtain a passage for Virginia directly. Probably I shall be there by the last of November. If my immediate attendance at New York should be requisite for any purpose, I will leave them with a relation near Richmond and proceed immediately to New York. But as I do not foresee any pressing purpose for that journey immediately on my arrival, and as it will be a great saving of time to finish at once in Virginia so as to have no occasion to return there after having once gone on to the Northward, I expect to proceed to my own house directly. Staying there two months (which I believe will be necessary) and allowing for the time I am on the road, I may expect to be at New York in February, and to embark from thence, or some eastern port. You ask me if I would accept any appointment on that side the water? You know the circumstances which led me from retirement, step by step & from one nomination to another, up to the present. My object is a return to the same retirement. Whenever therefore I quit the present, it will not be to engage in any other office, and most especially any one which would require a constant residence from home. The books I have collected for you will go off for Havre in three or four days with my baggage. From that port I shall try to send them by a direct occasion to New York. I am with great & sincere esteem Dr. Sir your affectionate friend and servant

P. S. I just now learn that Mr. Necker proposed yesterday to the National assembly a loan of 80. millions, on terms more tempting to the lender than the former, & that they approved it, leaving him to arrange the details in order that they might occupy themselves at once about the constitution.

To James Madison[1]
Paris, September 6, 1789.
Dear Sir,

I sit down to write to you without knowing by what occasion I shall send my letter. I do it because a subject comes into my head which I would wish to develop a little more than is practicable in the hurry of the moment of making up general dispatches.

The question Whether one generation of men has a right to bind another, seems never to have been started either on this or our side of the water. Yet it is a question of such consequences as not only to merit decision, but place also, among the fundamental principles of every government. The course of reflection in which we are immersed here on the elementary principles of society has presented this question to my mind; and that no such obligation can be transmitted I think very capable of proof. I set out on this ground which

---

[1] Recovering from an illness that had incapacitated him during the first week of September in 1789, in this letter to Madison Jefferson sets forth a political and legal doctrine remarkable for its boldness and simplicity. "The question," Jefferson began, "whether one generation of men has the right to bind another, seems never to have been started either on this or our side of the water. Yet it is a question of such consequences as not only to merit decision, but place also, among the fundamental principles of every government." Turning directly to the answer to this "fundamental" question, Jefferson continued, "I set out on this ground, which I suppose to be self-evident, 'that the earth belongs in usufruct to the living': that the dead have neither powers nor rights over it." This letter is significant, indeed it emerges as a central text in the Jeffersonian canon, because it represents what mattered most to Jefferson at a significant moment in his life: his expression of the widely known doctrine of "political relativism": each generation has the right to be free from the burdens assumed by the past generation and the concomitant duty to respect the same right of its successor. At one level the doctrine is an answer, albeit a remarkable one, to an aspect of the larger problem of intergenerational justice familiar to modern political theorists and lawyers: what rights and duties, if any, do generations owe to each other? Admittedly, Jefferson's endorsement of the rights of the present generation was hardly original, for it was a theme common among mid- to late eighteenth-century political writers influenced by republican ideology. Still, there was a measurable originality to Jefferson's articulation of the doctrine, as he himself claimed. Jefferson asserted a principle of political economy the extent of whose dynamism few of his contemporaries were prepared to accept — i.e., each generation is free to create its own social order and is under no constraints from actions taken by past generations. Jefferson went so far as to suggest that all constitutions and laws naturally expire and must be either reenacted or revised at the end of nineteen years, a period he calculated to be the life expectancy of any single generation. (Alexander 1997, 26-27)

I suppose to be self-evident, "that the earth belongs in usufruct to the living;" that the dead have neither powers nor rights over it. The portion occupied by any individual ceases to be his when himself ceases to be, and reverts to the society. If the society has formed no rules for the appropriation of its lands in severalty, it will be taken by the first occupants. These will generally be the wife and children of the decedent. If they have formed rules of appropriation, those rules may give it to the wife and children, or to some one of them, or to the legatee of the deceased. So they may give it to his creditor. But the child, the legatee or creditor takes it, not by any natural right, but by a law of the society of which they are members, and to which they are subject. Then no man can by natural right oblige the lands he occupied, or the persons who succeed him in that occupation, to the payment of debts contracted by him. For if he could, he might during his own life, eat up the usufruct of the lands for several generations to come, and then the lands would belong to the dead, and not to the living, which would be reverse of our principle. What is true of every member of the society individually, is true of them all collectively, since the rights of the whole can be no more than the sum of the rights of individuals. To keep our ideas clear when applying them to a multitude, let us suppose a whole generation of men to be born on the same day, to attain mature age on the same day, and to die on the same day, leaving a succeeding generation in the moment of attaining their mature age all together. Let the ripe age be supposed of 21. years, and their period of life 34. years more, that being the average term given by the bills of mortality to persons who have already attained 21. years of age. Each successive generation would, in this way, come on and go off the stage at a fixed moment, as individuals do now. Then I say the earth belongs to each of these generations during its course, fully, and in their own right. The 2d. generation receives it clear of the debts and encumbrances of the 1st., the 3d. of the 2d. and so on. For if the 1st. could charge it with a debt, then the earth would belong to the dead and not the living generation. Then no generation can contract debts greater than may be paid during the course of its own existence. At 21. years of age they may bind themselves and their lands for 34. years to come: at 22. for 33: at 23 for 32. and at 54 for one year only; because these are the terms of life which remain to them at those respective epochs. But a material difference must be noted between the succession of an individual and that of a whole generation. Individuals are parts only of a society, subject to the laws of a whole. These laws may appropriate the portion of land occupied by a decedent to his creditor rather than to any other, or to his child, on condition he satisfies his creditor. But when a whole generation, that is, the whole society dies, as in the case we have supposed, and another generation or society succeeds, this forms a whole, and there is no superior who can give their territory to a third society, who may have lent money to their predecessors beyond their faculty of paying.

What is true of a generation all arriving to self-government on the same day, and dying all on the same day, is true of those on a constant course of decay and renewal, with this only difference. A generation coming in and going out entire, as in the first case, would have a right in the 1st year of their self-dominion to contract a debt for 33. years, in the 10th. for 24. in the 20th. for 14. in the 30th. for 4. whereas generations changing daily, by daily deaths and births, have one constant term beginning at the date of their contract, and ending when a majority of those of full age at that date shall be dead. The length of that term may be estimated from the tables of mortality, corrected by the circumstances of climate, occupation &c. peculiar to the country of the contractors. Take, for instance, the table of M. de Buffon wherein he states 23,994 deaths, and the ages at which they happened. Suppose a society in which 23,994 persons are born every year and live to the ages stated in this table. The conditions of that society will be as follows. 1st. it will consist constantly of 617,703 persons of all ages. 2dly. of those living at any one instant of time, one half will be dead in 24. years 8. months. 3dly. 10,675 will arrive every year at the age of 21. years complete. 4thly. it will constantly have 348,417 persons of all ages above 21. years. 5ly. and the half of those of 21. years and upwards living at any one instant of time will be dead in 18. years 8. months, or say 19. years as the nearest integral number. Then 19. years is the term beyond which neither the representatives of a nation, nor even the whole nation itself assembled, can validly extend a debt.

To render this conclusion palpable by example, suppose that Louis XIV. and XV. had contracted debts in the name of the French nation to the amount of 10.000 milliards of livres and that the whole had been contracted in Genoa. The interest of this sum would be 500 milliards, which is said to be the whole rent-roll, or net proceeds of the territory of France. Must the present generation of men have retired from the territory in which nature produced them, and ceded it to the Genoese creditors? No. They have the same rights over the soil on which they were produced, as the preceding generations had. They derive these rights not from their predecessors, but from nature. They then and their soil are by nature clear of the debts of their predecessors. Again suppose Louis XV. and his contemporary generation had said to the money lenders of Genoa, give us money that we may eat, drink, and be merry in our day; and on condition you will demand no interest till the end of 19. years, you shall then forever after receive an annual interest of 1 125. per cent. The money is lent on these conditions, is divided among the living, eaten, drank, and squandered. Would the present generation be obliged to apply the produce of the earth and of their labor to replace their dissipations? Not at all.

I suppose that the received opinion, that the public debts of one generation devolve on the next, has been suggested by our seeing habitually in private life that he who succeeds to lands is required to pay the debts of his ancestor or testator, without considering that this requisition is municipal only, not moral, flowing from the will of the society which has found it convenient to appropriate the lands become vacant by the death of their occupant on the condition of a paiment of his debts; but that between society and society, or generation and generation there is no municipal obligation, no umpire but the law of nature. We seem not to have perceived that, by the law of nature, one generation is to another as one independent nation to another.

The interest of the national debt of France being in fact but a two thousandth part of its rent-roll, the paiment of it is practicable enough; and so becomes a question merely of honor or expediency. But with respect to future debts; would it not be wise and just for that nation to declare in the constitution they are forming that neither the legislature, nor the nation itself can validly contract more debt, than they may pay within their own age, or within the term of 19. years? And that all future contracts shall be deemed void as to what shall remain unpaid at the end of 19. years from their date? This would put the lenders, and the borrowers also, on their guard. By reducing too the faculty of borrowing within its natural limits, it would bridle the spirit of war, to which too free a course has been procured by the inattention of money lenders to this law of nature, that succeeding generations are not responsible for the preceding.

On similar ground it may be proved that no society can make a perpetual constitution, or even a perpetual law. The earth belongs always to the living generation. They may manage it then, and what proceeds from it, as they please, during their usufruct. They are masters too of their own persons, and consequently may govern them as they please. But persons and property make the sum of the objects of government. The constitution and the laws of their predecessors extinguished them, in their natural course, with those whose will gave them being. This could preserve that being till it ceased to be itself, and no longer. Every constitution, then, and every law, naturally expires at the end of 19. years. If it be enforced longer, it is an act of force and not of right.

It may be said that the succeeding generation exercising in fact the power of repeal, this leaves them as free as if the constitution or law had been expressly limited to 19. years only. In the first place, this objection admits the right, in proposing an equivalent. But the power of repeal is not an equivalent. It might be indeed if every form of government were so perfectly contrived that the will of the majority could always be obtained fairly and without impediment. But this is true of no form. The people cannot assemble themselves; their representation is unequal and vicious. Various checks are opposed to every legislative proposition. Factions get possession of the public councils. Bribery corrupts them. Personal interests lead them astray from the general interests of their constituents; and other impediments arise so as to prove to every practical man that a law of limited duration is much more manageable than one which needs a repeal.

This principle that the earth belongs to the living and not to the dead is of very extensive application and consequences in every country, and most especially in France. It enters into the resolution of the questions Whether the nation may change the descent of lands holden in tail? Whether they may change the appropriation of lands given antiently to the church, to hospitals, colleges, orders of chivalry, and otherwise in perpetuity? whether they may abolish the charges and privileges attached on lands, including the whole catalogue ecclesiastical and feudal? it goes to hereditary offices, authorities and jurisdictions; to hereditary orders, distinctions and appellations; to perpetual monopolies in commerce, the arts or sciences; with a long train of et ceteras: and it renders the question of reimbursement a question of generosity and not of right. In all these cases the legislature of the day could authorize such appropriations and establishments for their own time, but no longer; and the present holders, even where they or their ancestors have purchased, are in the case of bona fide purchasers of what the seller had no right to convey.

Turn this subject in your mind, my Dear Sir, and particularly as to the power of contracting debts, and develop it with that perspicuity and cogent logic which is so peculiarly yours. Your station in the councils of our country gives you an opportunity of producing it to public consideration, of forcing it into discussion. At first blush it may be rallied as a theoretical speculation; but examination will prove it to be solid and salutary. It would furnish matter for a fine preamble to our first law for appropriating the public revenue; and it will exclude, at the threshold of our new government the contagious and ruinous errors of this quarter of the globe, which have armed despots with means not sanctioned by nature for binding in chains their fellow-men. We have already given, in example one effectual check to the Dog of war, by transferring the power of letting him loose from the executive to the Legislative body, from those who are to spend to those who are to pay. I should be pleased to see this second obstacle held out by us also in the first instance. No nation can make a declaration against the validity of long-contracted debts so disinterestedly as we, since we do not owe a shilling which may not be paid with ease principal and interest, within the time of our own lives. Establish the principle also in the new law to be passed for protecting copy rights and new inventions, by securing the exclusive right for 19. instead of 14. years [a line entirely faded] an instance the more of our taking reason for our guide instead of English precedents, the habit of which fetters us, with all the political heresies of a nation, equally remarkable for its incitement from some errors, as long slumbering under others. I write you no news, because when an occasion occurs I shall write a separate letter for that.

To William Carmichael[1]
Paris, Sep. 12, 1789
Dear Sir,

I have duly received your favor of Aug. 13. and I have written to Francesco and Giuseppe Chiappe both, to assure them of the friendly light in which our government will view the restitution of the schooner from Salem, made by the emperor. I have lately received letters & papers from America to the 25th. of July. New York and N. Hampshire had elected their senators, so that that

---

[1] The three Chiappe brothers, Giuseppe, Girolamo (Geronimo), and Francisco, became involved in American affairs in North Africa at least as early as 1784. Apparently Italian in origin, Giuseppe was consul for Genoa and vice-consul for Venice at Mogador and Girolamo was consul for Venice and vice-consul for Genoa at Tangiers. The Chiappes had acted on behalf of the United States in 1784 when on 11 Oct. Sidi Mohammed, emperor of Morocco, impatient at the lack of progress in negotiating a treaty with the United States, had the United States brigantine *Betsey* seized. Thomas Barclay, who lodged with Giuseppe Chiappe during his time in Morocco, had appointed Francisco, Giuseppe, and Girolamo, American agents at Morocco, Mogador, and Tangiers, respectively, subject to the approval of Congress. (Boyd 1990)

branch of our legislature was complete. Congress had decided that the president should have no title of courtesy. The bill for the impost was past. That also for establishing an office of foreign affairs. Bills for establishing offices of war & of finance, for establishing a federal judicature, for the government of the western country, establishing a land office, for an impost on tonnage, for fixing the President's allowance at 25.000. & the Vice-president's at 5000. dollars a year, were so far advanced as to be near their passage. They had refused to establish a Secretary for the domestic departments. New York had passed a law appointing commissioners to agree with the state of Vermont on the conditions of its independence. None of the higher federal offices were yet filled.

With respect to the extraordinary expenses which you may be under the necessity of incurring at the coronation, I am not authorized to give any advice, nor does anybody, my dear Sir, need it less than yourself. I should certainly suppose that the representative of the U. S. at Madrid, was to do as the representatives of other sovereignties do, and that it would be viewed as the complement of our nation & not of its minister. If this be the true point of view, it proves at whose expense it should be. But my opinion would be viewed as an interested one, & therefore of no weight. In some letter which I had the honor of writing you a year & a half or two years ago (for having packed my letters I cannot name the date exactly) I took the liberty of saying what I thought would be prudent relative to the Algerine captives from that time forward. The two accompts you send me I will take with me to America, & undertake to place you at ease as to them. But I believe you cannot keep yourself too clear as to others. I will write you more fully when I shall have conferred with our government, and if you are not placed more at ease on other accounts it will not be that I have not a due sense of the necessity of it, nor that I shall be wanting in expressing that sense. I have received my leave of absence, & my baggage is already gone off. I shall follow myself in about 10. days, so as to sail about the last of the month, I am not certain whether from Havre or Lorient. Mr. Short being named Chargé des Affairs in my absence will be happy in your correspondence till I can resume it.

To Ralph Izard[1]
Paris, Sep. 18, 1789
Dear Sir,

I have received by Mr. Cutting your favor of April 3. In order to ascertain what proportion of your rice might be taken off by this country, I applied to the proper officer and obtained a statement of their importations of rice for a twelve month, and from what countries. This I inclose to you. You will observe it is between 81 and 82 thousand quintals, which I suppose to be about a fourth or

---

[1] Ralph Izard, diplomat, member of the Continental Congress and, as of this letter, a United States Senator from South Carolina, was an old friend of Jefferson's who was perhaps best known for pledging his large estate in South Carolina for the payment of war ships to be used in the American Revolutionary War. As reflected in his July 14, 1787 letter to William Carmichael, Jefferson was well aware of Izard's interest in the economic potential of South Carolina's rice crop. (Dodge and Koed 2005, 1316-1317)

fifth of your whole exportation. A part of this will always be from Piedmont, but yours may gain ground from two causes: 1st. It's preference over that of Piedmont increases. 2dly. The consumption increases. Paris and the seaport towns are the principal places of consumption, but most of all Paris. Havre therefore is unquestionably the deposit for it, because from thence it may come up the river, or be shipped to any foreign market as conveniently as from Cowes. I wish much you had a good merchant or consignee there. There is a brother of Cutting's there, of whom I hear good spoken, but I do not know him myself. All I know is that an honest, intelligent & active consignee there (or two of them) could do immense service to your countrymen.

When I received your letter I was too near the time of my departure to undertake to procure from Constantinople the intelligence you desired relative to that as a market for your rice. I therefore wrote to a merchant of my acquaintance at Marseilles engaged in the Levant and also in the American trade. I asked from him the prices current of Constantinople & of Marseilles for some years past. I inclose you his answer, giving only the present price at Marseilles, & the price of a particular cargo only at Constantinople. When I return here I will try through the French Ambassador at Constantinople to get more particular information, but we must get rid of the Algerines. I think this practicable by means honorable & within our power, but of this we will converse when I shall have the honor of seeing you at New York, which will be in February, if there be no particular cause for my going on there till I shall have arranged the private business which has rendered it necessary for me to visit my country.

I wish the cargo of olives spoken of in the enclosed letter, & which went to Baltimore, may have got on safe to Carolina, & that the one he is about to send may also arrive safe. This my dear friend should be the object of the Carolina patriot. After bread, I know no blessing to the poor, in this world, equal to that of oil. But there should be an annual sum steadily applied to that object: because a first and second essay may fail. The plants cost little; the transportation little. It is unremitting attention which is requisite. A common country laborer whose business it should be to prepare and pack his plants at Marseilles & to go on with them through the canal of Languedoc to Bordeaux and there stay with them till put on board a ship to Charleston, & to send at the same time great quantities of the berries to sow for stocks, would require but a moderate annual sum. He would make the journey every fall only, till you should have such a stock of plants taken in the country, as to render you sure of success. But of this too we will talk on meeting. The crisis of this country is not yet absolutely past. The unskillfulness of new administrators leaves the Capital in danger of the confusion which may attend the want of bread surrounded by a country which has just gathered in a plentiful harvest.

To The Secretary for Foreign Affairs (John Jay)[1]

---

[1] Although Jefferson was never fully aware of the extent of France's weakness and duplicity, he was not an undiscriminating adherent of the Revolution politically any more than he was philosophically. On the contrary, he recognized

Havre, Sep. 30, 1789

Sir,

No convenient ship having offered from any port of France I have engaged one from London to take me up to Cowes, and am so far on my way thither. She will land me at Norfolk, & as I do not know any service that would be rendered by my repairing immediately to New York, I propose, in order to economize time, to go directly to my own house, get through the business which calls me there, and then repair to New York where I shall be ready to reembark for Europe. But should there be any occasion for government to receive any information I can give, immediately on my arrival, I will go to New York on receiving your orders at Richmond. They may probably be there before me, as this goes by Mr. Trumbull, bound directly for New York. I inclose you herewith the proceedings of the National assembly on Saturday last, wherein you will perceive that the committee had approved the plan of Mr. Neckar. I can add from other sure information received here, that the assembly adopted it the same evening. This plan may possibly keep their paiments alive until their new government gets into motion; tho I do not think it very certain. The public stocks lowered so exceedingly the last days of my stay at Paris, that I wrote to our bankers at Amsterdam, to desire that they retain till further orders the 30,000 guilders, or so much of it as was not yet come on. And as to what might be already coming on I recommended to Mr. Short to go & take the acceptances himself, & keep the bill in his own hands till the time of paiment. He will by that time be able to see what is best to be done with the money.

In taking leave of Monsieur de Montmorin I asked him whether their West India ports would continue open to us awhile. He said they would be immediately declared open till February; and we may be sure they will be so till the next harvest. He agreed with me that there would be two or three months provision for the whole kingdom wanting for the ensuing year. The consumption of bread for the whole kingdom is two millions of livres tournois a day. The people pay the real price of their bread everywhere except at Paris & Versailles. There the price is suffered to vary very little as to them, & government pays the difference. It has been supposed that this difference for some time past has cost a million a

---

that under any ruler France's policies could conflict with the aspirations of the United States. The alliance with France notwithstanding, Jefferson's suspicions of imperialism were sufficiently aroused by a report of a French scientific expedition to the South Seas in 1785 for him to ask John Paul Jones to find out if the expedition had any designs on the west coast of America. Furthermore, Jefferson was willing to exploit the initial weakness that follows any upheaval, while he waited to exploit the future strength of a reformed France. For example, in this letter to Jay, with a suggestions of pleasure he expected famine and financial bankruptcy to yield America the opportunity to supply a starving Paris with salted provisions to be admitted duty free.. But the French were not mistaken in considering Jefferson a friend, for despite any considerations of self-interest, Jefferson's main hopes were centered in the new popular government, composed in large measure of America's friends, which would rebuild on the ruins of a mercantilism a structure of political and commercial collaboration between the two countries firm enough to secure the United States from future attacks by Britain. (Kaplan 1967, 33)

week. I thought the occasion favorable to propose to Monsieur de Montmorin the free admission of our salted provisions, observing to him particularly that our salted beef from the Eastern states could be dealt out to the people of Paris for 5. or 6. sols the pound, which is but half the common price they pay for fresh beef: that the Parisian paying less for his meat, might pay more for his bread, & so relieve government from its enormous loss on that article. His idea of this resource seemed unfavorable. We talked over the objections of the supposed unhealthiness of that food, it's tendency to produce scurvy, the chance of its taking with a people habituated to fresh meat, their comparative qualities of rendering vegetables eatable, & the interests of the gabelles.[1] He concluded with saying the experiment might be tried, & with desiring me to speak with Mr. Neckar. I went to Mr. Neckar, & he was gone to the National assembly. On my return to Paris therefore I wrote to him on the subject, going over the objections which Monsieur de Montmorin had started. Mr. Short was to carry the letter himself & to pursue the subject. Having observed that our commerce to Havre is considerably on the increase, & that most of our vessels coming there, & especially those from the Eastward are obliged to make a voyage round to the neighborhood of the Loire & Garonne for salt, a voyage attended with expense, delay, & more risk, I have obtained from the farmers general that they shall be supplied from their magazines at Honfleur, opposite to Havre, at a mercantile price. They fix it at present at 60 livres the muid,[2] which comes to about 15 sous, or 7½d sterling our bushel: but it will vary as the price varies at the places from which they bring it. As this will be a great relief to such of our vessels coming to Havre as might wish to take back salt, it may perhaps be proper to notify it to our merchants. I enclose herewith Mr. Neckar's discourse to the assembly which was not printed when I left Paris.

To James Rumsey[3]
Cowes, October 14, 1789
Dear Sir,
 I am honored with your favor of the 4th instant and will pay attention to what you say on the subject of the Barker's mill your friends beyond the water are about to erect. I am sincerely sorry not to have know[n] the result of your experiment for steam navigation before my departure. Tho I have already been detained here & at Havre 16. days by contrary winds I mu[st] hope that detention will not continue till your experime[nt] be tried. As I feel infinitely

---

[1] Gabelles were a type of tax in France before the Revolution of 1789.
[2] A method of measuring land in France based on the number of muids of seeds needed to sow a particular piece of land
[3] Jefferson considered James Rumsey "the most original and the greatest mechanical genius" he had ever seen. And, as reflected in this letter, Jefferson was clearly captivated by the results of Rumsey's much-heralded experiments with steam navigation, the trial of which was shortly scheduled to take place. But Jefferson sailed from Europe before he received any word. The experiment proved unsuccessful but Jefferson's intense interest in steam navigation was to continue until Robert Fulton and John Fitch finally made it practicable. (Martin 1961, 72; Schachner 1957, 383- 384)

interested in its success, would you be so good, my dear Sir, as to drop me a line on the subject as soon as the experiment shall be made. If directed to me at Richmond to the care of Mr. Alexr. Donald, & sent by a Virginia ship, I shall get it with certainty. As soon as your experiment shall be over Mr. Short will do for you at Paris whatever I could have done towards obtaining you a patent there.

To William Short[1]
Lynhaven Bay [Virginia], Nov. 21, 1789
Dear Sir,

Tho' a committee of American captains at Cowes had [de]termined we must expect a nine weeks passage, the winds [and] weather have so befriended us that we are come to an anch[orage] here 29. days after weighing anchor at Yarmouth, having bee[n] only 26. days from land to land. After getting clear of the etern[al] fogs of Europe, which required 5. or 6. days sailing, the sun broke out upon us, & gave us fine autumn weather almost cons[tant]ly thro the rest of the voyage, & so warm that we had no occas[ion] for fire. In the gulf stream only we had to pass thro' the squalls of wind & rain which hover generally over that tepid cur[r]ent: & thro the whole we had had nothing stronger tha[n] what seamen call a stiff breeze: so that I have now passed the Atlantic twice without knowing what a storm is. When we had passed the meridian of the Western islands, our weather w[as] so fine that it would have been madness to go 1000. miles out of our way to seek what would not have been better. So we determin[ed] to push

---

[1] For the return to Virginia, Jefferson's party, which included his two daughters, James Hemings, and James' sister Sally. John Trumbull had booked passage for them aboard the *Clermont*, which embarked from London and made a special stop at Cowes to pick up the Jefferson party. Once aboard the *Clermont*, they were plagued by seasickness for the first five days of the journey, but the remainder of the crossing turned out to be quite pleasant. In Jefferson's words, they experienced "the finest autumn weather it was possible to have the wind having never blown harder than we would have desired it." The crossing was uneventful, until the *Clermont* approached the Virginia capes, where thick fog made it impossible to locate a pilot boat. For three days they searched but to no avail. The captain of the *Clermont* finally decided to brave the capes and enter the Chesapeake on his own. Martha Jefferson remembered the experience well: "After beating about for three days the captain, who was a bold as well as an experienced seaman determined to run in at a venture without having seen the capes. We were near running upon what he conjectured to be the middle ground when we cast anchor at ten o'clock at night. The wind rose, the vessel drifted down dragging her anchors one or more miles, but we had got within the capes whilst a number of vessels less bold were blown off the coast some of them lost and all of them kept out three or four weeks longer. We had to beat up against a strong head wind which carried away our topsails and were very near being run down by a brig coming out of port who having the wind in her favor was almost upon us before we could get out of the way. We escaped however with only a loss only of a part of our rigging." Mooring safely at Norfolk on Monday afternoon, November 23, the Jeffersons disembarked, thinking their adventures over, but an hour or two later, before their luggage had been unloaded, the *Clermont* caught fire. The fire started in the middle steerage, and the flames burst through the cabin and out the windows. Fortunately, Jefferson's luggage escaped harm. (Hayes 2008, 383, 387-388)

on the direct course. We left the banks of Newf[oundland] about as far on our right as the Western islands on our left notwithstanding the evidence of their quadrants to the contrary some of the sailors insisted we were in the trade winds. Our sickness in the beginning was of 3. 4. or 5 days, severe enough. Since that we have been perfectly well. We separated from Mr. Trumbull's ship the evening on which I wrote you from the needles, & I never saw her more. Our ship is two years old only, excellently accommodated, in ballast, and among the swiftest sailors on the ocean. Her captain a bold & judicious seaman, a native of Norfolk, whose intimate knowledge of our coast has been of both confidence & security to us. So that as we had in prospect every motive of satisfaction, we have found it still greater in event. We came to anchor here because no pilot has yet offered. Being within 15. miles of Norfolk by land, I have some thought of going ashore here in the morning, & going by land to that city. I wrote this from hence in hopes some outward bound vessel may be met to which it may be consigned. My plants & shepherd dogs are well. Remember me to enquiring friends, and accept assurances of sincere esteem & attachment with which I am Dear Sir,

To The Secretary for Foreign Affairs (John Jay)[1]
Norfolk, Nov. 23, 1789
Sir,

I think it my duty to inform you that I am this day arrived here after a passage of 26 days from land to land. By the Montgomery [a ship name], Capt. Bunyan, which sailed from Cowes at the same time with us, I had the honor of addressing you and of sending you the Letter book & account book of Silas Deane, which I put into the hands of Mr. Trumbull, who I presume is arrived at New York. According to what I proposed in that letter I shall proceed first to my own house to arrange those matters which have called for my presence there, and, this done, go on to New York, in order for my embarkation: where I shall first have occasion to confer with you in order to take the sense of government on some subjects which require vivâ voce explanations. I hope to be with you as early as the season will admit a tolerable passage.

---

[1] Silas Deane, along with Benjamin Franklin and Arthur Lee, served as one of the first foreign diplomats from the United States to France. Recalled to the United States, Deane was forced to defend his financial affairs in Paris; and the interception and publication of his letters by the British, suggesting that the American cause was hopeless, further diminished his reputation. All but exiled from America, after the war, Deane lived in London where, in late 1787, he became bedridden from an unknown illness — some suggest it was poison — and did not fully recover until April 1789. His condition depleted his remaining money and forced him to depend on the charity of friends. In the summer of 1788, a Frenchman named Foulloy approached Jefferson in Paris with an account book and a letter book dating from Deane's time as a diplomat. Foulloy implied that he held the books as security for a debt; however, most believe that they had been stolen from Deane during his illness. Foulloy threatened to sell the books to the British government if Jefferson did not purchase them, which Jefferson eventually did after negotiating a greatly reduced price. (Schaeper 2011, 195–227)

EPILOGUE

When Jefferson, returning from France, disembarked at Norfolk, Virginia, on 23 November 1789, he learned from the newspapers that he had been appointed Secretary of State in the new Federal administration. But Washington's letter and commission nominating him to the post did not reach him until some three weeks later, at Eppington, the Virginia plantation home of his daughter Mary and her husband John Wayles Eppes. Jefferson was reluctant to accept.[1] In a December 15. 1789 letter to Washington he responded:

I have received at this place the honor of your letters of Oct. 13 and Nov. 30. and am truly flattered by your nomination of me to the very dignified office of Secretary of state: for which permit me here to return you my humble thanks. Could any circumstance seduce me to overlook the disproportion between its duties and my talents it would be the encouragement of your choice. But when I contemplate the extent of that office, embracing as it does the principal mass of domestic administration, together with the foreign, I cannot be insensible of my inequality to it: and I should enter on it with gloomy forebodings from the criticisms and censures of a public just indeed in their intentions, but sometimes misinformed and misled, and always too respectable to be neglected. I cannot but foresee the possibility that this may end disagreeably for one, who, having no motive to public service but the public satisfaction, would certainly retire the moment that satisfaction should appear to languish. On the other hand I feel a degree of familiarity with the duties of my present office, as far at least as I am capable of understanding its duties. The ground I have already passed over enables me to see my way into that which is before me. The change of government, too, taking place in the country where it is exercised, seems to open a

---

[1] O'Brien 1996, 69.

possibility of procuring from the new rulers some new advantages in commerce which may be agreeable to our countrymen. So that as far as my fears, my hopes, or my inclination might enter into this question, I confess they would not lead me to prefer a change.

But it is not for an individual to choose his post. You are to marshal us as may best be for the public good: and it is only in the case of it's being indifferent to you that I would avail myself of the option you have so kindly offered in your letter. If you think it better to transfer me to another post, my inclination must be no obstacle: nor shall it be, if there is any desire to suppress the office I now hold, or to reduce its grade. In either of these cases, be so good only as to signify to me by another line your ultimate wish, and I shall conform to it cordially. If it should be to remain at New York, my chief comfort will be to work under your eye, my only shelter the authority of your name, and the wisdom of measures to be dictated by you, and implicitly executed by me. Whatever you may be pleased to decide, I do not see that the matters which have called me hither will permit me to shorten the stay I originally asked; that is to say, to set out on my journey Northward till the month of March. As early as possible in that month I shall have the honor of paying my respects to you in New York. In the meantime I have that of tendering you the homage of those sentiments of respectful attachment with which I am Sir Your most obedient & most humble servant,

As a practical matter, Jefferson could not flatly refuse the appointment; but, neither was he prepared to wholeheartedly accept it. In fact, he much preferred his post in Paris. It was familiar, its lines well charted. The new office of Secretary of State, on the other hand, embracing a mass of domestic administration together with the foreign, presented a boundless sea of troubles, which he would admittedly enter with "gloomy forebodings from the criticisms and censures of a public" easily misinformed and misled, and from which he would wish to withdraw the moment the torrent rose. But, he acknowledged, "...it is not for an individual to choose his post. You are to marshal us as may best be for the public good." Jefferson thus threw the decision back to Washington, uncertain of what the outcome would be, but inasmuch as Washington had consulted his wishes, expecting he would be allowed to remain as he was.[1]

Jefferson, of course, accepted the appointment and, as Secretary of State, he soon found his approach to foreign affairs to be limited by Washington's preference for neutrality regarding the war between Britain and France. Jefferson favored closer ties to France, who had supported the United States during the Revolutionary War. Tension within Washington's Cabinet — notably with Secretary of the Treasury Alexander Hamilton, who favored an assertive central government — prompted Jefferson's resignation.

---

[1] Peterson 1975, 391.

In the end, Jefferson emerges as a seminal figure in American political thought. And although he was occasionally unrealistic about what the United States might achieve on its own, from a foreign policy viewpoint, he did not take the position that international conflict was an aberration, nor did he chose to ignore the interest of the state in security. On the contrary, Jefferson harbored a dominantly political perception of the world that clearly influenced his foreign policy decisions. One which, if necessary, would witness the selective application of political power and military action.[1]

In the final analysis, it may be reasonable to argue that it is Jefferson who, by virtue of his writings, is most often associated with the American conscience and who carries the moral character of the nation on his back. But, if so, is it really possible for a historical figure to bear this type of symbolic burden and still remain simply a person, and not something more? One can only wonder. [2]

Thomas Jefferson died on July 4, 1826, and was buried beside his wife in the cemetery on the sloping hillside at Monticello. He had drawn the design and left the instructions for a plain obelisk of coarse stone to mark his grave and requested as his epitaph "the following inscription, and not a word more":

Here was buried
Thomas Jefferson
Author of the Declaration of American Independence
of the Statute of Virginia for religious freedom
and Father of the University of Virginia.

He made this request "because by these, as testimonials that I have lived, I wish most to be remembered."[3]

---

[1] Stuart 1976, 171.
[2] Wood 2006, 99-100.
[3] Cunningham 1987, 349.

Works Cited

Abernethy, Thomas Perkins. *Western Lands and the American Revolution*. New York: Russell & Russell, 1959.

Abrams, Jeanne E., ed., *Revolutionary Medicine: The Founding Fathers and Mothers in Sickness and in Health*. New York: New York University Press, 2013.

Abrams, Jeanne E., ed., *Revolutionary Medicine: The Founding Fathers and Mothers in Sickness and in Health*. New York: New York University Press, 2013.

Adams, William Howard. *The Paris Years of Thomas Jefferson*. New Haven: Yale University Press, 1997.

Alexander, Gregory S. *Commodity & Propriety: Competing Visions of Property in American Legal Thought, 1776-1970*. Chicago: University of Chicago, 1997.

Appleby, Joyce and Terence Ball, eds. *Thomas Jefferson: Political Writings*. Cambridge, England: Cambridge University Press, 1999.

Bailyn, Bernard. *Faces of Revolution: Personalities and Themes in the Struggle for American Independence*. New York: Knopf Doubleday Publishing, 2011.

Baseler, Marilyn C. *Asylum for Mankind: America, 1607-1800*. Ithaca, NY: Cornell University Press, 1998.

Berman, Eleanor Davidson. *Thomas Jefferson among the Arts: An Essay in Early American Esthetics*. New York: Philosophical Library, 1947.

Bernstein, R.B. "Chapter Twenty-Six: Thomas Jefferson and Constitutionalism," *in A Companion to Thomas Jefferson*, ed. Francis D. Cogliano. Malden, MA: Wiley-Blackwell, 2012.

Beveridge, Albert J., *The Life of John Marshall*, vol. 2. Boston: Houghton Mifflin, 1916.

Boyd, Julian P., ed. "Editorial Note: Negotiations for a Treaty of Amity and Commerce with Portugal," Founders Online, National Archives *Founders Online, National Archives.* Princeton: Princeton University Press, 1990,

Brands, H.W. *The First American: The Life and Times of Benjamin Franklin.* New York: Anchor Books, 2000.

Brandt, Anthony. *Thomas Jefferson: Travels Selected Writings, 1784-1789.* Washington, D.C.: National Geographic Society, 2006. Kindle.

Brecher, Frank W. *Securing American Independence: John Jay and the French Alliance.* Westport, CT: Praeger, 2003.

Brodie, Fawn M. *Thomas Jefferson: An Intimate History.* New York: W. W. Norton, 1974.

Browning, Oscar and John Frederick Sackville Dorset, *Despatches from Paris, 1784-1790.* London: Offices of the Society, 1909.

Carman, Harry J. and Harold C. Syrett, *A History of the American People.* New York: Alfred A. Knopf, 1952.

Catanzariti, John. "Editorial Note: The Settlement of Jefferson's Accounts as Minister Plenipotentiary in France." *Founders Online, National Archives.* Princeton: Princeton University Press, 1990.

Central Intelligence Agency. "Intelligence in the War of Independence." *Intelligence Operations.* Washington D.C., 2015.

Chisholm, Hugh, ed. "Charles Alexandre De Calonne." *The Encyclopedia Britannica: A Dictionary of Arts, Sciences, Literature and General Information.* New York: Encyclopedia Britannica, 1910.

Combs, Jerald A. *The Jay treaty; Political Battleground of the Founding Fathers.* Berkeley: University of California Press, 1970.

Conrad, Dennis M. "Nathanael Greene."*World at War: Understanding Conflict and Society.* Santa Barbara: ABC-CLIO, 2015.

Coyle, David Cushman. *Ordeal of the Presidency.* Washington, DC: Public Affairs Press, 1960.

Cunningham, Noble E., Jr. *In Pursuit of Reason: The Life of Thomas Jefferson.* Baton Rouge: Louisiana State University Press, 1987.

Daynes, Ron W. "Chapter 1: George Washington: Reluctant Occupant, Uncertain Model for the Presidency," in *George Washington and the Origins of the American Presidency,* by Mark J. Rozell, William D. Pederson, and Frank J. Williams. Westport, CT: Praeger, 2000.

Deconde, Alexander. *Entangling Alliance: Politics & Diplomacy under George Washington.* Durham, NC: Duke University Press, 1958.

Dodge, Andrew R. and Betty K. Koed, eds. *Biographical Directory of the United States Congress, 1774-2005: The Continental Congress, September 5, 1774, to October 21, 1788, and* the Congress of the United States, from the First Through the One Hundred Eighth Congresses, March 4, 1789, to January 3, 2005, Inclusive. Washington, D.C.: U.S. G.P.O., 2005.

Dorfman, Joseph. "Thomas Jefferson: Commercial Agrarian Democrat," in The American Past: Conflicting Interpretations of the Great Issues, ed. Sidney Fine and Gerald S. Brown, vol. 1. New York: Macmillan, 1961.

Dreisbach, Daniel L. Thomas Jefferson and the Wall of Separation between Church and State. New York: New York University Press, 2002.

Ecker, Grace Dunlop. A Portrait of Old George Town. Richmond, VA: Garrett & Massie, 1933.

Egerton, Douglas R. Death or Liberty: African Americans and Revolutionary America. New York: Oxford University Press, 2009.

Elkins, Stanley and Eric McKitrick, The Age of Federalism. New York: Oxford University Press, 1995.

Ellis, Joseph J. The Quartet: Orchestrating the Second American Revolution, 1783-1789. New York: Knopf Doubleday Publishing. 2015.

Encyclopedia Britannica Online, s. v. "Jacques-Pierre Brissot. 2016.

Ferguson, James. The Power of the Purse: A History of American Public Finance, 1776-1790. Chapel Hill, NC: University of North Carolina Press, 1961.

Fladeland, Betty. Men and Brothers: Anglo-American Antislavery Cooperation. Urbana, IL: University of Illinois Press, 1972.

Ford, Paul Leicester, ed. The Works of Thomas Jefferson, Federal Edition, New York: G.P. Putnam's Sons, 1905. passim.

Foster, H. Thomas. "Benjamin Hawkins." Encyclopedia of Alabama. Birmingham: Alabama Humanities Foundation, 2013.

Freidel, Frank, and Hugh Sidey. "Thomas Jefferson," in The Presidents of the United States of America. Washington, D.C.: The White House, 2006.

Frisch, Morton J., and Richard G. Stevens. American Political Thought; The Philosophic Dimension of American Statesmanship. New York: Scribner, 1971.

Gallimore, Mark K. "Thomas Jefferson, the Barbary Pirates and the Law of Nations." Theses and Dissertations.

Bethlehem, PA: Lehigh University, 2003.

Gelles, Edith B. Portia: The World of Abigail Adams. Bloomington, IN: Indiana University Press, 1995.

Graebner, Norman A, Richard Dean Burns, and Joseph M. Siracusa, Foreign Affairs and the Founding Fathers: From Confederation to Constitution, 1776-1787. Santa Barbara, CA: Praeger, 2011.

Greene, John C. American Science in the Age of Jefferson. Ames, IA: Iowa State University Press, 1984.

Hartzler, Daniel D. *American Silver-Hilted, Revolutionary and Early Federal Swords According to Their Geographical Areas of Mounting.* Xlibris Corp, 2015.

Hatzenbuehler, Ronald L. "2: Thomas Jefferson," in *Popular Images of American Presidents,* ed. William C. Spragens. New York: Greenwood Press, 1988.

Hayes, Kevin J. *The Road to Monticello: The Life and Mind of Thomas Jefferson.* New York: Oxford University Press, 2008.

Hazen, Charles Downer. *Contemporary American Opinion of the French Revolution.* Baltimore: The Johns Hopkins Press, 1897.

Holton, Woody. *Forced Founders: Indians, Debtors, Slaves, and the Making of the American Revolution in Virginia.* Chapel Hill, NC: University of North Carolina Press, 1999.

Horne, Gerald. *The Deepest South: The United States, Brazil, and the African Slave Trade.* New York: New York University Press, 2007.

Houdon, Jean Antoine. "Jean Houdon to Virginia Governor Robert Brooke," 8 September 1796. Letter. Richmond: Virginia State Papers and Other Manuscripts.

Hutson, James H., ed. *Letters from a Distinguished American: Twelve Essays by John Adams on American Foreign Policy, 1780.* Washington, DC: Library of Congress, 1978.

Issacson, Walter. *Benjamin Franklin: An American Life.* New York: Simon and Schuster, 2003.

Jay, William. *The Life of John Jay: With Selections from His Correspondence and Miscellaneous Papers.* New York: J. & J. Harper, 1833.

Jefferson, Thomas, James Madison, and James Morton Smith. *The Republic of Letters: The Correspondence between Thomas Jefferson and James Madison, 1776-1826.* New York: Norton, 1995.

Jefferson, Thomas, to Honoré de Riquetti, Comte de Mirabeau, 25 August 1786, in *The American Ecclesiastical Review,* ed. Herman Joseph Heuser, vol 109. Washington, D.C.: Catholic University Press, 1943.

_____. *The Best Letters of Thomas Jefferson,* ed. J. G. De Roulhac Hamilton. Boston: Houghton Mifflin, 1926.

Jensen, Merrill. *The New Nation: A History of the United States during the Confederation, 1781-1789.* New York: Vintage Books, 1950.

Kaplan, Lawrence S. *Jefferson and France: An Essay on Politics and Political Ideas.* New Haven, CT: Yale University Press, 1967.

Ketcham, Ralph. *From Colony to Country: The Revolution in American Thought, 1750-1820.* New York: Macmillan, 1974.

Kierner, Cynthia A. *Martha Jefferson Randolph, Daughter of Monticello: Her Life and Times.* Chapel Hill, NC: University of North Carolina Press, 2012.

Kimball, Marie. *Jefferson, the Road to Glory, 1743 to 1776.* New York: Coward-McCann, 1943.

Kimball, Marie. *Jefferson: The Scene of Europe, 1784 to 1789.* New York: Coward-McCann, 1950.

Koch, Adrienne. *Jefferson and Madison: The Great Collaboration* New York: Alfred A. Knopf, 1950.

Koch, Adrienne. *The Philosophy of Thomas Jefferson.* Gloucester, MA: Peter Smith, 1957.

Kranish, Michael, *Flight from Monticello: Thomas Jefferson at War.* New York: Oxford University Press, 2010.

Kromkowski, Charles A. *Recreating the American Republic: Rules of Apportionment, Constitutional Change, and American Political Development, 1700-1870.* Cambridge, England: Cambridge University Press, 2002.

Lewis, James A. *Neptune's Militia: The Frigate South Carolina during the American Revolution.* Kent, OH: Kent State University Press, 1999.

Library of Congress. "James Madison's Ciphers." *The James Madison Papers, 1723-1859,* 2015.

_____. "Thomas Jefferson: Establishing a Federal Republic." 2015.

Lieber, Francis, E. Wigglesworth, and T. G. Bradford. *Encyclopædia Americana.* Philadelphia: Desilver, Thomas, & Co, 1835.

Lipsky, George A. *John Quincy Adams: His Theory and Ideas.* New York: Thomas Y. Crowell, 1950.

Looney, J. Jefferson. "Peter Carr." *Dictionary of Virginia Biography.* Charlottesville: Virginia Foundation for the Humanities, 2013.

Marble, Annie Russell. 1907. *Heralds of American Literature: A Group of Patriot Writers of the Revolutionary and National Periods.* Chicago: University of Chicago Press, 1907.

Martin, Edwin T. *Thomas Jefferson: Scientist.* New York: Collier Books, 1961.

Mason, Alpheus Thomas. *The Supreme Court: Palladium of Freedom.* Ann Arbor, MI: University of Michigan Press, 1962.

Massachusetts Historical Society. "William Stephens Smith." *Adams Biographical Sketches,* 2015.

McCormick, Alpheus Thomas Mason and Richard H. Leach, *In Quest of Freedom: American Political Thought and Practice.* Englewood Cliffs, NJ: Prentice Hall, 1959.

Moore, Andrew. "The American Farmer as French Diplomat: J. Hector St. John De Crèvecoeur in New York After 1783." *Proceedings of the Western Society for French History.* Vol. 39 (2011).

Moscow, Henry. *Thomas Jefferson.* Newbury, Connecticut: American Heritage New Word City, 2015.

O'Brien, Conor Cruise. *The Long Affair: Thomas Jefferson and the French Revolution, 1785-1800.* Chicago: University of Chicago Press, 1996.

Onuf, Peter, S. *The Origins of the Federal Republic: Jurisdictional Controversies in the United States, 1775-1787.* Philadelphia: University of Pennsylvania Press, 1983.

Padover, S.K. *The Revolutionary Emperor, Joseph the Second, 1741-1790.* New York: R. O. Ballou, 1934.

Parton, James. *Life of Thomas Jefferson: Third President of the United States.* Boston: James R. Osgood and Company, 1874.

Patterson, Richard S. 1956. *The Secretaries of State: Portraits and Biographical Sketches.* Washington, DC: U.S. Government Printing Office, 1956.

Peterson, Merrill D. "Thomas Jefferson and Commercial Policy, 1783-1793." *The William and Mary Quarterly,* Vol. 22, No. 4 (October, 1965)

Peterson, Merrill D. *Thomas Jefferson and the New Nation: A Biography.* London: Oxford University Press, 1975.

Ragosta, John A. "Chapter Six: The Virginia Statute for Establishing Religious Freedom," in *A Companion to Thomas Jefferson,* ed. Francis D. Cogliano. Malden, MA: Wiley-Blackwell, 2012.

Randall, Henry S. *The Life of Thomas Jefferson,* vol.1. New York: Derby and Jackson, 1858.

Randolph, Sarah N. *The Domestic Life of Thomas Jefferson. Comp. from Family Letters and Reminiscences, by His Great- Granddaughter, Sarah N. Randolph.* New York: Harper & Brothers, 1871.

Rayner, B. L. *Sketches of the Life, Writings, and Opinions of Thomas Jefferson.* New York: Francis and Boardman, 1832.

Reisz, Autumn. "Hogsheads: The Containers for Tobacco." Colloquium in U.S. Colonial History. Orlando: University of Central Florida, 2013.

Risjord, Norman K. *Chesapeake Politics, 1781-1800.* New York: Columbia University Press, 1978.

Rives, William C. *History of the Life and Times of James Madison.* Boston: Little, Brown and Company, 1870.

Rutland, Robert Allen. *The Birth of the Bill of Rights, 1776-1791.* Chapel Hill, NC: University of North Carolina Press, 1955.

"Saint-Lambert, Jean-François, Marquis De (1716-1803)". In *The Hutchinson Unabridged Encyclopedia with Atlas and Weather Guide.* Abington: Helicon, 2015. Online.

Schachner, Nathan. *Thomas Jefferson: A Biography.* New York: Thomas Yoseloff, 1957.

Schaeper, Thomas J. *Edward Bancroft: Scientist, Author, Spy.* New Haven: Yale University Press, 2011.

Smith, Jeffery A. *War & Press Freedom: The Problem of Prerogative Power.* New York: Oxford University Press, 1999.

Solomon, Susan, John S. Daniel and Daniel L. Druckenbrod. "Revolutionary Minds" *American Scientist.* Volume 95, Number 5 (September-October, 2007)

Spahn, Hannah. "Chapter Twenty-Three: Thomas Jefferson, Cosmopolitanism, and the Enlightenment," in *A Companion to Thomas Jefferson*, ed. Francis D. Cogliano. Malden, MA: Wiley-Blackwell, 2012.

Stanton, Lucia, "Chapter Sixteen: Thomas Jefferson- Planter and Farmer," in *A Companion to Thomas Jefferson*, ed. Francis D. Cogliano. Malden, MA: Wiley-Blackwell, 2012.

Steinberg, Allen. *The Transformation of Criminal Justice, Philadelphia, 1800-1880.* Chapel Hill, NC: University of North Carolina Press, 1989.

Taylor, C. James, ed. *Founding Families: Digital Editions of the Papers of the Winthrops and the Adamses,* Boston: Massachusetts Historical Society, 2015.

Taylor, Francis Henry. *Houdon in America: A Collection of Documents in the Jefferson Papers in the Library of Congress,* ed. Gilbert Chinard. Baltimore: Johns Hopkins Press, 1930.

The Columbia Encyclopedia, 6th ed. "Houdon, Jean-Antoine." New York: Columbia University Press, 2015.

Thomas Jefferson Foundation. "Archibald Stuart." Monticello, Home of Thomas Jefferson. October 2015.

_____. "Elizabeth House Trist." Monticello, Home of Thomas Jefferson. March 2016.

_____. "Mary Jefferson Bolling." Monticello, Home of Thomas Jefferson. March 2016.

_____. "The First Barbary War." Monticello, Home of Thomas Jefferson. October 2015.

Thomas, Charles Marion. *American Neutrality in 1793: A Study in Cabinet Government.* New York: Columbia University Press, 1931.

Thompson, James C. *Thomas Jefferson's Enlightenment: Paris 1785.* Alexandria: Commonwealth Book Publishers of Virginia, 2013.

Toth, Charles W., ed. *Liberte, Egalite, Fraternite: The American Revolution & the European Response.* Troy, NY: Whitston, 1989.

Tucker, Robert W., and David C. Hendrickson. *Empire of liberty: The Statecraft of Thomas Jefferson.* New York: Oxford University Press, 1992.

Turner, Frederick J. "The Origin of Genet's Projected Attack on Louisiana and the Floridas." *The American Historical Review.* Vol. 3, No. 4 (July, 1898)

U.S. Department of State. *About Thomas Jefferson and Monticello.* Paris, France: American Embassy, 2016.

Wallace, Anthony F.C. *Jefferson and the Indians: The Tragic Fate of the First Americans.* Cambridge, MA: Harvard University Press, 2001.

Walsh, Robert, ed. "Diplomatic Correspondence of the United States." *The American Quarterly Review.* Vol.16 (September and December, 1834)

Wayson, Billy L. "Chapter Nineteen: Thomas Jefferson and Affairs of the Heart," in *A Companion to Thomas Jefferson*, ed. Francis D. Cogliano. Malden, MA: Wiley-Blackwell, 2012.

Wilkins, Lee. "Madison and Jefferson: The Making of a Friendship." *Political Psychology*, Vol. 12, No. 4 (Dec., 1991).

Wiltse, Charles Maurice. *The Jeffersonian Tradition in American Democracy.* Chapel Hill, NC: University of North Carolina Press, 1935.

Winsor, Justin H. *The Westward Movement: The Colonies and the Republic West of the Alleghanies, 1763-1798. with Full Cartographical Illustrations from Contemporary Sources.* Boston: Houghton Mifflin and Company, 1897.

Winterer, Caroline. "Chapter Twenty-Four: Thomas Jefferson and the Ancient World," in *A Companion to Thomas Jefferson*, ed. Francis D. Cogliano. Malden, MA: Wiley-Blackwell, 2012.

Wintle, Michael. *An Economic and Social History of the Netherlands, 1800-1920: Demographic, Economic, and Social Transition.* Cambridge, England: Cambridge University Press, 2000.

Wollery, William Kirk . *The Relation of Thomas Jefferson to American Foreign Policy, 1783-1793.* Baltimore, MD: Johns Hopkins Press, 1927.

Wood, Gordon S. *Revolutionary Characters: What Made the Founders Different.* New York: Penguin Books, 2006.

_____. *Empire of Liberty: A History of the Early Republic, 1789-1815.* New York: Oxford University Press, 2009.

Woolery, William Kirk. *The Relation of Thomas Jefferson to American Foreign Policy, 1783-1793.* Baltimore, MD: Johns Hopkins Press, 1927.

Young, James P. *Reconsidering American Liberalism: The Troubled Odyssey of the Liberal Idea.* Boulder, CO: Westview Press, 1996.

Zagarri, Rosemarie. *Revolutionary Backlash: Women and Politics in the Early American Republic.* Philadelphia: University of Pennsylvania Press, 2007.

INDEX

Printed in the United States
By Bookmasters